Jessica Jones, Scarred Superhero

D1552839

Jessica Jones, Scarred Superhero

Essays on Gender, Trauma and Addiction in the Netflix Series

Edited by TIM RAYBORN *and* ABIGAIL KEYES

Foreword by Robert G. Weiner

McFarland & Company, Inc., Publishers
Jefferson, North Carolina

WORKS BY TIM RAYBORN FROM MCFARLAND

*A New English Music: Composers and Folk
Traditions in England's Musical Renaissance from
the Late 19th to the Mid–20th Century* (2016)

*Against the Friars: Antifraternalism
in Medieval France and England* (2014)

*The Violent Pilgrimage: Christians, Muslims
and Holy Conflicts, 850–1150* (2013)

ISBN (print) 978-1-4766-6684-6 ∞
ISBN (ebook) 978-1-4766-3157-8

LIBRARY OF CONGRESS CATALOGUING DATA ARE AVAILABLE

BRITISH LIBRARY CATALOGUING DATA ARE AVAILABLE

Front cover images © 2018 iStock

Printed in the United States of America

*McFarland & Company, Inc., Publishers
Box 611, Jefferson, North Carolina 28640
www.mcfarlandpub.com*

Table of Contents

Foreword

The Not Quite Super Jessica Jones

ROBERT G. WEINER

When writer Brian Michael Bendis and artist Michael Gaydos debuted Jessica Jones in 2001's *Alias* #1, it was clear that she was not an ordinary costumed Marvel superhero character. Yes, she had super powers. Yes, Bendis gave her a back story that included a costume and a code name: Jewel. Her back story included hanging out with the Avengers and being friends with Captain/Ms. Marvel (Carol Danvers). She was present when Peter Parker was bitten by that radioactive spider.

Yet, when Jones was first introduced in *Alias* #1, it was not as a costumed superhero, but rather as a private investigator (the origin came later). She was doing the typical job of a PI by investigating the cheating wife of a client (who then proceeds to take out his anger on Jones, much to his detriment). There were other things, too: Jones had a drinking problem, loved to have sex, was street smart, and talked with the crudeness of a sailor. As Jeph Loeb points out in the afterword to the *Alias Omnibus*, Marvel had published adult oriented comics before, but this was the first time the F-bomb was used repeatedly in one. Bendis did not pull any punches with this character. *Alias* was a series for adults; it was written as such and was part of Marvel's new MAX imprint for mature readers.

When I first read *Alias*, I thought that this was a Marvel character that was less than super. There was something more human, more relatable, and more honest about her than previous Marvel heroes. It wasn't that she was a flawed superhero; rather, she was a deeply flawed human being. Therein lies the dichotomy. All of us have struggles and have probably been in some of the situations Jones found herself in or at least know someone like Jones (albeit without the powers). She is relatable precisely because she is flawed (the Netflix series kept this aspect of her). Bendis was honestly taking Marvel comics further than they had been before, despite the fact that nearly all Marvel characters have some kind of flaw. Jones had lived a life filled with so many difficulties (including being abused by the villain known as the Purple Man/Killgrave) that she did not suffer fools. Her career as the superhero Jewel was less than stellar. Jones' relationships with others were often fraught with complications and her clients were sometimes difficult to deal with. At her core, though, she was a good person who, despite her problematic past, still wanted to do the right thing and make a life for herself.

To make Jessica Jones a private investigator was not much of stretch for Bendis. He had been writing crime related comics for years with *Fire* (1993), *Goldfish* (1994), *Jinx* (1996), *Torso* (1998, about true crime hero Elliot Ness) and *Powers* (2000). It is worth noting that Bendis' character Jinx is a female bounty hunter, and *Powers* features two police detectives who investigate murders related to those who have superpowers. *Powers* was first published by Image Comics and then by Marvel Comics' Icons imprint. Jessica Jones fit right into Bendis' tendency for gritty crime stories. The difference is that Jones would become a part of the Marvel Universe proper.

At first glance, that Marvel Studios and Netflix would produce *Jessica Jones* as a 13-part series seemed odd. Jones as a character was still minor and mostly unknown, but Netflix had seen tremendous success with their other original content, including *House of Cards* and *Orange Is the New Black*. Marvel's first Netflix series *Daredevil* was a bona fide hit and *Jessica Jones* followed suit. The series kept all of the angst of Bendis and Gaydos' original *Alias* run along with all of the adult content. Here was a Marvel series that was NC-16, a show that was definitely not typical children's Saturday morning cartoon fare. With Netflix, Marvel (and by extension Disney) did not have to worry about making the series palatable to the general public, unlike their movies, animated series, and other network television programs. This worked to the advantage of the series. Jones could be played just like she was in the original *Alias* comics, having the same problems and desires. Krysten Ritter's excellent performance was one of deadpan honesty. She, too, ultimately cared about the people around her as she learned what it meant to have superpowers, but not be "super" in the traditional sense. In the series, Jones has to make some hard choices that, for example, Spider-Man or Captain America or even Daredevil cannot or would not make.

Unlike the *Alias* comics, the 13 episodes of the Netflix series mostly revolve around the abusive dynamic between Jones and Kilgrave (renamed from Killgrave and played with a total lack of empathy by the exquisite David Tennant). Kilgrave is originally a Daredevil villain, and his back story with Jones is only given a couple of issues in the original *Alias* comic series. In the show, Kilgrave is the ultimate narcissistic villain. Jones even tries to teach him to do something selfless for its own sake, but this does not work. His obsession with her is painful to watch, and the abuse and continued rape that she endures at his hand does make for uncomfortable viewing. The dynamic between her and Luke Cage (played with terrific believability by Mike Colter) keeps the tension high and makes for a compelling romance. Time will tell how this plays out in future series; in the comics, Jones and Cage get married and they have a daughter.

Tim Rayborn and Abigail Keyes have assembled a finely crafted collection of essays on the *Jessica Jones* television series. The offerings are unique and provide scholars and fans with a useful and relevant collection. So kick back, read an essay, re-watch an episode of *Jessica Jones*, then repeat as needed. Find the humanity within yourself from this collection in conjunction with the Netflix series.

BIBLIOGRAPHY

Loeb, Jeph. "Jeph Loeb's Introduction from Alias Volume I Hard Cover," in Brian Michael Bendis and Michael Gaydos, *Alias Omnibus*. New York: Marvel, 2006. (The original introduction is reprinted as an afterword in the omnibus edition with no page numbers.)

Robert G. Weiner, the popular culture/humanities librarian at Texas Tech University, is the author of *Marvel Graphic Novels and Related Publications* (2008), editor of *Captain America and the Struggle of the Superhero* (2009) and coeditor of *Web-Spinning Heroics* (with Robert Moses Peaslee, 2012) and *Marvel Comics into Film* (with Matthew J. McEniry and Robert Moses Peaslee, 2016), all from McFarland.

Introduction

TIM RAYBORN *and* ABIGAIL KEYES

"They say everyone's born a hero. But if you let it, life will push you over the line until you're the villain. Problem is, you don't always know that you've crossed that line."[1]

Marvel's Jessica Jones barged onto our TV screens and laptops in November 2015, courtesy of Netflix, presenting a hard-drinking female protagonist who was sick of everyone's crap and wrestled with her own inner (and outer) demons. The show is the second of four overlapping series (the others being *Daredevil, Luke Cage,* and *Iron Fist*) culminating in a team-up series (*The Defenders*) focusing on "street level" heroes and their adventures. Though set in the same universe (the Marvel Cinematic Universe, which will also be referred to as the MCU throughout this book) as the mega-powered Avengers and other big-screen Marvel heroes, these television series bring a new level of grittiness and realism, as well a hefty dose of violence, to that shared universe, themes that are less prominent in the larger tent pole cinematic outings. Set in New York City, each of the four "defenders" grapples with different kinds of threats that at times seem miles away from the cosmic dangers of the films, but are no less evil in their villainy and their capacity to ruin and destroy lives.

Jessica is a hard-drinking, cynical woman who as a teenager gained unnatural abilities in an accident, giving her enhanced strength, jumping ability, and improved healing. But rather than don a costume and become a stereotypical crime fighter, she instead works as a private investigator, uncovering infidelities, serving court summons, and engaging in other such covert activities for the right price. It may not be noble, but it's a living. There is a distinct film noir feel to the show, but it overturns the stereotypes of that genre by making its tough-as-nails detective a woman. As the series opens, Jessica is dealing with difficult clients (by throwing them through her front

5

door), and spying on a potentially adulterous couple, not realizing that her world is about to be torn apart once again.

While Daredevil struggled against a corrupt crime lord, Wilson Fisk, determined to make over the neighborhood of Hell's Kitchen in his own image by destroying anything and anyone that got in his way, Jessica's villain is in many ways far more insidious, because of the very intimate nature of the character. The reclusive but dapper and charming Englishman Kilgrave presents viewers with an adversary unlike any seen in the MCU to date: someone who does not want to rule the world, but instead enjoys his ability to make people do whatever he wants them to, simply by speaking to them and commanding them to comply; they cannot refuse. He has always had everything that he wanted, and so has no empathy or compassion, and cannot form any kind of realistic view of the world.

We learn that Jessica had in the past fallen under his mind control, and was kept as a virtual slave for some period of time, doing whatever he wished. She was eventually able to break free from him, but is now haunted by memories of this abuse, taking only some comfort in believing that he is dead. Of course, this soon proves not to be true, and Kilgrave once again returns to menace her, her friends, and potentially all of New York.

The series uses this premise to examine several important themes, including abuse (physical, sexual and emotional), trauma, PTSD, rape culture, issues of consent, alcoholism, drug addiction, the plight of victims, and the importance of family. These are heavy topics, far removed from the usual fare that we have come to expect in comic book films and television. Indeed, this dark and mature tone sets the show apart from many of its counterparts. It immediately earned praise from a wide variety of sources, not only within comic fandom, but also from counselors, therapists, women's rights advocates, scholars of women's studies, and other related disciplines. Stars Krysten Ritter and David Tennant received much acclaim for their emotional and gut-wrenching performances, becoming icons within fandom. Indeed, viewers watched the show in large numbers (though Netflix does not normally release ratings information), and this popularity was enough for the show to receive a second season, airing on Netflix in 2018. Before that, Ritter reprised her role as Jessica in *The Defenders* series in 2017.

A richly-conceived and complex show such as this deserves deeper study and analysis, and this book helps to fill that need. This collection of essays by noted scholars examines different topics and aspects of *Jessica Jones* in considerable detail.

We begin with "'Even you can break': Jessica Jones as Femme Fatale," by Daniel Binns, which examines the themes of film noir in classic films, analyzing how the character of Jessica Jones is figured against the traditional noir archetype of the *femme fatale*. Rather than being a lure for the hapless "fall guy," Jessica switches between hardboiled antihero, struggling victim, and a "normal" thirty-something, embodying each role as the narrative dictates.

In "Elite and Famous: Subverting Gender in the Marvel Universe with *Jessica Jones*," Nicholas William Moll argues that Jessica Jones presents a form of superhero literature that subverts hierarchies of gender, class, and ideology frequently enshrined in costumed adventure narratives. In doing so, the essay explores the contrasts between *Jessica Jones* the television show and *Alias*, the comic it is based on, focusing on each incarnation's respective use of a wider Marvel Universe. Herein the limited scope of *Jessica Jones* is central. Where *Jessica Jones* focuses on antagonism measured in terms of the protagonist as an individual victim of sexual assault and domestic abuse, the contrasts offered by *Alias* invoke a global drama of aliens, costumed vigilantism, and mutants.

In "'AKA Occasionally I give a damn': Mirrored Archetypes and Gender Power in *Jessica Jones*," Aleah Kiley and Zak Roman argue that *Jessica Jones* subverts not only genre expectations, but also expectations about race, class, and gender. They conduct a review of the industry dynamics underpinning the creation of the series, promotional materials, and textual analysis of the first season of the show. With a specific focus on Jessica and her friend Trish Walker's relationship, as well as the interplay between diverse allies, this essay argues that *Jessica Jones* negotiates normative gender expectations and subverts power dynamics, while ultimately remaining ambiguous toward the anti-heroine.

In "*Jessica Jones*: Gender and the Marvel Phenomenon," Lillian Céspedes González looks at public reception of the show and the reasons behind its success. This essay focuses on the adaptation of the comic into a television series, and the popularity of the show within the wider context of the wave of new releases set in the Marvel Universe. The methodology includes reception and audience studies, cultural theory, and social analysis, as well as a case study using quantitative data gathered through a focus group/survey to obtain audience feedback on the show. Moreover, this essay looks at Jessica as a woman of the twenty-first century in superhero culture and how this reflects the deeper and wider changes within cultural dynamics.

"AKA Marvel Does Darkness: Jessica Jones, Rape Allegories and the Netflix Approach to Superheroes," by CarrieLynn D. Reinhard and Christopher J. Olson, considers how the Netflix direct-to-streaming model influences how producers can portray a superhero, particularly when compared to those produced within the confines of the traditional television model. It also considers how Netflix's political, economic, and technological construction allows for a more in-depth exploration of a very complex story, i.e., using superpowers as an analogy for rape and sexual assault. The essay also looks at how the mega-series is tailor-made for a specific niche audience, one more likely to accept the analogy depicted in the series. This tailoring results in a darker, more nuanced portrayal of Jessica Jones, but one that still fits within the overall shared cinematic universe that Marvel has constructed, while also depicting a unique and potentially more human expression of life in the MCU.

In "Sobriety Blows: Whiskey, Trauma and Coping in Netflix's *Jessica Jones*," Janis Breckenridge observes that Jessica's alcohol binges signify far more than a mere penchant for drinking to excess. In addition to a connection to post-traumatic stress disorder, Jessica's specific drinking habits (her frequent benders) underscore the numerous subverted gender roles, or recurring gender benders, at play throughout all thirteen episodes. This essay explores the intricate dynamics of traumatic memory, substance abuse and powerlessness—connecting the sense of victimization that results from mind control with the analogous feelings of powerlessness, both psychological and physiological, that come with chemical dependency—through the lens of trauma and addiction studies. Special attention is paid to narrative and visual strategies employed in the representation of alcohol and alcoholism on the television screen, particularly the recurring use of flashbacks, intertextual references, and specific filmic devices including strategic manipulation of lighting, focus, framing and composition.

Sharon Packer, in "Jessica Jones, Women and Alcohol Use Disorders," observes that, in spite of the obvious allusions to alcohol in the show and the online homages to Jessica Jones, there is no mention of the potential medical consequences of excessive alcohol consumption in women. Women who watch this series and who see the risk-taking, wise-cracking Jessica as a role model may emulate this alcohol-related behavior, without awareness of the grave consequences of excessive alcohol use. We can contrast the *Jessica Jones* series to the *Iron Man* comic book, where Tony Stark's character acknowledges his struggles with alcohol. Stark's AA allegiance becomes part of his persona. We can also compare *Jessica Jones* to another television series, *Arrow*, where the female lead, Laurel Lance, nearly ruins her legal career and estranges family and friends because of more slowly-evolving alcohol and pill problems. Laurel begrudgingly seeks treatment, attends meetings, and eventually accepts the aid of her recovering alcoholic, police officer father. In *Arrow*, the female lead's fall and redemption occur within a single season—the second. It remains unknown what lies ahead for the second season of the already successful *Jessica Jones*.

In "*Jessica Jones*'s Feminism: AKA *Alias* Gets a Fixed-It," Melissa C. Johnson compares the comic book and the television show, noting the influence of and revisions to the origin story as depicted in the Alias comics, particularly in regard to representations of rape, rape culture, gender, and sexuality. Preliminary analysis suggests that Kilgrave's sexual exploitation of Jones is used for titillation in the comics, while the television series carefully avoids that. Jones' physical strength, refusal to express or tolerate emotion, choice of profession, and wardrobe are all stereotypically male. Does this suggest that women have to behave like men in order to survive trauma and/or resist exploitation? The Jessica of the series is more damaged than the character of the comic book, and by the end of season one, she has not received a resolution to the damage that she suffered at the hands of Kilgrave. This interpretation casts her in a darker light, and ultimately gives her a somewhat less rich and full life than her comic book counterpart.

In "The Haunted Hero: The Performance of Trauma in *Jessica Jones*," Melissa Wehler notes the effective use of flashbacks throughout the series. When these flashbacks end, they leave the viewer with haunting images of Jessica lingering into the present. Using performance studies and trauma theory, the essay argues that the performance of trauma through the technical use of flashback in *Jessica Jones* demonstrates the fluidity of the survivor identity. Moreover, the author describes how these moments for Jessica Jones reassert the complexities of post-traumatic existence as the nexus of the victim past and survivor present become ghostly mirrors of one another, reflecting and refracting the traumatized identity.

Brian Fuller and Emily D. Edwards, in "Integrity, Family and Consent: The Ontological Angst of *Jessica Jones*," observe that the characters in the show negotiate a reality that is familiar to students of film noir. The genre's stylistic conventions are well suited to the ontological angst of a corrupt world, overflowing as it is with the dangers of sexual violence and the abuse of power. This essay explores the appeal of *Jessica Jones*, particularly to millennials. In the series, Jessica, a millennial herself, confronts issues of probity, family, and free will. Though she knows right from wrong and resolves to do the right thing, she resists the idea of being a hero and cannot be seen as a traditional "role model."

Courtney Lee Weida takes the position of comparing *Jessica Jones* to another popular female-centric television program, *Buffy the Vampire Slayer* in "From the Hellmouth to Hell's Kitchen: Analyzing Aesthetics of Women Survivors and Spaces in *Buffy the Vampire Slayer* and *Jessica Jones*." This essay explores connections, not only between the two title heroines, but also addresses comparisons of the female ensemble casts of each and the possibilities and problems that the shows present in the creation of female communities and space around areas of extraordinary strength and of human frailty. Both series represent symbolic, adoptive, or even magical sisterhood as defining roles and responsibilities of the female protagonists. The essay focuses on the feminist aesthetics of the superhero as a symbol of survival in both of these shows, showing that both Jessica and Buffy display great strength of character along with their physical powers.

In "Battling Bluebeard, Fighting for Hope: The Heroine's Journey," Valerie Estelle Frankel looks at the villainous character of Bluebeard, a nemesis of women in the classic tale, who kills a series of wives for disobeying him. The heroine of the story must fight back, protecting those emotional parts of herself, such as intuition and autonomy, that this creature most wants to control. The analogy to Kilgrave and his desire to control Jessica is clear. Jessica's attempt to live with him and persuade him to do good with his power represents a combination of guilt and obligation, and these feelings are the heroine's biggest trap in attempting to fight his evil. As with Bluebeard and the wives that he successively murders, Kilgrave is the savage male pleading with Jessica to devote her goodness to him and redeem him. Though the compassionate heroine is always tempted, she must learn to deny pity and turn her back on him. Further, she must, as in any heroine's journey, face her own dark side to emerge as a stronger person.

Finally, in "'Is that real or is it just in my head?' 'Both': Chronotopal Representations of Patriarchal Villainy and the Feminist Antihero in *Marvel's Jessica Jones*," Justin Wigard argues that Jessica Jones represents something rather unique in the Marvel Cinematic Universe: a feminist superhero whose conflicts expose problematic aspects of gender relations in society. She has the power of super strength, yet the villainy she faces is insidious and nearly invisible, which can be viewed as representations of patriarchy. Comparing the show with season one of *Daredevil*, the author observes that *Jessica Jones* offers a more gender-driven narrative. In addition to feminist theory, Wigard uses Mikhail M. Bakhtin's notion of the chronotope as a theoretical lens through which to view Jessica Jones, allowing for a reading of the show through its historical, cultural, and generic context. By viewing Jessica as a product of her historical position and cultural influences, we find that she acts as a champion of feminism. In response, the villains at work within the show operate as and represent agents of patriarchal oppression, suppressing Jessica's agency and identity. Each of Jessica's conflicts with these villains (Kilgrave and Will Simpson) is shown to subvert American gender norms.

This collection thus offers a look into many of the key themes found in the show, and can serve as a good point of departure for further study. Extensive notes and a full bibliography are included at the end of each essay to further that goal, should the reader desire additional information.

The Jessica Jones of television is unique in the vast world of superheroes: a flawed hero with powers who doesn't really consider herself to be a hero at all, who eschews the "super costume," and is far more concerned with the problems of daily life than the high-profile world of historic super soldiers, Norse gods, and billionaires in powered armor. Her story is still unfolding;

she returns for a second Netflix season in 2018, and appears in an ongoing monthly comic written by her original creator, Brian Michael Bendis, which debuted in 2016. Undoubtedly, we will see her continue to struggle against many more antagonists, both internal and external.

NOTE

1. *Jessica Jones*, season 1, episode 13, "AKA Smile."

"Even you can break"

Jessica Jones as Femme Fatale

Daniel Binns

Like its central character, the television series *Jessica Jones* is troubled. The show grapples with the depiction of trauma, post-traumatic stress disorder, and psychological and sexual abuse, and does so with a grungy, dirty, film noir aesthetic. The darkness and grittiness of the show, its self-declaration as neo-noir in style, and the tension at the heart of its protagonist, immediately calls to mind classic films noir of the 1940s and 1950s. An analysis of the figuration of female characters in *The Killers* (Robert Siodmak, 1946) and *Laura* (Otto Preminger, 1944) reveals that the show's influences combine to create a nuanced and complex protagonist.

The theoretical substructure of this work is a theory of genre that draws on the field of linguistics; in particular, the works of A. J. Greimas and Roland Barthes. From Greimas, I adopt the notion of the "utterance" and the "enunciation" as being key to observing the adherence to and subversion of generic tropes. From Barthes' near line-by-line deconstruction of Balzac's *Sarrasine* in *S/Z* (1970), I draw out the five codes of signification: the hermeneutic, the semic, the symbolic, the proairetic, and the reference. These codes are applied to the film noir genre, as well as read into the performance of Jones herself as a character; the refiguring of the *femme fatale* archetype also permits a brief discussion of the series as rape-revenge. This essay further charts the evolving history of female characters within popular culture, and how screenwriters and filmmakers can and frequently do draw on classical tropes and figurations to flesh out these intricate roles.

Jessica Jones: The Series and the Character

With varying degrees of success, *Jessica Jones* attempts to humanize and "ground" the Marvel Cinematic Universe. While certain elements of the Marvel franchise are present—persistent references to the "incident" in New York from *The Avengers* (2012), for instance, and the presence of Rosario Dawson's character from the show's companion series *Daredevil*—the larger set pieces and Jones' own superpowers are downplayed at first, in favor of a more intimate portrayal of the character.

Jessica Jones posits its lead character (Krysten Ritter) alternately as hard-boiled antihero—traditional noir protagonist—and struggling victim. On the one hand, Jessica is a busy private detective, running her own business with a reasonably high success rate. On the other, however, she is a victim of post-traumatic stress disorder, recovering from the experience of having been kidnapped, brainwashed, and controlled by the psychopathic Kilgrave (David Tennant). This tension is at the heart of the show, and it is argued here that the reconciling of these two disparate personalities occurs within the traditional noir archetype of the *femme fatale*.

The series begins with an inciting incident: the cold-blooded murder of an older couple, the Shlottmans, by their daughter, Hope. High-powered attorney Jeri Hogarth (Carrie-Ann Moss), who often throws Jones investigative work, gets her onto this case. For the first half of the series, events play out as a reasonably standard criminal investigation or procedural show. Jones follows up leads while attempting to reconcile with her old friend Trish Walker (Rachael Taylor). The key to the case is that the violence is out of character for Hope, and soon, similar incidents lead Jones and her colleagues to believe there is a connection between the various cases. That connection is Kilgrave, a man with the ability to control minds, and bend others to his will. Kilgrave and Jones have a history, and she soon realizes that her former captor is orchestrating everything to lure her back into his web.

Importantly for the Marvel Cinematic Universe, and for popular culture more broadly, Jessica Jones presents a female protagonist that is very much not a male surrogate. Jessica's traumatic history is certainly not relatable only to women. However, the series attempts to realistically portray the effects of physical, psychological, and sexual abuse on a female protagonist; the fact that this character appears in a high-budget comic book–based universe is almost secondary. The series and the character have attracted praise from victims facing similar ongoing struggles: a community that has felt marginalized by representations in blockbuster cinema until now. Kia Groom neatly sums this up:

> While it masquerades as a show about heroes and villains, ultimately, *Jessica Jones* is not a fantasy. It's the reality of existing in a patriarchal society that does everything it

can to silence, dismiss, and ignore women—that strips power and agency from us at every conceivable level: domestically, romantically, politically, legally, and in the media.[1]

This is a television series that wears its emotions, its psychology, on its sleeve. Jones does indeed have superpowers, but she herself is terrified of what they can do, given her experiences with Kilgrave. How, then, is the show filmed? How do you leverage a deep emotional character arc against a world where superpowers are supposedly the norm? The answer, I argue, lies in the style of neo-noir, itself a revival of classic film noir.

Consider the title sequence of *Jessica Jones*: an impressionistic rendering of a cityscape, featuring silhouettes getting up to all sorts of mischief in apartment windows, with an almost-abstract representation of the figure of Jessica walking through it all. The impressionist style is based around inference: by giving a hint—an "impression"—of the image, the subject, the viewer then decodes what that subject is. Thus, impressionism is based around what is hidden: the same could be said of both neo-noir and its antecedent, film noir.

Color is very much present throughout the series, as opposed to the traditional monochrome film noir aesthetic. This is as much due to advancements in film technology as it is to a desire to visually connect the television series to its source material, Brian Michael Bendis, Michael Gaydos, and Matt Hollingsworth's comic series *Jessica Jones: Alias*. A striking color palette is present in other neo-noir works such as *Basic Instinct* (Paul Verhoeven, 1992) and *Chinatown* (Roman Polanski, 1974); dynamic use of color is also prevalent in future noirs like *Blade Runner* (Ridley Scott, 1982) and *Total Recall* (Paul Verhoeven, 1990). In the case of *Jessica Jones*, color is used to differentiate Jones from all other characters—she is most often dressed in black, but occasionally in a dull grey or green; her clothes are also baggy, loose-fitting, comfortable, rather than cut to accentuate any aspect of her physicality. This is presented in contrast to nearly every other character: Trish, for instance, wears bright block colors in alternating professional and casual configurations; Mike Colter wears similar block colors, usually in tight-fitting shirts that accentuate his brute strength.

The starkest contrast to Jones' dull, functional wardrobe is that of Kilgrave himself. The comics' Killgrave has purple skin, the result of an accident in a chemical refinery.[2] In adapting the comic for television, the creators of *Jessica Jones* decided to set Kilgrave up with somewhat more realism: his skin is a regular human shade. His costumes, however, play with his comic counterpart's signature hue: David Tennant's Kilgrave is clad in fitted shirts and tailored suits in varying shades of purple, forming a perfect visual contrast to Jones' loose, muted clothing. I mention color—using costumes as an example—to consider neo-*noir*'s use thereof. Glitre suggests that, generally, neo-noir operates with a largely monochromatic palette, favoring expressionistic daubs of primary colors (reds, greens, blues) that "become more prevalent during scenes of dramatic conflict."³ This can be observed in some sequences that depict Kilgrave controlling Jones. Rather than a primary color, though, these sequences are usually liberally splashed with purple light.

Much of the series occurs at night, particularly the earlier episodes as Jessica works through the initial parts of her investigation. The darkened city of New York figures prominently in the series, almost becoming a character in and of itself. Jessica uses the city to her advantage; she knows it well and can move through it mostly unseen. Setting the series in the old Hell's Kitchen district of Manhattan further adds to this gritty, urban feel. Color, too, comes into play here: neon lights are put into bright contrast against a city in shadow.

Neo-noir, though, is not just an aesthetic. Abrams offers that neo-noir is not only a modern re-presentation of classic film noir tropes. It is a development and evolution of these tropes, and an even more intensive examination of the psyche and human subjectivity. Very often, per Abrams, this is cast against the backdrop of a future near or far (for instance, *Blade Runner*), but it can also be done contemporarily (such as in *Chinatown*). The protagonist of classic noir was the hardboiled detective, "not a flat character," says Abrams, "but hardly 'conflicted' in Shakespeare's sense."⁴ With neo-noir, however, we are given multi-dimensional, complex figures that must often attempt to reconcile disparate parts of their personality—just as this essay posits is occurring with Jessica Jones. This is the protagonist template of neo-noir. Abrams suggests: "The character is 'divided' against himself, although not so much emotionally, as in Shakespeare, as epistemologically: divided in time as two selves, and one is looking for the other."⁵ I am suggesting that the reconciliation of Jessica Jones' disparate mindsets—the hardboiled antihero and the trauma victim—occurs in her conscious figuration of herself as the *femme fatale*.

The Femme Fatale *in Film Noir*

With the translation of several American crime novels into French, and the subsequent French critical attention to Hollywood adaptations of those novels, film noir was born not only in name but in terms of a corpus of works.⁶ There remains contention about what precisely film noir is: a genre, a set of story structures, a visual style, or a "touchstone of popular culture," as Bould contends.⁷ Answering this conundrum is not the purview of this essay; suffice to say that film noir incorporates an incredibly wide body of story types, plot devices and tropes, and character archetypes. One such character archetype is the *femme fatale*.

The *femme fatale* is a troubled figure, not only in her films, but in the inevitable criticism of those films that follows. Janey Place sees the *femme fatale* as a pure object of male fantasy, and observes that in film noir, "women are defined *in relation* to men."[8] Place is well aware that this is a hugely male-centric—indeed phallocentric—lens on the world, but she also suggests that the *femme fatale* is a dynamic and active female character, allowing for appropriately nuanced portrayals. Doane suggests that the *femme fatale* is a "symptom of male fears about feminism"[9] and female empowerment; the aggression shown by these characters is a direct threat to patriarchal society. Elisabeth Bronfen sums up Doane's position: "[The *femme fatale*'s] ability to seduce the *noir* hero into undertaking actions that undermine his self-interests renders visible a radical fallibility of the masculine subject."[10] Yet Bronfen herself suggests that critics should not be so quick to write the *femme fatale* off as either symbol of masculine anxiety *or* fantasy. Indeed, Bronfen suggests it is the frequent tension at the heart of the archetype between these two positions that presents the opportunity for Place's dynamic and nuanced portrayals. The *femme fatale* "has no fixed place and no unequivocal meaning within the narratives of the classic *films noir*":

> The femme fatale has resiliently preserved her position within our image repertoire precisely because she forces the spectator to decide whether she acts as an empowered modern subject or is simply to be understood as the expression of an unconscious death drive, indeed, whether we are to conceive of her as an independent figure or merely as a figure of projection for masculine anxiety.[11]

The above critiques allow, perhaps, for an alternative view of the *femme fatale* as strong, independent, and powerful, a willful vehicle (and/or victim) of her own destiny. There is a tension at the heart of the archetype, a tension that I argue is encoded via semes. Semes are co-opted from Barthes here, and interpreted as individual cinematic gestures such as part of a performance, like a pointed look or gesture, or a lighting arrangement, or a line of dialogue. These semes are utilized by the filmmakers to construct character, plot, and emotion; the semes are then read or decoded by the audience. In the case of the *femme fatale*, the various semes deployed by the filmmakers position this character archetype as one with an implicit tension between male objectivity, male anxiety, and fierce and willful independence. Through the deployment and manipulation of semes, that tension is thus presented for the audience to interpret.

Further, this research posits that character archetypes—such as, presently, the *femme fatale* (later, the hardboiled detective is considered)—are symbolic groupings, also per Barthes' thinking. Rather than being a "field [that] can be entered from any number of points," however, I suggest that character archetypes are symbolic configurations that can be placed within any story structure.[12] That is not to say, however, that the *femme fatale* is a homogenous cardboard cut-out; this is borne out by the various critiques discussed earlier. Barthes himself says that the symbolic grouping is characterized by "multivalence and reversibility."[13] For the purposes of this essay, two configurations of the *femme fatale* are observed, and they are not mutually exclusive. The first is the sexual seductress: the honey trap that lures an unsuspecting character—typically male—into trouble or to their death; Place calls this "The Spider Woman."[14] The second is the *femme fatale* as an object-of-mystery. Her motives are hazy, her morals non-existent, her character wavers somewhere between angelic and demonic. An example of the sexual seductress would be Ava Gardner's Kitty Collins in Robert Siodmak's *The Killers* (1946), or Rita Hayworth's titular *Gilda* (Charles Vidor, 1946). The object-of-mystery figuration of the *femme fatale* can be observed in Otto Preminger's *Laura* (1944) or, to a lesser degree, in *Double Indemnity* (Billy Wilder, 1944). No matter the configuration, the *femme fatale* is a dangerous beauty. While she is sometimes a strong and independent character, such as Barbara Stanwyck's scheming Phyllis Dietrichson in *Double Indemnity*, her shrewd use of beauty and femininity to dupe can also belie a naïvety—a lack of awareness about the power she has or the long-term effects it may trigger. These inherent tensions can often make for thrilling stories and fascinating characters, and this is part of the attraction of classic noir. Here, I will examine scenes from *The Killers* and *Laura* in order to examine how both types of femme fatale are configured in terms of semes such as scripting, performance, and cinematic technique.

Ava Gardner's introduction as Kitty Collins in *The Killers* takes place at a party in a smoky apartment: an oft-utilized film noir location. Kitty is clad in an elegant, figure-hugging, floor-length black gown, her shoulders and arms notably bare. Much is made of film noir and monochromatic cinema's use of lighting and shadow to create a dynamically contrasting image; this scene is perhaps one of the reasons why. Gardner's pale skin is contrasted with the black of her hair and her dress, and her deep (presumably ruby) lipstick, and then set against the shifting grey haze of the smoke-filled room. She leans provocatively against a black baby grand piano, the curves of her lower body echoing the contours of the instrument, as she breathes the lyrics to "The More I Know of Love" alongside the accompaniment. Burt Lancaster's Ole Andreson (aka "the Swede") is clearly drawn to her, as is the audience. He immediately abandons his girlfriend, who is left to chat idly with one of the guests, as he stares, almost open-mouthed, at the engrossing spectacle of Kitty. The whole scene oozes sex. Kitty is very aware of the Swede's gaze, and seems to very much enjoy the attention. The lighting of the room, through the smoke haze, greatly emphasizes the contours of Kitty's body. This is an obvious example of Naremore's conception of an "erotic lighting" set-up.

Drawing on the lighting of older mystery films (and perhaps directly or indirectly from German Expressionism) erotic lighting is—according to Naremore—intended to visually represent and amplify the male's fear of female sexuality. The Swede's fear here is well-founded, but he cannot resist temptation. Kitty unlocks the carnal and the corrupt within him, and he is inevitably drawn to his death. Kitty is cast in this scene as a spectacle, an irresistible object of carnal desire. In subsequent scenes this is stripped away, as Kitty further draws the Swede into the conspiracy. In a scene near the end of the film, Kitty and the Swede consider making a break for it. Different semes are employed by the filmmakers here: the figure of Kitty as sexual being is played down, both in terms of Gardner's performance and in her appearance. Her makeup is much less severe, more naturalistic; her clothes are much more casual and functional; her hair, similarly, is arranged in a neat configuration for comfort rather than to complement, for instance, the black dress. However, this figuration of Kitty is yet another projection of male fantasy. In this case, Kitty is fulfilling the male's need for companionship and an almost maternal security; this is another ruse by Kitty to further lure the Swede to his demise, to take the fall.

Kitty Collins in *The Killers* is the archetypal *femme fatale*, a striking beauty, using her sex appeal and all aspects of her femininity to lure the unsuspecting male target to his doom. She is, however, a fragmented character. Her confidence wavers; she is being used as an instrument of control by the male characters, particularly her husband, Big Jim. Her recognition of herself as a tool gives her pause and causes her to doubt. The result is a fractured figure who ends up paying the price for trusting corrupted characters: Kitty must take the fall for her husband's crimes, as he does not exonerate her before his death.

Unlike the stylistic construction of Kitty, with high contrast to accentuate her eyes, hair, curves, and lips, the titular character in Preminger's *Laura* is rarely lit with anything other than all-encompassing, high-key lighting. This could perhaps be due to the film's being slightly older, or simply to Preminger's style. The resulting film, regardless, places more emphasis on character and performance than on striking visuals. This is not to say, though, that the film is without cinematic flair, particularly as regards its central female figure. For the film's first half, Laura Hunt is a specter: a supposed murder victim appearing only in remembered and recounted circumstances and, infamously and most crucially, in her likeness, the painting above her fireplace. Memories can be hazy and idealized, just as a painting's subject can be treated generously, if inaccurately, by its artist. The men that circle around Laura—her fiancé Shelby Carpenter (Vincent Price), her socialite guardian Waldo Lydecker (Clifton Webb), and the detective investigating her death, Lieutenant Mark McPherson (Dana Andrews)—project their own idealized desire onto the conveniently absent character. The painting over the fireplace becomes the real Laura, at least in their minds.

The object-of-mystery *femme fatale* is like a puzzle that must be pieced together; this is observed in *Laura*. Laura is the supposed murder victim, so it is her absent, lifeless corpse that forms the focus of McPherson's investigation. In unravelling the mystery of her death, McPherson also uncovers something of the truth about her life. The mystery of her death and the fascination of her life become intertwined in McPherson's mind. When he awakes from a drunken nap in Laura's apartment to find her there alive and well, the disbelief on his face is understandable. But this is soon replaced by a cool, calculated indifference as he resolves to uncover the truth. There is just enough time for him to order Laura to stay in the apartment and not contact anyone; this is partly done to manipulate the truth out of her friends and fiancé, but also, as McPherson says, "if anything should happen to you this time, I wouldn't like it."

Angela Martin notes that in *Laura*, it is not the central character that is active in luring the males to their doom; they do that all by themselves. "[I]t is the *male* characters whose shadows are thrown; it is the male characters who produce 'the fatal': Laura just brings out what is already there."[15] Martin also looks into the development of the film, noting that in Vera Caspary's original play, Laura Hunt was a much more rounded character. "I'd given Laura a heroine's youth and beauty but had added the strength of a woman who had, in spite of the struggle and competition of success in business, retained the feminine delicacy that allowed men to exercise the power of masculinity."[16] Where Martin goes on to suggest that much of this was lost in Preminger's adaptation, I (respectfully) disagree. Kitty Collins is a fragmented figure—much like, for instance, Lily Carver in *Kiss Me Deadly* (Robert Aldrich, 1955) or Brigid O'Shaugnessy in *The Maltese Falcon* (John Huston, 1941)—caught up in the machinations of a criminal plot. Laura, as played by Gene Tierney, is certainly youthful, vivacious, and beautiful, but is also a successful career woman, living alone and independently. It is only her *absence* that allows the men to exercise their masculinity—it is the male competitiveness and jealousy that drives the action, and this is a fracas that Laura sees herself (rightly) as being above.

There are parallels between *Laura*, *The Killers*, and *Jessica Jones*, which will be addressed before moving into a deeper analysis of Jones as noir character. Laura and Jessica, at least in their adult lives, have functioned primarily as the object of male interest, be it personal, sexual, or professional. At key moments, however, both characters declare their separation from this male domination. Laura declares herself to Waldo Lydecker (Clifton Webb), seeking an endorsement of a pen that her agency is advertising. When Lydecker refuses, Laura persists, until she finally reveals that she sought him out under her own initiative. Lydecker does not immediately soften, and it is not until later that he seeks Laura out to apologize. This vehement declaration of Laura's independence sets her apart. Further, she lives alone, clearly comfortable with her own space and, it should be noted, her own image, given her painting's privileged position in the house. In addition to the images projected on Laura by her male satellites, she too projects an idealized image of herself into the world. It is not until the end of the film, when Laura is finally depicted alone in her apartment that the mask falls away. Gene Tierney plays Laura here as exhausted, but relieved that the chain of events will be resolved soon; this relief gives way to terror, when Lydecker is suddenly in the parlor with her, a shotgun leveled at her face. Lieutenant McPherson, though, has figured out Lydecker's plan, and bursts back into the apartment in time to defend Laura—it is here that the film ends, order supposedly restored.

Jessica Jones presents the world with a version of herself as the world-weary (and world-wary), hard-drinking private eye. As her friend Trish repeatedly points out, though, this is not her true nature. The true Jessica is the hero, who wants to use whatever she can—be it her logic and deductive skills, or her superpowers—to help those in need or distress.

The character of Waldo Lydecker in *Laura* is also eerily similar to *Jessica Jones'* Kilgrave. Both Lydecker and Kilgrave are portrayed—by Clifton Webb and David Tennant respectively—as athletic, cultured, intelligent, cunning, and somewhat effete. Both are obsessed with their female targets. Their obsession leads them to greater and greater acts of transgression. Ultimately, both get their comeuppance, but it is certain that while revenge is satisfying, each victim will bear the visible scars of this obsession for the rest of their lives.

Kitty Collins is a fractured figure: very aware of her own powerful sexuality, but also powerless—and perhaps somewhat naïve—about the corrupt men that encircle and entrap both her and the Swede. The mask that Collins puts on is one of empowered femininity, but the truth is much sadder. Jessica Jones is an accomplished detective and a fiercely independent character and, as noted, she wears the mask of the hardboiled investigator. At the same time, she is understandably traumatized by her experiences with Kilgrave. The moment she realizes that her investigation may well lead her to her former tormentor, the trauma is inscribed on her face—that fractured visage becomes a defining feature of the character throughout the show. It is an expression that only the audience is aware of, for the most part, as Jessica mostly wears it only when she is alone. She realizes just in time that in order to stop Kilgrave, she must ditch the detective and put on the costume of the *femme fatale*. The *femme fatale*—whether sexual seductress or object-of-mystery—is always a fractured figure, a muddle of semes, hermeneutic codes, and symbolic groupings, struggling to come to terms with *her own* situation in the world. That her place in the world may be entirely dependent on male characters often creates a sense of, at its most benign, frustration or, at its extreme, mental breakdown; this makes for some incredibly complex characterizations. Jessica Jones is one such multifaceted figure.

Jessica Jones as Femme Fatale–*cum–Hardboiled Detective*

The translation of film noir—even neo-noir—to the television format is not without its complications. An intense two-hour study of a single character and their satellites must be expanded to incorporate various other sub-plots and secondary figures. The protagonist (or protagonists) should develop as the episodes progress; there should be some kind of denouement, with the hint of questions to be answered in subsequent seasons. Television studies tend towards some kind of theory of how the device functions in the home, how it engages audiences, and how it functions as a medium.[17] In the wake of the recent boom of "high quality" narrative television in the HBO era, more recent studies take form and narrative into account, even willfully ignoring the televisual aspects and instead focusing on the purely cinematic. Brian L. Ott shifts the study of television more towards a textual analytical angle, and, appropriately, these later studies co-opt terminology and theory from cinema studies in order to observe trends in characterization and representation: "[A]ny cultural commodity produced, distributed, and circulated by the entertainment industry can be approached as a text."[18]

The extended, serial form of television, though, cannot be ignored or underestimated in terms of its potential for deep character exploration and development, as well as playing the format for suspense and audience engagement. This is where, perhaps, the functional/medium-based conception of television merges somewhat with representational/formal analysis. This merger is even more pronounced in the era of streaming entertainment, and the phenomenon known as binge-watching: to be consumed in a large clump of episodes at a time or, ideally, across a whole day. *Jessica Jones* emerged in the wake of its companion Marvel series, *Daredevil*, but at the tail-end of a strong push by Netflix in terms of creating its own content. This began primarily with Beau Willimon's adaptation of the British television series *House of Cards*. Willimon's series was produced by David Fincher, who also directed the first two episodes of the series. Fincher's cinematic gravitas and influence is evident not only in his own two episodes, but across the entire series. *House of Cards* was intended by Fincher and Willimon (and by other executive producer and lead actor Kevin Spacey) to be binge-watched. Fincher says:

> If you're working in the movie business, you're thinking in terms of you have this two-hour form that requires a kind of ballistic narrative that doesn't always allow for characterizations to be that complex, or that deep, or that layered, or that you can reveal slowly and be as faceted. And I felt for the past ten years that the best writing that was happening for actors was happening in television. And so I had been looking to do something that was longer form.[19]

Jessica Jones is perhaps crafted around this binge-watch-ready model, but I would certainly argue that the darkness of its themes, and the investigative or procedural nature of its narrative, dissuade the viewer from gorging themselves. Like old pulp crime short stories, the series feels more appropriate one or two episodes at a time. That said, Perks has investigated how binge-watching can increase an audience's engagement with characters, and their immersion in the story-world. She posits a wardrobe metaphor as a way of conceiving the total suspension of disbelief that occurs with true immersion in a fantasy world, such as that presented by a television show or film:

> *Something* about the story has drawn us in so strongly that we emphasize the story world over the lived experience for a temporary stretch, dedicating time and effort to understanding its discourses as they mingle with our existing experiences and enduring discourses.[20]

I am questioning the degree to which this level of immersion can occur with *Jessica Jones*, but it must be remembered that, despite its oft-mentioned darkness and grittiness, it remains a series set in a world with superheroes. Similarly, the symbolic groupings and hermeneutic codes the series employs are drawn from another popular entertainment: films noir.

For roughly the first two thirds of the series, Jones is characterized *and* technically treated as the hardboiled antihero. However, at the end of the ninth episode, "AKA Sin Bin," a tremendous shift occurs not only for the character, but for the series as a whole. This episode is discussed in more depth shortly, but suffice to say that the end of this episode reveals that Kilgrave no longer has power over Jessica. From this moment, for the remainder of the series, Jones becomes cinematically treated as the *femme fatale*. She is still the antihero underneath, however. She is still the hardboiled detective *and* the superhero wanting to do good, thus certainly retaining the object-of-mystery trope.

Before this point, however, she is positioned by the narrative and the style as the typical noir protagonist; the cynical detective engaged in the initial stages of her investigation. Like Dana Andrews' Detective McPherson in *Laura*, Jones is a cynic, a heavy drinker, and seemingly ambivalent to the lofty ideas of love and happiness. Apart from the interviews of with Hope Shlottman, which usually take place during daytime visiting hours at the jail, Jessica's initial inquiries take place at night. As noted, Jones dresses herself in dark colors; this, combined with her dark hair, makes her at one with the night and the city. The notion of "hidden in plain sight"—the inherent advantage of being invisible—is played in Jessica Jones both in terms of Jones' configuration as operating outside standard law enforcement, but also in terms of fear. Kilgrave's power means that he can order anyone to do his bidding—Jones and her friends are constantly at a disadvantage, as they never know who is under Kilgrave's power or where he will pop up next.

The shift from the initial investigation to a broader focus on the Jones/ Kilgrave relationship is obviously a narrative turning point, but is also a key moment for the figuration of Jones' character. This shift occurs in "AKA Sin Bin." Jessica captures Kilgrave and locks him in a hermetically sealed tank. A few inches of water in the bottom of the tank have been rigged with an exposed wire, such that if Kilgrave tries to use his powers, the depression of a red button will electrocute him. Videos of Kilgrave's childhood torture are played repeatedly; Kilgrave looks dejected. Jessica constantly films the tank, aiming to lure Kilgrave into using his powers; he is, however, keenly aware of the trap she is laying. When Jessica enters the tank to give Kilgrave some food, she attempts to push Kilgrave's buttons, first sexually, then violently. The characterization of Jones is appropriately seductive in this moment: Jessica lowers her voice to a sultry, animalistic growl; her lips pout, and her posture becomes slinky, appearing on the one hand to succumb to Kilgrave's masculine presence, but also to wrap around and ensnare him in her own feminine one. "I know how you like to be touched," she purrs, as she draws her fingers softly across Kilgrave's chest. Kilgrave sees through the ruse—he refuses to use his powers. He is, however, undoubtedly aroused. "You have my full attention!" he beams.

The characterization of Jessica as slinky seductress is filmed in an alternation of mid-shots and closeups. Mid-shots accentuate Jessica's physical looseness in this moment—she wants Kilgrave to see her body move. Close-ups show Jessica's eyes, her exposed neck, and draw attention to her lips with her breathy utterances. The close-up is also an intimate framing, reiterating Jessica's attempts to overwhelm Kilgrave with her femininity. The hermetic tank is a confined space to begin with, but these moments cinematographically constrict that space even further. Jessica literally has Kilgrave up against the wall. It is then that the mood switches and Jessica begins to try to physically provoke Kilgrave into using his powers to protect himself. The space opens up once more as Jessica throws Kilgrave around it. The cinematographic expansion of the tank makes Jessica smaller as a figure within the frame, but the narrative irony is that she is more terrifying, given her control over the enlarged space. This is one of the key moments where Jessica is not shy about using her powers. Trish looks on as Jessica flips Kilgrave around like a rag doll, wondering whether or not she should electrocute them both and end the legally inadmissible torture. Jones' plan fails, however. While Jones is absent, Kilgrave manipulates Hogarth into freeing him. It is this failure, though, that allows Jones to realize that Kilgrave no longer has power over her. This is the moment when Jones shifts from hapless victim and begins to embody the "sexual seductress" from film noir. She is no less Kilgrave's victim, but one that has a key means of enacting revenge.

Rather than a *femme fatale* that uses her wiles to entrap a hapless everyman,

Jones activates the tropes of that same *femme fatale* in order to lure Kilgrave to his death. The tension of both the series and the character of Jones is released in the very moment Kilgrave's neck is snapped. This is an immensely satisfying conclusion to the arc of the series—for better or worse, though, the unanswered questions (and thus the potential for future stories/series) are left somewhat diminished in the viewer's mind. Jones is a layered projection here and throughout the series. Firstly, she is the object of Kilgrave's fantasy from a purely human, psychological perspective. Second, she has also been the controlled, subordinated, manipulated slave to Kilgrave's powers; this is what Kilgrave believes he has regained in the final episodes. Thirdly, she is faking this second projection in order to lure Kilgrave to his death. This ability to negate Kilgrave's control is not necessarily a superpower—certainly not a consciously activated one.

Jessica's performance of her prior, enslaved self is an inversion of Kilgrave's fantasy, permitting her to get close enough to make the final, fatal move. This subversion of the seductress archetype—not to mention the character of Jones herself—gives the series credence as an example of the rape-revenge film. Alex Heller-Nicholas's position is that the rape-revenge film is not its own genre; rather she posits that this is a narrative pattern that functions over or within other genres. Heller-Nicholas observes the narrative pattern particularly as it functions within the horror genre.[21] While the visual tropes differ from those of noir, and the narratives of horror rape-revenge films typically involve an incredibly gruesome finale, there are some similarities in terms of the depiction and eventual release of trauma. Claire Henry, in particular, notes that elements of rape-revenge are present in a number of erotic thrillers or neo-noirs, such as *The Girl with the Dragon Tattoo* (Niels Arden Oplev, 2009), *Irreversible* (Gaspar Noé, 2002), *The Book of Revelation* (Ana Kokkinos, 2006), or *The Disappearance of Alice Creed* (J. Blakeson, 2009).[22] Heller-Nicholas observes the varying representations of the sexual assault itself, from the implied, to the uncomfortably-prolonged direct portrayal, through to the rape surrogate; this latter being another form of physical or psychological torture or abuse.

The anti-heroine lies beneath all these projections and subversions, however. While still not entirely accepting of her true, good, nature, Jessica grudgingly admits that it feels good to help people. At the time of writing, however, it remains to be seen how this altruism will develop, or whether it extends only as far as the satisfaction of enacting revenge on Kilgrave. It is in combining the anti-heroine and the seductress archetypes—and filming the resulting character in an appropriately neo-noir way—that the deeper messages of *Jessica Jones* are most effectively put into relief. Jones oscillates wildly between the indulgence of her trauma and the denial of it, before realizing that she can leverage her power and her personality to defeat Kilgrave. The utterance of various semes throughout the corpus of film noir has been refined and enunciated in *Jessica Jones*. The complex neo-noir detective is rewritten here as a fiercely independent woman working to move on from her past. There is still a long way to go, but *Jessica Jones* is one more chapter in the proliferation of strong, complex, non-male characters in popular culture. *Jessica Jones* is very much set in the Marvel Universe, but it opens up a personal story unlike anything we have seen in that world before. Interestingly, as demonstrated here, it co-opts symbolic configurations, codes, and semes from film noir in order to do so.

NOTES

1. Kia Groom, "So You Married a Supervillain: Watching *Jessica Jones* as a Trauma Survivor." *The Mary Sue*. December 17, 2015, http://www.themarysue.com/watching-jessica-jones-as-a-trauma-survivor/. See also Jos Truitt, "Jessica Jones, or How To Make a TV Show About Trauma." *Feministing*. November 24, 2015, http://feministing.com/2015/11/24/jessica-jones-or-how-to-make-a-tv-show-about-trauma/; Kelley Calkins, "Why Is Jessica Jones Important?" *Huffington Post*. December 21, 2015, http://www.huffingtonpost.com/kelley-calkins/why-is-jessica-jones-impo_b_8846902.html.
2. This is not a misspelling; the additional 'I' in Killgrave is present in Bendis' and Gaydos' *Alias* series, as is Killgrave's first name, Zebediah. In the Marvel TV series, "Kilgrave" is the alias Kevin Thompson chose to distance himself from his traumatic childhood.
3. Kathrina Glithre, "Under the Neon Rainbow: Colour and Neo-Noir," in *Neo-Noir*, ed. Mark Bould, Kathrina Glitre, and Greg Tuck (New York: Columbia University Press, 2015), 17.
4. Jerold J. Abrams, "Space, Time, and Subjectivity in Neo-Noir Cinema," in *The Philosophy of Neo-Noir*, ed. Mark T. Conard (Lexington: University Press of Kentucky, 2007), 7.
5. Abrams, 7.
6. Rebecca R. House, "Night of the Soul: American Film Noir," *Studies in Popular Culture* 9, no. 1 (1986): 62.
7. Mark Bould, *Film Noir: From Berlin to Sin City* (New York: Columbia University Press, 2012), 108.
8. Janey Place, "Women in Film Noir," in *Women in Film Noir*, ed. E. Ann Kaplan (London: British Film Institute, 1998), 47.
9. Mary Ann Doane, *Femmes Fatales: Feminism, Film Theory, Psychoanalysis* (New York: Routledge, 1991), 2–3.
10. Elisabeth Bronfen, "Femme Fatale: Negotiations of Tragic Desire," *New Literary History* 35, no. 1 (2004), 113.
11. Bronfen, 114.
12. Roland Barthes, *S/Z* (Malden: Blackwell, 2002), 19.
13. Barthes, 19.
14. Place, 53.
15. Angela Martin, "'Gilda didn't do any of those things you've been losing sleep over!' The Central Woman of 40s Films Noir," in *Women in Film Noir: New Edition*, ed. Amy Kaplan (London: British Film Institute, 1998), 214.
16. Caspary, cited in Martin, 211–12.
17. See John Fiske and John Hartley, *Reading Television* (London: Routledge, 2003), 49–53.
18. Brian L. Ott, "Introduction: The Not TV text," in *It's Not TV: Watching HBO in the Post-Television Era*, ed. Marc Leverett, Brian L. Ott, and Cara Louise Buckley (New York: Routledge, 2008), 97.
19. Fincher, interviewed by Alan Sepinwall, "'House of Cards' Director David Fincher on Making 13 Hours for Netflix." *HitFix*. January 29, 2013, http://www.hitfix.com/whats-alan-watching/house-of-cards-director-david-fincher-on-making-13-hours-for-netflix. This inter-

view gives a lot of insight into translating cinematic directing to a serial format, and also the logistics of crafting a story over an extended period of time, intended to be consumed in a large chunk.

20. Lisa Glebatis Perks, *Media Marathoning: Immersions in Morality* (Lanham, MD: Lexington Books, 2015), 2.

21. Alex Heller-Nicholas, "The Violation of Representation: Art, Argento and the Rape-Revenge Film," *Forum* 13 (2011), 2. This is opposed to positioning rape-revenge as a sub-genre of horror, as Henry notes has been done by other critics.

22. Claire Henry, *Revisionist Rape-Revenge: Redefining a Film Genre* (New York: Palgrave Macmillan, 2014), 2–3.

BIBLIOGRAPHY

Abrams, Jerold J. "Space, Time, and Subjectivity in Neo-Noir Cinema." In *The Philosophy of Neo-Noir*, edited by Mark T. Conard, 7–20. Lexington: University Press of Kentucky, 2007.

Barthes, Roland. *S/Z*. Malden: Blackwell, 2002.

Bould, Mark. *Film Noir: From Berlin to Sin City*. New York: Columbia University Press, 2012.

Bronfen, Elisabeth. "Femme Fatale: Negotiations of Tragic Desire." *New Literary History* 35, no. 1 (2004): 103–116.

Doane, Mary Ann. *Femmes Fatales: Feminism, Film Theory, Psychoanalysis*. New York: Routledge, 1991.

Fiske, John, and John Hartley. *Reading Television*. London: Routledge, 2003.

Glithre, Kathrina. "Under the Neon Rainbow: Colour and Neo-Noir." In *Neo-Noir*, edited by Mark Bould, Kathrina Glitre, and Greg Tuck, 11–27. New York: Columbia University Press, 2015.

Groom, Kia. "So You Married a Supervillain: Watching *Jessica Jones* as a Trauma Survivor." *The Mary Sue*. December 17, 2015. http://www.themarysue.com/watching-jessica-jones-as-a-trauma-survivor/.

Heller-Nicholas, Alex. "The Violation of Representation: Art, Argento and the Rape-Revenge Film." *Forum* 13 (2011), 1–12.

Henry, Claire. *Revisionist Rape-Revenge: Redefining a Film Genre*. New York: Palgrave Macmillan, 2014.

House, Rebecca R. "Night of the Soul: American Film Noir." *Studies in Popular Culture* 9, no. 1 (1986): 61–83.

Martin, Angela. "'Gilda didn't do any of those things you've been losing sleep over!' The Central Woman of 40s Films Noir." In *Women in Film Noir: New Edition*, edited by Amy Kaplan, 202–228. London: British Film Institute, 1998.

Ott, Brian L. "Introduction: The Not TV text." In *It's Not TV: Watching HBO in the Post-Television Era*, edited by Marc Leverett, Brian L. Ott, and Cara Louise Buckley, 97–100. New York: Routledge, 2008.

Perks, Lisa Glebatis. *Media Marathoning: Immersions in Morality*. Lanham, MD: Lexington Books, 2015.

Place, Janey. "Women in Film Noir." In *Women in Film Noir*, edited by E. Ann Kaplan, 47–68. London: British Film Institute, 1998.

Sepinwall, Alan. "'House of Cards' Director David Fincher on Making 13 Hours for Netflix." *HitFix*. 29 January 2013. http://www.hitfix.com/whats-alan-watching/house-of-cards-director-david-fincher-on-making-13-hours-for-netflix.

Elite and Famous

Subverting Gender in the Marvel Universe with Jessica Jones

Nicholas William Moll

This essay explores the contrasts between the Netflix series *Jessica Jones* and its Marvel comic book source series, *Alias*. In doing so, it focuses on each incarnation's respective use of the wider Marvel Universe. While both texts make use of a protagonist struggling with the aftermath of abduction, abuse, sexual assault, and trauma, *Jessica Jones* does so in a limited scope that focuses on the main character as an individual victim of the super-powered criminal, Kilgrave. In contrast, *Alias* invokes a global drama of aliens, costumed vigilantism, and mutants—including the purple-skinned supervillain, Killgrave, also known as the Purple Man. In doing so, *Alias* engages a legacy of traditional notions of superhero characterizations, contrasting the protagonist Jessica with a wide range of mainstream superheroines such as Captain Marvel, Spider-Woman, and Phoenix. While the television adaption is frugal in its use of the Marvel Cinematic Universe, this essay argues that *Jessica Jones* presents a form of superhero literature that subverts hierarchies of gender, class, and ideology frequently enshrined in costumed adventure narratives.

Market and Celebrity

Jessica Jones, and its source text, *Alias*, are both set within an expanded Marvel Universe. That is to say, both operate as a small portion of a wider setting that is explored through other stories. For *Alias*, this wider Marvel Universe setting is positioned broadly across the company's range of superhero comic books. Indeed, a significant portion of Jessica's background in *Alias* is her close yet complicated relationship to the Avengers superhero team. While featured in *Alias*, the Avengers' adventures are detailed in their own, self-titled comic book. The television series, however, operates on a far more limited scope than its comic book counterpart. Similar to *Alias*, *Jessica Jones* is set within the wider Marvel Cinematic Universe (MCU), which includes films and television series produced by Marvel Studios and Netflix. Herein, *Jessica Jones* occurs in the space of *The Avengers*[1] films and their associated characters along with Netflix's *Daredevil*[2] television series. This is indicated by references made throughout *Jessica Jones* to "the flag waver" (Captain America), "the big green dude who's cruel" (the Hulk), and "the Incident" (the alien attack on New York depicted in *The Avengers*). While *Jessica Jones* also comes to feature Claire Temple, who is also included in *Daredevil*, this is the only overt character introduced from another source. The limitations of television's scope are thus evident in the manner through which *Jessica Jones* engages the expanded universe, through allusion—referring to characters through dialogue. In both comic book and television incarnations, the life of Jessica Jones occurs within a wider setting respectively.

Jessica Jones does not come to interact with the wider MCU but is instead tightly interwoven with characters featured in the series. These connections thus do not extend outside the series itself as they do in the *Alias* comic book, but instead feature Jessica's childhood friend (Trish Walker), her nemesis Kilgrave, and other individuals who are immediately connected to the protagonist's personal narrative and not the further evocation of an expanded universe. Furthermore, there is a sense that *Jessica Jones'* portion of the Marvel Cinematic Universe is unrealized. While Jessica is romantically involved with Luke Cage and Cage himself has acquired superpowers, he is not yet publicly acting as Power Man. Rather, he is simply Luke Cage, bartender. Similarly, Trish "Patsy" Walker, Jessica's close friend and confidant, has not yet taken on the comic book Patsy Walker's super-heroic identity as Hellcat. Will Simpson is also featured in *Jessica Jones*, a televisual counterpart to the MU's Frank Simpson. However, Simpson has yet to be identified or empowered as the supervillain Nuke, a foe of Captain America. Nor is *Jessica Jones'* Jeri Hogarth a male legal counsel to superheroes as per the comic book universe, but rather an unethical and pragmatic female lawyer. Even Kilgrave, with his mind-altering powers, is presented in a muted fashion for television, lacking the distinctive purple skin and ironic title (the Purple Man) of his comic book counterpart. Only Claire Temple, titled the Night Nurse within the comic book universe and an aid to injured superheroes, is similar to her comic book referent in role but not title. Thus, while there are a variety of prominent characters within *Jessica Jones* adapted from Marvel's range of comic books, they are introduced within the television series and contextualized into Jessica's life. As such, *Jessica Jones* is focused on a localized network rather than an expanded universe of characters, each with their own distinct and wholly separate narratives.

In contrast to *Jessica Jones*, *Alias* actively features Jessica interacting directly with characters such as Captain America, Captain Marvel, Ant-Man, Daredevil, and other established Marvel superheroes. The *Alias* series storylines do not simply draw on existing characters, but provide integral narratives about them that extend beyond Jessica's personal journey itself. For instance, in the storyline "B Level," Jessica Jones encounters an impersonator claiming to be Rick Jones, a former sidekick to Hulk and Captain America. Herein, *Alias* revisits several significant storylines of *Hulk*, *Captain America*, and *Avengers* comic books featuring the real Rick Jones such as the *Kree-Skrull War*.[3] Engaging in the vigorous patchwork of the Marvel Universe (MU), *Alias* functions as a node under R. Alberich, J. Miro-Julia, and F. Rosselló's definition[4]: that is, as a discernible point for specific concepts and ideas in the wider setting, the edges of which touch on the wider milieu of other key concepts and ideas embodied in comic book titles.[5] Links between individual nodes then solidify when "corresponding characters have jointly appeared" in multiple titles.[6] The effect is one of a "social structure" or hierarchy within which certain characters develop a higher currency—both commercial and cultural—than others, and in being more popular are more central to the MU.[7] Captain America, featured throughout *Alias*, had been the focus of not only numerous comic books, but film, videogames, toys, clothing, animation, and other franchise products since the 1940s. As such, Captain America is likewise positioned within the MU as one of the setting's foremost superheroes.

The value of certain characters over others, while based in market value and cultural currency, is likewise woven into *Alias*' narratives and depiction of the MU. Herein, certain characters are described by the media within the book as "elite and famous" superheroes,[8] that is, those characters widely popular within the real-world consumer marketplace and celebrated within their fictional settings, such as Captain America and Iron Man. These notable and iconic characters are separated in *Alias* from other protagonists that occupy a relatively unknown status in the market, lacking large multimedia franchises in their own right, and overlooked within their fictional settings, such as Jessica.

The integration of the wider MU positions the events depicted in *Alias* within a global context. However, the intervening presence of the wider setting also regulates the drama of *Alias* to a reclusive level of secondary spectacle. During *Alias*' 2001–2004 run, for instance, Earth is transformed into an intergalactic prison by the alien Kree,[9] Magneto attempts to exterminate all human life on Earth,[10] clones of Thanos attempt to destroy the universe,[11] and the Avengers are disbanded.[12] While Jessica is not featured in these events, they are present in the wider setting of *Alias*. The secondary nature of *Alias*, however, creates the effect of a wider intersection of nodes—an experience focused not on Jessica Jones herself but the wider collection of characters.

Superheroines

As part of the series' integration of the MU, throughout the *Alias* comic series Jessica is contrasted with mainstreamed, established superheroines drawn from the wider MU. On a basic level, this occurs through Jessica's encounters with various characters that exist within and have long-term histories in the mainstream Marvel continuity and various individual comic-book titles. Most notably, Captain Marvel (Carol Danvers),[13] two variations of Spider-Woman (both Jessica Drew and Mattie Franklin),[14] and Phoenix (Jean Grey).[15] Carol Danvers has appeared in a variety of self-titled and *Avengers* publications since her premier in 1968[16] as NASA security captain Carol Danvers, and under later adopted titles—Ms. Marvel from 1977[17] and Captain Marvel from 2012.[18] Similarly, both incarnations of *Spider-Woman* (Jessica Drew and Mattie Franklin) have featured as the protagonist of various *Spider-Woman* comic book series, in addition to their inclusion in both *Avengers* and *Spider-Man* publications since their 1977 (Drew)[19] and 1998 (Franklin)[20] premiers. Phoenix originally debuted as Marvel Girl in 1963 and has appeared throughout the *X-Men* franchise since.[21] Each of these three characters—Captain Marvel, Spider-Woman, and Phoenix—are linked to prominent Marvel comic books and are key features of the expanded setting. They are also archetypical superheroes in the sense that they possess both civilian and costumed identities, histories and legacies explicitly linked to other heroic characters, team memberships, an array of villains, and other typical features of superhero characterization.[22]

However, Jessica Jones lacks each of these features, premiering in *Jessica Jones: Alias* issue one in 2001 and lacking a costumed identity. Despite the title of the comic book as "*Alias*"—Jessica Jones, private investigator operates under no title save her name and occupation. Jessica also lacks many of the archetypical features of a superhero such as a rogue's gallery of villains and team memberships. As such, due to her lack of costumed identity and twenty-first century premiere, Jessica is automatically contrasted with other female protagonists featured in *Alias*.

In addition to these contrasts, Jessica is further distinct due to her lack of a direct male counterpart. Michael R. Lavin notes superheroines in Marvel comics are "often defined by their relationship to men," and points to the tradition of deriving superheroines from more established heroes both in terms of concept and origin.[23] She-Hulk, for example, is Hulk's cousin who gained her powers after a blood transfusion from her male counterpart. Captain Marvel is directly derivative of a pre-existing male, Captain Marvel (Dr. Walter Lawson) in both powers and original costume. Likewise, the Jessica Drew variation of Spider-Woman derived her powers from a spider-blood serum, similar to Spider-Man's origin with an injection of a radioactively altered spider's venom. In contrast, Mattie Franklin began as a minor character in *Spider-Man* comic books. Thus in many cases, superheroines share their status and identity as characters with other, male, protagonists, relegating them to a market side-line.[24] Lavin further notes that tethering female characters to male heroes makes superheroines glamorized but largely unnecessary, as their activities and roles as heroic figures are already occupied. Captain Marvel, Spider-Woman, and Phoenix therefore cannot be classified as "elite and famous" characters in and of themselves, but are certainly featured in the same hierarchy.

Just as in-universe celebrity for the character follows the market place, female protagonists are often outranked by male superheroes in terms of publication volume. Kristin J. Anderson and Donna Cavallaro note that this is in spite of female characters such as She-Hulk, Captain Marvel, Spider-Woman, and others who have enjoyed multiple incarnations within numerous self-titled comic book series published over prolonged periods.[25] Rather, male superheroes will see more regular and numerous publications of self-titled comic books than their female counterparts. Anderson and Cavallaro further argue that the superhero genre is conventionally enameled with traditional "American values and 'maleness,'" which further relegates female characters to a supporting role.[26] In doing so, Anderson and Cavallaro attribute lesser publication ranges to a comparatively lower quantity of female characterizations within comic books in general.[27] Within this structured hierarchy, superheroines are ranked as secondary in both characterization and marketplace significance to their male counterparts.

There is, however, no male counterpart or pre-existing character with which Jessica Jones shares a relationship. Rather, Jessica Jones premiered in *Alias* as a unique character. Indeed, the contemporary nature of Jessica's creation is noted by the Purple Man (Kilgrave in the television series). Referring to Jessica's 2001 origin but retroactive placement into the MU, the Purple Man describes Jessica metatextually as having a "contradictory nature." Indeed, *Alias* launches Jessica as an established character—placing her at the Baxter Building during the Fantastic Four's first battle with Galactus in 1966, in Midtown High School in 1962 with Peter Parker on the day he acquired his powers as Spider-Man, and her time as a hostage of the Purple Man during the villain's period in the 1960s and 1970s as a *Daredevil* foe.[28] Retrospectively placed into the MU and lacking a male antecedent character, Jessica stands in contrast to other female protagonists featured in *Alias* and the expanded universe.

The presentation of Jessica's femininity and sexuality further highlights the distancing of the character from other superheroines. The typical super-heroine is presented to audiences with a "voluptuous figure" of "thin waist and silicone breasts" emphasized by a revealing "'bathing costume' outfit."[29] While Jessica is shown to have engaged the archetypical superheroine image prior to the onset of *Alias* as Jewel, outside of flashbacks, Jessica is presented in the practical work attire of t-shirt, jacket, and jeans. Indeed, the candid presentation of Jessica's life throughout *Alias*, such as panels depicting the character utilizing the toilet, disrupts the typically exaggerated voluptuous image of the female MU protagonist.

Likewise, just as Jessica's image is that of a non-superhero, so too is this role highlighted in her activities and situation as a private detective. During Jessica's first date with Ant-Man (Scott Lang), the pair notices a battle between Spider-Man and Doctor Octopus in the street outside. When asked by Ant-Man if she wishes to intervene, Jessica comments that it is "not my thing," indicating a distinction between Jessica herself and typical superheroines. In doing so, Jessica Jones is positioned in opposition to the "blind though well-intentioned" crusade for justice typically associated with superhero activi-ties.[30] Rather, throughout *Alias*, justice is an abstract idea, defined by the police, state law, courts, and other legally and politically empowered entities rather than by Jessica herself. Storylines in both "Alias" and "Homecoming" demonstrate Jessica attempting to work with police, with varying degrees of success. Likewise, "Alias" and "Underneath" show Jessica working with S.H.I.E.L.D.[31] Jessica lacks the self-imposed mission or sense of service and as such is not positioned "beyond the power of the armed forces" and in range with the non-superhero—or "the normal"—characters of the MU.[32] While Jessica is a protagonist, the character is not presented within *Alias* as a superheroine in outlook or activity.

Alias' denial of the role and sexualized image typically attributed to super-heroines is followed in *Jessica Jones*. However, while *Jessica Jones* largely fol-lows the visual tropes of Jessica's presentation established in *Alias*, the contrast between the character and other superheroines is less pronounced due to the localized focus of the television series' expanded universe. Jessica Jones is the central character of the series, with the narrative focused strongly on the after-math of her abduction by Kilgrave. In the wake of her traumatic experience, television Jessica lives with a degree of fluidity, working hours of her choosing, defining her mixed home and work space on a day-by-day, case-by-case status. Likewise, in the second episode, when Jessica visits Luke Cage's bar and engages in intercourse with Cage himself, it is uncertain if the visit is part of a case, a personal quest, recreation, or some undefined mixture of all three.

Later in the series, with the revelation that Jessica murdered Cage's wife while under Kilgrave's control, distinction between the three objectives mentioned above becomes less clear. Luke Cage shifts back and forth from lead to case to lover. The result for Jessica, as Luke Cage notes, is a messy and indistinct bundle of motivations and activities. Likewise, Jessica's involvement with Jeri Hogarth is on one level professional—providing Jessica with casework—and on another, personal, with Jessica assisting in Jeri's divorce and the latter aiding in the pursuit of Kilgrave. Trish Walker is at once best friend, confidant, and sister to Jessica. If the superheroine is intended to embody "domesticity, motherhood and consumerism" as Lillian Robinson argues,[33] it is an embodiment denied in *Jessica Jones*. The fluid mix of professional and personal denies anyone from occupying a single, convenient role. As Robinson notes, however, the domestic ideals of the superheroine are associated stringently with mid-to-late twentieth century comic books.[34] And Jessica is explicitly contrasted with this era's superheroines in *Alias*. For *Jessica Jones*, however, the distinction is less overt than *Alias*, which actively presents Jessica in reaction against established superheroines and through the rejection of her own superhero past as Jewel. Within *Jessica Jones*, flashbacks reveal that the Jewel costume and name were created by Jessica's friend Trish Walker, but Jessica actively rejected both. While Jessica previously attempted a career as a superhero in *Jessica Jones*, she never engaged with a costume or secret identity akin to her comic book counterpart. In this sense, *Jessica Jones* presents a similar, albeit less overt, subversion and contrast with the established superheroine image featured in *Alias*.

Super-Noir

While Jessica Jones is super-powered in both *Alias* and *Jessica Jones*, in a setting focused on superheroes, the character is not a costumed vigilante. Rather, Jessica staunchly remains a private detective throughout both series. The relationship between the noir and superhero genres is not something particularly new in and of itself. Noir-like expansive urban landscapes controlled by greedy businessmen, organized criminals and corrupt politicians, are stock-tropes for many urban-focused superhero figures,[35] such as Batman, the Punisher, and Daredevil. Indeed, crime as a lifestyle and ideology along with the hero's struggle against it is part of the "mythology for comics."[36] However, while *Alias'* engagement of noir-aspects with the superhero genre is not in itself unique, the emphasis on noir that is awarded in *Alias* is quite distinct. Firstly, as noted above, Jessica herself is not a superhero but a private detective. Secondly, while many comic books engage noir-tropes, they tend to favor typical "four color" imagery over the "noir style" of presentation, shying away from the dark yet contrasting imagery, expressionistic landscapes and settings, and minimalist panels.[37] Yet, for *Alias*, noir is again emphasized with the genre's stylistic hallmarks following not only the narrative, but the artwork as well. Much of the series is presented in an expressionist tone, which favors scratchy, heavily-inked line work and inconsistent color tones, giving the comic a grimy effect. Likewise, the covers are largely designed following the principles of conceptual art and thus do not overtly appear to be those of a superhero comic book. Jessica's recollections of her time as a superheroine, however, are presented in the four color style emblematic of superhero comic books with defined, thin, lines and a limited but bright color pallet. The effect for *Alias* is a contrast with the wider MU setting between the noir imagery featured in *Alias,* Jessica herself, and other Marvel comic books.

The emphasis of a noir-style of artwork in *Alias* offers a stark contrast. From the 1970s onward the various stylistic conventions of Jack Kirby and Stan Lee's work on the *Fantastic Four* in the 1960s evolved, as noted by Douglas Wolk, into a "house style" that constituted a "right ('Marvel') way and wrong way to draw everything."[38] This style is defined by Wolk as developing into a, "pumped-up sort of photorealism, full of very beautiful people, accurate or at least convincing anatomy that showed the ripples and wrinkles of everything and freaky perspectives that heightened the drama."[39] The contrast of the Marvel style which dominates the majority of the publisher's comic books with *Alias* occurs on two fronts. Firstly, it distinguishes *Alias* as a distinct style of narrative within the wider drama of that comic universe. Secondly, the use of the Marvel style in flashbacks for Jessica's acquisition, early experimentation with her powers, and time as Jewel distinguishes the character's superhero past from her private detective present. The effect creates a distinct narrative space within *Alias* in which the understated and subtextual elements of the MU can be drawn to the fore.

Contrasted with both other MU protagonists and the visual imagery of the setting itself, *Alias* occupies a particular narrative space. From the standpoint of *Alias*' contrast with the wider MU, the comic book can be understood as what Scott McCloud defines as a "palatable" B comic book.[40] That is to say, it is a comic book that exists within the mainstream superhero genre but makes "progress" towards "genre diversity" in the shared universe and market space.[41] Not only is Jessica Jones within *Alias* not a superhero, the majority of *Alias*' storylines draw heavily from the noir genre with elements of the MU added.

Furthermore, the use of the noir genre throughout *Alias* actively subverts existing notions of hierarchy and character status. In the "Alias" storyline, for instance, Jessica uncovers a sex scandal concerning typically morally stalwart Captain America engaged in an affair with a married woman having simply, in his own words, "let my guard down."[42] Later, Jessica comes to work for Daredevil as a bodyguard in the pages of *Alias*[43] after his secret identity as Matt Murdock is exposed in *Daredevil* issue 32.[44] "Come Home"[45] sees a missing person investigation lead Jessica to a small town's persecution of people they wrongly perceive as mutants.[46] Additionally, "Underneath" (vol. 3) opens with *Daily Bugle* editor J. Jonah Jameson hiring Jessica to uncover the secret identity of Spider-Man and resolve the abduction of his adopted daughter, Mattie Franklin (Spider-Woman). This leads Jessica to the understated ability of super-powered characters within the MU to grow the narcotic MGH[47] within their bodies as a natural hormonal process. Thus through engagement with the noir genre, the enshrined status of "elite and famous" Marvel superheroes is tarnished and subverted in *Alias*. In respect to *Alias'* place in a wider MU, and Jessica's contrast with the setting's established superheroines, the noir aspect of *Alias* becomes an example of an "embryonic genre" hidden amongst the superhero tropes and motifs, but engaging its own "rich history and stylistic hallmarks" throughout the series.[48] *Alias* operates within a complex relationship of the noir and superhero genres that subverts the typical standards of the MU.

Jessica Jones, maintains the noir aspect of *Alias*. The series opens, for instance, with the conclusion of a case dealing with an adulterous lover. Over the course of *Jessica Jones*, Jessica herself undertakes a number of investigations for clients ranging from serving court chapters to missing persons. Through use of the wider Marvel Cinematic Universe, *Jessica Jones* attempts to establish a similar embryonic relationship between noir and the superhero genre as established in *Alias*. Yet, *Jessica Jones* is more stringently grounded in the noir genre than *Alias*. As noted earlier, television's Jessica actively rejected a super-heroic costume and identity as Jewel, and other characters are discernibly unrealized compared to their comic book counterparts. Likewise, the costumed "elite and famous" superheroes of the Marvel Cinematic Universe are absent from *Jessica Jones*, featured only through allusion and discussion with a mixture of concepts from awe to abject terror. This is particularly evident in the fourth episode, "AKA 99 Friends," when Audrey Eastman uses a fictive story of a cheating husband to lure Jessica into a trap. During their confrontation, Eastman expresses feelings of fear and terror at the prospect of a world of superpowers. *Jessica Jones* thus presents a similar but muted association with a wider MCU and greater emphasis on the noir genres. This is an association that in doing so, avoids the notions of gendered hierarchy that feature prominently, albeit subverted, in *Alias*.

Crime and Execution

The absence of established hierarchy in *Jessica Jones* is most prevalent through the prominence of Kilgrave and the manner in which the villain is addressed. While Kilgrave's comic book counterpart, the Purple Man, features within *Alias*, the character lacks the same significance within the comic book narrative. For television's Jessica Jones, the ongoing trauma of her abuse at Kilgrave's hands and the quest to bring the villain to some form of justice or, at the very least, personal resolution, is the driving plotline of the series. In contrast, for *Alias*, Jessica's confrontation with the Purple Man occurs in "The Secret Origin of Jessica Jones" and "Purple" story arcs and is two of five narratives that occupy the series. Occurring across issues twenty-two through twenty-eight, the finale of the series, "The Secret Origin of Jessica Jones" and "Purple" provide an explanation for Jessica's powers, her abandonment of her career as a superhero and complex relationship to the Avengers.

Further contrast resides with the portrayal of trauma between *Alias* and *Jessica Jones*. The comic book Jessica denies the Purple Man ever raped her (unlike her television counterpart who tells Kilgrave to his face that he raped her), instead describing herself as being "degraded." This process included the Purple Man compelling Jessica to "cry while I [Jessica] watched" him commit rape and "wish it was me [Jessica]" and "beg him [the Purple Man] for it [sex]" as well as pandering to the villain's whims.[49] The rationale that Jessica presents for the Purple Man's actions is framed in terms of revenge against Daredevil, Spider-Man, or whichever superhero had recently defeated the villain. In contrast with the Purple Man, *Jessica Jones*' Kilgrave is acknowledged to have raped Jessica, pursuing and seeking to hold her captive within an abusive domestic relationship. Where the Purple Man articulates disdain for Jessica, Kilgrave expresses affection, explaining in "AKA Top Shelf Perverts" that "I'm the only one who matches you. Who challenges you. Who'll do anything for you." Kilgrave further frames his affection in terms of romantic love for Jessica, noting in the same episode, "you made me feel something I never felt before. Yearning. I actually missed you." Unlike *Alias*, *Jessica Jones* features Kilgrave as an ongoing antagonist.

The contrast between *Alias* and *Jessica Jones* on this front is sharp. While both Kilgrave and the Purple Man respectively abduct Jessica, only Kilgrave is shown to explicitly rape her. The Purple Man's kidnapping, abuse, and degradation of Jessica and other unnamed victims in the "Purple" story arc are never addressed beyond the "implication of rape" in a manner Michael R. Lavin frames as typical of comic book villains.[50] It is implied or suggested to have occurred or replaced with some other form of sexually connotative torture, rather than explicitly addressed.[51] The Purple Man's abuse of Jessica can be read as a lateralization and sublimation of the "trend toward superheroines as sex objects," outlined by Lavin as prolific throughout superhero media.[52] But while Lavin notes aptly that often the superheroine or other female victim is "helpless at the hands of one villain or another,"[53] this is simply not the case for *Alias*. While initially helpless under the Purple Man's control, Jessica mentally recalls a previous encounter with Phoenix. Herein, Phoenix explains that she placed a mental "trigger" in Jessica's brain to override the Purple Man. All Jessica needs to do is "make the decision." With the Purple Man's control outranked by the actions of Phoenix as an extension of Marvel's "elite and famous" X-Men, in this moment Jessica chooses not to be helpless. As a result of this choice, Jessica simply renders the Purple Man unconscious in a single punch. Rather than the prolonged cat-and-mouse game between Kilgrave and Jessica Jones and the protagonists own lingering trauma shown in the television series, *Alias* resolves the threat and trauma presented by the Purple Man in a single, decisive action.

With *Alias'* swift rebuttal of the Purple Man, the comic book follows the typical depiction of abuse and its aftermath. Typically, television's depiction of rape, abuse, degradation, and the trauma that remains after such experiences as positioned by Lisa M. Cuklanz emphasizes "male avengers" of female victims.[54] In focusing on an aggressive response to "the problem or crime" of rape, "the experiences and feelings of the victim" are largely overlooked and resolved in a single moment's violence.[55] Despite its status as a comic book series and not television, we find that this is the case with *Alias*, as the series promptly ends mere pages after Jessica defeats the Purple Man. While the narrative of comic book Jessica Jones does continue several months later with the premier of *Jessica Jones: The Pulse*, the second series does not address Jessica's victimization by the Purple Man. Rather, *The Pulse* focuses on Jessica's pregnancy, announced in the final pages of *Alias*. Jessica's trauma in *Alias* simply ends with her triumphant, single, blow against the Purple Man. While the moment of retributive violence is, as outlined by Cuklanz, particular to a male-based revenge narrative in which the victim is often framed as "passive and silent,"[56] the outcome for *Alias* is the same, coming in the form of an unspoken undoing of the pain inflicted by the Purple Man. While *Alias* hints at Jessica's trauma following her ordeal with the Purple Man, it is quickly addressed and resolved in the finale of the series.

While Cuklanz asserts the perspective of a single moment of violent resolution is common to United States–like television narratives and their depictions of rape and trauma, it is not the one we see in *Jessica Jones*. In part, this is because simply eliminating Kilgrave himself does not alleviate the ambiguity surrounding the villain. When Patsy is ordered to "put a bullet in your head" by Kilgrave, for instance, one placed in the mouth is sufficient to fulfill the command. Likewise Kilgrave justifies fostering Malcolm's addiction to drugs with the explanation "I didn't make him do anything he didn't want to do. He was … he was an addict waiting to happen." As Frank Verano notes, examination of a supervillain's origin typically reveals something of the nature of the character.[57] In doing so, the relationship between the villains, their crimes, and the hero is explored.[58] The audience understands Kilgrave's origin as a human guinea pig in his parents' experiments. Yet this exploration of Kilgrave does not resolve the ambiguity that surrounds the character's crimes or define the nature of the villain's control aside from timeframe (initially twelve hours) and delivery (verbal command). Moreover, while Jessica is certain she was raped by Kilgrave, for Reva Connors' death, Kilgrave's order for Jessica to "take care of her [Reva]" shrouds the event in uncertainty. Popular culture's typical solution to sexual assault and its aftermath might be a violent confrontation,[59] but such action will not overcome the ambiguity surrounding Kilgrave.

Kilgrave's villainy does not operate on the world-threatening and ultimately visually spectacular scale of Loki, the Red Skull, Ultron, or other rivals for the characters referred to in *Alias* as "elite and famous." Despite his status as a super-powered rival for Jessica, Kilgrave lacks the grand design expressed commonly by supervillains such as the Red Skull in *Captain America: The First Avenger*[60] or Ultron in *Avengers: Age of Ultron*.[61] The lack of world-changing vision sees Kilgrave behave more akin to a conventional criminal, a clever, manipulative stalker, serial killer, rapist, and con artist. In this sense, just as Jessica herself is a private detective with superpowers, Kilgrave is likewise a super-powered conventional criminal. Robin S. Rosenberg frames such characters with the phrase "straightforward criminal," employing it to denote a character who "seeks either material gain—in money or valuable objects—or power and acts illegally to get it."[62] Such characters are generally equipped with less or restricted super-abilities and thus seemingly present, in Rosenberg's estimation, "less of a challenge for the superhero" in terms of providing a physical threat or confrontation.[63] And certainly what threat Kilgrave poses is one of a lingering sense of violation, not an overt physical one in the sense of Loki or *Guardians of the Galaxy*'s Ronan the Accuser respectively marshaling intergalactic armies.[64] Yet, because the threat posed by Loki or Ronan is—along with that of the Red Skull or *Iron Man 3*'s Mandarin[65]—essentially a fantastic spectacle for both the audiences and characters of those worlds, they call for an appropriately publicly spectacular response to combat their plots.

Supervillains in this sense present a "layered problem" for the superhero, on the one hand able to defeat the protagonist in single combat and on the other to pose some form of wider threat.[66] Yet, Kilgrave represents a form of "faceless or generic"[67] crime. Indeed the faceless aspect of Kilgrave is underscored visually when the character is shown only in shadow or from behind until episode three, "AKA It's Called Whiskey." Kilgrave's obfuscated identity and criminality is likewise emphasized by the absence of understanding of how Kilgrave's powers function and thus "it can't be explained, so it can't be believed" as Malcolm notes in "AKA You're a Winner!" Without the overt, intervening presence of an established hierarchy of "elite and famous" superheroes, *Jessica Jones* ultimately is mired in uncertainty.

The lack of an obvious solution is emphasized in the conclusion of *Jessica Jones*. While Hope has committed suicide, disavowing Jessica of responsibility, Kilgrave's death does not succeed in resolving the repercussions and problems for his victims. Some resolution is implied as Jessica is vindicated in the media and faces a torrent of calls for help from prospective clients. The lingering questions of unresolved trauma in *Jessica Jones*, however, avoid the "tasteless and irresponsible" portrayal of sex and violence Lavin associates with comic book superheroes.[68] Lavin notes that the traditional comic book portrayal of sexual violence frames the feminine body as both fragile and a subject for "sexual desire."[69] This combination of fragility and sexuality renders individual moments of female victimization as personal weaknesses for the victim. However, the ambiguity surrounding the actions of Kilgrave's victims—both male and female—and the lack of resolution from the traditionally definitive means of capturing or murdering the perpetrator presents audiences with an ongoing ordeal for Jessica. Within this ordeal, Jessica is characterized with the strength and resolve to continually revisit Kilgrave's actions and move towards an ideal of resolution. Through the presentation of an ambiguous and ongoing ordeal, *Jessica Jones* avoids the traditional portrayal of femininity and victimization associated with the superhero genre. In doing so, *Jessica Jones* presents a form of superhero literature that subverts hierarchies of gender, class, and ideology frequently enshrined in costumed adventure narratives.

Conclusion

The subversion of gender, class and ideology within *Jessica Jones* stands in stark contrast to the global drama of aliens, costumed vigilantism, and mutants offered by its source text, *Alias*. The use and presence of hierarchy, however, pervades both *Alias* and *Jessica Jones* through the presence of "elite and famous" superheroes, that is, those superheroes, typically male and featuring both celebrity within their respective setting and market value in the real world. Here the abundant presence of derivative superheroines regulates female characters such as Jessica to a secondary status. Jessica Jones in both comic book and television incarnations is contrasted sharply with superheroines of the MU and MCU respectively, both for her lack of typical superhero conventions and adherence to the noir genre. In employing this genre, *Alias* actively deconstructs this hierarchy through revealing an otherwise unseen side of established, mainstream Marvel superheroes. *Jessica Jones* however, goes one step further, actively avoiding focus on the existing status quo within the Marvel Cinematic Universe to focus instead on a localized network focused on Jessica herself and the problem Kilgrave presents. In doing so, *Jessica Jones* actively presents characters adapted from their comic book counterparts in an unrealized state within Jessica's fluid network of social, professional, and personal concerns. This absence of hierarchy features strongly in the manner in which *Jessica Jones* addresses Kilgrave. While *Alias* eliminates the Purple Man in a single, violent, moment, *Jessica Jones* presents an ongoing drama of trauma and the need for that trauma to be validated, acknowledged, and resolved prior to the final confrontation.

NOTES

1. *Marvel's Avengers*, directed by Joss Whedon (2012; South Yarra Walt Disney Studios Australia, 2012), DVD.
2. *Daredevil*, Drew Goddard, aired 2015, on Netflix.
3. Roy Thomas, "The Only Good Alien…" *Avengers* 1, no. 89 (1971).
4. R. Alberich, J. Miro-Julia, and F. Rosselló, "Marvel Universe looks almost like a real social network." eprint arXiv:cond-mat/0202174 (2002): 2.
5. *Ibid.*, 1–2.
6. *Ibid.*, 2.
7. *Ibid.*, 3.
8. Brian Bendis, *Jessica Jones: Alias* 1 (New York: Marvel, 2015), 79.
9. Kurt Busiek, *Maximum Security: Dangerous Planet* 1, no. 1 (2000).
10. Scott Lobell, "Prelude to Destruction." *X-Men* 2, no. 111 (2001).
11. Jim Stalin, "A Mad Calling!" *Infinity Abyss* 1, no. 1 (2002).
12. Brian Bendis, *Avengers Disassembled, Chaos* 1, no. 500 (2004).
13. Bendis, *Alias* 1: 9.
14. *Ibid.* 3: 28, 106.
15. *Ibid.* 4: 142.
16. Roy Thomas, "Where Stalks the Sentry!" *Marvel Superheroes Featuring Captain Marvel* 1, no. 13 (1968).
17. Gerry Conway, "This Woman, This Warrior." *Ms. Marvel* 1, no. 1 (1977).
18. Kelly Sue DeConnick, "Untitled." *Captain Marvel* 7, no. 1 (2012).
19. Archie Goodwin, "Dark Destiny!" *Marvel Spotlight* 1, no. 32 (1977).
20. Howard Mackie, "The Final Chapter Part Three of Four: The Triumph of the Goblin." *The Spectacular Spider-Man* 1, no. 263 (1998).
21. Stan Lee, "X-Men." *The X-Men* 1, no. 1 (1963).
22. Richard Reynolds, *Superheroes: A Modern Mythology* (Jackson: University Press of Mississippi, 1992): 12–16
23. Michael R. Lavin, "Women in comic books," *Serials Review* 24, no. 2 (1998): 94.
24. *Ibid.*, 162.
25. Kristin J. Anderson and Donna Cavallaro, "Parents or Pop Culture? Children's Heroes and Role Models." *Childhood Education* 78, no. 3 (2002): 162.
26. *Ibid.*
27. *Ibid*
28. Bendis, *Alias* 4: 23, 32, 84.
29. Reynolds, 80.
30. *Ibid.*, 14.
31. Strategic Homeland Intervention, Enforcement and Logistics Division. A fictional espionage, law-enforcement, and counter-terrorism agency within the Marvel Universe.
32. Reynolds, 14–15.
33. Lillian Robinson, *Wonder Woman: Feminisms and Superheroes* (New York: Routledge, 2004), 13.
34. *Ibid.*
35. Randy Duncan and Mathew J. Smith, *The Power of Comics: History, Form and Culture* (New York: Continuum Publishing International, 2009), 319, 516.

36. *Ibid.*, 391.
37. *Ibid.*, 516, 684.
38. Douglas Wolk, *Reading Comics: How Graphic Novels Work and What They Mean* (Cambridge, MA: Da Capo Press, 2007), 51.
39. *Ibid.*, 51–52.
40. Scott McCloud, *Reinventing Comics: How Imagination and Technology Are Revolutionizing an Art Form* (New York: HarperPerennial, 2000), 116.
41. *Ibid.*
42. Bendis, *Alias* 1: 64.
43. *Ibid.*
44. Bendis, "Out." *Daredevil* 2, no. 32 (2002).
45. Bendis, *Alias* 2.
46. Humans born with superpowers, a staple narrative trope from Marvel's *X-Men* comic books.
47. Mutant Growth Hormone. A fictional narcotic within the Marvel Universe that grants superpowers.
48. McCloud, 116.
49. Bendis, *Alias* 4: 90–94.
50. Lavin, 96.
51. *Ibid.*
52. *Ibid.*, 97.
53. *Ibid.*, 95.
54. Lisa M. Cuklanz, *Rape on Prime Time Television: Television, Masculinity and Sexual Violence* (Philadelphia: University of Philadelphia Press, 2000), 6.
55. *Ibid.*
56. *Ibid.*
57. Frank Verano, "Superheroes Need Supervillains." *What Is a Superhero?* (New York: Oxford University Press, 2013), 162.
58. *Ibid.*
59. Cuklanz, 6; Anderson and Cavallaro, 162.
60. *Captain America: The First Avenger*, directed by Joe Johnston (2011; South Yarra Walt Disney Studios Australia, 2011), DVD.
61. *Avengers: Age of Ultron*, directed by Joss Whedon (2015; South Yarra Walt Disney Studios Australia, 2015), DVD.
62. Robin S. Rosenberg, "Sorting Out Villainy: A Typography of Villains and Their Effects on Superheroes," *What Is a Superhero?* (New York: Oxford University Press, 2013), 197.
63. *Ibid.*
64. *Guardians of the Galaxy*, directed by James Gunn (2014; South Yarra Walt Disney Studios Australia, 2014), DVD.
65. *Iron Man 3*, directed by Shane Black (2013; South Yarra Walt Disney Studios Australia, 2013), DVD.
66. Paul Levitz, "Why Supervillains?" *What Is a Superhero?* (New York: Oxford University Press, 2013), 156.
67. *Ibid.*, 155.
68. Lavin, 96.
69. *Ibid.*, 93.

BIBLIOGRAPHY

Alberich, R., J. Miro-Julia, and F. Rosselló. "Marvel Universe looks almost like a real social network." eprint arXiv:cond-mat/0202174. (2002).
Anderson, Kristin J., and Donna Cavallaro. "Parents or Pop Culture? Children's Heroes and Role Models." *Childhood Education.* 78, no. 3 (2002): 161–168.
Bendis, Brian. "Avengers Disassembled, Chaos." *Avengers.* 1, no. 500 (2004).
_____. *Jessica Jones: Alias* 1. New York: Marvel, 2015.

_____. *Jessica Jones: Alias 2.* New York: Marvel, 2015.
_____. *Jessica Jones: Alias 3.* New York: Marvel, 2015.
_____. *Jessica Jones: Alias 4.* New York: Marvel, 2015.
_____. "Out." *Daredevil* 2, no. 32. 2002.
Busiek, Kurt. *Maximum Security: Dangerous Planet* 1, no. 1 (2000).
Conway, Gerry. "This Woman, This Warrior." *Ms. Marvel* 1, no. 1 (1977).
Cuklanz, Lisa M. *Rape on Prime Time Television: Television, Masculinity and Sexual Violence.* Philadelphia: University of Philadelphia Press, 2000.
DeConnick, Kelly Sue. "Untitled." *Captain Marvel* 7, no. 1 (2012).
Duncan, Randy, and Mathew J. Smith *The Power of Comics: History, Form and Culture.* New York: Continuum Publishing International, 2009.
Goodwin, Archie. "Dark Destiny!" *Marvel Spotlight* 1, no. 32 (1977).
Lavin, Michael R. "Women in comic books." *Serials Review* 24, no. 2. (1998): 93–100.
Lee, Stan. "X-Men." *The X-Men* 1, no. 1 (1963).
Levitz, Paul. "Why Supervillains?" In *What Is a Superhero?* 153–158. New York: Oxford University Press, 2013.
Lobell, Scott. "Prelude to Destruction." *X-Men* 2, no. 111 (2001).
Mackie, Howard. "The Final Chapter Part Three of Four: The Triumph of the Goblin." *The Spectacular Spider-Man* 1, no. 263 (1998).
McCloud, Scott. *Reinventing Comics: How Imagination and Technology are Revolutionizing an Art Form.* New York: HarperPerennial, 2000.
Reynolds, Richard. *Superheroes: A Modern Mythology.* Jackson: University Press of Mississippi, 1992.
Robinson, Lillian. *Wonder Woman: Feminisms and Superheroes.* New York: Routledge, 2004.
Rosenberg, Robin S. "Sorting out Villainy: A Typography of Villains and Their Effects on Superheroes." In *What Is a Superhero?* 196–297 (New York: Oxford University Press, 2013).
Stalin, Jim. "A Mad Calling!" *Infinity Abyss* 1, no. 1 (2002).
Thomas, Roy. "The Only Good Alien…"*Avengers* 1, no. 89 (1971).
_____. "Where Stalks the Sentry!" *Marvel Superheroes Featuring Captain Marvel* 1, no. 13 (1968).
Verano, Frank. "Superheroes need Supervillains" I.n *What Is a Superhero?* 159–166. New York: Oxford University Press, 2013.
Wolk, Douglas. *Reading Comics: How Graphic Novels Work and What They Mean.* Cambridge, MA: Da Capo Press, 2007.

Filmography

Avengers: Age of Ultron. Directed by Joss Whedon. 2015. South Yarra Walt Disney Studios Australia, 2015. DVD.
Captain America: The First Avenger. Directed by Joe Johnston. 2011. South Yarra Walt Disney Studios Australia, 2011. DVD.
Daredevil. Drew Goddard. 2015. Netflix.
Guardians of the Galaxy. Directed by James Gunn. 2014. South Yarra Walt Disney Studios Australia, 2014. DVD.
Iron Man 3. Directed by Shane Black. 2013. South Yarra Walt Disney Studios Australia, 2013. DVD.
Jessica Jones. Melissa Rosenberg. 2016. Netflix.
Marvel's Avengers. Directed by Joss Whedon. 2012. South Yarra. Walt Disney Studios Australia, 2012. DVD.

"AKA Occasionally I give a damn"

Mirrored Archetypes and Gender Power in Jessica Jones

ALEAH KILEY and ZAK ROMAN

Jessica Jones: Just had to be a hero didn't you.
Trish Walker: I learned it from you.
—"AKA I've Got the Blues"

Traditionally, male superheroes imbued with normative hypermasculine codes have defined the comic book hero archetype. Women's appearances in comic book universes tend to be limited to sexualized damsels in distress, feminized allies, or tough-as-nails badass villains, with their exaggerated sexuality acting as currency to gain access to the hypermasculine comic book realm. Similar to other mainstream media outlets, when strong women do appear, they are frequently represented in a sexualized manner, thereby taming female empowerment.[1]

Women's sexuality in comic universes is often a narrative device negotiated as a tool for domination, dehumanization, or, in some rare cases, empowerment.[2] Some strong women, often depicted as villains and allies, utilize normative feminine qualities to garner power and manipulate men to achieve their goals. Moreover, gender studies scholar Katy Gilpatric points out that women with physical power are often punished and forced to sacrifice their power to aid male counterparts, heroes, or humanity.[3] Thus when women are superheroes or strong leads, they are constrained by a distinctly limited heroism that must be qualified, aided, and validated by others.[4]

These trends are not isolated to comic book universes. Despite significant social and cultural shifts over the last forty years, in 2011, mainstream media outlets represented women in stereotypical and damaging ways similar to trends of the 1970s.[5] A 2013 study found that women only comprise 11 percent of movie protagonists.[6] Social psychologists Britney Brinkman and Allison Jedinak point out that it is not only stereotypical and underrepresentation on the screen and page, but there is a general "lack of representation of women in decision-making positions ... girls and women are often underrepresented, both as media figures and those responsible for creating the media."[7]

Tough female heroes or protagonists must often adopt masculine characteristics and actively deny their femininity to earn power, resolve narrative tensions, and accomplish their goals.[8] Notable examples such as Demi Moore in *GI Jane* (Ridley Scott, 1997) and Susan Sarandon and Geena Davis in *Thelma and Louise* (Ridley Scott, 1991), illustrate the ways in which the narrative arc of the film requires tough women to deny their femininity and fully embrace masculine qualities, physical traits, and normative behaviors. However, when tough women are able to express their femininity and perform masculinity at the same time such as in the case of Pamela Anderson in *Barb Wire* (David Hogan, 1996), they challenge simple adoption of masculine traits and present a transgressive powerful feminine subjectivity.

> On the one hand, she represents a potentially transgressive figure capable of expanding the popular perception of women's roles and abilities; on the other, she runs the risk of reinscribing strict gender binaries and of being nothing more than sexist window dressing for the predominantly male audience.[9]

Brown's assertions provide a useful frame to explore the presence of tough women on screen as complex articulations of contemporary femininity that either reinforce women's agency or reinforce heteronormative masculine desires and expectations.

Sexist Window Dressing?

Jessica Jones, Netflix and Marvel's joint web television series based on a Marvel comic book character, presents many challenges to industry stereotypes both on and off the screen. The thirteen-episode first season featuring two leading women, a private detective with super strength (Jessica Jones) and her best friend, a radio show host (Trish Walker), is produced, created, and written by Melissa Rosenberg, a well-established Hollywood screenwriter known for creating content about women and addressing gender disparities in the industry. In promotional materials and interviews, Rosenberg has expressed her appreciation for the complexity of Jessica's character as the first Marvel Cinematic Universe female superhero with her own series: "I love this character. That is an incredibly damaged, dark, complex female character that kicks ass."[10] Furthermore, in promotional buzz about the show, bloggers claimed that Rosenberg made other notably progressive choices by making Jessica's domineering lawyer employer "the definition of a power lesbian.... It's worth noting that the TV version changed the role of Jeri to female, as the comic character was a man. (Smart move, Melissa Rosenberg!)"[11]

However, while promoting the distinctiveness of the series, Rosenberg has distanced herself from a staunchly feminist stance and denied that the show is explicitly tackling "women's issues." She also said:

> There was never the intention of, "this is an issue series, we're dealing with issues." While issues of sexual assault and women in power are all issues that I certainly feel very passionately about taking on, the show's all about exploring the inner workings of Jessica Jones and her ensemble.[12]

Executive Vice President of Marvel Television, Jeph Loeb, reinforces this approach-avoidance stance of Jessica's role as a transgressive female figure. In a recent interview, Loeb revealed the decision to model Jessica after Jack Nicholson's famous *Chinatown* (1974) character, J.J. "Jake" Gittes, a distinctly troubled iteration of the masculine noir detective. Here, Loeb and Rosenberg reveal the tensions in *Jessica Jones* as vacillating between presenting a potentially transgressive female character and one rooted in male subjectivity and masculine expectations of the noir anti-hero.

> So much of *Chinatown* is about, you know, Jack Nicholson plays a guy who was a cop, something terrible happened to him, and now he has reinvented his life as a private detective.... I think the brilliance of what Brian [*Alias*/Jessica Jones creator Brian Michael Bendis] created, starting from that same concept—which is a woman who is a superhero, something terrible happens to her, and she tries to reinvent herself as a private detective, and then something happens and her world is then turned upside down again.[13]

The series challenges the often-predictable visual language of the comic book genre and embraces noir-esque elements. The gritty, unsanitized aesthetics of the dark, urban, and dystopian *Jessica Jones* iteration of New York allow the show to subvert both genre expectations and gender expectations at the same time.

Textual analysis of the first season, with a specific focus on Jessica and Trish's relationship, reveals that initially *Jessica Jones* establishes rudimentary gender binaries, but the show ultimately transgresses these stereotypical representations and presents a new understanding of women's lived realities and possibilities for agency and empowerment. Focusing on the relationship between Jessica and Trish presents a unique instance of the ways in which women can be powerfully in control and violently subjugated within the same narrative. As they negotiate the various dangers of physical, emotional, and psychological domination, Jessica and Trish are at once collaborative and supportive, united by their shared past, while also competitive and hurtful, isolated by their differences. In a complex illustration of contemporary gender dynamics, Jessica and Trish are forced to negotiate the violence and vulnerability of women's subjugation in two distinctly male-dominated genres (film noir and comic books) and ultimately reveal the ambiguous ways that women lose, negotiate, and reclaim power.

Simplistic Mirrors: Reinforcing Gender Binaries

Jessica as Gittes

In the first several episodes of the series, Jessica and Trish are presented as two rather diametrically opposing articulations of femininity. The world of *Jessica Jones* is somewhere in between the stylized noir and comic book dystopia. From the outset, Jessica is placed in these two traditionally masculine genres and framed as a masculine character archetype. The opening of "AKA Ladies Night" utilizes noir-style elements including a gritty urban location, skewed camera angles, chiaroscuro lighting, and saturated dark colors. Jessica's reflective and confessional first-person voice-over narration over scenes of her work as a private investigator taking pictures of cheating spouses, reveals her disillusioned and bleak view of humanity. As Loeb admits, these choices were not accidental, "The film that we always looked at was *Chinatown* … when Brian and Michael Gaydos created Jessica Jones [in *Alias* #1]—it opens with the opening scene from *Chinatown*. It's not even an homage, it's the scene."[14] Adapting these diegetic components from the *Alias* comic book series, the first episode quickly establishes Jessica, not as the *femme fatale* of film noir, but as the jaded Nicholson-esque anti-hero. In Jessica, they project the hard-boiled, hard-drinking, jeans and leather jacket-wearing, sexually-liberated, physically powerful, emotionally conflicted, protagonist.

Jessica is a cynical character who uses physical violence and adopts masculine codes to survive the peril of her everyday life and chosen vocation. In promotional material about the character of Jessica, Loeb noted, "She has real problems with a number of things that she abuses! And we're not shying away from that. There's no tidying her up."[15] These "problems," also read as masculine codes, establish Jessica as a masculine protagonist that actively resists and denies traditional feminine qualities: in "AKA Ladies Night" Jessica tells Trish not to have feelings, and conducts investigative work while sitting on the toilet; in "AKA Crush Syndrome" she bristles at wearing pink scrubs to gain entry into a hospital; in "AKA The Sandwich Saved Me" she and Trish debate an ultra-feminine superhero costume (discussed further below); and in "AKA WWJD" she scoffs at and tears up a purple sequin dress Kilgrave gives her.

However, Jessica is not without certain feminine qualities and throughout the show is made the object of male desire. Immediately following the first episode's establishing noir scene, Jessica finishes off a large glass of whiskey and proceeds to undress and reveal her trim body in black underwear and a tank top. In "AKA The Sandwich Saved Me" a flashback of Kilgrave's first encounter with Jessica, after she saves Malcolm from an almost fatal mugging, simultaneously establishes her not only as a sexual object, but also as a powerful force to conquer. Under Kilgrave's controlling gaze, he commands her by saying, "Come here, let me look at you." Jessica dutifully complies and Kilgrave assesses her stating, "Jesus, you're a vision! Hair and skin…. And, underneath it all that power!"

She often resists these advances in a dismissive and combative manner. In "AKA The Sandwich Saved Me" Jessica's milquetoast neighbor Ruben offers Jessica home-baked banana bread asking, "Do you like banana bread?" Glaring at him with a disgusted look, Jessica considers quickly, says, "No," grabs the plate, and slams the door in his face. In "AKA Top Shelf Perverts," after leaving Kilgrave, when he makes a romantic overture toward her she responds venomously, "You deranged prick, you've never loved anyone in your repulsive life." Not only does Jessica resist Kilgrave's powerful advances and Ruben's feeble admiration, but she also pursues and expresses her own sexual desire with focused determination and little concern for others. In the first three episodes, Jessica actively pursues Luke Cage, a bartender whose wife she murdered while under Kilgrave's mind control. During sex scenes between the two, Jessica frequently changes positions and intensity to satisfy herself sexually, thereby displaying power and domination rather than submission or passivity. Directly following their sexual encounters Jessica leaves Luke's apartment immediately, overwhelmed by her decision to gratify her desire rather than acknowledge her guilt.

These initial characterizations and early narrative devices of distancing from emotions, selfishly pursuing her physical desire, and acting callously toward others in conjunction with her representation as a sexualized object, establish Jessica's subjectivity as distinctly masculine without compromising her feminine desirability. The strength of her desirability in the face of her unconventional and aloof femininity is typified in "AKA The Sandwich Saved Me" when, despite many rejections, Ruben asks Jessica out to a movie while Malcolm is unconscious in the apartment elevator. In this unsanitized urban milieu, Jessica is thus both the merciless male subject and the coveted female object. Thus, in the first several episodes, Jessica-as-J.J. Gittes presents a troubled noir style anti-hero without problematizing that representation from a stronger feminine or feminist standpoint.

Trish as Patsy

Early in the season, much of Jessica's potentially transgressive femininity is counterbalanced by the softer and more heteronormative femininity of Trish. The show's creators Brandeis, Loeb, and Rosenberg drew from a particularly rare and distinctive romance comic character, Patsy Walker, to soften Jessica's rougher edges. Trish's identity as Patsy Walker is cemented through her intra-narrative child stardom as a television character of the same name. The publication history of the Patsy Walker character dates back to the early days of Marvel comics, when the teen-romance queen debuted in her own comic book *Patsy Walker* (1945–1965) and shortly after in spin-off comics *Patsy and Hedy* (1952) and *Patsy and Hedy: Career Girls* (1952–1967). These romance titles featured Patsy, an ultra-feminine young woman facing the heteronormative dramas of the day. Patsy promoted distinctively normative feminine predicaments including modern fashion trends and romantic melodramas; issues tackled such topics as Patsy's "fashion parade," her first fur coat, the troublesome "blonde tempest twins," Patsy and Hedy's overwhelming first jobs, secret admirers, first dates, and complicated romances with handsome and aloof men ("Buzz, my darling! You can't leave me now! I couldn't bear losing you again!").

Patsy emerged during a time when domesticity was highly promoted to buffer women's relegation back into the domestic sphere after their active involvement in the paid workforce during World War II. Patsy reinforced heteronormative desires and dramas, while distancing from critical engagement with issues around women's rights and the impacts of science and technology on women and their families, which was a focal point in the public consciousness during the 1950s and 1960s.[16]

The name Patsy Walker is a conspicuous one to Marvel fans who might recognize it as the alter ego of the comic book hero known as "Hellcat." In an effort to tap into the popularity of Patsy as well as the popular superhero comic genre, writer Steve Englehart took an essentially obscure character and "had her step into the role of the Cat [Hellcat], an ill-fated character that had debuted in her own title in 1974, which was subsequently canceled after only four issues."[17] Though the crossover appeal was not strong enough when writer Steve Engel revivified her initially, he was able to make her a more formalized superhero known as "Hellcat" in 1976's *The Avengers* #144.[18]

The Trish Walker of *Jessica Jones* still maintains many of the traditional antecedents of her romance comic femininity, but is updated and modernized in such a way that reflects the world that Rosenberg and Marvel have cultivated. The *mise-en-scène* of her New York apartment connotes a chic, highly-curated sense of style; even her judgmental and abusive mother remarks that she "always did have good taste—expensive, but good," upon first seeing her daughter's home. Trish is also impeccably dressed (especially when juxtaposed with Jessica's jeans-picked-up-off-the-floor look), and takes great care to manage her appearance through exercise (she practices yoga), diet (she is shown eating healthy foods), and fashion (her bed sheets and nightgown are made of silk). But unlike the Patsy Walker of the comics, Trish's more modern identity also negotiates these superficial qualities with civically engaged and socially minded concerns. For example, she expresses interest in booking Madeleine Albright for her radio show and her assistant reminds her that her audience "tunes out for politics," reiterating the tension between her crafted external image and her effort to expand normative expectations. These stylistic and narrative elements of her indirect characterization position Trish within a multivariate and neoteric form of femininity, while also remaining firmly ensconced within a heteronormative femininity.

Mars and Venus

Though decidedly a much more modern and moral version of Patsy Walker, the differences between Jessica and Trish are made starkly evident throughout the *Jessica Jones* environment. We see a salient example of this dynamic during a flashback in "AKA The Sandwich Saved Me." Trish is convinced that, to be a proper hero, Jessica needs to dress the part. Trish holds up a homemade costume telling Jessica, "This is it, this is the one!" to which Jessica replies, "The only place anyone is wearing that is trick or treating, or as part of some kinky role-playing scenario." Trish then models the Robinesque mask element of the outfit and assumes a faux-serious fighting pose. Jessica, rebuffing every angle, turns the mask around and says, "Try and hit me now." Even when Trish tries to appeal to the practicality of the costume, Jessica rejects it. "Fine. Be the naked superhero, that could be your alias," Trish tells Jessica in frustration. "Better than that name you came up with," Jessica snaps back. It is then revealed that Trish thinks that "Jewel" would be an appropriate moniker for a costumed hero. Letting no snarky opportunity escape her, Jessica says, "'Jewel' is a stripper's name, a really slutty stripper, and if I wear that thing, you're going to have to call me 'Camel Toe.'"

Jessica's judgment of a certain kind of framing or even a certain kind of sexuality seems to distance her from her own unapologetic sexual freedom. She clings to her femininity informed by masculine expectations and iconoclasm, but notably, she does not seem to believe that this is a freedom afforded to everyone. This exchange reinforces the tension between Jessica's troubled masculinity and Trish's normative femininity and masculinity. Here, Jessica's view of "strippers" purports a traditional stigma attached to sex work and reiterates the kind of passive femininity that Jessica actively eschews: that which is solely for the pleasure and satisfaction of men. Here, Jessica adopts an active subjectivity and resists being objectified on someone else's terms. Trish's response "Fine. Be the naked superhero…" further articulates Trish's inability to envision a female superhero outside feminine objectivity and desirability.

Moreover, the "Jewel" moniker is not simply fodder for a pithy joke. The name refers to a superhero alias that the comic book iteration of *Jessica Jones* has assumed at times during the character's history. And in the comic book version, Jessica's "Jewel" does indeed wear a costume that is identical to the one Trish presents. What is especially salient is that Trish acts as the salesperson for the costume. Even when we see her try on the mask and playfully throw a punch, she is not only endorsing the kind of normative superhero and gender tropes that Jessica rejects, but she may also be foreshadowing her own possible entree into the super realm.

Power Positions

Women who occupy central positions and display masculine forms of power in comic book narratives are often punished for their use of strength, brute force, and violence. In the face of these consequences, ultimately, many of these women subvert their own personal agency by sacrificing themselves for the sake of others.[19] As with many powerful female characters, there are consequences for Jessica's embrace of masculine qualities. She is unable to exist successfully as both a powerful man and empowered woman. Throughout the first five episodes, characters make frequent reference to Jessica as immoral, deviant, and troubled. Jessica is a constant disappointment to others and is frequently chastised for her inability to adequately fulfill either the masculine or feminine role.

In "AKA Ladies Night," her employer Hogarth explains that she refuses to consider her for a job because she is "volatile and erratic." She frequently asks for money from Hogarth who gives her jobs on the borderline of legality and morality. But even Hogarth—who is cunning, vengeful, and immoral— castigates Jessica for her behavior, "I have overlooked several complaints and kept your methods 'confidential.'" In "AKA The Sandwich Saved Me," Will Simpson (redolent of a deranged Captain America) asks Trish what she thinks of Jessica's boyfriends. Trish responds, "They never stick around long enough for me to form an opinion." Simpson replies, "Yeah, she probably scares guys off." Jessica's failed femininity is rooted in her problematic occupation of masculine subjectivity and adoption of aggressive behavior that malfunctions in a heteronormative construct.

Trish's more successful and normative femininity is offset by her lack of powers and further establishes the antipodal relationship between Trish and Jessica's gender characterization. Initially, Rosenberg was going to use superhero Carol Danvers (aka the super-powered "Captain Marvel") in Trish's role. However, as Marvel properties are regularly mined for upcoming productions (Brie Larson was cast as "Captain Marvel" for a motion picture), Rosenberg settled on Patsy Walker, a character without superpowers. Rosenberg found this to be "much more appropriate ... it was better that [Jessica's] best friend was not someone with powers. It actually ends up being a really great mirror for her."[20] The dynamic between the powerless and altruistic Trish and the powerful and jaded Jessica, establishes the failed femininity of Jessica as a masculine noir anti-hero.

Trish's altruism and heteronormative gender performance is rewarded in her characterization as a wealthy, successful, and adored celebrity and is playfully reinforced throughout the show. An instance occurs in "AKA Top Shelf Perverts" when Trish and Simpson debate Trish's proposition to spare Kilgrave's life and let him languish in jail:

> Simpson: That's naïve...
> Trish (*interjecting quickly*): ...and, idealistic and futile, but I want justice for my friend!
> Simpson: Wow, you just need a flag and a horse!
> Trish: And, I'll look goddamn good on it!

Here, Trish reinforces her selfless and sexual femininity that exaggerates the cynical self-centeredness of Jessica's failed femininity and hero qualities.

Jessica's failure as a superhero is rooted largely in her unwillingness to sacrifice herself for others. This selfishness is starkly contrasted to Trish's longing to sacrifice herself for the sake of helping others. Though the troubled anti-hero characterization reveals that trauma and pain are to blame for her self-interest, her lack of empathy and nurturing is teased out through Trish's desire to have powers. Trish frequently makes reference to wanting the powers that Jessica has, claiming she would be the hero that Jessica consistently fails to embody. In "AKA the Sandwich Saved Me," after Jessica uses her super strength to embarrass a man making advances toward Trish:

> Trish: You could use your abilities for something more useful.
> Jessica: Hey, I have an idea! Why don't *you* put on a cape and run around New York.
> Trish: You know I would if I could!
> Jessica: I don't get you! You have money, looks, a radio show, and creepy, if not, adoring fans. You're a freaking household name, what more do you want?!
> Trish: To save the world of course!

Trish's desire to nurture and save the world is magnified by her inability to do so and points to her limited agency within the world to effect change. In contrast, Jessica's ability to protect alongside her limited capacity for empathy exacerbates the tension between power, responsibility, and gender expectations.

Furthermore, Trish is frustrated by her lack of powers and provides several key moments in the series when she is reminded of her limited agency in the world. After Trish is tased by Kilgrave's bodyguards and she and Jessica are then outnumbered, Trish apologizes to Jessica: "One tase and I'm useless…. I'm just a goddamn radio talk show host." Jessica reiterates her lack of empathic nurturing: "I can't do that thing where I make you feel better. I don't know how." In these interactions, Trish's lack of powers amplifies the limitations of feminine caring without the strength and violence to protect. In the same way, Jessica's hesitance to express her emotions magnifies the limitations of masculine power without the empathy and self-sacrifice to nurture.

To Nurture and Protect

These early characterizations serve to present a relatively elementary gender binary at the start of the series, placing these two women at opposite poles of femininity. In addition to initial characterizations, the show presents Trish and Jessica as Marvel's "Odd Couple"; coding Trish as the refined and altruistic "good girl" and Jessica as the wild and selfish "bad girl." This is typified in a scene in "AKA Ladies Night" in which Trish attempts to convince Jessica to save the kidnapped Hope Shlottman from Kilgrave. Trish states, "I know one thing. You are far better equipped to deal with that animal than some innocent girl from Omaha. You're still the person who tried to do something." Maintaining her position of disaffected and troubled subject, Jessica retorts, "Tried and failed. That's what started this. I was never the hero that you wanted me to be." Here, we see this dualistic dynamic play out, with Trish presenting, as she does often, as the doting maternal figure, while Jessica maintains the role of petulant daughter. Thus, the early episodes of the season reinforce stereotypical understandings of gender, with Jessica's adoption of masculine subjectivity a troubled and violent muddle and Trish's occupation of feminine objectivity a gratifying and sacrificing endeavor.

Complicated Reflections: Transgressing Stereotypes

As the series progresses, it becomes clear that the conceptualization of Jessica and Trish as simple mirrors of opposing femininity is extremely limited. Through continued examination of their relationships, it becomes clear that the two female leads present complicated reflections of gender from distinctly women-centered points of view. This shift in perspective subverts Jessica as the male subject and female object and challenges the simpler reading of her as "sexist window dressing." Through the narrative integration of power and intimacy, Jessica and Trish both become female subjects that negotiate, resist, and challenge the forces that aim to harm, limit, and define them. Analyzing their varied and, at times, conflicting responses to violence and vulnerability, presents a new range of understanding of women's lived experiences.

Resisting and Renaming

In the superhero genre, violence is often transacted as power. Violence is frequently the primary method to exert influence, acquire power, and balance immorality.[21] Because violence has traditionally been reserved for male characters to wield for their benefit, women's use of violence is often coded as abnormal, monstrous, and threatening.[22] However, when violence is the primary form of narrative currency to gaining, asserting, reclaiming, and destabilizing power, it becomes a complex metaphor for exploitation, protection, retribution, resistance, and empowerment. Trish and Jessica both experience and use violence throughout the series. Examining the ways that violence surfaces in their intimate relationships demonstrates the complicated negotiation of violence and power in women's everyday lives.

As Jessica gains power realizing that Kilgrave can no longer control her mind, she begins to give voice to her experience of abuse and trauma during their relationship. In "AKA WWJD?" Jessica faces Kilgrave and accuses him of raping her throughout their relationship.

> **Kilgrave:** Which part of staying in five-star hotels, eating in all the best places, doing whatever the hell you wanted, is rape?
> **Jessica:** The part where I didn't want to do any of it! Not only did you physically rape me, you violated every cell in my body and every thought in my goddamn head.
> **Kilgrave:** That's not what I was trying to do.
> **Jessica:** It's doesn't matter, I don't care what you were trying to do. You raped me again and again and again.
> **Kilgrave:** How was I supposed to know, huh?! I never know if someone is doing what they want or what I tell them to.

Kilgrave's bewilderment about Jessica's perspective reveals the way in which male power obscures women's standpoints as well as minimizes issues of coercion, exploitation, and consent. Kilgrave's assertion that by taking advantage of the lifestyle he offered, Jessica both consented to and deserved to be violated, perpetuates victim-blame rape myths often reinforced in comic books.[23] Despite his mind control powers at work, Kilgrave still blames Jessica for not resisting him more clearly.

By directly naming her experience as rape, she shifts the assault of mind control from the symbolic realm into the real world experience of gender violence. Jessica's refusal to back down from naming her experience is a pointed moment of resistance and agency in the show. Perhaps more important than the act of killing him, Jessica needs to recover the lost moments and experiences during her time under his control when she was unable to define her own reality. Resisting Kilgrave's powers, perspectives, and definitions allows Jessica to reclaim the common silencing of women's experiences. In this scene, the symbolic realm of mind control powers and superhero fantasies fade away as Jessica and Kilgrave expose the harsh realities of rape, domination, and erasure.

Traversing the Tightrope

Revisiting Trish through the lens of violence and intimacy reveals that she is not the contented and self-possessed beauty queen of her predecessor in print. Rather, she is often preoccupied with the awareness of her subjugated positionality. The world Trish inhabits is far from the sanitized fantasies about men named "Buzz," her gentlemanly love interest in the Patsy Walker comics. While she negotiates the unwanted sexual advances of fans and stalkers, the modernized Trish is emotionally worn and weighted by her coding as an object of male desire. Often the harassment Trish faces harkens back to her childhood star persona, thereby exposing the sexualization of young girls and sexual objectification of women. A scene in "AKA The Sandwich Saved Me" is an illustration of this dynamic.

A brazen man in a bar approaches Trish and Jessica and begins making advances toward Trish when he recognizes who she is: "I watched your show! [*starts singing*] '*It's Patsy! It's Patsy! I really wanna be your friend*' Yeah, Patsy taught me how to hold a remote with one hand and box the bald-headed bishop with the other." Trish's discomfort with this man, who is eventually subdued by Jessica, makes clear that the Trish Walker of *Jessica Jones* must walk a tightrope of traditional femininity, while also encountering a dark noir comic book world that Patsy of the 1960s could not have imagined. Trish's uncomfortable and disturbing experiences with sexual aggression evince the centralization of a woman's point of view that becomes paramount toward the latter half of the series.

As the show progresses, Trish continues to balance the dynamics of vulnerability, desire, and femininity in ways that Jessica simply and forcefully rejects. In stark contrast to Jessica's reaction to Kilgrave, Trish consents to an intimate relationship with Simpson after he attempts to kill her while under Kilgrave's control. While in this "Kilgraved" state, Simpson is able to break through her elaborate security system by manipulating Trish into opening the door herself. In a violent scene, despite her efforts and self-defense training, Simpson physically dominates, assaults, and nearly strangles Trish to death. Jessica rushes in and saves Trish's life. Once the effects of Kilgrave's powers wear off, Simpson feels ashamed and attempts to make amends with Trish.

In "AKA 99 Friends," Simpson appears at her door and offers her a gift. They share an intimate conversation on either side of her heavily armored door. Trish eventually opens his gift to find an unlicensed gun. He quietly states, "I just want you to feel safe." With a look of satisfaction, Trish points the gun at his image in her security screen. Shortly after, Trish again opens her door and allows him in. The next time we see them together they have become sexually intimate, romantically involved, and have joined forces to help Jessica defeat Kilgrave.

The relationship between Trish and Simpson follows a complicated trajectory rooted in its painful origins and violent beginnings. The gun Simpson gives her captures both his admission that he may be unable to keep his violence at bay and Trish's acceptance of that vulnerability. Trish's door as a metaphor for her strength, security, and power is breached by her own decision to let him in, which initiated both the assault and their subsequent relationship. Upon finding them together in "AKA 99 Friends," Jessica points out the irony of the situation: "He's also the guy that was filled with remorse about attacking you until he decided to turn it into a booty call." Throughout the series, Trish constantly questions Simpson's motives, behaviors, and methods with an underlying vulnerability that suggests he might harm her again. She lives with the shadow of violence woven throughout her relationship. Simpson is thus never the comforting and steady protector that Jessica proves to be for Trish.

Through exploring the role of violence in both Trish and Jessica's intimate relationships, we are able to see critical insights into domination, exploitation, empowerment, and resistance. Although Jessica is inherently imbued with strength and power, she is vulnerable to the potential domination and exploitation of those powers. Through resistance and making Kilgrave accept her standpoint and experience, Jessica shows a way to reclaim her power. Jessica offers possibilities for resistance by taking control of what happens to and how she uses her body. She both names her experience of rape and uses violence at her discretion. Through this narrative we see a distinctly female perspective and validation of women's lived experiences. While her superpowers invite the imagined experience of retribution and resistance within the MCU, her unrelenting and unapologetic testimony reorients our understanding to women's real-world experiences and offers a powerful demonstration of naming her experience and placing responsibility squarely on the assailant.

Trish presents a different offering rooted more in the nuanced and complicated realm of intimacy and violence; without superpowers, she must engage in a much more complex and precarious negotiation of these elements. She often opens the door, welcoming in vulnerability and taking extreme measures to protect against what walks through the door and into her bed. However, by opening herself up to this vulnerability Trish is also able to see the potential for redemption and incremental change that is often required for socio-cultural change. These two characters' intimate connection to gendered violence, despite their different life positions, points to the way that women must often negotiate intimacy, violence, and resistance in their daily lives.

Nurtured Protector

One of the series' most robust thematic threads is the deep bond and protective instincts that both Jessica and Trish have for each other. However, to reduce Jessica and Trish to stereotypical sketches of the physical rescuer and the emotional nurturer respectively (as early episodes suggest) is to belie their actual relationship.

In "AKA I've Got the Blues," we get the obligatory comic book origin story of how the pair came to know one another, and learn that Trish didn't support taking an orphaned Jessica into the Walker home. Standing over a semi-conscious Jessica she tells her mother, "It's not fair, I don't even know her. We just go to the same school. I don't want to do this!" Her career-conscious stage mother then reminds Trish that it will be a good public relations move to offset her recent misbehavior at a nightclub. Although an unlikely messenger of truth, Ms. Walker leans down to comfort Jessica: "Hi Jessie. I know you must be confused right now, but everything's gonna be OK. Patsy's gonna save you." In many ways "Patsy" does save Jessica, just as Jessica will reciprocate to the person who essentially becomes her only family.

Later in the episode, after Jessica gets hit by a truck, we see Trish-as-nurse; patching up her friend and making sure she rests, at one point telling her, "You're strong, but you can break." Trish then prods Jessica about her moral and emotional parameters as the protector:

> **Trish:** What if he [Kilgrave] took someone you loved? Would you let them die?
> **Jessica:** Lucky me…. I don't have too many of those. Don't worry, I'm not just keeping you around because you have pull with the morgue attendants.
> **Trish:** You're still lookin' out for me, huh?
> **Jessica:** I can protect the one, or two, people I care about.

As Jessica lies on Trish's couch, we flash back again to their adolescence in the Walker house. We overhear a young Trish say, "I'm sick of all this Patsy shit!" as she bickers with her mother about her career. Jessica is upset by the fighting and breaks a sink, discovering her powers. Young Trish walks into the bathroom and questions Jessica, only to find her holding a chunk of marble sink above her head. A few lines into the scene, Jessica gets Trish to admit that her mother cut her, calling Ms. Walker "a dangerous nut job ... she just stabbed you!" Trish then redirects the conversation onto Jessica's impossible strength:

> **Trish:** Did the car accident cause it [her powers]?
> **Jessica:** I have no idea. And if you tell anybody, I'm going to tell everyone that you're a pathetic victim of child abuse.
> **Trish:** Don't you dare.
> **Jessica:** They'll make a Lifetime movie about it. (*Fakes sincerity*) *Stolen Childhood: The Patsy Walker Story.* I'd be saving you.
> **Trish:** Shut up!
> **Jessica:** Then it's a standoff.
> **Trish:** Ok deal. I don't tell, and you don't save me.

But of course, this is only a very early hint at the lifelong reciprocal support that the two will come to know. Jessica and Trish are trying to empower each other, but at the same time they are conscious to navigate within the parameters implicitly set by hegemonic/cultural forces. As young girls, they still play within the seemingly unquestionable rules of a patriarchal society. While Trish wants to adhere to more normative modes, sweeping all of her maternal strife and abuse under the rug, Jessica has no reservations about identifying the abuse as what it is, and calling it by name. Here the show explicitly goes out of its way to highlight what will be a perpetual (at least until the conclusion of Season 1) pattern for the two leads: abuse (in several forms), a covering/burying of the abuse, and protection from the abuse.

In one last flashback, we see Ms. Walker forcing Patsy to engage in bulimic vomiting:

> **Trish:** Stop it! I don't want to do this.
> **Ms. Walker:** You shouldn't have eaten all of that pizza. Then we wouldn't have to.
> **Trish:** Stop it!
> **Ms. Walker:** The camera adds ten pounds, you know that. You want them to call you "Fatsy"?
> **Jessica** (*stepping in*): Stop it!
> **Ms. Walker:** Get out, this is private.
> **Jessica:** Let. Her. Go.
> **Trish** (*overwhelmed, in tears*): Jess, get out.
> **Ms. Walker:** This is family business. You're not part of any family.
> **Trish:** You promised not to save me.

Jessica: I can't help it.
Jessica then throws Trish's mother into the hallway where she hits the wall hard. Jessica looks back at Trish.
Trish: Now she knows.
Jessica: Good.

The backstory here is especially salient because we see in explicit terms how both of these people have common scars; and that in turn, they find in one another the only true panacea, the only true haven they can consistently rely on to soothe and repair themselves. A few scenes later in the episode, the viewer is reminded of this constant mirrored support they have for each other when we see Jessica vigilantly posted at Trish's hospital bed (after the effects of Simpson's "red pill"), just as Trish had been at her bedside earlier. The show clearly lets viewers know that, despite Ms. Walker's cruel assertion years before, Trish and Jessica are indeed family. In fact, the final episode, "AKA Smile," cements this powerful bond between Jessica and Trish more completely.

During the final confrontation, after a brainwashed army of party cruise patrons are ordered to halt their mêlée, Kilgrave torments Jessica by noting that she would "do anything to protect" Trish. He then lists a number of abusive and violent things he plans to do with Trish before falling for Jessica's clever play-acting in which he believes that Jessica is back under his control. The final sequence and secret code-word to acknowledge that neither Trish nor Jessica are "Kilgraved" is a telling one:

> **Kilgrave** (*shocked; walking away from Trish*): God, it's true isn't it. You would let me take your beloved sister. God, it's finally over. You're mine now. No more fighting, no more of these ugly displays, you'll be with me now. Look, after a while, however long it takes, I know, I know you will feel what I feel. Let's start with a smile.
> *Jessica gives him a big smile. Kilgrave is giddy. He whispers in her ear—*
> **Kilgrave:** Tell me you love me.
> *Jessica tilts her head past Kilgrave's, so she's looking at Trish and says—*
> **Jessica:** I love you.
> *Jessica then picks Kilgrave up by his face. Then coldly says—*
> **Jessica:** Smile.
> *She then breaks Kilgrave's neck.*

In this move, not only do we know that indeed Jessica would "do anything" for Trish, but also the "I love you" delivery is yet another confirmation of how much Trish and Jessica are true family. The show also completes the narrative arc of how the characters felt when they first met: from Trish balking at the prospect of having an orphan sibling, to both women demonstrably thinking more of the other than of themselves. In a moment of vulnerability and tension for both women, Jessica is able to communicate her feelings to Trish, while ever so slightly still keeping her protective mask of toughness through the mode of the code word. It does not take long to confirm that

Jessica would indeed "do anything" to protect Trish. Thus, the ability to voice their emotions, validate their experiences, and defend themselves from harm, which was not fully accessible during their childhood, now becomes fully realized. In turn, both Trish and Jessica challenge the dominant ideas of masculine toughness and feminine emotionality, standing confidently in their own agency, vulnerability, and power.

Conclusion

In comic books and action films, power has often been synonymous with violence. In these worlds, using violence has become a primary means through which women control their lives and free themselves from dominating forces. We see this acted out frequently in *Jessica Jones,* as Jessica is capable of physically and sexually dominating powerful men. Her physical power and use of violence is the method through which she protects Trish and destroys Kilgrave. This limited way of expressing female power is often reduced to a masculine type of aggression; these align with the parts of the show that force Jessica's *Chinatown*-esque toughness and reinforce the embracing of masculinity for power.

However, *Jessica Jones* makes other offerings that suggest power can be reclaimed and actualized in different ways, grounded in women's lived experiences. Through Jessica and Trish's relationship, we are able to see women in control of their bodies, their choices, and their minds. We also see these women negotiating ways to name and define their experiences of trauma, assault, and abuse. Rather than a heteronormative rescue fantasy, it is through embracing one another's imperfect traits as well as facing their own painful realities that they are able to fully be in control of their bodies, their realities, and their destiny.

Jessica Jones presents a heroine rooted in the vulnerability of gender power dynamics. Displaying an assertive and, at times, forceful, feminine subjectivity and exposing vulnerabilities related to gender, subverts the expectations and tropes typically inherent of noir. Furthermore, by Jessica adopting the disillusioned, Gittes-style P.I., she subverts the traditional masculine cynicism after being damaged by a vindictive woman. Rather, Jessica's disillusionment comes from her experience of being a woman in a male-dominated world. The genre subversion allows for a critical reimagining of both the noir and superhero genre that reveals the gender dynamics inherent in these archetypes.

By subverting the mirrored images of one another, Jessica and Trish are able to assert their positionality rooted in lived experiences of differing femininities that are both required to defeat Kilgrave. Jessica is able to claim her power by acknowledging her vulnerability and Trish is able to assert her power through failing to be limited by her vulnerability. Here we see two offerings of ways to assert and resist gender binaries rooted in power dynamics and negotiating the rough terrain that women experience in a male-dominated world.

The tension between Trish's powerlessness and Jessica's superpowers exposes the vulnerabilities and strengths in both characters. Trish models the type of agency achieved through dogged effort despite dramatic limitations and overwhelming risk. She reveals to Jessica what it means to tirelessly negotiate a world hostile toward women. Due to her abilities, Jessica is able to avoid the pervasive, pernicious and, at times, subtle aggressions faced by women in everyday life. Only through her relationship with Trish is she reminded of the stakes of emotional connection and personal agency in a patriarchal sphere (especially given the comic book and noir infrastructure). By finally embracing her desire to nurture *and* protect Trish, Jessica must acknowledge the vulnerabilities of loss and fragility of love, in the face of a dangerous, violent, and unpredictable reality.

NOTES

1. Britney G. Brinkman and Allison Jedinak, "Exploration of a Feminist Icon: Wonder Woman's on U.S. Media," *Sex Roles* 40 (2014): 434–435.

2. Andrew J. Friedenthal, "*My* Wonder Woman: The 'New Wonder Woman,' Gloria Steinem, and the Appropriation of Comic Book Iconography." In *Crossing Boundaries in Graphic Narrative: Essays on Forms, Series and Genres*, edited by Jake Jakaitis and James Wurtz (Jefferson, NC: McFarland, 2012), 188–206.

3. Katy Gilpatric, "Violent Female Action Characters in Contemporary American Cinema," *Sex Roles* 62 (2010): 734–746.

4. Shannon Austin, "Batman's Female Foes: The Gender War in Gotham City," *The Journal of Popular Culture* 48, no. 2 (2015): 285–295.

5. Rebecca L. Collins, "Content Analysis of Gender Roles in Media: Where Are We Now and Where Should We Go?" *Sex Roles* 64 (2011): 290–298.

6. Britney G. Brinkman and Allison Jedinak, "Exploration of a Feminist Icon: Wonder Woman's on U.S. Media," *Sex Roles* 40 (2014): 434–435.

7. *Ibid.*, 435.

8. Jeffrey A. Brown, "Gender, Sexuality, and Toughness: The Bad Girls of Action Film and Comic Books," in *Action Chicks: New Images of Tough Women in Popular Culture*, edited by Sherrie A. Inness (New York: Palgrave MacMillan, 2004), 47–74.

9. *Ibid.*, 47.

10. Alanna Bennett, "'Jessica Jones' and 'Daredevil' Nab the Perfect Writers for Netflix Runs," *Bustle* (November 2011), accessed August 4, 2016, http://www.bustle.com/articles/8824-jessica-jones-daredevil-nab-the-perfect-writers-for-netflix-runs.

11. Trish Bendixon, "*Jessica Jones* is a Queer-Inclusive, Feminist Superhero Series," *AfterEllen* (August 2016), accessed August 5, 2016, http://www.afterellen.com/tv/462901-jessica-jones-queer-inclusive-feminist-superhero-series.

12. Dominic Patten, "Marvel's 'Jessica Jones' EP Melissa Rosenberg on Luke Cage, Season 2, 'Supergirl' & Gender Parity in Hollywood," Deadlinewww (November 2015), accessed July 24, 2016, http://deadline.com/2015/11/jessica-jones-spoilers-marvel-melissa-rosenberg-krysten-ritter-luke-cage-1201628832/.

13. J. Siuntres, "Marvel TV's Jeph Loeb on *Daredevil, Shield, Agent Carter, Jessica Jones*, & *Luke Cage*; Greg Pak on *Superman, Hulk,* and More," *Word Balloon* (July 2015), accessed June

20, 2016, http://wordballoon.blogspot.com/2015/07/marvel-tvs-jeph-loeb-on-daredevilshield.
html.
    14. *Ibid.*
    15. John Boone, "We asked Marvel's Head of Television About Everything From 'Agent
Carter' to 'Iron Fist,' and He Answered," *Entertainment Tonight* (July 2015), accessed August
16, 2016, http://www.etonline.com/news/168025_exclusive_interview_with_the_head_of_
marvel_tv_jeph_loeb/.
    16. Lisa Yaszek, *Galactic Suburbia: Recovering Women[apost]s Science Fiction* (Colum-
bus: Ohio State University Press, 2008), 1–65.
    17. Jonathan Miller, "Hellcat Cometh," *Back Issue* 40:2 (2010): 61, accessed July 17, 2016,
https://issuu.com/twomorrows/docs/back_issue__40/2.
    18. *Ibid.*, 62.
    19. Shannon Austin, "Batman's Female Foes: The Gender War in Gotham City," *The
Journal of Popular Culture* 48, no. 2 (2015): 285–95.
    20. Steve Watts, "Captain Marvel[apost]s Carol Danvers Was Originally on *Jessica Jones*,"
IGN (November 19, 2015), accessed August 16, 2016, http://www.ign.com/articles/2015/11/20/
captain-marvels-carol-danvers-was-originally-on-jessica-jones
    21. Katy Gilpatric, "Violent Female Action Characters in Contemporary American Cin-
ema," *Sex Roles* 62 (2010): 734–46.
    22. Shannon Austin, "Batman's Female Foes: The Gender War in Gotham City," *The
Journal of Popular Culture* 48, no. 2 (2015): 285–95.
    23. Tammy Garland, Kathryn A. Branch, and Mackenzie Grimes, "Blurring the Lines:
Reinforcing Rape Myths in Comic Books," *Feminist Criminology* 11, no. 1 (2016): 48–68.

BIBLIOGRAPHY

Austin, Shannon. "Batman's Female Foes: The Gender War in Gotham City." *The Journal of
    Popular Culture* 48, no. 2 (2015): 285–295.
Bendixon, Trish. "*Jessica Jones* is a Queer-Inclusive, Feminist Superhero Series." *AfterEllen*,
    August 2016.http://www.afterellen.com/tv/462901-jessica-jones-queer-inclusive-feminist-
    superhero-series> (5 August 2016).
Bennet, Alanna. "'Jessica Jones' and 'Daredevil' Nab the Perfect Writers for Netflix Runs."
    Bustle, November 2011. http://www.bustle.com/articles/8824-jessica-jones-daredevil-
    nab-the-perfect-writers-for-netflix-runs (4 August 2016).
Boone, John. "We asked Marvel's Head of Television About Everything From 'Agent Carter'
    to 'Iron Fist,' and He Answered." *Entertainment Tonight*, July 2015. http://www.etonline.
    com/news/168025 _exclusive_interview_with_the_head_of_marvel_tv_jeph_loeb (16
    August 2016).
Brinkman, Britney G. and Allison Jedinak. "Exploration of a Feminist Icon: Wonder Woman's
    on U.S. Media." *Sex Roles* 40, no. 9 (2014): 434–435.
Brown, Jeffrey A. "Gender, Sexuality, and Toughness: The Bad Girls of Action Film and
    Comic Books." In *Action Chicks: New Images of Tough Women in Popular Culture*. Edited
    by Sherrie A. Inness. New York: Palgrave MacMillan, 2004.
Collins, Rebecca L. "Content Analysis of Gender Roles in Media: Where Are We Now and
    Where Should We Go?" *Sex Roles* 64 (2011): 290–298.
Friedenthal, Andrew J. "*My* Wonder Woman: The 'New Wonder Woman,' Gloria Steinem,
    and the Appropriation of Comic Book Iconography." In *Crossing Boundaries in Graphic
    Narrative: Essays on Forms, Series and Genres*. Edited by Jake Jakaitis and James Wurtz.
    Jefferson, NC: McFarland, 2012.
Garland, Tammy, Kathryn A. Branch, and Mackenzie Grimes. "Blurring the Lines: Reinforc-
    ing Rape Myths in Comic Books." *Feminist Criminology* 11, no. 1 (2016): 48–68.
Gilpatric, Katy. "Violent Female Action Characters in Contemporary American Cinema."
    Sex Roles 62 (2010): 734–746.
Miller, Jonathan. "Hellcat Cometh." *Back Issue* 40, no. 2 (2010): 61. https://issuu.com/
    twomorrows/docs/ back_issue__40/2 (17 July 2016).
Patten, Dominic. "Marvel's 'Jessica Jones' EP Melissa Rosenberg On Luke Cage, Season 2,

'Supergirl' and Gender Parity In Hollywood." Deadlinewww, November 2015. <http://deadline.com/2015/11/jessica-jones-spoilers-marvel-melissa-rosenberg-krysten-ritter-luke-cage-1201628832/> (24 July 2016).

Siuntres, J. "Marvel TV's Jeph Loeb on *Daredevil, Shield, Agent Carter, Jessica Jones,* & *Luke Cage*; Greg Pak on *Superman, Hulk,* and More." *Word Balloon,* July 2015. http://word balloon.blogspot.com/ 2015/07/marvel-tvs-jeph-loeb-on-daredevilshield.html (20 June 2016).

Watts, Steve. "Captain Marvel's Carol Danvers Was Originally on *Jessica Jones.*" IGN, 19 November 2015. http://www.ign.com/articles/2015/11/20/captain-marvels-carol-danvers-was-originally-on-jessica-jones (16 August 2016).

Yaszek, Lisa. *Galactic Suburbia: Recovering Women's Science Fiction.* Columbus: Ohio State University Press, 2008.

Jessica Jones

Gender and the Marvel Phenomenon

LILLIAN CÉSPEDES GONZÁLEZ

Jessica Jones was one of those series that many of us perhaps did not expect. In the larger Marvel Universe, Jessica did not even have a comic book series under her exclusive name until October 2016. Instead, she was created as the main character for the narrative of the *Alias* series (2001–2004) by Brian Michael Bendis and Michael Gaydos.[1] It was one of the first series launched under the Marvel MAX imprint, producing explicit material for mature readers. The comic book series focuses on Jessica as a private investigator, with Bendis and Gaydos developing a noir-crime narrative rather than a straightforward superhero plot. According to Booker, "the fact that she was once a minor member of the superhero team The Avengers allows her access to her former world despite the loss of her powers, and allows her encounters with characters in the lower tiers of Marvel's pantheon during gritty crime investigations, which in turn offers a clever walk along the border of the two genres."[2] Jessica's story continued in *The Pulse* (2004–2006), concerning the investigative journalists working at "The Pulse," a weekly section of the newspaper, *The Daily Bugle*. In this arc, Jones acts as a specialist consultant for the journalist team. However, for what concerns the TV series, *The Pulse* narrative is not on the menu as of yet.

Returning to *Alias*, what was novel for this type of narrative was that it took the reader to the "street level," allowing them to experience the lives of supers (or ex-supers in this case) from a more familiar point of view.[3] In addition, due to the series' mature content, Bendis could allow himself to be blunt about certain topics, such as Jessica's alcohol problem, which is also reflected in the Netflix series, although perhaps in a more subtle and less brutal manner.[4] Then, we also have the issue of rape and abusive control brought into the story by the character of Killgrave—the Purple Man character who abducts and abuses Jones, creating the main plot for the last six issues of the series.[5] Therefore, they poured all this content into a mixer and *Marvel's Jessica Jones* was born. But Jones did not simply happen; she succeeded and has become a fan favorite. If we consider the growing number of Marvel products, as well as other superhero franchises with female leads such as Supergirl, what is it that has made this show so popular?

The Marvel Phenomenon

Marvel's popularity increased radically after the success of the Avengers' first cinematic installment in 2012.[6] That is not to say that Marvel was not popular before, however; the Avengers crystallized the company's drive during the last decade. In the early 2000s, Marvel was trying to recover from a crippling financial crisis that almost left them bankrupt.[7] Therefore, there was a need to take a firmer grasp over their products in a way that would become more profitable, whilst still being satisfying for their fans. Thus, in 2005, Marvel changed from an enterprise that was selling rights to different studios, into producers in their own right, turning the tables on the hierarchies of Hollywood and convergence cinema.[8] Moreover, Marvel had become self-conscious of their image due to a run of bad movies under their license, such as *Daredevil* (Mark Steven Johnson, 2003) and *Elektra* (Rob Bowman, 2005). According to Marvel's executives, these products failed due to the lack of control they had over the creative decisions in the production process. Therefore, by creating their own studio, they would be able to rectify these issues and have direct input.[9]

Due to the active nature of fan cultures, subjects such as adaptations need to meet the fans' approval, at least to some degree.[10] Moreover, Marvel is a multifaceted enterprise that not only produces comic books and movies, but also several different products derived from their original content such as toys, collectables, and many other kinds of merchandise. Thus, they needed to ensure that the success of their films would line up with their other licensed items in the market, maximizing profit and acquiring ultimate control over multimedia content.[11] Marvel emphasized a way that would allow them to be successful in the end: their multiverse, the crossover narrative where all things Stan Lee-approved take place. This strategy had been used in the 1990s, with the multitude of cartoon adaptations from comic books, the most prominent example of which was the X-Men television series that aired on Fox Kids. Liam Burke believes that it was these original animations that formed the bridge between comics and blockbuster movies.[12]

With Marvel Studios formed, a new wave of their own productions came to the screen. In their first release, *Iron Man* (Jon Favreau, 2008), Marvel made clear their crossover strategy with Nick Fury's invitation to Tony Stark to join the Avengers Initiative.[13] By creating this multiverse, Marvel achieved what Chuck Tryon notes is the concept of "incompleteness" in convergence cinema.[14] In this way, the audience feels like the story is not whole until they have all the pieces of the puzzle. This drives them to keep on watching movies and finding other products such as TV series, videogames, comics, and other media, to eventually get hold of the complete narrative. And here is where Netflix comes into play.

Streaming Killed the Broadcasting Star? Netflix and Marvel's Jessica Jones

By the mid–2000s, Netflix established itself as a streaming platform, moving away from their earlier DVD mailing services, allowing customers to access thousands of movies through their membership charges rather than the traditional fee per movie business practice.[15] Since then, their subscriber numbers have skyrocketed. According to Netflix's own website, the number of members at a global level in 2014 was over 50 million.[16] The success of their original content TV series has earned the streaming service Emmys and a loyal audience that keeps on increasing. The Netflix phenomenon and the practice of binge-watching have become popular socio-cultural practices amongst TV consumers that are changing the audience viewership.[17] In fact, Uricchio goes a step further and states that, "Netflix offers new ways to think about taste and genre."[18] This is precisely what attracted Marvel and Netflix to cooperate on the production and distribution of *Jessica Jones* and its predecessors. By 2013, Marvel's talent for transmedia storytelling became not only noticeable in their films, but also through their videogames and TV series, and the Netflix effect was something they could not ignore.[19] The agreement was struck between the two companies to create the cycle of series for *The Defenders*, which would incorporate the productions of shows based on *Daredevil*, *Jessica Jones*, *Luke Cage*, and *Iron Fist*.[20]

Similar to Bendis' ideas for *Alias*, the decision to focus on these "street heroes" stemmed from the public's lack of familiarity with these more mundane figures.[21] Thus, testing the waters with the release of *Daredevil* in 2015, the success of this enterprise has proven that the Netflix phenomenon is real and a potential game changer for television. In addition, it has expanded the Marvel Cinematic Universe dynamic, making it accessible for a different type of audience and allowing the company's presence into our living rooms. This is something that cannot be ignored. According to Cornejo Stewart, the incorporation of Netflix into the Marvel equation has been key for the appropriate development of cross-over narratives and character exchange, as displayed in *Daredevil* and *Jessica Jones*.[22]

The success is apparent through the positive reception of *Marvel's Jessica Jones*. According to Cornejo Stewart: "The reception of the series has been excellent both on behalf of the public and the critics. It has also managed to create a lead role for a superheroine in a genre often dominated by male roles."[23] Moreover, this is backed up by online review websites and aggregators such as Rotten Tomatoes, which gives the series a solid 93 percent.[24] Furthermore, web-based Internet Movie Database (IMDB) gives the series a conservative, yet well-earned 8.3 out of 10.[25] Nevertheless, a critics' review of television series between 2014 and 2015 provides further insight into the show and its popularity. Comparing the ratings of Daniel D'Addario (*Time*), Mike Hale (*The New York Times*), and the review aggregate website Metacritic, one can appreciate that *Jessica Jones* has not made it into the top 10 of any of these. However, it is described as an interesting and good show, but not a ground breaker, or a series that happens once in a lifetime.[26] The series is clearly good enough to attract a large audience, for reasons which Opam notes: "By placing its stellar female cast in this murky underworld and letting them shine in a way Marvel has never done before, it stands head and shoulders above the company's other marquee properties to become one of the best new shows out this year. *Daredevil* was great by Marvel standards. *Jessica Jones* is just great."[27] Thus, the gender factor becomes the third ingredient for this strong superhero cocktail.

Jessica Jones: Women and Change in Comics and Superhero Culture

Marvel's Jessica Jones opens with a pale skinned, dark haired, angry, and disillusioned young woman, living in a completely trashed apartment in the Hell's Kitchen neighborhood of Manhattan. With a flat that doubles up as her office for her private investigation services, we find that Jessica lives a pretty unglamorous life, where bottles of whiskey are abundant and sanitation seemingly lacking.[28] She lives on her own, isolated. It is not until the very end of the first episode of season one that we find out she has some sort of support, in the figure of Trish Walker.[29] That aside, the only other person who genuinely cares for her throughout the narrative is not revealed to be a friend until much later. Neighbor Malcolm Ducasse cares for Jessica once he is away from Kilgrave's influence, and truly bonds with her; he also overcomes his drug addiction thanks to Jones' help. In "AKA Top Shelf Perverts," following Kilgrave's murder of Ruben, it is Ducasse that orchestrates things to disrupt Jessica's risky plan of getting herself locked up in a top security prison in order to expose Kilgrave.[30] Moreover, nothing Jessica does in the series goes according to plan. Her attempts to catch Kilgrave end in disaster and usually have severe consequences for others. Her relationships are incredibly flawed and damaged. In many ways, she is more of a hazard than anything else.

There is only one way out, which Hope Shlottman (a recent victim of Kilgrave who Jessica is hired to find after her parents report her disappearance) already predicted in episode ten, when she goads Jessica to fight fire with fire and kill their abductor to end their suffering, and then takes her own life.[31] Ultimately, this confrontation was a self-fulfilling prophecy. The few instances where we get to see the display of Jones' powers always highlight her unnatural strength. When Kilgrave threatens to kidnap and control Trish, who is the only person Jessica seems to honestly care for, all her self-restraint is put aside, and with little remorse, the deed is done: she breaks his neck.[32] What this brief summary of the series attempts to demonstrate is that this is not the average television series with a female lead. In fact, it is nothing like other comic book shows with female leads, such as *Supergirl* or *Agent Carter*. Even the filming is different: in these latter two shows, there are vibrant colors, humorous scenes, and a degree of naivety and comfort. But in *Marvel's Jessica Jones* there is just a bleak, ever constant shade of grey.

Jessica Jones signifies the changes that some scholars are trying to highlight within the field of gender studies and geek subcultures such as comic books, and superheroes in particular. For decades, feminist criticism has taken over the matter of gender representation in sequential art. Lavin explains how, "during World War II, patriotic super-heroines captured the attention of an unexpected audience of new readers, both male and female."[33] The likes of Wonder Woman or She-Hulk were considered to exist in duality as role models and sex objects at the same time.[34] Similarly, Stabile supports the idea that since the 9/11 attacks, the superhero industry has focused on the protection of the weak and salvation of the secular society, illustrating a great deal of sexism and militarized cultural behaviors.[35] For her this becomes perfectly represented by the television series *Heroes*, where the only main female lead is the cheerleader Claire, who has only the power of self-healing. Stabile advises that the materialization of her statement becomes real in the advertisement line for the series, "Save the cheerleader. Save the World," thus portraying women in need of protection and using the cheerleader as an ideal portrayal of American secular society.[36] In many ways, this suggests and exemplifies that the "beautiful soul" narrative still applies to our society and it is most visible in female heroines. This type of plot device is often used to explain "women's relationship with war through history, describing women's innocence of and abstention from war."[37]

Moreover, Britain endorses the idea that this principle is also used as a mechanism for portraying women fighting against terrorism, particularly female soldiers in recent military conflicts such as in the U.S. invasion and occupation of Iraq.[38] Furthermore, it emphasizes how these women are under a high threat of becoming victims of sexual violence and rape, and are always presented as girls rather than women, who are fulfilling their dreams or using the army to survive. Despite them being capable members of the military, they are still the ones in need of saving, usually by their male colleagues.[39] So at the same time, we have this constructed reality of what a superheroine should be: both of supernatural abilities, yet a victim of her own nature, both with the capability to inspire women and others in the spirit of true feminism, yet undermined by its objectification. So how does Jessica Jones fit in here? Put simply: she does not.

Some could argue that her vulnerability and PTSD due to Kilgrave's influence depicts her within the beautiful soul narrative, but Jessica needs nobody to save her. In fact, she saves herself: she breaks from his control, and eventually she defeats him. Her acquaintances help her achieve her goals. They do not do the work for her, though; they perform an act of reliance, not replacement, and her representation is not objectified or sexualized.

We must not confuse Kilgrave's control over Jessica with sexualization: it is abuse, and no different to the domain he establishes over others, if perhaps accentuated due to his fascination with her. She is not treated differently in that respect to anyone else. Kilgrave uses his powers indiscriminately; the focus on sexual abuse is a social commentary relevant to a modern audience engaging with the series. It is not an original character trait; Jessica's trauma is acquired following the narrative arc with her abuser (likewise, there was a Jessica in *Alias* before and after the Purple Man), which is also reflected by the flashbacks in the series and through conversations with Trish. Moreover, the actual portrayal and imagery of Jessica in the series is hardly a fashion statement or a cry for sexual attention. In almost every scene she wears the same outfit: generic jeans, boots, plain t-shirt, black leather jacket, and a scarf.[40] Carolyn Cocca's analysis of depictions of women in mainstream (DC and Marvel) comics between 1993 and 2013 shows that "women were portrayed in non-realistic sexualized poses and/or with their breasts or buttocks falling out of their clothes in 25.18% of the 4670 panels in which their bodies were drawn."[41] As a comic book adaptation, it would be logical to expect trends in the paper medium to transfer into the television representation. Yet, none of the characters are portrayed in this way. In fact, any glimpses of exposed flesh coming from Jessica or Trish are because of their performance of the sexual act,[42] which are driven by the narrative and not as the consequence of their objectification. If we compare Jessica with Cocca's study on sexualized female superheroines, she passes the test.

Therefore, what becomes transparent with *Jessica Jones* is that the issue of representation is changing. On this subject, Lavin concludes that female leadership in comics is becoming a clear trend, and negative portrayals are decreasing.[43] Moreover, Cocca emphasizes that "the sensibility of the 'third wave' of feminism, encouraging analysis, critique and production of pop culture through humor and irony, seems to have made inroads among comic readers who see the objectification and will critique that objectification through parody."[44] This goes back to previous statements reflected in this essay. We have established that geeks, fans, and comic book collectors are active audiences that must be pleased. An important aspect of the redesign of Batgirl's and Spider-Woman's outfits was due to fan reactions and their feedback to the publishers.[45]

Lars Konzack, expert in geek and computer culture, states that this culture generates "a communication network with its own literary and cultural critical apparatus: a coherent, scholarly alternative to established academia with cultural ties that transcend it."[46] As a self-reflective community, with products created by geeks for geeks, change is bound to happen as society evolves. Moreover, as with many stigmatized social groups, there is a phenomenon of developed sympathy and inclusion of others who may also be excluded. In this way, as more women get involved in geek culture practices, the tendencies become moderated by their presence and need for representation. Consider another successful television series, *The Big Bang Theory*. Raewyn Campbell (PhD candidate, University of Wollongong, Australia) advises that female participants are reclaiming their place in geek culture, and this is seen with the inclusion of characters such as Bernadette or Amy, who are funny, fleshed out, and embody the diversity which exists within geek environments and social groups.[47]

The society of the twenty-first century has changed. The same principles that allowed Marvel and Netflix to become successful enterprises, revolutionizing their own fields, are reflected in their audience base. Particularly since the 2010s there are a growing number of fantasy and sci-fi series and comic books, with lead female roles that bring forward a plurality of women of different backgrounds to the forefront of the geek narratives.[48] *Rat Queens*, *Orphan Black*, or the web series *RWBY* are letting female outcasts into society, giving them a place to belong and flourish, to become active members of said society, and even its saviors.[49] The women of the twenty-first century are not Diana Prince; many of them are their own versions of Jessica Jones and Trish Walker. Their communities need them; and they are finally being heard. The rise of geekdom is here: the dawn of outcast females in splendor.

Viewer Feedback on Marvel's Jessica Jones

The theories presented on this study keep referring and driving us back to the audience, the fans, and their self-reflective nature. Therefore, this essay would be incomplete without an analysis of what the audience actually has to say on the show. For that purpose, a viewer feedback form was created by the author and circulated online via Google Drive between 8 June 2016 and 17 July 2016 producing a total of 45 individual responses.[50] The survey aims to collect information regarding the viewers' participation in geek culture, i.e., whether they read comic books or watch any other superhero movies/ series, as well as their knowledge of *Jessica Jones* prior to the series. Moreover, with respect to their opinions on the actual series, they were given different topics discussed within this text such as popularity, the Netflix effect (i.e., the binge-watching of shows), or the portrayal of gender, in order to gauge how these matters are understood from a viewer's viewpoint. While the small sample size means that this is not a scientific study, the results are interesting.

Identifying the Audience

Due to the stigmatization issues mentioned earlier regarding comics, binge-watching on Netflix, or just the presence of a female heroine, there was a need to understand what kind of people were actually watching this series. The age range is wide, with the oldest member being born in 1960 and the youngest in 1998.[51] I believe this confirms Benjamin Woo's theory that, "geek culture comprises people within a whole range of ages and life stages," unlike the patterns shown in other subcultures.[52] With regards to their nationalities, the vast majority of the respondents identified themselves as American citizens, followed by the group composed of ten British people.[53] This is perhaps not so surprising, considering that the comic book industry flourished in the United States and spread quickly to other English-speaking countries with strong cultural traditions of cartooning, such as the British Isles. Finally, when asked about their sex identification, the group showed a relatively even split with 55.6 percent of the participants being male, and the remaining 44.4 percent as female.[54] Regarding the viewers' experience with other geek culture items, the results portray more variety in the replies.

Thirty-four individuals identified themselves as comic book readers, while only eight participants advised they did not read these. Interestingly, the remaining three took the option other. The individual replies belong to a British female born in 1983, an American male citizen born in 1985, and an American female citizen born in 1977. Both females advised that they used to read comics in the past, but not anymore, while the male advises: "Sometimes graphic novels," as a differentiation from comic books.[55] Moreover, the negative replies came both from male and female participants, demonstrating that the gender inclusivity is a reality.

When questioned if the viewers watched any other Marvel shows, the reply was overwhelmingly positive with only four negative answers and an encouraging "Not at the moment, but will do."[56] From the reply summary, it becomes apparent that there is an indisputable audience favorite: *Daredevil,* followed closely by *Agents of S.H.I.E.L.D.*[57] Despite the popularity of *S.H.I.E.L.D,* it is clear that Cornejo Stewart was correct in establishing that the popularity of Netflix series such as *Daredevil* highlights the new ways of producing and consuming series that do not follow the traditional pattern of television viewership.[58]

Concerning the question that asked individuals whether they considered themselves fans of any other comic or superhero franchise, the results were most disparate. Only three participants advised they did not have an interest in these, which coincides with some of the negative replies for the Marvel series question.[59] The rest of the 42 answers refer to so many different tendencies that no data amalgamation would do them justice. Therefore, we will use here a few of the replies in full as representatives of this variety. An American male citizen born in 1981 replied, "I'm sorry, can I say most? Not so much the DCCU (movie), but the DCAU (animated shows), the MCU, CW/DC shows (now including *Supergirl*) I watch."[60] In addition, a Lithuanian participant advised, "TV shows: *Gotham, Arrow,* but will check out others such as *Flash* and *Daredevil.* I don't remember, there are so many! Movies: everything ever released. Even the very first, old ones. Some of them I will never watch again as they were bad."[61] These replies reflect that there is so much cultural capital within this industry that it is hard to amass, but at the same time the abundance caters for many tastes, keeping a happy and engaged audience.

Jessica Jones Before Marvel's Jessica Jones: *What the Audience Knew About It*

This was the only part of the survey which was not compulsory, as the surveyor understood that not everyone that has seen the series may have also read *Alias* or *The Pulse.* This area of the survey included only two sections: "Have you read any Jessica Jones comics?" (34 responses) and "How do you feel regarding the adaptation of the comic book series to the screen?" (28 responses). The data from the 34 individuals who completed the first section showed that 61.8 percent of these participants had not read any of the comic books.[62] With regards to the adaptation question, two types of answers have been identified: those belonging to the 13 individuals who confirmed their reading of the comic books, and those of people who, despite not having read the original sources, still voiced their opinions on the nature of adaptation to the screen. Regarding the answers of the 13 comic readers, the survey results provide us with 13 positive replies towards the adaptation of the character and the series as a whole. For instance, an American male citizen born in 1977, who had read the comics, stated, "I was cautiously optimistic about the adaptation, and I found myself delighted at how they used this alternate medium (i.e., television) to explore aspects of Jessica Jones that either the comic did or did not fully exploit. I am usually quite critical of such adaptations, but I felt this was masterfully done."[63] A British female born in 1994 who had also read the comics said she felt "it was done very well—especially considering Marvel didn't have the rights to aspects of the comics. Purple Man was made far more realistic and therefore far more convincing. Jessica was more self-loathing in the show compared to the comic but made sense considering the differences in time frame and dealing with the events. Normally wouldn't be happy to add a rape plot but was one of the few shows to deal with it in an appropriate way."[64] Although these are just samples, the feeling expressed in the rest of the replies is of a similar nature. Even though most of the participants acknowledge and are aware of changes to the plot, narrative, or certain aspects, they recognize them in a positive light, usually for the benefit of the audience and improvement of the comic in areas that were left unclear or perhaps not investigated in as much depth.

In addition, like the female subject's response above, many felt that the sexual assault material was dealt in a respectful, approachable manner. Considering these commentaries come from both genders, it is fair to establish that once again, the audience takes responsibility for the content they are provided and they are willing to explore risky subjects, even those that may be gender sensitive, with objectivity. Moreover, even the replies regarding adaptation from the viewers who did not have a knowledge of the comics are equally positive and reflect that the show was enjoyable and approachable without prior information on the subject.[65] It is likely that the approach from a "street hero" perspective and the noir script made it easier to engage for those who were not aware of *Alias* or *The Pulse*.

By making the superhero a closer approximation to the viewer, in contrast to a mutant or an alien from with a long-standing story arcs such as Thor or the X-Men, the extended universe becomes a product to explore afterwards without the prerequisite of having an acquired taste for the subject. The crossover narrative makes it easier for the viewer to enter a world perhaps unknown to them from different access points that suits the audience and not the producers. Replies such as "Haven't read these (yet) but I was pleased to see a female superhero protagonist," suggest that the success of the series may grow interest in the franchise and acquire new fans retrospectively.[66]

Viewer Opinions of Marvel's Jessica Jones

The surveyor asked the question to ascertain whether the viewers would have still watched the show if it had not been available through Netflix/online. Due to the Netflix effect discussed earlier, this needed to be addressed with regards to the popularity of the show and the implications this would have on the audience. The results show the following: 44.4 percent of the respondents confirmed they would have watched it otherwise, followed by a striking 31.1 percent who replied with indecision (maybe), and 15.6 percent who gave a straight negative answer.[67] Moreover, the individuals were given an "other" option, in case they felt the three previous choices did not reflect their views on the subject. A total of four out of the 45 participants selected this reply.[68] It seems the viewers would have kept in mind the following issues when deciding to watch the show if it was not on Netflix/online: how well was it rated, how accessible it was, and whether they could still watch it under their own terms. A British male born in 1993 advised, "I think I would have watched it if the series went out weekly on UK television, but I think I would have located a digital copy so that I could watch on my MacBook 'in my own time,' rather than having to rely on my television and not-always-reliable Digibox recorder to view it."[69] Thus, what is clear from the results is that audience convenience is a definite factor to consider with regards to the show's popularity.

The last section of the survey tried to ascertain the audience viewpoint of certain topics; the first one being their feelings towards Jessica as a character, their familiarity with her, and if they found her relatable. All the replies were overwhelmingly positive. Only five participants provided answers that advised they did not know about their feelings in this respect or that they did not relate with the character at all.[70] One of the participants summarizes the view: "Directly no. I have not been a victim of control as she had. Although her reaction and subsequent actions are understandable."[71] For the remaining 40 individuals, their appreciation of Jessica seems compelling. An American male citizen born in 1967 stated, "I definitely think over the course of the series we get a chance to not only know Jessica, but feel for her. She's relatable in a certain sense, but as a man, I can't pretend to know what she's been through."[72] This view is replicated in several of the other male participants, and although it is not reflective of the majority, it highlights the arguments presented earlier by Campbell and that are discussed in more depth by Brown and Loucks. They note that the increase of women in the superhero/comic book industry, both producing and consuming these products "can open up important new avenues to explore."[73] The reply of a British female born in 1994 agrees with this theory. She states that Jessica "felt a much more realistic character—why [while] I admire and enjoy other characters, they often aren't relatable because they're generally to [too] perfect. I could see myself and others I know much more in Jessica than I normally would. Her reactions were much more human and realistic. She didn't have some superior moral code, she had realistic reactions."[74]

Following up on this subject, the viewers were asked if they felt that the narrative of the series allowed them to bond with Jessica. A total of 11 participants did not provide fully positive answers. Their views can be summarized in the following way: these participants did not feel that a "bond" was the actual relationship they had established with the character. There is a trend between the two types of answers provided along those lines: those who did not bond but rather empathize because the character's attributes did not allow them to establish this relationship, and/or those who did not bond due to their detached viewership. The following statement from an American citizen female born in 1991 is representative of this sentiment. She advises, "I don't know if bond is the right word. I would say empathize maybe, but I don't feel like I have any kind of relationship with her different than that of any other fictional character."[75] The remaining 24 answers were happy to admit there was a bond with the character. For example, there were replies such as "Yes, I wanted her to succeed, to recover from trauma, to be the hero and protect other people" as well as "Yes as she is shown to be very flawed despite the fact she has superpowers."[76] These feelings towards Jessica echo the words of Cornejo Stewart in her study of the Netflix effects. According to her, one of the pillars of the compelling story is the supreme character interpretation that combines irony and cynicism with fragility and vulnerability, whilst still portraying a certainly not defenseless and confident Jessica.[77]

Regarding Gender

Moving on to subject specific questions about the series, the participants were asked about their opinion concerning how the gender matter is treated on the show. Moreover, the question prompted them to think about if they believe it was representative of modern society or perhaps of comic/superhero culture.[78] Only seven out of 45 participants did not contribute to the discussion from a fully positive perspective; some felt they could not express an opinion on the subject. Interestingly, all of these seven subjects were identified as males.[79] Their replies varied from "I really don't have/can't formulate an opinion on this," to more detailed replies such as "Trans-individuals were unrepresented, but that's pretty common. I didn't feel like any of the characters behaved in ways that did not reflect aspects of gender performance in modern society."[80] Whether this is due to their personal viewership or it is reflective of a gender divide is something difficult to assess with the sample provided.[81] With regards to the remaining 38 replies, there was a general consensus that the strong characters played by Jessica and Trish reflected on modern feminism and female agency in a positive light. One of the most detailed answers comes from an American male citizen born in 1968 explaining that "Jessica Jones and Supergirl are both breaking new ground in terms of appealing directly to a female audience. Jones, because she is on Netflix, can do this in a more mature and thoughtful way, while Supergirl tends to be more celebratory (a tone which also has its place). So we have a female superhero, her female supporting cast, and antagonists (Kilgrave, Nuke) who represent forms of toxic masculinity. This, in my opinion, is why the show resonated so strongly with female audiences, why they insisted Kilgrave was the best villain in the Marvel stable: because at last we had a villain who symbolized a problem female audiences don't just recognize but face daily. I have not thought about the tv [sic] show as a metaphor for comic book culture; I think this may be too narrow of a reading. I don't think Jessica Jones is written for traditional comic book fans—by which I mean middle-aged, white men. I have no data to back this up, but my suspicion is that most women who watch this show do not buy monthly comics."[82] In addition, there is the statement of a Canadian female, born in 1992, who states, "I felt the show had a very modern perspective on gender, and focused strongly on gender specific violence and the fear that women experience in the world. Hope was an example of how trauma can change a person."[83]

This is representative of the scholarly argument supported by Brown and Loucks. They advise that the increasing female contribution to the comic industry is allowing the development of alternative narratives moving away from previous misogynistic/sexist attitudes, and allowing superheroines to headline their own stories with far more success than in previous generations.[84] These tendencies correlate to the last compulsory question of the survey which addresses the popularity of the series.

Why Is Jessica Jones as a Series So Popular?

This was an open question, as the surveyor did not want to impose a specific reason or set of reasons on such a reactive audience. Moreover, the answers provided usually point to more than one reason, yet they follow the same patterns.[85] The participant's answers identified the following subjects as the reasons for the success of the series:

- The strong female characters and different approach to gender related subjects such as abuse.

- The proximity to the viewers' reality and thematic composition that is relatable to everyday life, as opposed to traditional superhero stories.
- The production values of the show: good script, acting, and filming.
- The marketing: this is a Marvel brand product on Netflix.

In addition, a few minor subjects were reflected upon by a few participants such as the mature content and darker tone of the series, as well as star appeal, particularly because of the presence of David Tennant.[86] All these factors were addressed in the previous section of this study. However, it is noticeable that although these ideas are well-ingrained in the audience, the academic work still has a great deal to catch up with. The scholarly work in these fields is growing but it lacks cohesion, due to the revisionism imposed on fields such as comic book, film, and gender studies. The attitudes voiced by those like Kirkpatrick or Scott are holding us back from understanding these cultural phenomena and reflecting upon flourishing fields which are bound to dominate certain spheres of interdisciplinary studies throughout the twenty-first century. Kirkpatrick and Scott's reductionist views express that although fields such as the above are changing from a sociocultural, and even industry standard perspective, academia cannot afford to move forward due to the concern for a "predictable parade of elisions, evasions, and errors."[87]

As stated earlier by Lonzack, geek culture (including all its variants such as comics, fan cultures, gamers, and other areas) has its own "alternative intellectual milieu," which moves forward with the products and times.[88] As scholars, we should be embracing and partaking in these new areas of research with the same positive attitude that the participants of the survey have deployed toward *Jessica Jones*. Holding on to antiquated, narrow arguments instead of developing new methodologies may impede us from comprehending these new cultural tendencies in a never-static society bound to keep on reinventing itself through new subcultures, technologies, and ideas. What has become clear out of this research is that the audience still holds a great deal of power. Jessica Jones would have not been successful if the factors advised previously had not been relevant from the point of view of the viewers.

As a corollary for the survey and the study, it is worth looking at the answers provided to the last question asked to the participants. This was not a compulsory part of the questionnaire, and it was simply an open statement for those who felt they had something else to say regarding Jessica Jones and the discussion, that perhaps was not included in the other sections. A British female born in 1994 said, "To me Jessica Jones is the new standard on writing female characters—they don't have to always be likable or perfect, as long as they're three-dimensional. It served well as introducing Luke as a character and I can't wait for his show. Also despite being a *Doctor Who* nerd I can't look at Tennant in the same way." Encouragingly, an American female citizen born in 1976 replied, "I generally don't watch sci-fi but loved every minute of this series." The evidence concurs. Females have now a space within geek culture to express themselves, the rule of patriarchy is being rectified, and instead of cowering, new generations have a chance to stand up for themselves, with new role models and different aspirations.

Geek subculture is addressing issues that mainstream tendencies are still reluctant to face in an appropriate manner. A plethora of cultural products is imposing itself over our social trends, transgressing backgrounds and demographics. The people have a voice, and they are being heard, including those who live in the stigmatized fringes of society. The world of academia is shifting. Within a few years we may experience the same effects that are widespread in geek culture such as the fan-author evolving into the fan-scholar. Perhaps this is the only way to bridge the divide between academia and the public, and leave behind our self-imposed elitist cultural behaviors, for we are both. The superhero can be a normal guy. The heroine can save herself and break the rules. We can all be Jessica Jones, scholars included.

NOTES

1. Brian Michael Bendis and Michael Gaydos, *Alias #1–#28* (New York: MAX 2001–2004).
2. M. Keith Booker, *Encyclopedia of Comic Books and Graphic Novels: Volume A-L* (Santa Barbara: Greenwood, 2010), 124.
3. Adam J. Noble, "Meta-Comics and Libraries: Should Libraries Buy Them?" in *Graphic Novels and Comics in Libraries and Archives: Essays on Readers, Research, History and Cataloguing*, ed. Robert G. Weiner (Jefferson, NC: McFarland, 2010), 206, article in full at 202–208.
4. Stanton Peele, writing for *Psychology Today*, points out that throughout the first season, although we see the character drink more than eat, or sleep, he believes that this is more of a plot device and a coping mechanism for the character to deal with her traumas rather than a social commentary on substance abuse like in series such as *Breaking Bad* or *The Knick*. For more information see: https://www.psychologytoday.com/blog/addiction-in-society/201512/jessica-jones-alcoholism.
5. Bendis and Gaydos, *Alias*.
6. Daniele Giannantoni, "Netflix & Marvel Studios: Come Costuire una Realta Serial," *Corso di Laurea Magistrale in Lingue e Culture per la Comunicazione Internazionale*, Università degli Studi della Tuscia (2014/2015), 133.
7. Derek Johnson, "Cinematic Destiny: Marvel Studios and the Trade Stories of Industrial Convergence," *Cinema Journal* 52 (2012): 9.
8. Johnson, "Cinematic Destiny," 9.
9. *Ibid.*, 10.
10. Liam Burke, "Sowing the Seeds: How 1990s Marvel Animation Facilitated Today's Cinematic Universe," in *Marvel Comics into Film: Essays on Adaptations Since the 1940s*, ed. Matthew J. McEniry, Robert Moses Peaslee, and Robert G. Weiner (Jefferson, NC: McFarland, 2016), 114.
11. Johnson, "Cinematic Destiny," 10–11.
12. Burke, "Sowing the Seeds," 116.

13. Johnson, "Cinematic Destiny," 7.
14. Chuck Tryon, *Reinventing Cinema: Movies in the Age of Media Convergence* (New Brunswick: Rutgers University Press, 2009), 18–20.
15. David Pogue, "A Stream of Movies, Sort of Free," *The New York Times*, January 25, 2007, accessed July 15, 2016, http://www.nytimes.com/2007/01/25/technology/25pogue.html?_r=0.
16. "About Netflix," Netflix, accessed July 15, 2016, https://media.netflix.com/en/about-netflix.
17. Rachel E. Silverman and Emily D. Ryalls, "Everything Is Different the Second Time Around: The Stigma of Temporality on *Orange Is the New Black*," *Television & New Media* (May 5, 2016): 1, accessed July 15, 2016, DOI: 10.1177/1527476416647496.
18. William Uricchio, "Film, Cinema, Television … Media?" *New Review of Film and Television Studies* 12/3 (2014): 277.
19. Giannantoni, "Netflix & Marvel Studios," 133.
20. *Ibid.*, 134–134.
21. *Ibid.*, 133.
22. Josefina Cornejo Stewart, "El Caso de Netflix (2012–2015). Nuevas Formas de Pensar la Producción, Distribución y Consumo de Series Dramáticas," Tesis Doctoral, Universitat Ramon Lull (2016), 3–4.
23. "La serie ha tenido una excelente respuesta por parte del público y la crítica y ha logrado posicionar a una superheroína dentro de un género donde suelen predominar los papeles masculinos." Translation by Lillian Céspedes González. *Ibid.*, 135.
24. "Marvel's Jessica Jones," Rotten Tomatoes, accessed July 15, 2016, https://www.rottentomatoes.com/tv/jessica-jones/s01/.
25. "Jessica Jones," IMDB, accessed July 15, 2016, http://www.imdb.com/title/tt2357547/.
26. Cornejo Stewart, "El Caso de Netflix," 9.
27. Kwame Opam, "Review: Jessica Jones is the Complex (Super) Heroine We've Been Waiting For," *The Verge*, last modified November 19, 2015, http://www.theverge.com/2015/11/19/9760514/jessica-jones-review-marvel-netflix-krysten-ritter.
28. *Marvel's Jessica Jones*, "AKA Ladies Night." Season 1/1. Directed by S. J. Clarkson. Written by Melissa Rosenberg. Netflix, November 20, 2015.
29. *Ibid.*
30. *Marvel's Jessica Jones*, "AKA Top Shelf Perverts." Season 1/7. Directed by Simon Cellan Jones. Written by Jenna Reback and Micah Schraft. Netflix, November 20, 2015.
31. *Marvel's Jessica Jones*, "AKA 1,000 Cuts." Season 1/10. Directed by Rosemary Rodriguez. Written by Dana Baratta and Micah Schraft. Netflix, November 20, 2015.
32. *Marvel's Jessica Jones*, "AKA Smile." Season 1/13. Directed by Michael Rymer. Story written by Jamie King and Scott Reynolds. Teleplay by Scott Reynolds and Melissa Rosenberg. Netflix, November 20, 2015.
33. Michael R. Lavin, "Women in Comic Books," *Serials Review* 24/2 (1998): 94.
34. Lavin, "Women in Comic Books," 94.
35. Carol A. Stabile, "'Sweetheart, This Ain't Gender Studies': Sexism and Superheroes," *Communication and Critical/Cultural Studies* 6/1 (2009): 86.
36. Stabile, "Sexism and Superheroes," 86–88.
37. Laura Sjoberg, "Women Fighters and the 'Beautiful Soul' Narrative," *International Review of the Red Cross* 92 (March 2010): 54.
38. Melissa Brittain, "Benevolent Invaders, Heroic Victims, and Depraved Villains: White Femininity in Media Coverage of the Invasion of Iraq," in *(En)Gendering the War on Terror*, ed. Krista Hut and Kim Rygrel (London: Ashgate, 2006), 73–96.
39. Sjoberg, "Women Fighters," 57–66.
40. *Marvel's Jessica Jones*, created by Melissa Rosenberg. Netflix, November 20, 2015.
41. Carolyn Cocca, "The 'Broke Back Test': A Quantitative and Qualitative Analysis of Portrayals of Women in Mainstream Superhero Comics, 1993–2013," *Journal of Graphic Novels and Comics* 5/4 (2014): 415.
42. *Marvel's Jessica Jones*, passim.
43. Lavin, "Women in Comic Books," 99.

44. Cocca, "The 'Broke Back Test,'" 421.

45. Ellen Kirkpatrick, and Suzanne Scott, "Representation and Diversity in Comics Studies," *Cinema Journal* 55 (Fall 2015): 122–123.

46. Lars Konzack, "The Origins of Geek Culture: Perspectives on a Parallel Intellectual Milieu," in *Wyrd Con Companion Book 2014*, ed. Sarah L. Bowman (Costa Mesa: WyrdCon, 2014), 52.

47. Raewyn Campbell, "'I Can't Believe I Fell for a Muppet Man': Female Nerds and the Order of Discourse," in *Smart Chicks on Screen: Representing Women's Intellect in Film and Television*, ed. Laura Mattoon D'Amore (Lanham, MD: Rowman & Littlefield, 2014), 180.

48. Lillian Céspedes González, "The Quartet of Empowerment: Embracing the Female Outcast," paper presented at the Centre for Gender Studies Spring Symposium, University of Winchester, March 5, 2016.

49. *Ibid.*

50. Lillian Céspedes González, "Jessica Jones Viewer Feedback Survey," distributed between June and July 2016, *Google Drive*, https://docs.google.com/forms/d/e/1FAIpQLScat-7SHQW76V9qkbUzvQs5AgxYavEInxD-pKfle_0rstQHjg/viewform.

51. There are also five extra replies that have the year of birth as 2016. Whether this was accidental or purposeful it is difficult to say. However, two of the participants did contact the surveyor individually, and advised that due to filling in the survey on their phones, the calendar option did not work well for them and defaulted to 2016. Nonetheless, they confirmed their years of birth to be within that age range.

52. Benjamin Woo, "Nerds, Geeks, Gamers, and Fans: Doing Subculture on the Edge of Mainstream," in *The Borders of Subculture: Resistance and the Mainstream*, pt. 2.

53. The rest of the replies include three Canadians and one Lithuanian, with the remaining five answers being controversial. Two subjects identified their nationality as white, whilst other two advised they were European, and the remaining one wrote the word Caucasian in this answer. Whether this highlights the lack of importance of nationality in a phenomenon which is being influenced by globalization, or the personal convictions of individuals affected by recent socio-political events, is something difficult to assess. Nevertheless, this may be a subject to consider and reflect upon future audience studies.

54. Although provided the option to include other, reflecting individuals who may consider themselves transsexuals, transgender or fluid, this was not an option taken by anyone, unlike previous audience studies undertaken by the surveyor.

55. Lillian Céspedes González, "Jessica Jones Viewer Feedback Survey Metadata," distributed between June and July 2016, *Google Drive*, https://docs.google.com/spreadsheets/d/13ZTN_iYvF_g3mNmeS07rlVkcLJW7x00vGks4jfI_nJE/edit?usp=sharing.

56. *Ibid.*

57. *Ibid.*

58. Cornejo Stewart, "El Caso de Netflix," 96.

59. Céspedes González, "Survey Metadata."

60. Notice how most of the fans represented by this subject use the fan known abbreviations such as DCAU (DC Animated Universe) or MCU (Marvel Cinematic Universe) as a general expression of their fandom, which perhaps to a non-familiar reader may seem confusing.

61. Céspedes González, "Survey Metadata."

62. Céspedes González, "Survey Metadata." One can only infer that the 11 remaining individuals who did not participate in this question are also an indicator of their lack of awareness of the comics.

63. Céspedes González, "Survey Metadata."

64. *Ibid.*

65. *Ibid.*

66. *Ibid.*

67. *Ibid.*

68. *Ibid.*

69. *Ibid.*

70. *Ibid.*

71. *Ibid.*
72. *Ibid.*
73. Jeffrey A. Brown, and Melissa Loucks, "A Comic of Her Own: Women Writing, Reading and Embodying through Comics," *ImageText: Interdisciplinary Comics Studies* 7 (2014): 4, accessed July 15, 2016, http://www.english.ufl.edu/imagetext/archives/v7_4/introduction.shtml.
74. Céspedes González, "Survey Metadata."
75. *Ibid.*
76. *Ibid.*
77. Cornejo Stewart, "El Caso de Netflix," 322.
78. These were subjects that were drawn from the previous research and academic debates elaborated in this essay. The surveyor wanted to identify whether the viewers did connect with the same discussion than the scholarly circles in order to establish a pattern.
79. Céspedes González, "Survey Metadata."
80. *Ibid.*
81. Not all participants were equally active in all answers, nor were these seven individuals. However, it is worth noting that one of them, an American citizen born in 1972 replied to a fair number of the questions with "Alas, I haven't watched the series." This has been taken into consideration when interpreting the data.
82. Céspedes González, "Survey Metadata."
83. This individual's reply is significant in opposition to that of the previous statement as she identified herself not only as an avid comic reader, but with prior knowledge of the Jessica Jones comic books, unlike the previous participant who although reads comic books, had not engaged with *Alias/The Pulse*. There were other replies that back up the position of the Canadian subject, although the surveyor is aware this could simply be a case of fan culture reflecting a citizenship to a multiverse.
84. Brown, and Loucks, "A Comic of Her Own," 2–3.
85. That is with the exception of two subjects, both males: the previously referred individual with the lack of knowledge on the series, and another male who did not seem aware of the show's popularity. He was also identified as a comic non-reader or geek culture participant, so this is likely to be due to his cultural context and citizenship.
86. Céspedes González, "Survey Metadata."
87. Kirkpatrick and Scott, "Representation and Diversity," 121.
88. Konzack, "The Origins of Geek Culture," 55.

BIBLIOGRAPHY

Bendis, Brian Michael, and Gaydos, Michael. *Alias* #1¬–#28. New York: MAX, 2001–2004.
Booker, M. Keith. *Encyclopedia of Comic Books and Graphic Novels: Volume A-L.* Santa Barbara: Greenwood, 2010.
Brittain, Melissa. "Benevolent Invaders, Heroic Victims, and Depraved Villains: White Femininity in Media Coverage of the Invasion of Iraq." In *(En)Gendering the War on Terror.* Edited by Krista Hut and Kim Rygrel, 73–96. London: Ashgate, 2006.
Brown, Jeffrey A., and Loucks, Melissa. "A Comic of Her Own: Women Writing, Reading and Embodying through Comics." *ImageText: Interdisciplinary Comics Studies* 7 (2014): 1–7. Accessed July 15, 2016. http://www.english.ufl.edu/imagetext/archives/v7_4/introduction.shtml.
Burke, Liam. "Sowing the Seeds: How 1990s Marvel Animation Facilitated Today's Cinematic Universe." In *Marvel Comics into Film: Essays on Adaptations Since the 1940s.* Edited by Matthew J. McEniry, Robert Moses Peaslee, and Robert G. Weiner, 106–117. Jefferson, North Carolina: McFarland, 2016.
Campbell, Raewyn. "'I Can't Believe I Fell for a Muppet Man': Female Nerds and the Order of Discourse." In *Smart Chicks on Screen: Representing Women's Intellect in Film and Television.* Edited by Laura Mattoon D'Amore, 179–192. Lanham, MD: Rowman & Littlefield, 2014.
Céspedes González, Lillian. "Jessica Jones Viewer Feedback Survey," distributed between

June and July 2016, *Google Drive*, https://docs.google.com/forms/d/e/1FAIpQLScat-7SHQW76V9qkbUzvQs5AgxYavEInxD-pKf1e_0rstQHjg/viewform.

Céspedes González, Lillian. "Jessica Jones Viewer Feedback Survey Metadata," distributed between June and July 2016, *Google Drive*, https://docs.google.com/spreadsheets/d/13ZTN_iYvF_g3mNmeS07rlVkcLJW7x00vGks4jfI_nJE/edit?usp=sharing.

Céspedes González, Lillian. "The Quartet of Empowerment: Embracing the Female Outcast." Paper Presented at the Centre for Gender Studies Spring Symposium, University of Winchester, March 5, 2016.

Cocca, Carolyn. "The 'Broke Back Test': a Quantitative and Qualitative Analysis of Portrayals of Women in Mainstream Superhero Comics, 1993–2013." *Journal of Graphic Novels and Comics* 5/4 (2014): 411–428.

Cornejo Stewart, Josefina. "El Caso de Netflix (2012–2015). Nuevas Formas de Pensar la Producción, Distribución y Consumo de Series Dramáticas." Tesis Doctoral, Universitat Ramon Lull, 2016.

Giannantoni, Daniele. "Netflix & Marvel Studios: Come Costuire una Realta Serial." Corso di Laurea Magistrale in Lingue e Culture per la Comunicazione Internazionale, Università degli Studi della Tuscia, 2014/2015.

IMDB. "Jessica Jones." Accessed July 15, 2016. http://www.imdb.com/title/tt2357547/.

Johnson, Derek. "Cinematic Destiny: Marvel Studios and the Trade Stories of Industrial Convergence." *Cinema Journal* 52 (2012): 1–24.

Kirkpatrick, Ellen, and Scott, Suzanne. "Representation and Diversity in Comics Studies." *Cinema Journal* 55 (Fall 2015): 120–124.

Konzack, Lars. "The Origins of Geek Culture: Perspectives on a Parallel Intellectual Milieu." In *Wyrd Con Companion Book 2014*, edited by Sarah L. Bowman, 52–59. Costa Mesa: WyrdCon, 2014.

Lavin, Michael R. "Women in Comic Books." *Serials Review* 24/2 (1998): 93–100.

Marvel's Jessica Jones, created by Melissa Rosenberg. Netflix, November 20, 2015.

Netflix. "About Netflix." Accessed July 15, 2016. https://media.netflix.com/en/about-netflix.

Noble, Adam J. "Meta-Comics and Libraries: Should Libraries Buy Them?" In *Graphic Novels and Comics in Libraries and Archives: Essays on Readers, Research, History and Cataloguing*, edited by Robert G. Weiner, 202–208. Jefferson, NC: McFarland, 2010.

Opam, Kwame. "Review: Jessica Jones is the Complex (Super) Heroine We've Been Waiting For." *The Verge*. Last modified November 19, 2015. http://www.theverge.com/2015/11/19/9760514/jessica-jones-review-marvel-netflix-krysten-ritter.

Pogue, David. "A Stream of Movies, Sort of Free." *The New York Times*, January 25, 2007. Accessed July 15, 2016. http://www.nytimes.com/2007/01/25/technology/25pogue.html?_r=0.

Rotten Tomatoes. "Marvel's Jessica Jones." Accessed July 15, 2016. https://www.rottentomatoes.com/tv/jessica-jones/s01/.

Silverman, Rachel E., and Emily D. Ryalls. "Everything is Different the Second Time Around: The Stigma of Temporality on Orange is the New Black." *Television & New Media* (May 5, 2016): 1–14. Accessed July 15, 2016. DOI: 10.1177/1527476416647496.

Laura Sjoberg, "Women Fighters and the 'Beautiful Soul' Narrative." *International Review of the Red Cross* 92 (March 2010): 53–68.

Stabile, Carol A. "'Sweetheart, This Ain't Gender Studies': Sexism and Superheroes." *Communication and Critical/Cultural Studies* 6/1 (2009): 86–92.

Tryon, Chuck. *Reinventing Cinema: Movies in the Age of Media Convergence*. New Brunswick, New Jersey: Rutgers University Press, 2009.

Uricchio, William. "Film, Cinema, Television ... Media?" *New Review of Film and Television Studies* 12/3 (2014): 266–279.

AKA Marvel Does Darkness

Jessica Jones, Rape Allegories and the Netflix Approach to Superheroes

CARRIELYNN D. REINHARD *and*
CHRISTOPHER J. OLSON

As of this writing, Jessica Jones is one of only two female lead characters featured in the Marvel Cinematic Universe (MCU). The other is Peggy Carter, protagonist of the now-cancelled television series *Agent Carter*, which portrays the MCU's beginnings rather than its current setting. As such, Carter's exploits speak less to the contemporary world, even as they address the lack of female action heroes headlining movies and television shows. In *Jessica Jones*, the eponymous lead character also draws attention to this issue; though, perhaps more importantly, her exploits address a problem that contemporary women face on a daily basis: rape culture. Indeed, the entire first season of the series seems built to specifically address this issue, because it uses comic book tropes to comment on real world concerns and thus functions as a social allegory.

Given that female characters rarely headline any of the various transmedia products that comprise the MCU, it becomes important to consider why Marvel chose to use *Jessica Jones* for such an allegorical purpose. This essay examines different aspects of *Jessica Jones* to better understand the show's position in and relationship to the rest of the MCU. These aspects include the source material that inspired the series, which offers insight into how the character was constructed in the original Marvel Universe. This essay also considers how *Jessica Jones* results from Netflix's agreement to produce series featuring Disney/Marvel characters, and how this agreement in turn led to the creation of a Marvel Netflix Universe (hereafter referred to as the MNU) that exists in relation to the MCU. Finally, this essay considers how the MNU's production practices provide showrunners with more leeway to construct *Jessica Jones* as a social allegory, and how this allegorical nature sets the series apart from the MCU's other transmedia products. These considerations can illuminate how the MNU operates in relationship to the larger MCU.

Jessica Jones in Comics

Jessica Jones, now known in the Marvel Comic Book Universe as Jessica Campbell Jones Cage, debuted in *Alias* #1 (originally published November 2001), the first series from Marvel's MAX imprint for adult readers. Created by Brian Michael Bendis and Michael Gaydos, *Alias* ran for a total of 28 issues between 2001 and 2004. The series ended in part because Bendis wanted Jessica Jones to encounter more well-known characters like Captain America[1] and Spider-Man, but the series' adult content and R-rated stories prevented such crossovers.[2] Thus, Bendis brought *Alias* to a close, and Jessica Jones migrated to Bendis' more mainstream title *The Pulse*.

In the comics, Jones received her powers from exposure to radioactive chemicals after her family's car collided with a military convoy while traveling to Disney World.[3] As in the Netflix series, Jessica's family was killed and she spent months in a coma. Jones later spent time as the superheroine Jewel until Killgrave[4] (also known as the Purple Man) used his pheromone powers to turn her into his unwilling slave.[5] For eight months, Jones endured physical, emotional, and mental abuse at the hands of the deranged supervillain, until a confrontation with the Avengers and the Defenders freed her mind from his control.[6] Nevertheless, following this traumatic experience, she opted to end her career as a costumed adventurer in favor of becoming a licensed private investigator. The series opens a few years after these events, with Jones running her own detective agency, Alias Investigations.

The MNU: Subset of the MCU

Debuting on Netflix on November 20, 2015, *Jessica Jones* adapts the Killgrave story from the comic book series and functions as another piece of the MCU, which itself represents Disney/Marvel's attempt to develop a grand transmedia narrative. According to Henry Jenkins, such storytelling "is the art of world making."[7] A transmedia approach to storytelling involves using different media to tell one overarching story; each media product provides information on a different aspect of the overall storyworld, but all aspects converge to provide a coherent story, requiring consumers to actively seek out the different parts of the story.[8]

The MCU fits this definition as a transmedia narrative. As Colin Harvey writes, "despite its title [the MCU] incorporates not only feature films but also short films, live-action televisions and comic books."[9] The MCU's transmedia storyworld was initially introduced in *Iron Man* (Jon Favreau, 2008), which featured a post-credits teaser that introduced both Nick Fury (Samuel L. Jackson) and the Avengers Initiative. This storyworld was then further established across five subsequent films: *The Incredible Hulk* (Louis Leterrier, 2008), *Iron Man 2* (Jon Favreau, 2010), *Thor* (Kenneth Branagh, 2011), *Captain America: The First Avenger* (Joe Johnston, 2011), and *Marvel's The Avengers* (Joss Whedon, 2012). As of the end of 2017, eleven more films have been released,[10] with at least seven more planned[11]; three traditional television series have been released,[12] with three more planned[13]; five Netflix series have been released,[14] with more planned.[15]

The various movies, television series, short films, and comic books relate to one another and serve to either form the central storyline of the MCU (as in the case of the movies) or expand upon and add to that storyline (as in the case of the television series and other media products). This approach provides fans with the core story through the movies, but also offers them an expanded experience if they opt to engage with the rest of the transmedia storyworld. Furthermore, the different media products also serve as marketing tools for one another, because they encourage consumers to engage with each aspect of the transmedia narrative beyond the core films. Indeed, the MCU succeeds both critically and commercially because it "relies on the structures Marvel has developed for crossmedia production."[16] Moreover, the MCU transmedia storyworld also represents a concerted and expansive effort to adapt several decades of material from the Marvel Universe. Such an endeavor necessitates the deployment of "numerous techniques of adaptation, while at the same time extending the storyworld intramedially across the various films in the franchise and transmedially outward to live action television and comics."[17] In other words, the MCU's transmedia narrative suggests the need for such a construction to fully adapt over six decades' worth of source content.

The MNU functions as part of the MCU, though one designed to take advantage of the unique production capabilities offered by Netflix. In 2013, Disney/Marvel announced that they would release a *Daredevil* series on Netflix on April 10, 2015, and announced other series shortly thereafter, including *Jessica Jones*, *Luke Cage*, and *Iron Fist*.[18] These four series would lead to an eventual miniseries based on *The Defenders* comic books that first appeared in December 1971. Following the character's success in the second season of *Daredevil*, Netflix began planning a *Punisher* series that would soon join the other shows in the MNU.[19]

While connected to the transmedia narrative established by Disney/ Marvel in the MCU, the MNU exists in a pointedly different corner of that increasingly larger storyworld. Significantly, the character of Agent Coulson (Clark Gregg) has yet to appear in any of the Netflix series. This transnarrative character has appeared in several of the MCU films (including *Iron Man*, *Thor*, and *The Avengers*), and is featured prominently in the ABC television series *Agents of S.H.I.E.L.D.* As such, Coulson connects the various parts of the MCU,[20] and his absence thereby suggests that the MNU remains somewhat separate from the rest of the transmedia storyworld.

Furthermore, Netflix structures storytelling somewhat differently than the older media used to produce the MCU proper. As a process of adaptation, transmedia storytelling requires producers to consider the different characteristics of the various media used to produce each part of the overall story.[21] Put simply, Netflix and cinema both have their own particular advantages and disadvantages that force producers to tell stories in different ways. Yet, the producers of the MNU would not have had access to this sort of production model had Netflix not made the transition from content distributor to content provider.

Established in 1997, the company began as a DVD-by-mail rental system in 1998.[22] Netflix's early business model focused mainly on the distribution of already produced content through deals with content providers, from independents to Hollywood studios; this model accompanied the company's expansion into streaming video in 2007.[23] Over the years, more streaming companies emerged, including some owned by the same content providers who supplied Netflix with their online offerings. By 2010, Netflix started to rethink their business model when they noticed their suppliers were increasingly withholding content, dealing with rival platforms, or simply developing their own streaming services.[24] In reaction to changing circumstances, Netflix began the restructuring process to become a content provider. Producing original programming became the company's new business model, which in turn allowed Netflix "to control costs and create exclusives that none of its competitors will ever be able to carry, drawing subscribers onto its rolls, and off of theirs."[25] Netflix started offering such original programming in 2012 with *Lilyhammer*, but the service truly established itself as an alternative to traditional television production models with *House of Cards* in 2013.

Now known as Netflix Originals, such programming represents an alternative to traditional television networks. Netflix can offer its content to targeted audiences, allowing producers to tailor their series and movies to highly specific audiences. Such production techniques align Netflix with cable networks that produce content for niche audiences, (i.e., The Disney Channel for children or ESPN for sports fans). However, these models differ in that Netflix has the ability to house all of these niche networks under one banner, allowing them to reach a much wider consumer-base than any single cable network. In a sense, then, Netflix operates as its own media conglomerate, able to house numerous content providers under one roof.

Furthermore, this model allows the producers to express themselves in ways unavailable elsewhere. Netflix has fewer top-down restrictions on writers and producers, and they forego the sort of network executive notes that could potentially interfere with creative decisions.[26] Additionally, because Netflix does not broadcast over the air or via cables, its content is not beholden to Federal Communications Commission regulations that might impact the streaming content.[27] Thus, much like pay cable channels such as HBO or Showtime, Netflix is not affected by the same sort of restrictions regarding explicit violence and sexuality that govern traditional broadcast networks. Most significantly, Netflix posts all available episodes of a series at the same time, allowing viewers to "binge" an entire season in a short period of time, rather than having to wait a week between each episode.[28] This on-demand, all-at-once distribution model represents the most significant departure from traditional television, and these characteristics feature highly in the construction of *Jessica Jones* and its relationship to the MCU.

The characteristics described above become the focus of the analysis in this essay, which argues that the structure of Netflix sets the MNU apart from the larger MCU, particularly in how the MNU tells its stories. The darker, more adult tone of the MNU series represents a departure from the rest of the MCU, which is primarily aimed at a broader, more mainstream audience. Additionally, this characteristic allows the MNU to more closely mirror the modern approach to writing comics. Modern Marvel comics are written with an eye toward collected editions, which allow for the consumption of multiple issues at once, much like the Netflix shows written for block programming binge-watching. In comparison, the movies that make up the MCU more closely resemble one-shot stories or original graphic novels. Thus, the MNU series tell more complex and adult-focused superhero stories, and the first season of *Jessica Jones* serves as a prime example of this tendency.

Allegory and Jessica Jones

Jessica Jones marks the first time the character has been seen outside of the comics. One of Marvel's lesser-known superheroines, Jones has not received as much mainstream attention as characters like Black Widow, Phoenix, the Invisible Woman, or Captain Marvel. Jones is also unique because she is the first Marvel superheroine to headline a piece of the MCU,[29] and her story becomes all the more important when considering what it does or doesn't say, and how it says these things.

Of the five series produced for Netflix, only *Jessica Jones* features a superheroine as the lead or even primary character. Showrunner Melissa Rosenberg originally pitched the series to ABC in December 2010.[30] In May 2012, however, the network's president passed on the series, even though Rosenberg claimed she toned down the series' adult tone to better align with the network's other offerings.[31] The Netflix series allowed Rosenberg to maintain this adult tone and showcase the darker storytelling possibilities that accompany it.

Jessica Jones follows the title character's attempts to save a young girl and to stop the manipulation and crimes of Kevin Thompson, who calls himself Kilgrave (David Tennant). In the first episode, Jessica Jones (Krysten Ritter) accepts the case of finding missing college student Hope, only to learn that Kilgrave is using her to reach Jones, the only woman he has ever loved. In the series, Jones and her best friend, Trish Walker (Rachael Taylor),[32] work together to capture Kilgrave. Along the way, Jones also develops a romance with Luke Cage (Mike Colter),[33] which becomes complicated when he discovers Jones killed his girlfriend, Reva Connors (Parisa Fitz-Henley), while under Kilgrave's mind control. This traumatic event allowed Jones to break free from that control, and since then, Kilgrave has been trying to get her back. As the series reveals, he will to do anything to gain control over her once more.

The first season of *Jessica Jones* functions as an allegory for rape. Jones' struggle to overcome Kilgrave utilizes a personal and sociocultural rape allegory to tell Jones' origin story. On a personal level, the show portrays a woman's struggle to overcome a traumatic past experience, in this case being a victim of mind control forced to do things against her will. Though told in fantastical strokes, this allegory reflects the experiences that many women around the world have faced after being raped and made to feel as though they have no agency in their own lives. It also tells the story, in similar fantastical strokes, of how women can cope with the trauma in ways that are self-destructive and in ways that actually help them manage the guilt and anxiety associated with such trauma. Underneath the story of mind control, outrageous medical experiments, and superhuman strength lies the very real process of a woman with psychological damage experiencing the ups and downs of healing.

At the same time, *Jessica Jones* functions as an allegory for rape culture. The concept of rape culture suggests that certain behaviors become normalized in a society or culture and serve to permit or excuse rape. For example, victim-blaming, or saying that women's choices to drink excessively or wear certain clothing, serves to absolve rapists of guilt, and women can subsequently internalize the idea that their own behaviors caused the assault to occur.[34] Kilgrave's victims engage in such self-blame repeatedly throughout *Jessica Jones*, while Jones makes them focus their anger on Kilgrave instead. Additionally, Kilgrave acts with impunity, as if he believes he has the right to inflict his will on others without question. He believes that he loves Jones, and that the type of "affection" he can show will make her love him in return. As such, Kilgrave embodies the idea of the male rapist who believes that women should simply serve the whims of men. Moreover, he represents the type of man who believes that domestic abuse can cement a woman's affection. Thus, he stands in for a type of toxic masculinity and misogyny that perpetuates rape culture.[35]

The Netflix series has apparent connections to the comics from the beginning, with Kilgrave's hallucinatory appearances draped in the purple that identifies him as the comic book supervillain The Purple Man. The series references Luke Cage's unbreakable skin and super-strength. For fans who may only know the MCU, the series links to the overall transmedia storyworld in the first episode, when Jones delivers a summons by lifting a car's rear off the ground. Frightened, the driver exclaims that she is "not normal" and threatens to tell the world about her powers. Thus the first episode makes it clear that the world of *Jessica Jones* knows about superpowered humans, indicating that this story occurs sometime after *The Avengers* when the Battle of New York made such enhanced individuals common knowledge.

Yet, *Jessica Jones* never fully trades on the fantastic to the extent that the MCU does. The series uses standard origin story tropes to introduce a character just learning how to deal with her newfound powers, but the show does not focus on the discovery and use of these powers. Instead, the series focuses on Jones learning how to control Kilgrave's powers rather than on how she obtained her own superpowers, which are limited in this adaptation. The show primarily concerns Jones' efforts to stop Kilgrave even as she struggles to overcome the trauma she experienced while under his control. Thus *Jessica Jones* only ostensibly operates as an origin story; the series depicts a woman becoming a hero, but rather than learning to control her powers, she must learn to control her fear.

Ritter has described the series as "a psychological thriller first and a superhero show second."[36] Her description indicates that the series' overall tone downplays the fantastic in favor of a more grounded portrayal that emphasizes the psychological issues of people dealing with trauma. Ritter expanded on this description by saying, "She's rough around the edges so getting to spend time with her and see her be vulnerable and process the weight of her world is what makes the character so likeable."[37] These descriptions highlight just how much the series focuses on the Jones' complex characterization and her relationships with the other characters.

Jones does not lead an easy life, nor can she effortlessly overcome her inner demons or the wicked man bent on controlling her. Instead, her relationships come and go, almost on a daily basis, and her own moral character strengthens and weakens over the series. Indeed, as one critic noted, "*Jessica Jones* highlights the role of human will in relationships and in moral judgment."[38]

Her powers do not allow her to easily save the day, because her strength and ability to jump (she does not yet fly in Season One as she does in the comics) are useless against a criminal who possesses the ability to control her mind and her actions. No amount of fisticuffs will stop Kilgrave when he can simply freeze her fists with a whispered word. Jones' conflict with Kilgrave requires her to develop and use her other skills as a private investigator, primarily her intelligence, though, even that could prove inadequate if her fear overwhelms her cunning.

The series' opening moments establish Jones' character by linking her with film noir tropes.[39] Jessica Jones opens with a voiceover that serves as the introduction to the character; a saxophone plays low on the soundtrack, and the viewer hears Jones talking about her job finding cheating spouses before she ever appears onscreen. These film noir tropes clearly align her with a particular characterization that becomes complicated due to Jones' gender, which does not fit with this traditionally masculine style. This gender conflict sets up Jones' complexity, preparing viewers to expect something different from this character. The series masculinizes Jones through her brusque behavior, alcohol abuse, and cynicism. By distancing herself from other people, Jones seeks to establish herself as a capable, stoic individual whose intelligence can solve any problem. Initially, she appears to be another in a long line of masculinized female characters.[40]

Yet, masculinization is not Jones' defining characteristic. Instead, her characterization comes more from her sense of alienation due to her powers, which set her apart from "normal" humans. Her neighbor Malcolm observes that she uses sarcasm to keep people at a distance. For instance, Jones pushes Walker away to protect her, but Walker's strength lies in refusing to leave Jones alone. This alienation explains why she forms a close bond with Cage, because they share such uniqueness. Jones' drinking borders on alcoholism, but she drinks mainly to suppress her traumatic memories. Indeed, when Walker admits that she hates feeling paranoid about Kilgrave and wonders how Jones handles it, Jones retorts, "It's called whiskey." In many ways, Jones' masculine tendencies seem like affectations that she performs to cope with the trauma she experienced during her time as Kilgrave's victim.

Thus, rather than another masculinized superheroine, Jones becomes a woman dealing with deeper problems of guilt and post-traumatic stress disorder (PTSD) that stem from losing her entire family when she was a child and, most importantly for the series, her violation by Kilgrave.[41] According to one critic, "what works about Jessica Jones is its understanding of how, particularly, Kilgrave's crimes fit into Jones's identity as a woman."[42] Indeed, Jessica Jones conforms more to a typical female revenge story or avenging-woman narrative[43] than the adolescent male power fantasies normally presented in superhero comic books or the films that comprise the MCU proper.

The series deals explicitly with issues of rape, survivor guilt, and PTSD, and the series fully explores these issues throughout the first season. The true nature of Jones' trauma emerges in first episode, as she sits on a fire escape and spies on Cage. She experiences a vision of Kilgrave visiting her and immediately suffers a panic attack; she calms herself by reciting the street names from her childhood and taking a swig of whiskey from a thermos. Later in the same episode, Jones suffers another panic attack; after she presumably passes out drunk, Kilgrave appears next to her and licks the side of her face. Jones wakes with a start, and again recites the street names to calm herself. Later she locates the restaurant where Kilgrave took Hope and recognizes it, triggering a flashback that reveals Kilgrave once took Jones to that same restaurant. This memory provokes yet another panic attack, which causes Jones to run away. Afterward, Walker suggests that Jones' actions result from her PTSD and suggests that Jones should return to therapy. Thus, the show establishes early on that Jones experienced some traumatic event in her past, and the following episodes unveil what happened to her.

Jessica Jones explores these issues and their related concerns as Jones learns how to deal with this trauma and thus succeed in her heroic quest. Rather than learning how to control or use her powers, Jones must learn how to control her life and her mind, and thereby become more powerful than Kilgrave. As such, the story focuses on Jones learning to accept what happened to her and to use this knowledge to prevent others from suffering a similar fate. The first episode explicitly addresses an important aspect of handling such trauma: the need to gain control. Indeed, victims can learn to deal with their lingering fears when they confront what happened. In the first episode, Jones wants nothing more than to run away instead of confronting Kilgrave again. However, after seeing what he did to Hope, Jones decides to stop Kilgrave rather than spend her life running. She decides to take control and confront the traumatic events of her past, which research indicates allows sexual assault victims to deal with their PTSD.[44]

In the second episode, Jones realizes that she cannot stop Kilgrave on her own; she can only succeed if she accepts help from others. Therefore, she finally stops pushing Walker away and starts seeking help from others by disclosing what happened to her. Delayed disclosure of the ordeal can exacerbate PTSD,[45] and by opening up to others Jones takes another step in healing because she asserts control over her recovery process.[46] By the third episode, Jones can look Kilgrave in the eyes, and she gains knowledge about his weaknesses, which in turn helps her overcome her own. At this point, she becomes more willing to face the past and recall what happened to her and what she did (including killing Cage's wife, Reva). Yet, she still cannot confront Kilgrave on her own, and thus she spends more time manipulating and alienating others. For instance, in the fourth episode, Jones lashes out at the members of a support group for Kilgrave's victims. She scolds them for not dealing better with their pain, but her anger indicates that she has not yet dealt with her own pain. Nevertheless, by the fifth episode, Jones' panic attacks grow weaker and it takes less time to calm herself, and by the end of the episode she can face Kilgrave.

By the sixth episode, however, Jones' newfound relationship with Cage seemingly ends when she finally confesses that she killed Reva. Cage calls Jones "a piece of shit," and she breaks down and has to recite the street names to calm herself. This incident represents the first breakdown not caused by Kilgrave, and reveals that Jones' relationship with Cage likely improved her sense of self-worth and allowed her to deal with her traumatic past. Cage's reaction to her confession causes her guilt issues to resurface and leaves her feeling worthless. Research on PTSD indicates that such self-blame can derail a rape survivor's healing process.[47] In the next episode, her damaged self-esteem leads her to withdraw from her friends and try to atone for her actions by turning herself in to the police for the murder of her neighbor, Ruben.

The storyline's progression across the first season suggests a recognition that those on the path to recovery often experiences lapses. Jones' mental health improves throughout the series, but in ways that demonstrate that healing does not occur in a straight line, but rather a jagged line that sometimes curves back on itself, as setbacks may occur alongside of or in place of progress. Much of this jaggedness emerges in how *Jessica Jones* comments on the choices people make throughout their lives. For instance, during the first half of the season, Jones believes Kilgrave commanded her to kill Reva. Yet, he explains that he never told Jones to kill Reva, just to "take care" of her. This revelation suggests that Jones harbored a dark side long before she ever met Kilgrave, and it caused her to interpret "take care of her" as "kill her." This revelation also suggests that even though Kilgrave controlled her mind, and therefore her ability to choose to leave him, Jones still retained some choice in how she performed his commands. Perhaps deep down she realizes that she interpreted and performed Kilgrave's command this way, and now blames herself for Reva's death, even if she could rationalize her actions as resulting from Kilgrave's control. In the healing process, self-reflection and acceptance allow individuals to understand how their choices led to their current predicament. Until Jones realized the darkness in herself and the guilt she has carried around since her family's death, she could not fully move forward.

This progress also requires confronting what happened in the past, and acknowledging the experience for what it was. This confrontation occurs in the eighth episode when Kilgrave lures Jones to her childhood home and tries to convince her that he did not rape her. Kilgrave paints a tragic back-story for himself when he explains that he gained his powers after his parents conducted horrific experiments on him. Thus, the show presents an obstacle to Jones' recovery and complicates the topic of rape by depicting the rapist's complexity and providing him with a backstory meant to explain his actions. By the end of the episode, however, Jones chooses not to trust Kilgrave. From then on, her choices arise less from guilt or fear as they had from the beginning, and more from a need to enact justice in the name of all of the people Kilgrave wronged by robbing them of their ability to choose.

In this way, Jones' character arc involves learning how to deal with choices. In the beginning, her fear of Kilgrave and her guilt and anger over what she did under his control drive her choices. Later, she realizes how her inner darkness—a combination of survivor's guilt and loneliness—drives the choices that impact her relationships. While she never directly addresses this darkness, she does embrace it as a form of inner strength and identity that helps her take down Kilgrave. On her path to becoming a hero, however, she must learn to make the choices a hero would make, including relying on and forming relationships with others. Yet, this becomes complicated given the nature of Kilgrave's powers, because Jones does not know who to trust. For example, in the twelfth episode, Kilgrave controls Cage's mind and uses him to emotionally manipulate Jones. When Jones learns the truth, Kilgrave chides her by saying that she "chose wrong; you always have." Yet, she made the heroic choice, because she chose to believe that love can save the day. Choosing otherwise would align her with Kilgrave and set her on the path of the villain. Later, in the final episode of the season, Jones and Walker establish a code word that will prove Jones has not fallen under Kilgrave's control. Jones suggests "I love you," a phrase she would not normally say, and this indicates how important this relationship has become to her. Moreover, this incident suggests that Jones can now make the right choices, such as allowing the people in her life to help her.

Ultimately, Jones' struggles to deal with her choices lead her to become a superhero. In the final episode, she meets the nurse Claire Temple (Rosario Dawson) at the hospital, who worries that Jones might act stupidly out of guilt. Jones asserts that she does not feel guilty about assaulting Cage at the end of the previous episode. Temple responds with "I want everything to be my fault, good or bad. It means I have some control." Jones says that Temple does not have such control, and while Temple seems to realize this, she nevertheless responds to Jones' cynicism by saying, "But it keeps me dreaming I can change things for people." This declaration indicates that Temple represents optimism, in opposition to Jones' cynicism. Like Agent Coulson in the initial MCU films, Temple operates as a lynchpin character in the MNU, and her words function as a lesson Jones must internalize; if Jones wishes to become a hero capable of stopping Kilgrave in a just and ethical fashion, she needs to realize that she cannot control everything and that she must choose to keep trying to help others.

Yet, because of the darkness still lingering inside of her, she kills her arch-nemesis rather than bring him to justice. In the end, Jones' superhero origin story ends much like other female revenge narratives, in which the rape survivor hunts down her attacker(s) and enacts her own brand of justice. In this series, however, this revenge narrative does not simply fulfill Jones' desire for closure, but also serves to protect others. In effect, her revenge narrative allows her to save the city, and perhaps even the world, making her a true superhero.

By grappling with rape and rape culture in the guise of a superhero series, *Jessica Jones* brings these issues to the attention of a wider audience and shines a light on the damage both cause to everyone in a community. The personal allegory helps viewers understand the experiences of those who have had to deal with such trauma in their lives. The sociocultural allegory helps viewers see which elements in the world around them need to be changed to prevent these experiences from continuing to happen. More so, the series does all this without challenging Jones' account of what Kilgrave did to her; unlike many rape victims who come under the scrutiny of the court of public opinion, not to mention legal justice systems,[48] no one doubts what Kilgrave did to her, and thus no one challenges her account of the rape. This lack of a challenge validates Jones' experience and, by extension, the trauma suffered by other rape survivors. The series has an important place in the MCU because of this allegorical nature, and because of what the allegories are about. Yet, *Jessica Jones* would not have been possible were it not for the unique characteristics offered by the MNU in comparison to the MCU.

The MNU versus the MCU

The MNU follows a direct-to-streaming model that facilitates a storytelling structure more akin to a miniseries, and allows the creators to establish a darker, more adult tone than that found in the majority of MCU characters and narratives, which are generally more fun, colorful, and family-oriented. *Jessica Jones* was not the first series to do this, as the characteristics of the MNU emerged with *Daredevil*, which has been described as more street level than the MCU.[49] Others have described it as "more of a crime drama or legal procedural than it is a superhero story."[50] Such descriptions suggest that the series was designed to better replicate the types of genres found on television, and by extension Netflix. Yet, neither the series nor the MNU itself completely divorce themselves from the conventions established in the MCU. *Daredevil*'s executive producer Steven DeKnight envisioned the series as a "hybrid of a TV procedural and Marvel's cinematic levity—and with a lot more broken bones and spilled blood than ABC's *Agents of S.H.I.E.L.D.*"[51] Thus, while the series has a darker, more violent tone, it was nevertheless still intended as part of the same transmedia storyworld.

The tone and theme of *Jessica Jones* matches that of *Daredevil*. While more of a detective series with intense violence and heavy themes, *Jessica Jones* still clearly exists within this larger MCU, and the show highlights the Marvel approach to storytelling; that is, the studio developed a shared universe that reflects a house style driven primarily by the producers (similar to the studio system of the 1930s and 1940s), but the characterizations and narrative structures display a diversity that more closely reflects the comic book source material. The difference lies in how the Netflix model allows showrunners to push the boundaries of the Marvel house style and thus offer a more nuanced depiction of the central character. As such, *Jessica Jones* has room to use superpowers and supervillains as allegories for complex issues like rape and sexual assault.

As an adaptation, the TV series focuses on the later issues of the comic book series *Alias*, primarily those that detail Jones' experience with Killgrave. In issues #24–28,[52] Jones must confront her past and help the other survivors of Killgrave's actions. The comic book presents a shorter account of this experience than the one portrayed in the TV series, and differs in other key aspects as well, such as in how Jones ultimately ends Killgrave's threat to New York City. The biggest difference, however, occurs in issue #25, when Jones tells Cage about the eight months she spent under Killgrave's control. She explains that Killgrave never raped her; he just made her watch him rape other women and made her continually beg him to rape her. Even in the R-rated comic book series, which Jeph Loeb said showed the "underbelly of the Marvel Universe,"[53] the series could not go all the way and depict a woman dealing with the trauma of being a rape survivor. As a comic book series, even one meant for mature audiences,[54] *Alias* still carried the baggage of the medium's history as children's entertainment, primarily because it involved relationships with and cameos of well-known superheroes such as Ant Man and Captain America. Netflix freed *Jessica Jones* of such baggage and provided the time and space necessary to depict this complex, allegorical story.

Beyond simply setting up tensions for the hero to overcome, *Jessica Jones* uses allegory to provide viewers with insight into the title character and her origin. The rape allegory becomes central to understanding Jones and her struggle to become a hero in this world. While viewers likely came to the series because of its relationship to the MCU, they would find a story unlike anything else in that transmedia storyworld. According to Ritter, "[creator Melissa Rosenberg] approaches it with an incredibly flawed, complicated character.... I think having the Marvel mythology will appeal to a larger audience ... but the focus was always on Jessica Jones and what's true to her and her world."[55] *Jessica Jones* tells a personal story in a way that the movies have thus far not.

The MCU tends to use allegory more for the purposes of building the universe in which these interconnected stories occur. For example, the allegorical nature of *Captain America: Winter Soldier* and *Captain America: Civil War* focused on the relationship between citizens, superheroes, and governments, and this in turn established the parameters and conflicts of the overall cinematic universe. The MNU uses allegory more for character-building, and indeed the series have more allowance to do so because they exist peripherally to the MCU even as they reference it. The focus on characters first appeared in *Daredevil*, which established this mode of storytelling by exploring why a hero without superpowers is so driven to protect Hell's Kitchen despite the physical toll.[56] While the MCU's draw could lie with the characters or the spectacle, the appeal in the MNU lies primarily with the characters, rendering their appeal similar to the soap opera genre, which is itself similar to comic books.

Much like television soap operas, comic books feature a serialized storytelling format, often featuring big events, that nevertheless focuses on the actions and lives of the characters. Viewers and readers of both come to know their favorite characters rather intimately, and thus the appeal lies not with the spectacle of the events but rather in how these events impact the characters. While the MCU's use of allegory tends to function more as social commentary, even that takes a back seat to big budget, crowd-pleasing spectacle. Conversely, the MNU's focus on character-building allows for the sort of personal allegory seen in *Jessica Jones*, and this in turn allows the MNU more latitude to tell stories that concern women's issues.[57]

This difference becomes clear when comparing Jones' story of sexual assault with a similar story told in the MCU proper. In *The Avengers: Age of Ultron*, Black Widow—the MCU's only other major superheroine at the time—recounts being sterilized without her consent, and now she considers herself as a monster. While Black Widow appears to have found her own coping mechanism for dealing with personal trauma, the film does not have the time to sufficiently explore her trauma, despite its 141-minute runtime. As one critic observed, "[t]he problem with the Black Widow plotline … is that the big-screen Marvel movies are so laughably overstuffed, so intent on overwhelming the audience, that they can't possibly do justice to anything so serious."[58] Conversely, *Jessica Jones* has the time to focus solely on the title character's trauma and her struggle to cope, and the series does not have to offer big-budget spectacle designed to appeal to a broad audience. Without these constraints, the series can more fully explore this complex feminine issue through the presentation of a nuanced and ultimately rather "real" superhero.

As such, the series functions as a counterpoint to the larger MCU, which has thus far focused mainly on telling male-based stories of redemption and revenge. *Jessica Jones* also portrays a story of redemption and revenge, but the scale and scope of the main character's story is more personal and less concerned with saving the world. Whereas *Daredevil* focuses more on a hero saving the city in his origin story, *Jessica Jones* focuses mainly on the lead character's attempts to become a better person by learning how to deal with a past trauma and its continuing repercussions in her life. While this personal struggle mirrors the portrayals of her male counterparts in the MCU, the connections drawn between rape culture and Jones' struggle allow the series to have more sociocultural relevance than the other stories and characters presented thus far in the MCU.

Furthermore, this focus on the personal fallibility and struggles of the title character reflects the long-standing Marvel Comics approach to storytelling—an approach that set the company apart from its major competition, DC Comics, in the 1960s. *Daredevil* star Charlie Cox commented on how the show's dark nature was more aligned with the source material.[59] Similarly, *Jessica Jones* retains its comic roots because its origin story focuses less on Jones learning how to be a superhero and more on her struggling to make a living as a detective while dealing with her PTSD. Given the MNU's focus on the personal lives of its characters, Jessica Jones was far better suited for life in the MNU than the MCU. Thus, *Jessica Jones* reflects the MNU's ability to better adapt the storytelling found in comic books.

More than that, the series replicates the serialized storytelling format of comic books, and thereby demonstrates that Netflix is the medium best suited to adapt this characteristic. Whereas other detective series or crime procedurals routinely feature a new crime to investigate and a new criminal to prosecute in each episode, *Jessica Jones* focuses primarily on the central story.[60] Throughout the series, all thirteen episodes focus on stopping Kilgrave, the lynchpin behind everything that happens. This storytelling format represents a new trend in television storytelling: the "totally serialized drama."[61] This format goes beyond the type of serialized television seen within the past decades on broadcast television, in which a single episode might feature its own central storyline, but a background storyline or "running plot" would connect it to other episodes.[62]

Because Netflix releases all episodes at once, removing the need to wait for weekly installments, binge-watching becomes not only possible but promoted as the best consumption practice to engage with their extensive streaming library. The viewers' ability and desire to binge-watch "means creators are increasingly viewing a season as a unit, free from the need to make every episode have its own story or theme."[63] This practice means that producers can tell a complex serialized drama over multiple episodes, because viewers can watch all of the episodes as closely together as they like. The ability to watch episodes thusly means that there may be no reduction in lost knowledge about what happened on previous episodes, so the stories can become more detailed and thus more complex. As Ritter notes, "The thing about Netflix is that you get more minutes in your episode because there are no commercial breaks. You have time to let things breathe and be quiet. You get to see an entire scene play out instead of just jumping halfway in."[64] In a sense, a television season now can be seen as one long movie, a sort of long-form storytelling in which creators can spend more time exploring complex personalities and themes.[65]

This long-form approach to storytelling harkens back to miniseries and soap operas, but also to the serial formatting of comic books; beyond the miniseries or mega-series special events stories, superhero comics have been dominated for decades by serialized, universe-building, canonical stories that avoid any sense of the passing of real time. In this type of long-form storytelling, "the Marvel universe orders events in a timeline, and the characters accumulate an experience that they did not have at the beginning; in other words, a consistency of narrative occurs across several separate issues."[66] This storytelling approach can provide readers with a unified and coherent universe in which characters appear to have a memory similar to real people.[67] This cohesion has allowed Marvel comics to tell more complex stories with interweaving subplots and vast casts of characters. The MNU replicates this approach to storytelling, because it allows, through binge-watching, a form of sequential storytelling not offered by the MCU proper; the movies' fragmented nature allows for the possibility that audiences could potentially engage with the transmedia storyworld at different entry points and in the wrong temporal order.[68] The MNU's format brings structure to the storytelling and allows producers to tell complex stories because viewers will likely engage with them as planned.

Furthermore, such long-form storytelling illustrates the MNU's ability to adapt the complex stories of the comics without having to leave out as much source material as the MCU's cinematic adaptations. Given the format of the MNU, the different series have the latitude to include more elements from the original source material because they do not face the same temporal limitations as a two-hour film.[69] The films are by their nature required to be more "loose adaptations" where "key elements are liable to be retained, whether these are characters, archetypes or themes."[70] While the MCU "is highly selective in choosing which elements of the originating storyworld of the Marvel Comics to vertically remember and which to ignore, these elements are then horizontally remembered by other parts of the MCU."[71] The MCU's transmedia storytelling allows for the expansion of the space and the telling of a more complex story across multiple movies, while the MNU's long-form storytelling tells a complex story across multiple episodes in one season—a temporal expansion that allows more source material to be remembered and explored in more depth. Indeed, *Jessica Jones* is all about remembering—remembering the past, remembering the trauma, remembering one's personal strength—and then moving forward based on those memories.

Yet, it cannot be forgotten that, although unique, the MNU is another part of Disney/Marvel's transmedia storyworld. The MCU and the MNU exist as part of a directed transmedia storytelling strategy in which Disney/Marvel retains the rights to and strictly controls all aspects of the storyworld.[72] Nevertheless, the MNU represents the larger strategy that aims to utilize different mediums to tell different stories from Marvel's comic book universe in an effort to ultimately reach the largest possible audience, and thereby develop the biggest consumer-base. While the films must be more selective in what parts from the comic book universe they can show, the overall transmedia storyworld can show more of these parts, adapting both the light and the dark parts of the comics and tailoring them to specific audiences. Thus, at this time, the MNU serves as the darker, more mature section of the MCU, bringing in an audience who appreciate these series and their focus on personal stories and sociocultural issues. That could change, however, if Disney/Marvel decides to target a different audience through Netflix. After all, a transmedia strategy hinges on adaptability, as the differences between the MNU and MCU demonstrate.

Conclusion

In transmedia approaches to storytelling, different media require creators to use a variety of adaptation strategies when translating a text from one medium to another. While the MCU may focus more on superhero genre tropes, the MNU can more accurately replicate the conventions of comic book storytelling, which hinges on seriality. The MNU functions as part of the transmedia storyworld developed by the MCU, but the production and distribution practices employed by Netflix allow for innovative approaches to storytelling. The MCU focuses on building awareness of the universe and franchise with a broader audience while the MNU provides darker, more complex characters and themes that ultimately create realistic depictions of both. Given the longer, more serialized nature of the MNU, shows like *Daredevil* and *Jessica Jones* can tell more expansive stories that spend more time with characters in a condensed setting, which in turn allow for more detailed examinations of complex stories, themes, and allegories.

At the same time, the MNU shows blur the lines between adaptation and transmedia storytelling because even though *Jessica Jones* and the rest of the MNU function as part of Disney/Marvel's transmedia storytelling, they also represent a clearer adaptation of comic book style storytelling than that seen in other parts of the MCU. Transmedia storytelling focuses more on "intercompositional approaches at the expense of intracompositional approaches,"[73] and this manifests in how the MCU's movies and television shows feed into one another. Thus far the MNU shows have remained separate from the MCU; they have referenced the MCU, but nonetheless stand apart from it. They have, however, fed into one another, forming a team series in the MNU (*The Defenders*) akin to the team series in the MCU (*The Avengers*). While replicating the same type of story convergence seen in Phase One of the MCU,[74] the MNU tells stories in an entirely different way and therefore it resides in its own unique corner of the Disney/Marvel storyworld.

Currently, it is unclear if Disney/Marvel will attempt to integrate the MNU and the MCU. It could be that by the time the MCU finishes Phase Three, with the massive adaptation of the *Infinity Gauntlet* story, the superheroes of the MNU may need to join in the galactic fight against the villainous Thanos, though this currently does not seem to be the plan. In any case, the MNU will most likely continue to produce complex and mature series similar to *Jessica Jones*. In the fantastical transmedia storyworld of the MCU, the MNU operates as its closest link to the grim realities of the contemporary world. As such, it provides the MCU with the opportunity to remain grounded, and to remember that Marvel Comics originally succeeded because creators focused on character rather than spectacle.

NOTES

1. Although Jones' first case involves politicians attempting to frame Captain America, and leads to her earning Cap's respect. For more, see Brian Michael Bendis (w) and Michael Gaydos (a), *Alias* #1–5, in *Jessica Jones: Alias Vol. 1*, ed. Jennifer Grünwald (New York: Marvel Entertainment, 2015), 1–118.

2. John R. Parker, "'Alias' Jessica Jones: A Critical Look Back at Marvel's Mature Readers Hero and New Netflix Star," *Comics Alliance*, last modified November 5, 2014, http://comicsalliance.com/alias-omnibus-review, accessed July 22, 2016.

3. Brian Michael Bendis (w) and Michael Gaydos (a), "The Secret Origin of Jessica Jones (Part 1 of 2)," in *Jessica Jones: Alias Vol. 4*, ed. Jennifer Grünwald (New York: Marvel Entertainment, 2015), 11–21.

4. In the comic books, the character's name appears as Killgrave, while the TV series modifies it to Kilgrave.

5. Brian Michael Bendis (w), Michael Gaydos (a), and Mark Bagley (a), "Purple (Part 2 of 5)," in *Jessica Jones: Alias Vol. 4*, ed. Jennifer Grünwald (New York: Marvel Entertainment, 2015), 71–93.

6. Brian Michael Bendis (w), Michael Gaydos (a), Mark Bagley (a), and Art Thibert (a), "Purple (Part 3 of 5)," in *Jessica Jones: Alias Vol. 4*, ed. Jennifer Grünwald (New York: Marvel Entertainment, 2015), 95–117.

7. Henry Jenkins, *Convergence Culture: Where Old and New Media Collide* (New York: New York University Press, 2006), 21.

8. *Ibid.*

9. Colin Harvey, *Fantastic Transmedia: Narrative, Play and Memory Across Science Fiction and Fantasy Storyworlds* (New York: Palgrave Macmillan, 2015), 64.

10. *Iron Man 3* (Shane Black, 2013); *Thor: The Dark World* (Alan Taylor, 2013); *Captain America: The Winter Soldier* (Anthony Russo and Joe Russo, 2014); *Guardians of the Galaxy*

(James Gunn, 2014); *Avengers: Age of Ultron* (Joss Whedon, 2015); *Ant-Man* (Peyton Reed, 2015); *Captain America: Civil War* (Anthony Russo and Joe Russo, 2016); *Doctor Strange* (Scott Derrickson, 2016); *Guardians of the* Galaxy Vol. 2 (James Gunn, 2017); *Spider-Man: Homecoming* (Jon Watts, 2017): and *Thor: Ragnarok* (Taika Waititi, 2017).

11. *Black Panther* (Ryan Coogler, 2018); *Avengers: Infinity War* (Anthony Russo and Joe Russo, 2018); *Ant-Man and the Wasp* (Peyton Reed, 2018); *Captain Marvel* (Anna Boden and Ryan Fleck, 2019); a fourth, untitled *Avengers* film (Anthony Russo and Joe Russo, 2019); a *Spider-Man* sequel (2019); and a third *Guardians of the Galaxy* film (James Gunn, 2020).

12. *Agents of S.H.I.E.L.D.* (2013-); *Agent Carter* (2015–16); and *The Inhumans* (2017-).

13. *Cloak and Dagger* (2018-); *The Runaways* (2018-); and *The New Warriors* (2018-). *Damage Control* (originally planned for 2016) is now apparently in limbo. A *S.H.I.E.L.D.* spinoff, *Marvel's Most Wanted*, was not picked up by ABC in 2016.

14. *Daredevil* (2015-); *Jessica Jones* (2015-); *Luke Cage* (2016-); *Iron Fist* (2017-); and *The Defenders* (2017-).

15. *The Punisher* (2017-) is the next Netflix series.

16. Harvey, *Fantastic Transmedia*, 81.

17. *Ibid.*

18. David Lieberman and Nellie Andreeva, "Netflix Picks Up Four Marvel Series & a Mini Featuring Daredevil, Jessica Jones, Iron Fist, Luke Cage for 2015 Launch," *Deadline*, last modified November 7, 2013, http://deadline.com/2013/11/disney-netflix-marvel-series-629696.

19. James Hibberd, "Marvel's *The Punisher* Spin-off Ordered by Netflix," *Entertainment Weekly*, last modified April 29, 2016, http://www.ew.com/article/2016/04/29/punisher-marvel-netflix.

20. Harvey, *Fantastic Transmedia*, 83.

21. *Ibid.*, 64.

22. "About Netflix," Netflixwww, accessed August 2, 2016, https://media.netflix.com/en/about-netflix.

23. *Ibid.*

24. Nick Summers, "Ted Sarandos' High-Stakes Gamble to Save Netflix," *Newsweek*, last modified May 14, 2012, http://www.newsweek.com/ted-sarandos-high-stakes-gamble-save-netflix-65063.

25. *Ibid.*

26. Summers, "Ted Sarandos."

27. *Ibid.*

28. *Ibid.*

29. While strong, capable, and heroic, Peggy Carter does not have superpowers, and is therefore not a superhero.

30. Michael Schneider, "'Twilight' Screenwriter Sets Marvel Adaptation for TV," *Variety*, last modified December 17, 2010, http://variety.com/2010/tv/news/twilight-screenwriter-sets-marvel-adaptation-for-tv-1118029209.

31. Kirsten Acuna, "How 'Jessica Jones' Made It to Netflix After ABC Nixed the Show," *TechInsider*, last modified November 17, 2015, http://www.techinsider.io/jessica-jones-was-supposed-to-be-on-abc-2015–11.

32. In the Marvel Comics Universe, this character is known as Patsy Walker, aka Hellcat.

33. Luke Cage is known as Power Man in the Marvel Comics Universe, where Jones and Cage had a daughter together and eventually married.

34. Kate Harding, *Asking for It: The Alarming Rise of Rape Culture—and What We Can Do About It* (Cambridge, MA: Da Capo Press, 2015), 141.

35. *Ibid.*, 52.

36. Eliana Dockterman, "Jessica Jones Star Krysten Ritter on Why the Superhero Will Never Wear Heels," Timewww, last modified November 30, 2015, http://time.com/4126495/jessica-jones-star-krysten-ritter-interview.

37. *Ibid.*

38. Beth Felker Jones, "Battling wills," *Christian Century*, March 2, 2016, 43.

39. In his introduction to the comic book series *Alias*, Jeph Loeb describes the series as "comic book noir," indicating that this aesthetic choice has been with the character from the beginning. For more, see Jeph Loeb, "Introduction," in *Jessica Jones: Alias Vol. 1*, ed. Jennifer Grünwald (New York: Marvel Entertainment, 2015), n.p.

40. These masculinized female characters recur throughout the so-called "avenging woman narrative." For more, see Lara Stache, "When a Man Writes a Woman: Audience Reception of the Avenging-woman Character in Popular Television and Film," in *Fan Girls and the Media: Creating Characters, Consuming Culture*, ed. Adrienne Trier-Bieniek (Lanham, MD: Rowman & Littlefield, 2015), 71–75.

41. Research suggests that experiencing trauma as a child can increase the severity of PTSD in cases of sexual assault. For more, see Sarah E. Ullman, Henrietta H. Filipas, Stephanie M. Townsend, and Laura L. Starzynski, "Psychosocial Correlates of PTSD Symptom Severity in Sexual Assault Survivors," *Journal of Traumatic Stress* 20, no. 5 (2007): 828.

42. Daniel D'Addario, "Jessica Jones Is Marvel's Most Nuanced Heroine Yet," Timewww, last modified November 19, 2015, http://time.com/4120228/jessica-jones-review-netflix-marvel.

43. Stache, "When a Man Writes a Woman," 71–75.

44. Patricia A. Frazier, Heather Mortensen, and Jason Steward, "Coping Strategies as Mediators of the Relations Among Perceived Control and Distress in Sexual Assault Survivors," *Journal of Counseling Psychology* 52, no. 3 (2005): 275.

45. Ullman et. al., "Psychosocial Correlates of PTSD," 828.

46. Frazier, Mortensen, and Steward, "Coping Strategies," 275.

47. For more, see Ullman et. al., "Psychosocial Correlates of PTSD," 828 and Frazier, Mortensen, and Steward, "Coping Strategies," 272.

48. Tara Roeder, "'You have to confess': Rape and the Politics of Storytelling," *Journal of Feminist Scholarship* 9 (2015): 19.

49. Brian Truitt, "Marvel's 'Daredevil' is dark Netflix series," USATodaywww, last modified April 9, 2015, http://www.usatoday.com/story/life/tv/2015/04/06/daredevil-netflix-tv-on-set/25343355.

50. Eliana Dockterman, "Here's How Netflix's *Daredevil* Fits Into the Greater Marvel Universe," Timewww, last modified April 10, 2015, http://time.com/3815524/daredevil-netflix-marvel-universe.

51. Truitt, "Marvel's 'Daredevil.'"

52. Brian Michael Bendis, Michael Gaydos (a), Mark Bagley (a), and Art Thibert (a), *Alias* Issues #24–28, in *Jessica Jones: Alias Vol. 4*, ed. Jennifer Grünwald (New York: Marvel Entertainment, 2015), 47–141.

53. Loeb, "Introduction," n.p.

54. *Ibid.*

55. Dockterman, "Jessica Jones."

56. Truitt, "Marvel's 'Daredevil.'"

57. For more, see D'Addario, "Jessica Jones."

58. *Ibid.*

59. Truitt, "Marvel's 'Daredevil.'"

60. We should note that in two episodes, Jones does take another case, which means she investigates something other than Kilgrave. However, even in these episodes, she believes the case links back to Kilgrave.

61. Jaime Weinman, "The stand-alone episode meets its end," *Maclean's*, last modified December 26, 2015, http://www.macleans.ca/culture/television/the-stand-alone-episode-meets-its-end.

62. Veronica Innocenti and Guglielmo Pescatore, "Changing Series: Narrative Models and the Role of the Viewer in Contemporary Television Seriality," *Between* 4, no. 8 (2014).

63. Weinman, "Stand-alone episode."

64. Dockterman, "Jessica Jones."

65. Weinman, "Stand-alone episode."

66. Marcello Serra, "Historical and Mythical Time in the Marvel and DC Series," *The Journal of Popular Culture* 49, no. 3 (2016): 647–48.

67. *Ibid.*

68. Harvey, *Fantastic Transmedia*, 89.
69. *Ibid.*, 73.
70. *Ibid.*
71. *Ibid.*, 92.
72. *Ibid.*, 187.
73. Harvey, *Fantastic Transmedia*, 66.
74. Following the release of *Iron Man*, Marvel announced they would release their films in different groupings that comprised separate arcs known as phases. Phase One introduces the MCU, and spans several films beginning with *Iron Man* and ending with *The Avengers*. Phase Two chronicles the aftermath of the Battle of New York and introduces several new characters, starting with *Iron Man 3* and concluding with *Ant-Man*. Phase Three takes place after Ultron's attack and deals with the fragmentation of the Avengers, and begins with *Captain America: Civil War* and ends with the upcoming fourth *Avengers* film. For more, see Caroline Siede, "A beginner's guide to the expansive Marvel Cinematic Universe," AVClub-www, last modified July 23, 2015, http://www.avclub.com/article/beginners-guide-expansive-marvel-cinematic-univers-221909.

Bibliography

"About Netflix." Netflixwww. Accessed August 2, 2016. https://media.netflix.com/en/about-netflix.
Acuna, Kirsten. "How 'Jessica Jones' Made it to Netflix After ABC Nixed the Show." *TechInsider*. Last modified November 17, 2015. http://www.techinsider.io/jessica-jones-was-supposed-to-be-on-abc-2015-11.
Bendis, Brian Michael (w), and Michael Gaydos (a). *Alias* #1–5. In *Jessica Jones: Alias Vol. 1*, edited by Jennifer Grünwald, 1–118. New York: Marvel Entertainment, 2015.
Bendis, Brian Michael (w), Michael Gaydos (a), Mark Bagley (a), and Art Thibert (a). *Alias* #24–28, in *Jessica Jones: Alias Vol. 4*, ed. Jennifer Grünwald (New York: Marvel Entertainment, 2015), 47–141.
D'Addario, Daniel. "*Jessica Jones* Is Marvel's Most Nuanced Heroine Yet." Timewww. Last modified November 19, 2015. http://time.com/4120228/jessica-jones-review-netflix-marvel.
Dockterman, Eliana. "Here's How Netflix's Daredevil Fits Into the Greater Marvel Universe." Timewww. Last modified April 10, 2015. http://time.com/3815524/daredevil-netflix-marvel-universe.
Dockterman, Eliana. "Jessica Jones Star Krysten Ritter on Why the Superhero Will Never Wear Heels." Timewww. Last modified November 30, 2015. http://time.com/4126495/jessica-jones-star-krysten-ritter-interview.
Frazier, Patricia A., Heather Mortensen, and Jason Steward. "Coping Strategies as Mediators of the Relations Among Perceived Control and Distress in Sexual Assault Survivors." *Journal of Counseling Psychology* 52, no. 3 (2005): 267–78.
Harding, Kate. *Asking for It: The Alarming Rise of Rape Culture—and What We Can Do About It.* Cambridge, MA: Da Capo Press, 2015.
Harvey, Colin. *Fantastic Transmedia: Narrative, Play and Memory Across Science Fiction and Fantasy Storyworlds.* New York: Palgrave MacMillan, 2015.
Hibberd, James. "Marvel's *The Punisher* Spin-off Ordered by Netflix." *Entertainment Weekly*. Last modified April 29, 2016. http://www.ew.com/article/2016/04/29/punisher-marvel-netflix.
Innocenti, Veronica and Guglielmo Pescatore. "Changing Series: Narrative Models and the Role of the Viewer in Contemporary Television Seriality." *Between* 4, no. 8 (2014): 1–14.
Jenkins, Henry. *Convergence Culture: Where Old and New Media Collide.* New York: New York University Press, 2006.
Jones, Beth Felker. "Battling wills." *Christian Century*, March 2, 2016.
Lieberman, David, and Nellie Andreeva. "Netflix Picks Up Four Marvel Series & a Mini Featuring Daredevil, Jessica Jones, Iron Fist, Luke Cage for 2015 Launch." *Deadline*. Last modified November 7, 2013. http://deadline.com/2013/11/disney-netflix-marvel-series-629696.

Loeb, Jeph. "Introduction." In *Jessica Jones: Alias Vol. 1*, edited by Jennifer Grünwald, n.p. New York: Marvel Entertainment, 2015.

Parker, John R. "'Alias' Jessica Jones: A Critical Look Back at Marvel's Mature Readers Hero and New Netflix Star." *Comics Alliance*. Last modified November 5, 2014. http://comicsalliance.com/alias-omnibus-review.

Roeder, Tara. "'You have to confess': Rape and the Politics of Storytelling." *Journal of Feminist Scholarship* 9 (2015): 18–29.

Schneider, Michael. "'Twilight' Screenwriter Sets Marvel Adaptation for TV." *Variety*. Last modified December 17, 2010. http://variety.com/2010/tv/news/twilight-screenwriter-sets-marvel-adaptation-for-tv-1118029209.

Serra, Marcello. "Historical and Mythical Time in the Marvel and DC Series." *The Journal of Popular Culture* 49, no. 3 (2016): 646–59.

Siede, Caroline. "A beginner's guide to the expansive Marvel Cinematic Universe." AVClubwww. Last modified July 23, 2015. http://www.avclub.com/article/beginners-guide-expansive-marvel-cinematic-univers-221909.

Stache, Lara. "When a Man Writes a Woman: Audience Reception of the Avenging-woman Character in Popular Television and Film." In *Fan Girls and the Media: Creating Characters, Consuming Culture*, edited by Adrienne Trier-Bieniek, 71–75. Lanham, MD: Rowman & Littlefield, 2015.

Summers, Nick. "Ted Sarandos' High-Stakes Gamble to Save Netflix." Newsweekwww. Last modified May 14, 2012. http://www.newsweek.com/ted-sarandos-high-stakes-gamble-save-netflix-65063.

Truitt, Brian. "Marvel's 'Daredevil' is dark Netflix series." USATodaywww. Last modified April 9, 2015. http://www.usatoday.com/story/life/tv/2015/04/06/daredevil-netflix-tv-on-set/25343355.

Ullman, Sarah E., Henrietta H. Filipas, Stephanie M. Townsend, and Laura L. Starzynski. "Psychosocial Correlates of PTSD Symptom Severity in Sexual Assault Survivors." *Journal of Traumatic Stress* 20, no. 5 (2007): 821–31.

Weinman, Jaime. "The stand-alone episode meets its end." *Maclean's*. Last modified December 26, 2015. http://www.macleans.ca/culture/television/the-stand-alone-episode-meets-its-end.

Sobriety Blows

Whiskey, Trauma and Coping in Netflix's Jessica Jones

Janis Breckenridge

The wildly popular and critically acclaimed debut season of the Netflix original series, *Jessica Jones*, brings a gritty superhero narrative to the home television screen. Featuring a sadistic villain who abuses his mind control powers to dominate others, the show consistently emphasizes the characters' struggles to overcome feelings of powerlessness in the face of hardship, adversity, and loss while downplaying superhuman traits. In fact, not only does the "super" remain understated in *Jessica Jones*, doubt is also frequently cast upon the label of "heroic" altogether. Nearly every character grapples with a traumatic past; the distinct but easily recognizable manifestations of post-traumatic stress disorder (PTSD) that emerge after personal experiences of violence and abuse become a vital thread unifying all thirteen episodes.

Jessica alone has survived multiple traumas since childhood: a tragic car accident that killed her parents and brother followed by prolonged hospitalization while comatose, adoption into an abusive and exploitative household and the unwitting discovery of exceptional physical abilities. These traumatic incidents culminate with her recent abduction and mistreatment at the hands of the sociopathic Kilgrave, whose insidious powers not only allow him to impose his will indiscriminately upon others but also to confuse and manipulate their desires, overriding their needs and wishes with his own. As such, notions of self-worth together with questions of choice, control and responsibility—issues that, not coincidentally, are also central to substance abuse—become pivotal thematic elements of the show.

The eponymous character's so-called gifts include exceptional strength, amazing speed, extraordinary jumping prowess (treated ironically as a poor substitute for the ability to fly) and a seemingly superhuman tolerance for alcohol consumption.[1] Jessica displays an incredible resistance to the vast quantities of hard liquor she relentlessly consumes. Nevertheless, despite being described by other characters as erratic, volatile, short-fused, out of control, a lush, and a mess of a woman, she proves herself to be an adept private investigator, albeit by employing highly unorthodox methods and unconventional means. Nonetheless, the bottle maintains a constant presence (most notably on her desk, nightstand, and kitchen counters) in the squalid New York apartment that doubles as office space for Alias Investigations, her one-woman detective agency. The whiskey decanter, intimately and directly tied to the lingering, debilitating effects of past traumas, quickly comes to denote another of Jessica's remarkable powers—that of repression—and arguably becomes as conspicuous a side-kick as her lifelong friend and adoptive sister, Trish Walker.

The pervasive presence of overturned glasses and empty bottles serves as a stark reminder of the haunting presence of Jessica's dark past and an ever-present testament to one of her many coping mechanisms: drinking as self-medication. Yet, ironically, Jessica often finds herself in a supporting role to others' efforts to overcome addiction or stay in recovery. The series incorporates numerous interconnected plots and subplots that directly relate trauma to substance use disorders, so many that the digital media site *Vox Culture* featured a post bluntly titled "Marvel's Jessica Jones Is More About Addiction and Relapse Than It Is About Superheroes." Following drug addiction as a response to childhood abuse, Trish struggles to stay clean while her lover, Will Simpson, falls back on the strength-enhancing pills supplied to help him quickly overcome severe physical injuries. Even more notably, Jessica's formerly drug-addicted neighbor Malcolm Ducasse, hooked against his will, experiences agonizing self-doubt, questioning whether he was always an addict-waiting-to-happen as supervillain and supplier, Kilgrave, contemptuously asserts. Jessica herself frequently resorts to a simple thought-stopping technique typical of that prescribed in cognitive behavioral therapy (CBT), reciting street names near her childhood home. This suppressive strategy, an avoidance behavior which provides temporary escape from self-defeating or obsessive thoughts and thus allows functionality, remains highly controversial.[2] To this end, Jessica refers to her therapist as a quack and offhandedly dismisses the value of this "proven" method of managing PTSD, even as she relies on alcohol to play a similar role.

This essay proposes a gendered framework from which to examine Jessica's alcoholism in relation to PTSD. Close readings of key scenes allow for special attention to be paid to visual strategies employed in the representation of alcohol and alcoholism on the television screen, including coded intertextual references as well as strategic manipulation of lighting, focus, and composition. The recurring use of flashbacks, considered through the lens of trauma theory, is shown to be a particularly effective filmic device for reproducing the processes of traumatic memory. Ultimately, by exploring the intricate dynamics of PTSD and substance abuse, this essay connects the haunting degradation that results from utterly dominating mind control with the analogous feelings of powerlessness, both psychological and physiological, that come with chemical dependency.

"It's called whiskey"

Throughout the first season, the fact that Jessica frequently (re)turns to liquor's numbing effects as a way to cope with symptoms of anxiety, depression, high alert, and intrusive memories remains contextualized in a social environment in which visual, narrative, and auditory references to alcohol are ubiquitous. Transitions between sequences, particularly within Jessica's apartment, repeatedly allude to the protagonist's alcoholism with lingering shots explicitly composed of and/or framed by images of empty bottles and glasses; careful manipulation of focus further highlights their presence. Occasionally the camera assumes the unusual perspective of the glass or bottle. These point-of-view shots, especially when depicting Jessica in unconscious states, suggest a unique narrative positioning that confers a sense of power, domination, and control onto the liquor.[3]

Similarly, several secondary characters are openly associated with excessive consumption of alcohol (including a bus driver, an ambulance driver, and a doorman) even as accusations of drunkenness are frequently proffered as an explanation when outsiders inconveniently perceive the atypical realities inherent to the superhero world. In short, alcohol consistently provides a quick and easy way not only to avoid pain but also to evade detection. Following a bar fight in which an assailant discovers his unbreakable skin, Luke Cage convinces his (seemingly sober) attacker that he is drunk, therefore not in his right mind and he should forget the whole thing. A free round on the house ensures that all will overlook the highly unusual incident. When a doorman, often blamed for negligence, questions Trish's lie regarding the presence of bodies in her apartment, her seemingly offhand remark that "he drinks" instantly discredits the man, leading to the immediate dismissal of his (accurate) assessment.

The show's climax features numerous victims of mind control who witness, first-hand, as Jessica murders Kilgrave; however, many also happen to be partiers from a booze cruise and it is assumed that the testimony of drunken brawlers would not be taken seriously. Manipulating (perceptions of) excessive or habitual alcohol consumption can thus provide protective safeguards. Drinking seems to provide a related, albeit self-destructive, sense of relief for Jessica in light of her traumatic past. Jessica repeatedly insists that the palliative or calming effect achieved by drinking allows her to function.

Indeed, through the first half of the season, despite the pervasive presence of liquor, Jessica remains a highly functional alcoholic. Her excessive drinking rarely becomes a significant element of the plot development and her addiction only occasionally elicits comments from others. Nonetheless, numerous friends and acquaintances recognize her reliance on alcohol as a form of self-medication and periodically call into question its efficacy as a coping mechanism. Likewise, her binge drinking has not gone unnoticed by fans and critics, especially on internet entertainment and social news media sites. Within one week of the show's premier Emily Canal posted *Forbes*' calculation of how much money Jessica Jones spends on booze during the first season while Daniel Dalton, a staff member at BuzzFeed, posted a cleverly captioned photographic log documenting Jessica's alcohol intake. By carefully examining labels and compiling a list of brands consumed episode by episode, it is ultimately determined that her drink of choice is blended whiskey. Such evidence upholds one of Jessica's many pithy quips, one that provides the title for the third episode and could readily serve as the tagline for the entire first season: when asked how she handles it, she immediately replies—"It's called whiskey."

Jessica's binges signify far more than a mere penchant for drinking to excess. Her specific drinking habits—the frequent *benders*—underscore the numerous subverted gender roles—the recurring *gender* benders—at play across the thirteen episodes. What's more, the specific brands that Jessica consumes speak volumes. The protagonist maintains the steady and constant companionship of Teacher's, Cutty Sark, Jim Beam, Maker's Mark, Wild Turkey, Heaven Hill, and Old Grand-Dad. Although whiskey has long been considered "a man's drink," recent publications, both popular and scholarly, have exposed the inherent gender bias behind assuming whiskey to be "the drink of power brokers."[4] All the same, as Emma Barnett, Women's Editor for *The Telegraph* cites, "It's a little like if a woman orders a pint of Guinness; there's nothing wrong with it—but it's still a statement."[5] Moreover, Jessica's apparent preference for the fictional Winston serves as a sly intertextual nod or subtle wink of conspiracy with knowing viewers. This label, recognized in Dalton's post as an homage to the well-known "Demon in a Bottle" story arc, was originally featured on the cover of Marvel's *The Invincible Iron Man* #128 as Tony Stark's drink of choice. For comic book fans, this stands as an unequivocal warning of the devastating toll that alcoholism can take—Stark's binge drinking nearly costs him his company as well as his long-term friends—but also offers the promise and possibility of recovery.

Not only have society pages noted a trend for women's increasingly strong relationship to hard liquor, studies in psychology have begun to focus on the correlations between gender and trauma-related substance abuse. As Judith Herman notes in *Trauma and Recovery: The Aftermath of Violence— from Domestic Abuse to Political Terror*, "Not until the women's liberation movement of the 1970s was it recognized that the most common post-traumatic disorders are those not of men in war but of women in civilian life."[6] It is beyond the scope of this essay to offer an in-depth discussion of this research, however, a sobering supposition introduces a thorough literature review titled "Gender Differences in Posttraumatic Stress Disorder," namely that "most studies on posttraumatic stress disorder (PTSD) in the general population have found higher rates of PTSD in women than in men."[7] Even more alarming are the authors' concluding remarks, which state that studies examining comorbidity (the simultaneous presence of two chronic conditions) of post-traumatic stress disorder with alcohol and/or drug abuse have shown that women who experience interpersonal violence—survivors of sexual abuse, physical abuse, and rape, rather than combat—show a "greater use of alcohol to manage trauma-related symptoms like intrusive memories and dissociation."[8]

Not coincidentally, *Jessica Jones* effectively dramatizes these specific sequelae or indicators by chronicling the devastating, long-term effects of coercion, domestic violence, and sexual assault. Throughout the first season, Jessica's alcoholism serves as a recurrent visual reminder of past trauma; however, focusing attention on the behaviors and cyclical thought patterns associated with PTSD, Jessica's current experience remains somewhat dissociated from a specific embodied cause. Much like the blended whiskey that serves as Jessica's drink of choice, intense survivor guilt fuses with the nearly overwhelming emotional impacts of having survived sexual abuse even as the intrusive symptoms of post-traumatic stress disorder remain intricately linked with the progressive dependency inherent to chronic alcoholism.

Whole Lotta Booze for Such a Small Woman

Flashbacks, a narrative device that allows for fragmented and non-chronological storytelling, play a significant role in *Jessica Jones*, aptly replicating the processes of traumatic memory. Mere minutes into the first episode, "Ladies Night," the viewer witnesses two key sequences that establish an explicit link between traumatic memory and alcohol with respect to the protagonist, an unequivocal tie that will gradually intensify as the season progresses. Both function as establishing scenes, but only partially introduce the viewer, visually and aurally, to the traumatic backstory that informs the protagonist's present condition. These truncated and non-contextualized glimpses into Jessica's abusive relationship with Kilgrave ultimately frustrate comprehension, deliberately impeding the viewer from fully grasping and understanding images that flash across the screen. Rapid flashbacks present sudden and incomplete fragments rather than fully developed narrative sequences, exemplifying Jessica's own "unclaimed experience" while increasing dramatic tension and suspense. In her book of that title, trauma theorist Cathy Caruth explains that "the painful repetition of the flashback can only be understood as the absolute inability of the mind to avoid an unpleasurable event that has not been given psychic meaning in any way."[9] For this reason, although fleeting (each segment lasts fewer than ten seconds), these flashbacks cause prolonged and profound disruption for Jessica; neither she nor the spectator can make coherent, integrated sense of these haunting memories. The recurring filmic device, then, aims to re-create the ongoing, debilitating effects of a traumatic past that persistently erupts into the present.

In the first such scene, Jessica tosses a camera into her messenger bag, fills a metal water bottle with Jim Beam, and nonchalantly leaps onto a fire escape to spy through her camera lens into the windows of an apartment building across the street. Throughout this sequence, highly reminiscent of Alfred Hitchcock's *Rear Window*,[10] point-of-view shots are intercut with images of Jessica reacting to what she sees and photographs; the viewer shares her voyeuristic gaze, effectively identifying with her subjective perspective. Tellingly, Jessica turns away from the very sexual encounter she has come to expose and as she closes her eyes, a slow zoom and dramatic transformation in the background neon's tonality—from realistic, warm pink-orange hues to sinister, cool purples and blues—signal entry into her subconscious. Significantly, the change in hue allows for increased contrast together with an erasure of details; thus the visual strategy paradoxically suggests a sharply vivid yet simultaneously tentative and amorphous memory. The soundscape provides a marked change of tempo to accompany the abrupt shift in tonality; the reverberation of an accelerating heartbeat overlaps with extradiegetic music that becomes increasingly strident while rushing to a harsh crescendo. At the same time, a shadowy male figure abruptly enters the frame from the left to assertively (and, for the viewer, mysteriously) declare in an uncanny voice with an unnatural echo-like quality that she knows she wants to do it.

Unlike a typical flashback, the intrusive memory takes places in precisely the same frame as the narrative action, still within the tight confines of the fire escape and in the present moment. Abruptly altering this objective reality with Jessica's subjective experience effectively illustrates the insidious nature of past trauma's irruption into daily routines. A lightning sharp, quick zoom followed by a jarring jump cut, functions as a trigger for the audience— rapidly returning to a now-defamiliarized scene and startling viewer passivity.

Jessica's frantic gasping indicates intense emotional turmoil until the deliberate recitation of street names creates a rhythmic incantation that allows her breath to gradually slow. Significantly, Jessica then takes a swig of Jim Beam.

A subsequent and deliberately parallel sequence combines the same key elements—the intrusion of the male figure, the calming recitation of street names, and the presence of liquor—unambiguously linking traumatic recall and personal coping mechanisms. A resounding rap tune with lyrics that brazenly celebrate drinking without moderation ("fucked up / watch everybody get / watch everybody get") provides a fitting prelude.[11] A powerful auditory transition, the song adeptly connects two seemingly disparate scenes while simultaneously capturing the paradox of Jessica's supernatural strength combined with the hazards of her outstanding drinking ability.

The beat can first be heard as Jessica triumphantly pronounces, "Mr. Gregory Spheris, you've been served," having just exhibited her physical capabilities and professional prowess in response to belittlement from an arrogant misogynist; only afterwards do the lyrics fade in, anticipating Jessica's struggle with alcoholism. Jessica is subsequently shown passed out on her desk, inverted glass in hand; a computer screen provides backlighting. As before, the camera slowly zooms in and oneiric blue-purple hues replace the realistic, warm glow of the computer monitor. Once again maintaining the present place and time, the man enters from the right pulling Jessica's hair back and, without warning, obscenely licks her face. Jessica leaps up so quickly that a bottle crashes loudly to the floor and, struggling to regulate her breathing, she slowly and methodically begins to recite the street names as a calming mantra.

These brief and disconnected evocations, narrative flashbacks so abrupt and decontextualized as to remain virtually inexplicable to the viewer, typify the haunting nature of traumatic memory. Considered to be "unclaimed" both for escaping immediate comprehension and for remaining outside of conscious control, the memory of a traumatic event or "the history that a flashback tells" can best be understood as "a history that literally *has no place*, neither in the past, in which it was not fully experienced, nor in the present, in which its precise images and enactments are not fully understood."[12] Traumatic recall disrupts the survivor's efforts to carry out daily routines, establish or maintain relationships or even sleep; in much the same way, these unique narrative flashbacks suddenly interject a traumatic event into the present (rather than transport the viewer back to the past) and thus complicate linear time, temporal progression, and chronological storytelling within the series.

With trauma (defined as suffering or witnessing sudden, catastrophic, and unexpected events) the reaction (re)occurs in the form of hallucinations, dreams, thoughts, or involuntary behaviors and can only begin to be grasped consciously *after* the actual experience.[13] Survivors often find themselves overcome by inescapable, recurring memories, often affective or sensory (auditory, visual, tactile, olfactory) that reproduce emotional intensity and resist linguistic registers and assimilation into a coherent structural whole. Only later can the subject begin to construct a communicable personal narrative. As Anne Whitehead further explains in the introduction to *Trauma Fiction*: "Insufficiently grasped at the time of its occurrence, trauma does not lie in the possession of the individual, to be recounted at will, but rather acts as a haunting or possessive influence which not only insistently and intrusively returns but is, moreover, experienced for the first time only in its belated repetition."[14]

Typically, in correlation with the severity and duration of the trauma, with time and distance, both the frequency and the intensity of intrusive memories slowly begin to diminish, allowing the survivor to progressively integrate disjointed memories. In *Jessica Jones*, the viewer can only infer the extent of what happened to the protagonist; comprehension is restrained by the scope and nature of the suppressed memories and Jessica's (in)ability to reconcile them. The recurrent use of flashbacks offers the viewer limited exposure to and understanding of the harrowing ordeals that Jessica has endured; only with increasing duration and narrative content can the spectator hope to piece the fragments together to create a more complete backstory. The strategic storytelling device, then, effectively replicates Jessica's own attempts to come to terms with her traumatic past.

A Mess of a Woman?

Jessica Jones successfully interlaces an evocative representation of the emotional impact inherent to traumatic recall with a compelling portrayal of the acute disintegration intrinsic to late stage alcohol abuse. In fact, the show projects marked similarities between clients who willfully deny the very facts they hire Jessica to uncover, a general populace that prefers not to confront the uncomfortable truths of difference in their midst, and an addict's lack of awareness of the ruinous effects of their habits. Jessica is no exception. The narrative arc suggests multiple ways in which alcoholism is a highly complex, progressive, and degenerative disease as the spectator witnesses Jessica struggle to maintain control of her personal as well as her professional life.[15]

At the same time, the distinctions between affective disorders related to PTSD (shame, self-loathing, and guilt) and self-destructive behaviors associated with alcoholism (risk taking and isolation) become increasingly indistinguishable and indeterminate. The codependency of excessive drinking with symptomatic anxiety, depression, and a constant state of high alert result in a seemingly inescapable cycle: alcohol calms anxiety, anxiety impairs judgment; feelings of self-loathing and guilt demand alcohol while excessive drinking leads to increased isolation and shame. In short, linking these symptoms also brings together the correlative thematic concerns of power, control, and coping with trauma. The overlap in symptoms and behaviors makes it hard for the viewer, and perhaps even Jessica, to distinguish the dominating psychopathology: PTSD or alcoholism? Coping mechanism or self-destructive behavior? Hero or alcoholic?

The central episodes of the first season highlight the protagonist's steady unraveling as she begins to lose control of various aspects of her life. While this descent assumes diverse forms, two patterns emerge: first, Jessica's apparent weakness, the "kryptonite" that Kilgrave repeatedly wields against her, is to protect others no matter the cost to herself and second, with each setback or failure her alcohol dependency intensifies. A case in point: Jessica inspires Malcolm to detoxify and introduces him to a support group; to further protect him she sends pictures of herself daily to Kilgrave in exchange for Malcolm's safety. With this "voluntary" act she once again relinquishes control to her nemesis to satisfy his desires, forfeiting both autonomy and privacy; such sacrifices generate renewed feelings of subjection and ultimately lead to a role-reversal with Malcolm who, in a telling reprise scene, now helps Jessica when he finds her passed out in the elevator, bottle in hand. This unambiguous allusion to Malcolm's devastatingly chronic addiction presages the potential severity of her own self-destructive path. Similarly, in order to save an innocent bus driver (whose blamelessness remains complicated by a habit of drinking on the job), Jessica confesses responsibility for the death of Luke's wife, albeit under Kilgrave's power. Luke's subsequent and absolute rejection fuels even more excessive drinking coupled with increasingly overt references to the attendant affective processes of shame and guilt, both symptomatic of late-stage alcoholism. It remains uncertain, however, whether these feelings correspond to actions committed under Kilgrave's influence or to being habitually under the influence.

Midseason, a decisive turning point in the storyline shows Jessica surrounded by bottles while obsessively repeating the names of streets, this time to no avail. Soon thereafter what has been a reassuring auditory technique—the verbal recitation of street names as a repressive, thought-stopping process—becomes a foreboding visual cue. Kilgrave receives the keys to his new home and a slow pan out reveals the surrounding street signs, identifying this location as Jessica's parent's home and literally mapping Jessica's soothing mantra to a specific geographic location. This nostalgic space previously denoted an idyllic, happy, and stable (although perhaps highly romanticized) childhood; however, what was once called upon as a safe haven, a comforting and protective refuge that offered wholeness in the form of unconditional love and support, now takes on sinister overtones. His literal possession of the domestic space carries immense symbolic import for Jessica: loss of control over a past that previously had been untouched and untouchable by her arch-enemy and, more importantly, loss of what had been a seemingly reliable, though simplistic, coping mechanism. Learned in therapy and passed on to Hope Shlottman, Kilgrave's most recent victim, the repressive technique can no longer be effective.

Not coincidentally, the following episode ("AKA Top Shelf Perverts") opens with Jessica cast in the stereotyped portrayal of the down-and-out alcoholic; cut off at a bar for excessive drinking and literally tossed out onto the street, Jessica lands in a pile of trash next to a homeless man. A self-destructive mantra replaces the former therapeutic device, whereby Jessica verbalizes a decreased sense of self-worth and amplified feelings of self-loathing. Repeating Luke's derogatory language, Jessica insists that she is a piece of shit and shit stinks, believing herself to be garbage deserving of public shaming. As her personal life unravels, her professional performance likewise deteriorates; Jessica loses emotional as well as physical control when an impassioned diatribe regarding the extent of the shame she would do absolutely anything to avoid results in dropping a woman on subway tracks, unintentionally carrying out a threat that was meant only to intimidate.

Significantly, Jessica simultaneously begins to display signs of impairment from excessive consumption for the first time: stumbling home, struggling with the lock, repeatedly dropping her keys, and blacking out in public. Arguably, however, her binge drinking reaches a climax when, while "choosing" under duress to cohabitate with Kilgrave in her childhood home (hoping to know his whereabouts, curtail his harmful acts and ultimately capture him), she defiantly refuses a specially-prepared meal to instead consume a liquid dinner ("AKA WWJD?"). Confronted with the severity of her drinking by her former assailant and ongoing aggressor, Jessica indignantly retorts that alcohol is the only thing that can get her through a day after what he has done to her, explicitly putting into words what has been a primarily visual association for the viewer between past trauma and current chemical dependency. This accusation unequivocally links the enduring impact of physical rape and psychological torment—complete and total violation—with her maladaptive, albeit vital and indispensable, coping mechanism of drinking to excess. Exteriorizing uncontainable rage, frustration, and desperation, Jessica smashes a wine bottle against the dining room wall. The shattered glass vividly reflects a shattered psyche.

In addition to severe depression, deep-seated shame, and unresolved anger, Jessica grapples with intense feelings of guilt. These internalized sentiments manifest themselves externally through self-harming behaviors including the self-deprecating mantra, extreme risk-taking, and excessive drinking; clinically, these compounded, dysregulated affective processes remain strongly associated with both PTSD and substance abuse disorders. Once again, the audience comes to gradually appreciate the ever-present weight of these deleterious emotions primarily through the strategic employment of narrative flashbacks. As shown through a series of recovered memories in combination with a revelatory nightmare, Jessica faces survivor guilt for unintentionally causing the car wreck that killed her family and feels she must atone. She similarly struggles with devastating self-recrimination regarding her involuntary involvement in the death of Luke Cage's wife, Reva, combined with the deliberate concealment of her perceived culpability when she subsequently establishes a sexual relationship with him. Vomiting in the street following their first erotic encounter (and, not coincidentally, immediately after discovering Reva's photograph in his medicine cabinet) can be read as an abject act that effectively reflects internalized disgust with herself together with the physical effect of intoxication. Ultimately, Jessica assumes personal responsibility for each of Kilgrave's recent victims, blaming herself for failing to kill her sociopathic adversary in the past—a decisive incident that, together with Reva's death, she relives repeatedly through its relentless irruption into her everyday thought processes. The intensity of the trauma is re-experienced, as if for the first time, with each repetition. Nevertheless, a closely interconnected series of linked flashbacks gradually reveals the details of what happened as Jessica slowly recovers these repressed memories.

Distinct stylistic techniques utilized to present the corresponding narrative flashbacks not only reflect their diverse thematic content but also become reliable indicators for interpreting Jessica's emotional well-being. Sudden, brief flashes that unexpectedly intrude into the narrative can offer profound insight into the disruptive nature of traumatic memory. As discussed before, these startling intrusions often aim to reflect affective interior states (as experienced in the past as well as in the present). The jarring filmic techniques employed when Jessica confronts memories of being under Kilgrave's domination—discordant soundscapes, rapid zooming out, and disconcerting lighting effects—disturb and disorient the viewer (as the memories do Jessica) while dramatically reinforcing the unsettling quality of traumatic recall.[16] These visual and auditory strategies reinforce the storyline, not merely telling but *showing* how these traumatic events remain omnipresent and beyond Jessica's control.

In contrast, traumatic events further removed in time (events that have been more fully processed) as well as non-traumatic memories are presented in a more integrated fashion and without special effects. The events of Reva's death and Jessica's failed confrontation with Kilgrave continually haunt her, as evidenced by the recurrent nature of their psychological and narrative returns. Unlike the repressed memories of sexual assault, however, as the show progresses, these repeated visual sequences become increasingly longer and provide enough information to steadily coalesce into a cohesive narrative. While traumatic, these are memories that Jessica consciously works through in an effort to more fully understand what took place, regain personal autonomy and control, and ultimately, overcome her adversary.

Similarly, flashbacks pertaining to Jessica's family and the tragic car accident offer repeated but increasingly longer narrative segments that eventually reveal the entire story, including the decisive moment in which young Jessica's actions distract her father and bring about the crash; it is thus implied that she has gradually come to terms with the survivor guilt associated with the loss of her family. Moreover, a compelling inversion of the temporal format previously utilized with traumatic flashbacks occurs. Although once again dramatizing internal processes related to traumatic recall, the past is no longer seen to intrude upon the present; instead, a mature Jessica "re-lives" the scene, appearing in her childhood home to carefully observe the family members' interactions (including her younger self) as they depart on the fatal journey. Visually superimposing the present onto the traumatic past in this way effectively casts the audience in the role of eye-witness while strategically placing attention not only on memory retrieval but, more importantly, on Jessica's recovery process.

Maybe It's Enough

Ostensibly, the first season of *Jessica Jones* revolves around the protagonist's ongoing efforts to rescue and protect Hope Shlottman, a wholesome young track star whose situation mirrors Jessica's traumatic experiences under Kilgrave's sociopathic control and domination. As such, the storyline follows a structuring element or plot device typical of superhero narratives whereby the supervillain abducts an innocent girl and uses her to bait the protagonist; in this case, Jessica feels responsible for Hope's fate and believes that she alone remains capable of defeating the malevolent foe. However, the fact that Kilgrave deliberately chooses Hope (not a friend or loved one but a stranger) as a surrogate to recreate Jessica's traumatic experiences following her unprecedented escape from his devastating psychological and sexual abuse and, even more significantly, openly recognizes the young athlete (whose abilities can never rival Jessica's gifts) as the living embodiment of Jessica's guilt, radically complicates the genre's basic narrative arc. Further transcending the standard plotline, Jessica resolves not to vanquish or kill her adversary, but instead to seek vindication and attain some amount of closure for both Hope and herself. In many ways, her determination to "make things right" in the face of widespread disbelief regarding Kilgrave's culpability can be understood to speak to the challenges of successfully prosecuting sexual assault cases in the existing criminal justice system. Much as survivors bear the burden of presenting substantial evidence against perpetrators of sexual violence, Jessica takes on the daunting task of providing legally documented proof of his guilt not only to demand justice for his crimes but also, and more importantly, to exonerate Hope (and, by extension, herself).

By the end of *Jessica Jones'* first season, the eponymous heroine has successfully outwitted her nemesis, proven herself capable of caring for as well as protecting others, and adeptly resolved numerous cases in her role as a private investigator. Moreover, Jessica has repeatedly proven mastery of the four skills she facetiously considers to be essential for an effective PI: punching, kicking, drinking, and talking shit. All the same, the debut season refuses to end on a triumphant or optimistic note. Jessica literally loses Hope. While the girl's dramatic suicide frees Jessica to simply eliminate Kilgrave, she remains saddled with guilt for surviving what Hope did not.[17] Moreover, despite having saved Malcolm from drug addiction and protecting Trish as she strives to stay drug free, the protagonist has yet to confront her own self-destructive behaviors related to alcohol consumption. In this way, although Kilgrave's death would seem to provide narrative resolution, it seems more accurate to suggest that the first season of *Jessica Jones* instead ends with an unsettling cliffhanger.

Fittingly, the show's closing sequence remains fraught with tensions and oppositions. A narrative voiceover, in which Jessica questions the ability to perceive the fine line distinguishing heroes from villains, confronts the viewer with her as yet unresolved and perhaps unresolvable sense of self-worth. A well-conceived set design physically reflects this persistent inner turmoil. Her apartment, uncharacteristically neater and tidier due to Malcolm's supportive intervention, is almost unrecognizable; yet demolished bookcases and the wall behind her workspace, riddled with bullet holes, serve as overt reminders of the persistent traces, physical and psychological, that will linger following the traumatic events she has recently survived. To this end, an overwhelmed Jessica is shown seated at her desk, a half-consumed bottle at her side. Pouring a mugful of whiskey, Jessica systematically deletes a series of frantic voicemails from potential, albeit desperate, clients; Malcolm, in contrast, gently responds to an incoming call by extending an offer to help.

Not coincidentally, the final image mirrors a key scene from the season's introductory sequence. An homage to the original comic, the show's opening vignette incorporates a traveling shot that slowly advances along the narrow confines of the apartment building's hallway towards Jessica's office. As the camera approaches, two shadowy figures, obscured by the frosted glass that advertises her PI business, suddenly come into sharp relief as Jessica tosses a belligerent male client through the glass in self-defense. She closes the case (and the scene) by cheekily bringing up the bill, a low-angle shot reinforcing her strength and power. The open-ended conclusion adeptly inverts this depiction. Now the camera slowly moves away, retreating down the hallway and framing a sharply-focused Jessica (joined by Malcolm) within the jagged contours of the repeatedly damaged or broken Alias Investigations logo. The technique effectively isolates the characters, distancing the spectator and offering an increasingly diminutive perspective of the beleaguered protagonist. In this way, the visual composition suggests resignation and powerlessness, reinforcing her sense of despair when inundated with calls from people begging to be saved.

The similarly urgent pleas imply the existence of infinite personal dramas and tragedies which, while overwhelming, signal income potential, the opportunity to help others and, in extradiegetic terms, the promise and possibility of additional seasons for the television series. At the same time, however, the incessant demands—which seem to overlap and compound, beyond all control—aptly reflect the recurrent pervasiveness of trauma, the cycle of addiction and, ultimately, the comorbidity of PTSD and substance abuse. Tellingly, for this viewer at least, the prophetic words that inaugurate the opening sequence, though conspicuously absent, continue to reverberate throughout this closing scene; with respect to her clients, Jessica states that once you know something is real you face a choice to either do something about it or continue denying it. We will have to stay tuned to see if Jessica is ready to accept the reality of her alcoholism and "fool herself" into believing she is the hero that we all believe her to be.

NOTES

1. Alcohol/ism is not a new topic to be explored within the superhero genre. Among the more notable examples: Tony Stark/Iron Man "Demon in a Bottle," Logan/Wolverine, Flash Thompson/Venom, Carol Danvers/Ms. Marvel, Mathew Murdock/Daredevil. In *Buzzkill* Ruben acquires his powers from alcohol while Ethan Falls, a retired superhero, grapples with alcoholism in *After the Cape*.

2. Thought suppression involves the conscious act of preventing intrusive thoughts or, put simply, the deliberate effort to *not* think about something. However, the possibilities of rebounding or of hyper-accessibility become potential dangers whereby the opposite occurs and the undesirable thought later recurs even more frequently and with increased intensity.

3. The technique effectively visualizes F. Scott Fitzgerald's well-known and oft-cited quip, "First you take a drink, then the drink takes a drink, then the drink takes you."

4. See Minnick.

5. See NPR's "Not Just a Man's Drink: Ladies Lead the Whiskey Renaissance," and the *Telegraph*'s "Why Is Whisky Still a 'Man's Drink'?"

6. Judith Herman, *Trauma and Recovery: The Aftermath of Violence—from Domestic Abuse to Political Terror* (New York: Basic Books, 2015), 28.

7. Olff, et al., "Gender Differences in Posttraumatic Stress Disorder." *Psychological Bulletin* 133, no. 2 (2007): 183.

8. *Ibid.*, 197.

9. Cathy Caruth, *Unclaimed Experience: Trauma, Narrative, and History* (Baltimore: Johns Hopkins University Press, 1996), 59.

10. This metatextual tableau further showcases architectural features such as doorways and window casings that evoke the panel arrangement or standard layout for a comic book page. The deliberately self-conscious gesture becomes overt as Luke Cage, dressed in an orange t-shirt that unquestionably calls to mind Power Man's superhero costume, lingers tantalizingly, perfectly framed in a backlit window. Similarly, the purple tonality associated with Kilgrave is a direct nod to his comic book identity as the Purple Man.

11. The closing credits do not specifically reference this song. Although I have been unable to identify the original source I find the segment to be reminiscent of Lil Wyte's "Fucked Up," a song that exalts excessive drinking, specifically whiskey and vodka. It is also important to note that hip hop in general, both as a musical genre and as a subculture, has come to signify rebellion as well as glorify masculinity. As such, the brief interlude further underscores Jessica's power as a female superhero and the show's frequent subversion of gender roles and stereotypes.

12. Caruth, "Introduction," *Trauma: Explorations in Memory* (Baltimore: Johns Hopkins University Press, 1995), 153.

13. Caruth, *Unclaimed Experience*, 11.

14. *Ibid.*, 12.

15. In early stages, drinking is no longer a social activity and instead becomes a method of emotional escape, an attempt to control mood and overcome inhibitions, stress, anxiety, depression; as a consequence of increased drinking, tolerance increases and more alcohol must be consumed for the same results—drinking gradually becomes a dependency rather than a matter of choice. With later stages, shame becomes characteristic, often leading to denial and isolation. Avoidance and the deterioration of interpersonal relationships are characteristic of third-stage alcoholic behavior. Final stages involve chronic loss of control not only of consumption but of physical reactions and one's personal and professional lives.

16. This technique is evident not only during the fire escape and workspace flashbacks discussed previously, but also as Jessica walks along a hotel hallway to rescue Hope Shlottman. A shrill fire alarm and bright flashing lights create an environment of panic, chaos and confusion for evacuating guests. Facing additional fears of her own, Jessica remains nearly paralyzed by terrifying, spasmodic images of her tormentor as past and present map onto each spatially (she too was held captive by Kilgrave in five star hotels) as well as temporally.

17. Hope's decision to kill herself remains highly complex and can be interpreted in multiple ways, including as an act of self-sacrifice, a form of escapism, a way to end unbearable and never-ending suffering, and a method to regain power and control.

BIBLIOGRAPHY

Abad-Santos, Alex. "Marvel's Jessica Jones is more about addiction and relapse than it is about superheroes." November 24, 2015. http://www.vox.com/2015/11/24/9791206/jessica-jones-addiction.

Aubrey, Allison. "Not Just a Man's Drink: Ladies Lead the Whiskey Renaissance." NPR. December 29, 2014. http://www.npr.org/sections/thesalt/2014/12/29/371652827/ladies-lead-whiskey-renaissance-as-distillers-and-new-tipplers.

Barnett, Emma. "Why is Whisky Still a 'Man's Drink'?" *The Telegraph*. October 11, 2013. http://www.telegraph.co.uk/women/womens-life/10372412/Why-is-whisky-still-a-mans-drink.html.

Canal, Emily. "Forbes Calculated How Much Jessica Jones Spends on Booze." November 25, 2015. http://www.forbes.com/sites/emilycanal/2015/11/25/netflix-jessica-jones-whiskey-drinking/#14150fa69aef.

Caruth, Cathy. "Introduction." In *Trauma: Explorations in Memory*, edited by Cathy Caruth, 151–157. Baltimore: Johns Hopkins University Press, 1995.

_____. *Unclaimed Experience: Trauma, Narrative, and History*. Baltimore: Johns Hopkins University Press, 1996.

Dalton, Daniel. "Here is Everything Jessica Jones Drinks in 'Jessica Jones.'" Buzzfeed. November 26, 2015. http://www.buzzfeed.com/danieldalton/is-it-still-ladies-night.

Herman, Judith Lewis. *Trauma and Recovery: The Aftermath of Violence, from Domestic Abuse to Political Terror*. New York: Basic Books, 2015.
Jessica Jones. Created by Melissa Rosenberg. Tall Girls Productions, 2015. https://www.netflix.com/browse?jbv=80002311&jbp=1&jbr=1.
Minnick, Fred. *Whiskey Women: The Untold Story of How Women Saved Bourbon, Scotch, and Irish Whiskey*. Dulles, Virginia: Potomac Books, 2013.
Olff, Miranda, Willie Langeland, Nel Draijer, Berthold P. R. Gersons, and Cooper, Harris. "Gender Differences in Posttraumatic Stress Disorder." *Psychological Bulletin* 133, no. 2 (2007): 183–204.
Whitehead, Anne. *Trauma Fiction*. Edinburgh: Edinburgh University Press, 2004.

Jessica Jones, Women and Alcohol Use Disorders

SHARON PACKER

What do *Jessica Jones* the superhero and Virginia Slims the cigarette have in common? More than it seems, on the surface.

"You've come a long way, baby," or so said the Virginia Slims cigarette ads from the 1960s. Phillip Morris launched this wildly successful campaign in 1968, if one uses financial success as a definition of "success." In that same year, the historic women's liberation conference convened in Illinois; second wave feminist activists protested the Miss America pageant in Atlantic City; influential local feminist publications emerged, including Chicago's *Voice of the Women's Liberation Movement* newsletter and the New York Radical Women's *Notes from the First Year*. *Ms.* magazine, the well-known glossy national magazine, would have to wait until 1972.

The Virginia Slims brand capitalized on the cache of the feminist movement and marketed slender "feminine" cigarettes to newly "liberated" women. The same manufacturer—Phillip Morris—pitched the Marlboro brand to men, and introduced the iconic macho "Marlboro Man" in 1954. Sadly, the best-known Marlboro man, the one in the cowboy hat silhouetted against the sunset, developed lung cancer, but became an ardent anti-smoking advocate before he expired. The Virginia Slims brand hinted at "equal opportunities" for women, and implied that it could level the gender-segregated tobacco playing fields. Virginia Slims promised women opportunities to smoke as many cigarettes as men, without mirroring the Marlboro Man image.

The upshot? Phillip Morris' marketing campaign succeeded in more ways than one. It sold women on smoking. It also sold women opportunities to "share" the risks of nicotine and cotinine exposure that were previously the province of males. The comparatively innocuous Victorian era "snuff," used to ward off "vapours" and other enigmatic female maladies, was long gone.

121

In response to these Virginia Slims ads (and accompanying social changes), lung cancer rates among women soared over the decades that followed. Smoking rates among women had already inched upward in the 1950s, shortly after World War II, but the appeal of Virginia Slims imagery and slogans merged "feminine" and "feminist" and pushed smoking rates and cigarette purchases far forward. These newly "won" opportunities to partake of this carcinogen carried other consequences. Rates of COPD (chronic obstructive pulmonary disease) among women skyrocketed as well. COPD— also known as "emphysema"—kills slowly, and painfully, whereas lung cancer claims lives quickly. Death follows in 18 months after diagnosis, on average.

Over time, the dire health consequences of this ad campaign garnered as much press as the cigarettes themselves. The ad campaigns became the subjects of study for innumerable academic articles. The government-sponsored American Cancer Institute and Center for Disease Control (CDC) posted statistics for professionals and the public. As clever advertisers expanded market share, they enriched the tobacco industry overall and Philip Morris in particular, but women lost lives to cancer and COPD, as well as cardiovascular disease, which is also increased by tobacco usage.

The American Cancer Society (ACS) reports that the "risk of lung cancer among women increased during the last 50 years for women smokers" because "women began to smoke more like men, by starting younger and smoking more cigarettes per day."[1] The ACS website notes that the "full effects of smoking do not become apparent for 50 years"—and so there was a lag in observing the effects of increased smoking in women. It cites a study published in *New England Journal of Medicine* on January 24, 2013.[2] In contrast to men, whose risks of dying from lung cancer peaked in the 1980s and have since stabilized as the overall smoking rates dropped in the U.S., female deaths from lung cancer continue to rise as of 2013.[3] Those deaths reflect women's increased likelihood of starting to smoke since the 1970s, and also the fact that women have harder times quitting smoking than men do after starting, and so they have more cumulative years of exposure to nicotine and its byproducts after they start.[4]

Let us see how these seemingly unrelated factoids relate to *Jessica Jones,* superhero and subject of a highly successful Netflix series of 2015.[5] We have 50 years of observation and research about tobacco use, health trends, and women, but we don't have statistics related to a newly conceived TV series about a hard-drinking (and loose-loving) female private eye. The CDC has hard data to show that advertising alcohol to teens in particular is especially effective in inducing them to drink. In contrast, according to relatively recent Cochrane Reviews, the jury is still out with respect to the benefits—or risks— of restricting alcohol advertising overall.

In many ways, *Jessica Jones* serves as a de facto ad campaign for several brands of alcohol, since dozens of labels are prominently displayed on screen as she downs bottle after bottle. We can speculate about the potential consequences of Jessica Jones' popularity and extrapolate about the potential influence that her personal habits may have on her many fans, with the caveat that this is still only speculation and extrapolation. However, we have many hard medical facts on alcohol, women, and fetuses on hand. Let us discuss the possibilities below.

Jessica Jones's first season on the streaming service Netflix earned rave reviews—and a return season.[6] Even Forbes Magazine sang the praises of *Jessica Jones*. Forbes contributor Mark Hughes wrote: "Review: *Jessica Jones Is the Best Show on TV*" (November 21, 2015).[7] A mere thirteen episodes made their mark on spectators and on the truly super-powered suits behind the scenes, for it is they who ultimately act as judge and jury and decide a show's fate for the future.

In response to this positive reception, Jessica will reappear and take more bows. In 2017, she shared the small screen with Luke Cage, Daredevil, and Iron Fist in *The Defenders*. To accommodate *The Defenders* series as well as previously scheduled shows about other Marvel characters, *Jessica Jones* must wait until 2018 for a solo show encore. Some speculate that the well-received small screen shows will give way to a feature length film. Either way, the celluloid future of this otherwise minor comic book superhero looks bright, even if her hypothetical health concerns could be compromised, as we will discuss at length later.

The super-powered private eye had attracted hard-core comics fans, via the 28 issues of *Alias* (2001–2004). Yet it was the Netflix series that introduced the comic book character to a wider audience. Thanks to Netflix, spectators see images of a hard-drinking, hard-boiled female detective who downs bottles of hard alcohol without apparent consequences. Sometimes she consumes two bottles, not just one. Her superpowers supposedly permit her to drink larger quantities of inebriating liquids than most. She never develops alcohol poisoning, and never needs emergency room care, as many drinking equivalent amounts might. She does not even have motor vehicle accidents—or get killed by oncoming cars, which is probable, since 70 percent of pedestrian fatalities are legally intoxicated at the time of their fatal accident, with blood alcohol levels above the legal limits.

Apart from her remarkable alcohol tolerance, the extent of Jessica's superpowers remains unknown. She can lift an automobile effortlessly and her punches are strong enough to stop a healthy heart from beating (as happened when she hit Luke Cage's fiancée, Reva). Jessica has increased resistance to physical injury, like Wolverine. She can fly, or at least control her falling, should she so choose, although she usually chooses not to. It is unclear if she is bulletproof, like Superman. She often attempts Good Samaritan–like savior acts, similar to Superman or Luke Cage, even though she is a private eye for hire and so more similar in spirit to Luke Cage, Hero for Hire, and her future lover. Occasionally, she succeeds as a Good Samaritan, as occurred when she intervened to stop her neighbor's death by hanging. At other times, she arrives too late, in spite of her best efforts. Her earliest case in the series, concerning a missing NYU student, ended badly, with the entranced girl dying a grisly death from self-inflicted wounds while in prison. Jessica succeeds in identifying the source of the student's strange behavior—not surprisingly, it was Kilgrave, Jessica's mind-controlling nemesis—but she fails in preventing the inevitable and cannot override Kilgrave, at least not in the beginning. Jessica's friends, adoptive family, neighbors, and colleagues comment on her drinking problem, but she is indifferent to their insults.

Some Internet fans catalogue her "alcoholic accomplishments" online, as if they were posting trophies on a wall. One website alone shows 28 screen shots of different alcoholic beverages aired in the first season alone. The liquor labels are easily identifiable. Some names are purely fictional, and one is an homage to Tony Stark's iconic blurry-eyed image behind a bottle. Enough liquor labels are real enough to constitute "product placement" and presumably add valuable advertising revenue—as well as subliminal (or not so subliminal) signals to spectators of all ages. According to the CDC, younger audiences are especially susceptible to alcohol advertising and TV superheroes attract teens, who are less likely to be hard-core comic book readers than their older counterparts.[8]

Jessica meets potential clients, tails their targets, lives in a tawdry apartment and maintains her own office. She converses with neighbors and shows concern about their welfare. She chastises a drug-using neighbor and encourages his recovery—while she drinks. She also meets strangers in bars and beds them of her own volition. Jessica needs no coercion to cavort with men she just met—with the notable exception of Kilgrave, the show's supervillain, accused of raping Jessica after immobilizing her via his mind control powers. Yet she never suffers the sexual assaults that abound among female binge drinkers in real life (who are not super-powered).[9] Since she is super-powered, she does not sprain ankles when tripping down stairs, and suffers no bruises when falling down drunk.

She even encounters Luke Cage, a "Hero for Hire" and star of his own Netflix show. Cage had been a 70s-era comic book icon and an outgrowth of the Blaxploitation trend in both cinema and on television. He remains the most popular Black superhero to date, even though he no longer sports his signifying Afro hairdo and in-your-face yellow bandana.

Cage is an ex-con who was convicted of crimes he did not commit (according to the comics' originals). He was emblematic of the Black Power movement of his era, and a reminder of Attica prison riots in upstate New York. His character recollects a variety of unethical medical experiments—but the *Jessica Jones* TV show provides only a silhouette, not a full portrait. A very tall and heavily-muscled black man, Cage sprang himself free from prison (known as "The Cage") after he acquires superpowers from a medical experiment gone awry. Promised early parole for his efforts, Cage volunteered for a study of a vaccine intended to offer immunity to all illness. When a vindictive prison guard deliberately overdosed him with chemicals, Cage emerged with rock-hard skin and super-strength. His new-found power permits him to break through cement prison walls, and to surmount metaphorical social barriers in the outside world.

In *Jessica Jones*, Jessica snoops on Luke while working as a private eye. She has been hired to gather evidence about Luke's dalliance with a married woman. To prove infidelity to the woman's husband, she photographs Cage and his lover. Afterwards, she joins Cage at the bar that he both tends and owns. He is a man who minds his own business. He keeps a low-profile and avoids unwanted attention of authorities. He does not welcome Jessica's uninvited visits, although he does not rebuff her sexual advances—until he learns that Jessica dealt a lethal blow to his beloved. He is unmoved after she explains that she acted under the influence of the mind-controlling Kilgrave, without intent to kill Cage's fiancée.

Jessica is never sexually or even emotionally exploited by Luke Cage, although she repeatedly references a previous rape, not by Cage but by Kilgrave. Kilgrave uses mind control to make people do his bidding and, via telekinesis, he moves whole bodies or body parts with his mind. In the comic book version, Jessica becomes pregnant with Cage's child, unintentionally, for she is still paired with Ant-Man during the time of her dalliance with Cage. That detail did not surface on Marvel's TV show, but it is surely salient to our review of alcohol's effects on women and on fetal alcohol syndrome and fetal alcohol spectrum disorder.

Neither Jessica nor any of the many other characters she encounters connect her problem drinking to PTSD (post-traumatic stress disorder) and flashbacks related to Kilgrave's assault—although substance abuse subsequent to sexual trauma is prevalent in real life. No one links her excessive alcohol consumption to early life losses, which predispose to life-long depression. Depression, in turn, increases risks for alcohol use disorders.

Yet we know that Jessica was orphaned at a young age when her family was en route to a Disney World vacation. He father was driving but became distracted by back seat fighting between Jessica and her brother. He lost control of the car, careened into an army transport, presumably loaded with radioactive material. Jessica spent months in a coma, unaware that her mother, father and brother had been killed in the car accident. Jessica was also unaware of her exposure to radioactive waste or its alleged ability to confer super-powers. However, the well-schooled spectator and superhero fan has encountered similar scenarios, such as with the characters of Spider-Man, Daredevil, the Hulk, and the Fantastic Four and is therefore able to suspend disbelief while watching or reading *Jessica Jones* and witnessing Jessica's superpowers emerge months after the accident.[10]

After Jessica regains consciousness, she is adopted by the Walker family. Spectators have access to this backstory and are thereby empowered to make inferences about Jessica's early life losses and her alcohol "problem"—should they know about correlations between early deaths of parents, later life depression, and depression's link to excess alcohol use. These issues need not concern Jessica, and they do not, because Jessica does not view her excessive consumption as a "problem," not in the first season. Her friends and associates often express different opinions, and make subtle, sometimes derisive, comments about her drinking.

Medical and Psychiatric Consequences of Women's Alcohol Use on Women

In spite of all the allusions to alcohol, and the online homages to Jessica Jones, there is no mention of the potential medical consequences of excessive alcohol use in women. Perhaps that omission reflects society's ignorance about gender-specific consequences of alcohol—apart from alcohol's teratogenic effects and advisories against alcohol use by pregnant women. Or perhaps it would interfere with the story line, or lessen the potential profitability of product placement.

Yet alcohol carries many medical as well as psychiatric side effects. Excess alcohol use predisposes users to depression and makes persons with bipolar disorder cycle more frequently. Excess drinking results in temporary memory loss (known as "blackouts") as well as shrinkage of the brain. Research suggests that women are more vulnerable than men to the brain damaging effects of alcohol use, and the damage tends to appear after shorter periods of excessive drinking for women than for men. Women get drunk faster than men (not having Jessica's superpowers). They develop neurotoxic symptoms after one-third less alcohol consumption than men do, meaning that a woman who consumes two drinks has as much memory loss or cognitive impairment as a man who consumes three drinks, and so on.

Neurotoxicity is an important issue in alcohol use disorders. Alcohol can cause several types of neuropathic syndromes. Alcoholic neuropathy occurs in some persons, and results in nerve pain or palsies. Wernicke's encephalopathy or Korsakoff psychosis are the most extreme consequences, and include ocular nerve paralysis, psychosis, and dementia. Full-blown Wernicke-Korsakoff Syndrome (WKS) is less common today, and it typically occurs in conjunction with vitamin deficiencies that coexist with extreme alcohol use and chronic intoxication, with consequent neglect of personal care and nutrition. Moreover, Wernicke Syndrome can exist without the Korsakoff component.

Other less common alcohol-related neurological syndromes exist, including central pontine myelinolysis, and Marchiafava-Bignami disease, which affects circumscribed parts of the brain. "Confabulation" can occur in advanced alcohol use disorders. In "confabulation," memory-impaired persons respond to prompts about past events by embellishing life experiences that they never experienced in the first place. Their "tall tales" can appear very similar to the deceptive behavior of inveterate liars or con artists, although their intent is not to deceive. Alcoholic hallucinosis is also dramatic in its own right, in that it often includes visions of wild animals or other horrific apparitions (instead of the pleasant "pink elephants" that were once associated with alcohol withdrawal, at least in the eyes of the public imagination). Seizures and visions can develop during the delirium tremens (DTs) of alcohol withdrawal. All in all, descriptions of neurological consequences of alcohol use disorders occupy many pages, if not full chapters, in neurology texts and are by no means limited to pure psychiatric problems.

Were that not enough, it should be noted that women develop cirrhosis twice as often as their male counterparts who drink the same amounts of alcohol for the same periods of time. Women are also at greater risk for potentially deadly alcohol-related cardiomyopathy than men, and so heart muscles of females who consume excessive alcohol give way much sooner than male drinkers' hearts—even when those women drink less than their male counterparts. Premature cardiovascular disease—such as heart attacks and strokes—are aided and abetted by alcohol.

Breast cancer is promoted by alcohol, which is a realistic concern for many women, considering that 11 percent of all American women develop breast cancer at some time in their lifetimes.[11] The risk of breast cancer increases as alcohol use increases. Breast cancer is sometimes treatable but is often deadly, as well as disfiguring. Treatments themselves are typically uncomfortable, at the very least, if not also excruciating.

Several other alcohol-potentiated cancers, such as liver cancer, lung cancer, esophageal cancer, colon cancer, and various oral-facial cancers, affect in women as well as men.

All these somatic consequences occur, in addition to increased rates of depression—and of treatment-resistant depression. Persons with alcohol use disorders face significantly greater risk of suicide overall, even when not intoxicated—but intoxication increases the odds of completed suicide. Sexual assault, such as "date rape," is much more prevalent in binge drinking college women. In summary, the potential medical consequences of alcohol use disorders should not be underplayed and exist apart from the more obvious psychiatric consequences—such as depression, disinhibition, dementia, and date rape.

Women who watch the *Jessica Jones* series and regard the risk-taking, wise-cracking Jessica as a role model run the risk of mirroring this alcohol-related behavior. Persons who are already in vulnerable psychological states may be more prone to mimicking idols in the media. Unlike cigarette wrappers that carry disclaimers about lung cancer, or even restaurants that post warnings about drinking during pregnancy, this series offers no warnings about potentially grave consequences that accompany excessive alcohol use. It potentially encourages alcohol use.

Alcohol's Role in Fetal Alcohol Syndrome and Spectrum Disorders

In contrast to the lesser-known health consequences of alcohol on women, the potential impact of alcohol on the developing fetuses is well-documented. Fetal alcohol syndrome or FAS did not enter the medical nomenclature until 1973, when the prestigious British publication, *The Lancet,* published groundbreaking research about distinctive facial features as well as neurodevelopmental delays observed in children exposed to alcohol in utero. Many years passed before scientists recognized that "fetal alcohol syndrome" exists on a continuum, and that "fetal alcohol spectrum disorder" (FASD) is equally important and even more prevalent, even though its signs and symptoms are not as extreme as full-blown FAS and even though distinguishing facial features are subtler. These unfortunate infants show developmental delays, behavioral problems, cognitive impairment, plus an array of other medical complications that may appear to be unrelated. Besides upping the chances for FAS or FASD, drinking while pregnant increases the odds for miscarriage, stillbirth, prematurity, and sudden infant death syndrome (SIDS).[12] Premature birth is not simply a chronological inconvenience—prematurity carries many medical and neuropsychiatric risks, including lower average IQ and more learning problems later in life.

More recent data from 2015–2016 prompted the American Academy of Pediatrics to add more categories of alcohol-related pediatric problems, including "Alcohol-Related Birth Defects" (ARBD), which may affect the heart, kidneys, bones and/or spine, hearing, and vision. "Alcohol-Related Neurodevelopmental Disorder (ARND)" refers to persons who do not have the distinctive facial features or growth problems of FAS or FASD, but who may have intellectual disabilities, behavior or learning problems, and/or nerve or brain abnormalities. "Partial Fetal Alcohol Syndrome (pFAS)" is yet another recently-recognized category. This term is used to describe persons who do not meet full criteria for FAS but who have a history of prenatal alcohol exposure and some—but not all—of the facial abnormalities, as well as growth problems or CNS abnormalities.[13]

Out of concern for future victims of FAS and FASD, the CDC recommends complete abstinence from alcohol for women of childbearing age who do not use contraception, for two reasons: one, because half of all pregnancies are unplanned, and secondly, because four to six weeks typically pass before confirmation—or even suspicion—of pregnancy. Alcohol exposure during that critical developmental time period can result in a lifetime of consequences—for the fetus. For females who become pregnant under 18 years of age, 75 percent do not plan their pregnancy, and so are even less capable of protecting fetuses from such toxins. As it stands, CDC data shows that 10 percent of women overall drink while pregnant.[14]

The CDC recommendations spurred public and occasional professional protests, with some obstetricians on Sermo.com (a confidential, physician-only discussion board) charging that this approach treats all women as "baby factories," without regard to individual plans for pregnancy and inferring that "every woman" is one of the 50 percent of women who do not plan their pregnancies.[15] Some patently irresponsible articles appeared in the general press. In October 2014, *Cosmopolitan* magazine published an article by Michele Ruiz, entitled "Why I Drank When I was Pregnant."[16] Ruiz argues that better-educated, slightly older (over 30 years old) middle class women are more likely to drink when pregnant than their less-educated and less-affluent counterparts. The article avers that doctors "trust" these better-educated women to set limits better and to avoid bingeing. Though a personal communication, the author of this article learned that the *Cosmopolitan* article author is a *Jones* fan. This author [SP] was relieved to learn that this *Cosmopolitan* article attracted widespread public condemnation in various online forums and that it was not embraced as "received wisdom."

We can contrast the *Jessica Jones* series to *Iron Man* and Tony Stark's anti-alcohol, pro-recovery approach. Tony Stark acknowledges his struggles with alcohol both in the comics and the films. The movies make repeated allusions to 12-step programs and practices. Stark's Alcoholics Anonymous (AA) allegiance is an inseparable part of his persona, just as his suit is inseparable from his self. A comic book cover of his sitting behind a bottle, his eyes bloodshot, has become iconic.

We can also compare *Jessica Jones* to another television series that aired around the same time that she premiered. In *Arrow* (based on DC Comics' *Green Arrow* series), a female lead, Laurel Lance, nearly ruins her legal career and estranges family and friends because of her slowly-evolving alcohol over-use. Laurel's covert career as Black Canary is not adversely effected by alco-hol—although Laurel's lifespan is cut short because of her Black Canary activities.

In contrast to *Jessica Jones*, who perseveres in her drinking career and seemingly succeeds, *Arrow*'s Laurel begrudgingly seeks treatment. During the course of the show, Laurel progresses from law student to attorney to Assistant District Attorney. After lashing out and losing her job, she attends meetings, struggles to stay sober, and accepts the aid of her father, a police detective who himself started out with a drinking problem but eventually found his way to recovery, via AA. We witness several scenes of both District Attorney Laurel Lance and her father, Detective Lance, sitting in circles and speaking at AA meetings. Their gradual transformations, to problem drinkers and to sobriety advocates, make this more credible.[17] There is no dashing into phone booths for a quick change of costume and a quick change of heart.

In *Arrow*, the female lead's fall and redemption occur only within the second season. It is unknown what lies ahead in the second season of the already successful *Jessica Jones*, but it causes concern that some spectators may base their own behaviors on this season. Considering that comics writers typically respond to fans' reactions, and adapt their plot lines and character traits and even costumes to popular demand, there is still a chance that public health advocates may press their opinions to modify Jessica's drinking habits—without adversely impacting her superpowers. Hopefully, this will occur before she conceives and carries Luke Cage's baby. But who knows: superhero stories are not sermons or Sunday school stories.

Notes

1. www.cancer.org. "Risk of Lung Cancer Death During Last 50 Years for Women Smokers," accessed online, November 6, 2016. Note that medical statistics are generally expressed in relative, rather than absolute, numbers. These numbers are not "adjusted" for confounding variables, such as the likelihood that smokers are more likely to drink alcohol, which also increase cancer risks. Smokers of any gender have a 3-fold greater risk for *any* cancer.

2. M.J. Thun, B.D. Carter, D. Feskanich, et al., "50-Year trends in smoking-related mortality in the United States," *New England Journal of Medicine* 2013: 368, accessed online November 6, 2016.

3. www.cancer.org. "Risk of Lung Cancer Death During Last 50 Years for Women Smokers," accessed online, November 6, 2016.

4. Thun. Thun notes that other factors have confounded risks from smoking in the last 20 years. Notably, public health campaigns against smoking were less effective among persons of lower SES (socioeconomic status), which affects or reflects other behaviors. In other words, more educated and affluent persons became less likely to smoke, while smoking rates remained unchanged in persons of lower socioeconomic status. Those persons are statistically less likely to practice preventive health measures or get regular physical exams or avoid other risky behaviors, and are more likely to live in environments that may expose them to other carcinogens

5. Keith Nelson, Jr., "Jessica Jones Is Four Times More Popular on Twitter Than The Man in the Castle," November 24, 2015, http://www.digitaltrends.com, accessed online August 15, 2015.

6. http://www.imdb.com, accessed online August 15, 2015.

7. Mark Hughes, "Review: *Jessica Jones is the Best Show on TV*," www.forbes.com, November 21, 2015, accessed online August 15, 2016.

8. Inconsistent local bans on hard liquor television advertising evolved in response to concerns about the influence of alcohol ads on underage drinking, but a relatively recent (2014) Cochrane Review finds inconclusive evidence and recommends completion of more reliable research before recommending—or refuting—alcohol advertising restrictions. Cochrane Reviews are regarded as the "Gold Standard" in medical literature, for each review scrutinizes previously published conclusions for accuracy and consistency and other relevant methodological data. See N. Siegfried, D.C. Plenaar, J.E. Ataguba J. Volmink, T. Kredo, M. Jere, C.D. Parry, "Restricting or banning alcohol advertising to reduce alcohol consumption in adults and adolescents," Cochrane Database of Systematic Reviews 2014, November 4, 2014 (11), accessed online August 7, 2016.

9. Department of Health and Human Services. Tenth Special Report to the U.S. Congress on Alcohol and Health [PDF-264KB]. Bethesda, MD: National Institutes on Alcohol Abuse and Alcoholism; June 2000; M. Mohler-Kuo, G.W. Dowdall, M. Koss, H. Wechsler, "Correlates of rape while intoxicated in a national sample of college women," *Journal of Studies on Alcohol* 65:1 (2004): 37–45; A. Abbey A. "Alcohol-related sexual assault: A common problem among college students," *J Stud Alcohol Suppl* 14 (2002): 118–128.

10. Marvel.com, http://marvel.com/universe/Jones,_Jessica#ixzz4Emsg7d6J, accessed online November 6, 2016.

11. S.A. Smith-Warner, et al., "Alcohol and breast cancer in women: A pooled analysis of cohort studies," *JAMA* 279: 7 (1998): 535–540.

12. S.C. Wilsnack, A.D. Klassen, R.W. Wilsnack, "Drinking and reproductive dysfunction among women in a 1981 national survey," *Alcohol Clin Exp Res* 8:5 (1984): 451–458.

13. http://www.healthychildren.org, accessed November 6, 2016. Healthy children.org is powered by the American Academy of Pediatrics but is geared toward the general public, accessed online November 6, 2016.

14. http://www.cdc.gov/vitalsigns/fasd; http://www.cdc.gov/alcohol/fact-sheets/womens-health.htm; http://www.cdc.gov/vitalsigns/bingedrinkingfemale/index.; http://www.cdc.gov/vitalsigns/alcohol-poisoning-deaths/index.html; http://www.cdc.gov/alcohol/fact-sheets/womens-health.htm, accessed online August 7, 2016.

15. http://www.sermo.com, accessed November 6, 2016.

16. Michele Ruiz, "Why I Drank When I was Pregnant," *Cosmopolitan* October, 2014, accessed online, November 6, 2016.

17. Another contemporary television series, *Person of Interest*, depicts the protagonist's descent into alcoholism and homelessness, his near-miraculous recovery after he regains his sense of purpose through the help of his billionaire benefactor. Ex-CIA agent and trained murderer John Reese later regresses and slides back into alcohol abuse after the murder of his comrade-in-arms and eventual love object, Detective Jose Carter. Going full circle, the same detective whom Reese once rescued from alcoholism and corruption goads Reese into returning to the world and abandoning his days at the bar. These trends counter the trend evinced in *Mad Men* and *Jessica Jones*.

BIBLIOGRAPHY

Abbey, Antonia. "Alcohol-related sexual assault: A common problem among college students." *Journal of Studies of Alcohol and Drugs Supplement* 14 (2002): 118–128.
American Academy of Pediatrics. http://www.healthychildren.org. Accessed November 6, 2016.
Bendis, Brian Michael. *Alias* (comics). Marvel, 2001–2004.
CDC, "alcohol/fact-sheets." http://www.cdc.gov/alcohol/fact-sheets/womens-health.htm.
CDC, "alcohol-poisoning-deaths." http://www.cdc.gov/vitalsigns/alcohol-poisoning-deaths/index.html.
CDC, "binge-drinkingfemale." http://www.cdc.gov/vitalsigns/bingedrinkingfemale/index.
CDC, "Fetal Alcohol Spectrum Disorder." http://www.cdc.gov/vitalsigns/fasd.

CDC, "womens-health." http://www.cdc.gov/alcohol/fact-sheets/womens-health.htm, accessed online August 7, 2016.

Department of Health and Human Services. Tenth Special Report to the U.S. Congress on Alcohol and Health [PDF-264KB]. Bethesda, MD: National Institutes on Alcohol Abuse and Alcoholism; June 2000; accessed online August 7, 2016.

Hughes, Mark. "Review: *Jessica Jones* is the Best Show on TV." www.Forbes.com. November 21, 2015, accessed online August 15, 2016.

Jones, Kenneth L., and David W. Smith. "Recognition of Fetal Alcohol Syndrome in Early Infancy." *The Lancet* 7836 (1973): 999–1001. November 3, 1973, Vol. 302, accessed online November 6, 2016.

Marvel.com. *Jessica Jones.* http://marvel.com/universe/Jones,_Jessica#ixzz4Emsg7d6J, accessed online, November 6, 2016.

Mohler-Kuo, M., Dowdall, G.W., Koss, M., Wechsler, H. "Correlates of rape while intoxicated in a national sample of college women." *Journal of Studies on Alcohol and Drugs* 65: 1 (2004): 37–45.

Nelson, Keith, Jr. "Jessica Jones is Four Times More Popular on Twitter than The Man in the Castle." November 24, 2015. http://www.digitaltrends.com, accessed online August 15, 2015.

Packer, Sharon. *Superheroes and Superegos: The Minds Behind the Masks.* Westport, CT: Praeger/ ABC-Clio, 2010.

Packer, Sharon. "Comics & Medicine: A Conference ... or a Movement?" *Psychiatric Times*, August 2014. http://www.psychiatrictimes.com/cultural-psychiatry/comics-and-medicine-conference%E2%80%A6or-movement. August 24, 2014.

Packer, Sharon. "*Luke Cage* and Race-Based Unethical Medical Experiments." *History of Medicine Online*, Priory Medical Journals. December 2014.

Packer, Sharon. "*Luke Cage* and Race-Based Unethical Medical Experiments." Paper presented at the annual Graphic Medicine Conference, sponsored by Johns Hopkins, Baltimore, June 23–25, 2014.

Ruiz, Michele. "Why I Drank When I was Pregnant." *Cosmopolitan*, October 2014, accessed online, November 6, 2016.

Siegfried, N., Plenaar, D.C., Ataguba, J.E., Volmink, J., Kredo, T., Jere, M., Parry, C.D. "Restricting or banning alcohol advertising to reduce alcohol consumption in adults and adolescents." *Cochrane Database of Systematic Reviews*, November 4, 2014 (11), accessed online August 7, 2016.

Smith-Warner, S.A., et al. "Alcohol and breast cancer in women: A pooled analysis of cohort studies." *JAMA* 279: 7 (1998): 535–540.

Thun, M.J., B.D. Carter, D. Feskanich et al. "50-Year Trends in Smoking-Related Mortality in the United States," *New England Journal of Medicine* 368 (2013): 351–364. January 24, 2013, accessed online November 6, 2016.

Wilsnack, S.C., Klassen, A.D., Wilsnack, R.W. "Drinking and reproductive dysfunction among women in a 1981 national survey," *Alcoholism: Clinical and Experimental Research* 8: 5 (1984): 451–458.

Jessica Jones's Feminism
AKA Alias Gets a Fixed-It[1]
MELISSA C. JOHNSON

Jessica Jones has been hailed as a feminist television series because the main character, Jessica Jones, is a woman with superpowers who doesn't dress in a ridiculous leotard and has rejected super heroism and stereotypical gender expectations to become a private investigator who lives and works alone. Jessica drinks hard, curses, has sex on her own terms, and is sardonic, prickly, and hard-boiled in the manner of Humphrey Bogart in *The Big Sleep*. She wears ill-fitting and none-too-clean jeans, a tank top, combat boots, and a black leather jacket. Her clothing choices are practical and comfortable, and she is completely unconcerned with her appearance or the approval of others. She does most of her detective work with a camera, shoe leather, and the Internet, but solves her cases or takes out the bad guys with her exceptional speed and strength when necessary. Jessica has meaningful dialogue and relationships with other women as well as non-romantic relationships with men—passing the Bechdel test. Her flaws also emphatically demonstrate that she is no Mary Sue.[2]

Many of these elements echo the characterization of Jones in the *Alias* series of comics for mature readers by her creators Brian Michael Bendis and Michael Gaydos, but there are significant departures in the television adaptation of the comic. In part, these departures are the result of the change in medium and the constraints put upon the television series by various licensing agreements, but they are also a corrective to the overtones of sexism in the comics and collectively reflect showrunner Melissa Rosenberg's attempt to use Jones's story as a vehicle for depicting the effects of sexism, rape culture, and rape on women's lives and ambitions.

In both the *Alias* comics and the television series, Jones suffers emotional trauma and abandons her ambition to be a superhero after being psychologically enslaved for eight months by the Purple Man (comics) or Kilgrave (television show),[3] a mind-controlling villain whom she ultimately defeats in both story lines. In both genres, Kilgrave exploits Jones sexually, humiliates her, and forces her to do his dirty work while she is under his control, but the television series specifically describes what he has done as serial rape and characterizes Jones as a rape survivor suffering from post-traumatic stress disorder (PTSD). This shift has been described by both Rosenberg and Bendis as a conscious departure from the original comic source material.[4] Melissa Rosenberg describes the shift not only as result of her efforts to adapt the superhero-dominated world of the comic to the world of the Marvel Cinematic Universe which is more realistic and has a more "grounded tone," but also as springing from her desire to explore the story of "a survivor and her healing, to the degree that she does"[5] and her resolve to avoid "doing the honeypot"—a common television trope in which a female detective vamps it up to catch a suspect—and to avoid depicting rape from a male point of view.[6] What neither explicitly says is that Bendis and Gaydos have done the honeypot with Jessica Jones and—despite Bendis' protestations to the contrary—have also depicted rape from a male point of view by both underplaying its existence and significance, and by refusing to call it rape.

In the comics, Jones's captivity under Killgrave's power does not explicitly or technically include rape, but does include being forced to watch Killgrave sexually exploit others and being forced to beg him to have sex with her. Certainly, it might be argued that this is metaphorical rape or tantamount to rape, but to counter that interpretation, Bendis has the Jessica Jones character emphatically make the distinction between what she has experienced and rape in response to the questions asked by both of her romantic partners. In Volume 3, Issue 18, when Scott Lang asks if Jones was raped when they are discussing her recent experience of having Madame Web read her mind, she becomes angry and says, "Such a guy thing to say!! A girl has a secret in her past—she must have been raped!!" When she reveals her past with Killgrave to Luke Cage in Volume 4, Issue 25, he is more gentle in his questioning, never saying the word rape, and she gives him the full details of her experience with Killgrave, Interestingly, she also doesn't describe Killgrave's treatment of her or his rape of "college girls he would pull off the street" as rape either, simply saying, "he fucking made me stand there and watch him fuck other girls."

This is one of the places where Bendis and Gaydos, in an attempt to avoid sexism and rape culture, grievously enact it. Bendis has stated that he did not present Killgrave as a rapist or Jessica as a rape survivor because it is not his place as a man to do so and that "there was just a lot of raping going on" in comics at this time "and I thought there was a much more complex and dangerous road to go down that doesn't have that in it, and as a male creator, do that: teach by example."[7] It is unclear what Bendis thinks he is teaching by example in *Alias*, but he appears to be teaching that if comic creators don't use the word rape, it's acceptable to depict rape. Bendis's female character—and by association, her creators—fails to recognize that Killgrave is committing rape when he has sex with college girls he pulls off the street, manipulates them to have sex with each other, and forces Jessica to watch while making her wish she were being forced to have sex with him. In the Netflix series, however, Rosenberg has Jones explicitly confront Killgrave and name what he has done rape in "AKA WWJD," as can be seen in the following exchange:

> **Kilgrave:** We used to do a lot more than just touch hands.
> **Jones:** Yeah. It's called rape.
> **Kilgrave:** What? Which part of staying in five-star hotels, eating in all the best places, doing whatever the hell you wanted, is rape?
> **Jones:** The part where I didn't want to do any of it! Not only did you physically rape me, but you violated every cell in my body and every thought in my goddamn head.
> **Kilgrave:** That's not what I was trying to do.
> **Jones:** It doesn't matter what you were trying to do. You raped me. Again and again and again!

In addition, Rosenberg, gives one of Killgrave's "college girls he has pulled off the street," a name, a family, a history, and a central role in the first season. Hope Shlottman is a young woman abducted by Killgrave, whom Jessica rescues from the same five-star hotel where he used to take her when she is hired by Shlotman's parents to find her. Tragically, Shlottman is still under Killgrave's control and murders her parents when they come to pick her up from Jessica's apartment. Like Jessica, Hope also clearly identifies what Killgrave has done to her as rape in "AKA You're a Winner." When Shlottman is begging Jessica to help her abort the fetus she carries, she says, "Every second it's there, I get raped, again and again." It is hard not to read this as a corrective to the comic.

Even more egregious than failing to name rape for what it is, Bendis and Gaydos visually depict the scene of Killgrave forcing Jessica—while dressed as a pornographic Catholic schoolgirl in a short skirt and unbuttoned blouse—to watch two nude women have sex on a pile of money for the titillation of their largely male audience. I suppose that Bendis could argue that this panel does not depict rape—since Killgrave is fully dressed and not involved in the sex going on. However, Jessica is drawn with pink, spaced-out eyes to indicate that she is under Killgrave's control, and he is shouting at her with his back to the viewer. The effect of this is that Killgrave does not confront or displace the viewer in the scene, allowing the viewer to ogle the nude "college girls" and Jessica, and put himself in Killgrave's place as the one in control of the minds and bodies of all three women. This panel, part of the satiric Jewel comic called *Purple Haze* included in Volume 4, Issue 24, is simply the nadir of the objectification of women in this "satire" of conventional comics.

Different in style and coloration, the comic is created by "Bashful Brian Bendis" and "Magnificent Mike Gaydos Art Boy" and features Jewel/Jessica Jones in a form-fitting costume in stereotypical female comic book poses delivering insipid lines such as "I tell ya thank goodness for flying! It gives me a minute to stop thinking about looking for a job or the fact that I just can't find a boyfriend. What's a girl got to do in this town to find a decent guy?" By presenting this as satire of the type of sexist comic *Alias* attempts to rise above, Bendis and Gaydos may hope to be hailed as progressive and even feminist comic artists. Certainly, *Alias* and *The Pulse* are an improvement on the limited and exploitative portrayal of women in many comics. However, in addition to using satire only to replicate the offenses of the object being satirized, Bendis and Gaydos also sometimes fall into the same patterns they satirize in the "straight" portions of *Alias*.

In *Alias*, Jessica Jones is not only involved in two textbook honeypot scenarios, but she is also depicted as an air-headed boy-crazy teenager and as a paranoid, emotionally erratic, sexually promiscuous, self-loathing, and insecure woman dependent on male approval.

Jessica is involved in two honeypot scenarios in *Alias*. Both occur in Volume 3 when she is trying to track down Mattie Franklin, the third Spider Woman, who has fallen under the sway of a drug dealer named Denny Haynes who has addicted her in order to use her flesh as a drug. In order to infiltrate the club where the drug dealer is partying, Jones has to put on makeup and a skimpy dress, and then she has to submit to an inspection of another woman to determine if she is attractive enough to be introduced to Denny. Even though Jessica thinks, "God forgive me for what I am about to do," the comic devotes most of a page to depicting her in the getup in a sultry pose. Later, when she teams up with Jessica Drew to track down Mattie, both Jessicas flirt with the desk clerk at the hotel where he is staying, pretending to be prostitutes in order to get access to the room. Needless to say, Rosenberg stands behind her resolution and Jessica solves her cases through good detective work, violence, and intimidation—never resorting to the honeypot. In a scene in "AKA Crush Syndrome," Jones actively refuses a mechanic's expectation that she will flirt with him or be nice to him to get information. He calls after her, "Rude girl is lonely girl," and she responds, "Counting on it." As Rosenberg explains in an interview, "she doesn't use her sexuality; she simply has a sexuality to her," and the television series allows her to express that sexuality in refreshingly non-voyeuristic and stereotypical ways, unlike the comic.[8]

In Issue 1, Volume 1 of *Alias*, Jessica gets drunk in Luke Cage's bar and then goes home and has sex with him—just as she does in the first episode of the television series, "AKA Ladies Night." However, the sex they have is very different in the two media. In the comic, the focus is on Jones as a sexual object and Cage is not depicted except in the last panel where his back is to the viewer, thus allowing the viewer to position himself as Cage. Based on her thoughts and her facial expression, Jones doesn't appear to be experiencing much pleasure in this sex act, although she initiated it. Her thoughts also show that she is more concerned with Cage's experience than with her own, and that for her, the sex is more masochistic than satisfying She thinks that Cage will regret having sex with her because she's a friend and also presumably because she's intoxicated. Ultimately, though, she continues because she just wants "to feel something. It doesn't matter what. Pain. Humility. Anger. I just want to feel something different." She also describes what is happening from what she imagines to be Cage's perspective in thought bubbles: "Because he'll also look back and remember this was the one night that I let him do anything he wanted. And even though he'll know it's wrong, he'll smile to himself."

These lines represent sexual intercourse as an interaction in which the woman has the power over what is allowed, but also an interaction in which women are objects which things are done to, rather than mutually involved partners. In subsequent encounters with Cage, Jones is depicted as needy, jealous, and emotionally erratic—regretful about this hook-up and yet tentatively available for another one like it. In Volume 1, Issue 2, Jones visits Cage's apartment in the early morning hours after the murder of the missing woman she is trying to locate, only to find Cage with another woman and unwilling to talk to her. Afterward, she sits on the stairs crying. Recounting these events later to Carol Danvers in Issue 6, she says, "I have done such stupid, stupid things with guys lately. Just a really pathetic mixture of just needy and just—just stupid—like you wouldn't believe."

When she encounters Luke again in Volume 2, Issue 15, she is angry and combative and he takes her to task for not recognizing that she is a consenting adult who initiated sex with him, that they have no commitment to one another, that he has helped her out, and that she is angry at herself rather than him. In essence, he makes her anger and jealousy seem unreasonable and illogical, thereby invalidating them. He also refuses to acknowledge that her drunkenness might have affected her judgment. In the end, she is the one to apologize, and he rewards her by asking her out to dinner, but she turns down him down because she has a date with Scott Lang. In their next encounter in Volume 4, Issue 25, Jessica wakes up in in her underwear in Cage's apartment with no memory of how she got there and immediately checks to see if she has had sex with someone that she didn't know. After "kidding" with her that she has "gang-banged the New Warriors," Cage reveals to her that she has drunkenly crashed through his window, compared him unfavorably to Matt Murdock, and told Luke to go fuck himself. It is at this point that she confides her history with Killgrave to him, and he comforts her and offers to handle Killgrave for her, but she says she has to do it on her own. The dynamic of their relationship throughout the series is that Jessica is unstable, erratic, unreasonable, and often impaired by drinking and Luke comforts her and helps her despite this. As Luke says when they ultimately get together at the end of Volume 4, "You frustrate me. You frustrate the shit out of me. But, no let's not get into that. We both know you're like a bat out of hell around me half the time."

There is only one sex scene between Cage and Jones in the comics, but there are three in the television series and those scenes do not presume a male viewer or objectify Jones. The first is in "AKA Ladies Night" and begins similarly to the one in the comics—in Luke's bar with a drunken Jones. However, the sex between the two is presented as far more mutually pleasurable and Cage as more tender and solicitous out of fear of harming Jones with his super strength. In both this sex scene and the two which follow in "AKA It's Called Whiskey," the camera objectifies Cage far more than Jones, lingering over his body in a way that is more typical of the way female bodies are shot and drawn. In all three scenes, the sex is presented as realistic and mutual, rather than as designed for the pleasure of a viewer, and Jones is, in many ways, the dominant partner. Additionally, rather than seek Cage out, Jones actually tries to keep her distance from him in order to protect him from Kilgrave and from the knowledge that she has killed his wife, Reva Connors. She goes to his apartment at the end of "AKA It's Called Whiskey" and breaks the relationship off, telling him, "I can't come in. Ever. This isn't right." When he responds, "Feels right to me," she says, "I have business. Unfinished. And you've been through too much for me to…." Although they briefly reunite in "AKA You're a Winner," it is Cage who pursues Jones. She is far more focused on freeing Hope, protecting Trish, and making amends for her murder of Reva than she is on having a romantic relationship with Cage.

In the comic, Jones is engaged in her work, but is also obsessed with romantic relationships, which she always seems to miscalculate or mishandle because she is so angry and erratic as a result of the traumas she has experienced. In the Volume 4, Issue 22, flashback to her origin story, we meet a teenaged Jessica who has a huge crush on Peter Parker, but Peter is barely aware of her existence. When he becomes aware of her, she angrily rejects him for his sympathy over the death of her family. Jones is also briefly rejected not only by Cage, but also by the sheriff of Lago, with whom she has a one-night stand following Cage's rejection, and by Scott Lang, whom she begins dating after her one-night stand with the sheriff.

Her attractiveness to these men wanes when she is needy, angry, upset, or demanding—anything other than smiling and willing to please. With the sheriff, the sex itself is not depicted, but it is once again initiated by a drunken Jones and regretted by both Jones and the sheriff. He locks her in a cell afterward and tells her the next day, "I don't know what you are used to—but that was a bit much for me, so...." Following this conversation, Jessica has a bizarre, teary, one-sided dialogue with someone, ostensibly herself, but perhaps Killgrave or even the readers of the comic, in the mirror of a diner in which she repeatedly says, "Fuck You!" and blames that "you" for wanting to see her naked and fucking some guy. She is clearly ashamed and regretful, and she angrily rejects the sheriff's apology, discounting the idea that he could really like her.

Similarly, in Volume 2, Issue 8, she becomes angry at Scott when he tries to get her to talk about what has happened between her and Madame Web and her memories of Killgrave, which have surfaced as a result of the experience. In response to her anger, he doesn't call her for six weeks, or return her apology calls, telling her in Volume 3, Issue 21, when he returns, "I'm sorry. I freaked! That night all I was trying to do was listen to you and be there for you, but you screamed and stormed out. I just—life's too short for shit like that. I made a promise to myself. I said life's too short for crazy. I said this long before I met you. And—and—and in you come ... into my life and you're all about crazy." Although she temporarily reconciles with both Lang and Cage, she has to apologize for being a crazy erratic woman to do so—to be forgiven more than she has to forgive.

Jones's relationship with Killgrave in the comics also exposes the character to sexist critique by him and by extension by the reader. In her conversation with Cage about her experience with Killgrave, Jessica explains that Killgrave enslaved and made her beg him for sex as a way of enacting revenge on other superheroes that had beaten him. In the embedded *Purple Haze* comic, he calls her Jewel costume her "stupid, fucking slut costume" and calls her a "stupid, stupid, little bitch" when she is under his control. Despite this, when she is in a coma and Jean Grey of the X-Men communicates with her telepathically, Jones says that Killgrave loved her "in his own way" calling to mind stereotypes about women in abusive relationships or women who are attracted to "bad boys."

In Volume 4, Issue 27, when Jones visits Killgrave in prison, he describes the visit as if they are in a comic book in which Jessica is the main character and he asks her if she gets a "perverse thrill out of getting undressed in front" of her readers and says, "You beg for their love while you act like a whore in front of them. Because you are a whore! You're the biggest whore in the history of the medium.... You're their dirty whore." In Issue 28, when she falls under his power again, he forces her to believe he has killed Scott, and says, "And this is just the first in what I hope will be many, many reminders of just how special you are to me and how much I detest your whore ways." These repeated accusations from Killgrave that Jessica is a "whore," when coupled with the comic's representation of Jones's drunken one-night stands with Cage and the Sheriff, tacitly give the reader permission to associate Jessica with sexist stereotypes about women who have casual sex. In addition, when Killgrave forces Jessica to imagine her worst nightmare, she imagines her friend Carol Danvers (Ms. Marvel)[9] in bed with Luke and Scott—reinforcing her characterization as a jealous woman whose primary concern is her romantic relationships.

In the television series, Jones is an object of obsession for Kilgrave, rather than a tool for his revenge, and she is an object of deep affection for Cage, as well as Ruben and Malcolm (both of whom are her neighbors), who embrace rather than regret her independence and her shortcomings. While this verges a bit into heterosexual female fantasy—being the object of all men's attention and love—it also demonstrates that women can express their full humanity and still be accepted and loved (both romantically and platonically) by good men who are willing to help them overcome trauma. Of course, Kilgrave is not a good man, and his "love" for Jessica is expressed through abusive control in the past and extortion and gaslighting in the present. As multiple commentators have observed, Kilgrave's character uses the emotionally manipulative and controlling tactics of long-term abusers in his interactions with Jessica. Her inability to get anyone to believe Hope's story or her own is a commentary on the skepticism that many abused women have to endure.[10] In the series, Kilgrave is not set up as a figure whose opinions about Jessica the audience should agree with in any way. His gaslighting is exposed for what it is and Jessica is allowed to provide a corrective to his versions of events, both in the conversation about rape quoted above and to his accusation that she stayed with him of her own free will in "AKA The Kumbaya Circle Jerk."

Additionally, there is no criticism of Jessica's expressions of her sexuality in the Netflix series, either by herself or by others (with the exception of her neighbor Robyn's unfounded accusation that she is a cougar pursuing her younger brother, Ruben in "AKA Crush Syndrome"). However, the Jewel identity is criticized for being "slutty" by Jones herself. In a flashback in "AKA The Sandwich Saved Me." Jones rejects the Jewel costume when it is presented to her as a possible superhero identity by Trish. She says, "Jewel is a stripper's name, a real slutty stripper and if I wear that thing you're going to have to call me camel toe." She also demonstrates how impractical the costume is for fighting by having Trish put on the mask and then using it to block her vision. The difference here is that she actively rejects the sexy female superhero persona that she is given in *Alias* as impractical and a ridiculous male fantasy rather than being labeled as a slut by a man for wearing it. In the two flashbacks in which we see Jessica acting as a superhero before her experiences with Kilgrave, she is dressed as a hoagie sandwich and in her regular street clothes. In the same way that Jones's relationships with men and her superhero past have been stripped of their sexist overtones in Rosenberg's adaptation of the comic, Jones's relationships with other women have undergone the same revision.

In the *Alias* comics, Jessica's closest female friend is Carol Danvers. She has several photos of them together back in her Jewel days in her office. This relationship has been troubled by an event that is never fully revealed, but when Jessica contacts Carol for help in an investigation in Volume 1, Carol says, "See? I'm supposed to rise above it right? I'm supposed to pretend that you didn't treat me like crap at a time when you treating me like crap was the last thing I needed." Later, Carol apologizes for her anger and unwillingness to help, writing in an email, "I really hate the way I behaved today. It's the cold medicine, my period, all kinds of other things," reinforcing the stereotype that women's erratic behavior is the result of their hormones (Jessica is also accused of "being menstrual" by Lord Kevin Plunder in Volume 4, Issue 24 when she refuses to take his case).

In the comics, the friendship between these two women does not pass the Bechdel test with flying colors. When Carol and Jessica get together for lunch, their conversation is all about Jessica's romantic interests and love life, with a brief detour into fashion and hairstyles. In the only other conversation they have in the *Alias* comics, Jessica is angry that Carol has referred a group of Killgrave's victims to her and they get in an argument that doesn't make a lot of sense, but that dredges up their past history. Although Carol says, "Guess what, you're one of my best friends on the planet," during this exchange and Jessica later tells Cage that Carol is her friend, their friendship is not depicted as particularly functional or supportive.

Because of licensing issues, Rosenberg was not able to use the character of Carol Danvers in *Jessica Jones*, so she brought in a foster-sister character named Trish Walker as a substitute.[11] Trish Walker shares a name with Hellcat from the Marvel Universe, but has not yet manifested any powers in the series. The relationship between Trish and Jessica is much closer than that between Carol and Jessica. In Rosenberg's version of Jessica's backstory, Jessica was adopted by Trish's mother, Dorothy Walker, after the death of the Jones family in order to drown out some negative press around Trish, who was at that time called Patsy and was the star on a children's television program called *It's Patsy!* Dorothy was abusive and Jessica became Trish's protector. Trish returned the favor after Jessica escaped from Kilgrave, offering her a home and making sure she went to therapy. However, Jessica moved out and broke off contact with Trish six months before the *Jessica Jones* series begins because as she says she needed "some breathing room." They are reunited when Jessica goes to Trish for money to flee town when she realizes Kilgrave has returned a year after her death. Here and throughout the series, Trish serves as Jones's "better angel," encouraging her to use her powers for good, to rescue Hope, to battle Kilgrave, and to aid Kilgrave's other victims. Jessica decides to stay and fight rather than flee. From that point forward, despite Jessica's initial reluctance based on her desire to protect Trish, the two work as a team to try to free Hope Shlottman and capture Kilgrave. Most of their interactions and conversations are about this work, as well as their relationship and history with one another. They only mention their romantic interests in passing and they do not have catty fights like Danvers and Jones in the comics. They love, support, and prioritize one another over the men in their lives.

Despite these examples of sexist objectification and stereotyping, the Jones of the comic book is also portrayed as an independent survivor who is heroic in her own right—not a sidekick and not arm or eye candy. Jones has been traumatized by her experience with Killgrave and its fallout, but has recovered to the extent that she is usually able to function in her day-to-day life except on the infrequent occasions when she is triggered by being reminded of her superhero past and/or of Killgrave and resorts to binge drinking and one-night stands. Even at her lowest points, she finds comfort and meaning in her relationships with others and is portrayed as altruistic and as an agent of justice. Ultimately, with the help of Jean Grey, she shakes off Killgrave's mind control and kills him, freeing her to begin a future with Luke Cage, the father of the child she is expecting. The Jones of the television series is altogether a more damaged and isolated figure, actively combating full-blown PTSD through excessive daily drinking, repeating a street-mapping mental exercise she's learned from a former therapist to battle her flashbacks and hallucinations, shutting her foster sister Trish and others out of her life, and focusing obsessively on her work. While Jones doesn't seem to be having much fun in either genre, in the first season of the television series she rarely shows humor and only experiences pleasure in sexual encounters with Luke Cage—a pleasure that is shadowed by guilt over killing his wife. Although she ultimately defeats Kilgrave at the end of the first season, there is no real catharsis for her or the audience because it is clear that this action will not rectify the damage she has suffered.

The television series does an excellent job of showing the terrible consequences of rape in Jessica Jones' PTSD, substance abuse, fear, and self-loathing, but the emphasis on how she has been damaged undercuts the strength and resilience of the character created by Bendis and Gaydos and undermines some of the pleasure the audience might feel in the feminist elements of the show, elements that include reversals of some of the more sexist tropes and scenes in the comics. Despite Jessica's ultimate triumph over Kilgrave in the final episode of the series and her successful efforts to protect her foster sister, despite her hot sex with fellow superhero Luke Cage, and her give-no-fucks attitude about what is expected of her as a woman by men and other women, she is presented primarily as Kilgrave's victim, as a woman whose life has been ruined by a man taking power over her. While the comic book version of Jessica Jones too often falls into stereotypes about women, objectifies and stereotypes Jones and other women, and presents Killgrave's sexual exploitation of women for titillation, it also gives Jones a fuller, richer life than the first season of the television series, but it may only do so because it refuses to recognize the full impact of rape on the lives of women.

NOTES

1. Grateful thanks to Dr. Thomas J. Nelson for his valuable feedback on an early draft of this essay.
2. The Bechdel test, also known as the Bechdel-Wallace test, first appeared in a conversation between two female characters in Alison Bechdel's comic strip *Dykes to Watch Out For* in 1985. In order to pass the Bechdel test, a film most feature two female characters who have a conversation about something other than a man. A Mary Sue is an idealized and flawless character, commonly female, whose achievements are unrealistic and are often seen as wish fulfillment on the part of the author.
3. The name is spelled Killgrave in the comics and Kilgrave for the television series. I use Kilgrave when referring to the television character or both representations and Killgrave when referring to the character from the comics alone.
4. Evan Narcisse, "Brian Michael Bendis Talks Powers, Jessica Jones, Civil War II and Much More," *IO9*, June 21, 2016, http://io9.gizmodo.com/brian-michael-bendis-talk-powers-jessica-jones-civil-1782377411.
Laura Hurley, "How Jessica Jones' Creator Feels about the Show's Biggest Change from the Comics," *Cinemablend*, June 30, 2016, http://www.cinemablend.com/television/1529159/how-jessica-jones-creator-feels-about-the-shows-biggest-change-from-the-comics.
5. Libby Hill, "'Jessica Jones' Showrunner Melissa Rosenberg Talks Rape, Adaptation, and Female Sexuality," *LA Times*, November 22, 2015, accessed September 4, 2016, http://www.latimes.com/entertainment/herocomplex/la-et-hc-st-jessica-jones-melissa-rosenberg-rape-female-sexuality-20151120-story.html.
6. Maureen Ryan, "'Jessica Jones' Showrunner Melissa Rosenberg Talks about Her Tough Heroine," *Variety*, November 20, 2015, accessed September 4, 2016, http://variety.com/2015/tv/features/jessica-jones-marvel-melissa-rosenberg-1201644912/.
7. Hurley.
8. Jon Dekel, "How Marvel's Jessica Jones Pairs Feminism with Superhero Noir," *National Post*, November 20, 2015, http://news.nationalpost.com/arts/television/how-marvels-jessica-jones-pairs-feminism-with-superhero-noir.
9. In the *Alias* series, published from 2001 to 2004, Carol Danvers was still Ms. Marvel. In 2012, she became Captain Marvel and in 2014 Kamala Khan became Ms. Marvel.
10. Delia Harrington, "Marvel's Greatest Villain: Killgrave and Abuse on Jessica Jones," *Feministing*, December 1, 2015, http://feministing.com/2015/12/01/marvels-greatest-villain-killgrave-and-abuse-on-jessica-jones.
11. Brett White, "'Jessica Jones' Showrunner Reveals Why Captain Marvel Had to Go," *CBRwww*, November 20, 2015, http://www.cbr.com/jessica-jones-showrunner-reveals-why-captain-marvel-had-to-go.

BIBLIOGRAPHY

Bendis, Brian Michael, and Michael Gaydos. *Jessica Jones: Alias*. Vols. 1–4 ed. New York: Marvel Worldwide, 2015.

Berlatsky, Noah. "In 'Jessica Jones,' Marvel Takes on the Biggest Villain of Them All—the Patriarchy." *Quartz*, November 29, 2015. http://qz.com/559803/in-jessica-jones-marvel-takes-on-the-biggest-villain-of-them-all-the-patriarchy.

Dekel, Jon. "How Marvel's Jessica Jones Pairs Feminism with Superhero Noir." *National Post*, November 20, 2015. http://news.nationalpost.com/arts/television/how-marvels-jessica-jones-pairs-feminism-with-superhero-noir.

Harrington, Delia. "Marvel's Greatest Villain: Killgrave and Abuse on Jessica Jones." *Feministing*, December 1, 2015. http://feministing.com/2015/12/01/marvels-greatest-villain-killgrave-and-abuse-on-jessica-jones.

Hill, Libby. "'Jessica Jones' Showrunner Melissa Rosenberg Talks Rape, Adaptation, and Female Sexuality." *Los Angeles Times*, November 22, 2015. http://www.latimes.com/entertainment/herocomplex/la-et-hc-st-jessica-jones-melissa-rosenberg-rape-female-sexuality-20151120-story.html.

Hurley, Laura. "How Jessica Jones' Creator Feels about the Show's Biggest Change from the Comics." *Cinemablend*, June 30, 2016. http://www.cinemablend.com/television/1529159/how-jessica-jones-creator-feels-about-the-shows-biggest-change-from-the-comics.

Narcisse, Evan. "Brian Michael Bendis Talks Powers, Jessica Jones, Civil War II and Much More." *IO9*, June 21, 2016. http://io9.gizmodo.com/brian-michael-bendis-talk-powers-jessica-jones-civil-1782377411.

Rosenberg, Melissa. 2015. *Jessica Jones: Season 1*. Netflix, November 20.

Ryan, Maureen. "'Jessica Jones' Showrunner Melissa Rosenberg Talks about Her Tough Heroine." *Variety*, November 20, 2015. http://variety.com/2015/tv/features/jessica-jones-melissa-rosenberg-1201644912.

White, Brett. "'Jessica Jones' Showrunner Reveals Why Captain Marvel Had to Go." CBRwww, November 20, 2015. http://www.cbr.com/jessica-jones-showrunner-reveals-why-captain-marvel-had-to-go.

The Haunted Hero

The Performance of Trauma in Jessica Jones

Melissa Wehler

In episode three, "AKA It's Called Whiskey," Jessica Jones is reunited with the heretofore phantom Kilgrave, the Purple Man, in a scene that brings the character's traumatized past flooding back into an ever-polluted present. Jessica, now on the hunt for Kilgrave, manages to track and save police sergeant Will Simpson from Kilgrave's thrall. In saving Will, she is brought face-to-face with Kilgrave for the first time since her escape. As she gazes at him—and him at her—the pair are brought back together in both past and present in a moment of flashback. The viewer is jerked unceremoniously back to another moment where Jessica uses her superhuman strength, but unlike the present where her powers position her as savior and hero, the viewer sees Jessica's dark past as victim and villain.[1] The flashback ends, leaving the viewer with the haunting images of Jessica lingering in the present. The Jessica the audience now sees has changed. Not necessarily in character, but in the perception of her character. This past traumatic experience has changed Jessica, and now, it has changed us.

Throughout the series, these moments of flashback position Jessica's character as a traumatic hero whose past is constantly reasserting itself and rewriting itself in the present. Like many traumatic characters, trauma occurs not in the physical, perceptible plane of the material world, but in the complex world of the psyche where the rules of reality exercise far less control. As a result, trauma can be difficult if not impossible to represent. In order to concretize the phantoms of memory, the series uses a variety of flashback techniques in order to manifest the otherwise inaccessible world of Jessica's trauma. The result of which is that her world is haunted by specters from her

145

past that move and live in front of her often without demarcation or acknowledgment of their place in her chronology. They superimpose themselves on her everyday surroundings, forcing her to relive painful memories and act on them in the present. As a haunted hero, Jessica symbolizes the fluidity of the traumatic identity as she stands at the nexus of her victim past and her survivor present.

This essay evaluates the performance of trauma through the lens of cultural criticism by the application of psychoanalysis, performance theory, and trauma studies in a strictly literary and symbolic context. As a critical and cultural critique, the argument herein makes no claims regarding the medical or clinical definitions, symptoms, and treatment of trauma nor is it an attempt to diagnose the figurative character at the center of its analysis. Terms such as post-traumatic stress disorder (PTSD) are borrowed from the medical and clinical authoritative texts but are applied strictly to illuminate the figurative representation of the series.

Obviously, in literary and cultural studies, the shadow of Freud looms large in the discussion of trauma theory, and it was through these influences that conversations about trauma began to extend beyond the physical pain of traumatic injury into the ways trauma affects the mind. Freud introduces the concept of *nachträglichkeit* in *A Project for a Scientific Psychology* (1895) and again that same year in *Studies on Hysteria* (1895), but does not fully develop it. In *Sexuality in the Aetiology of the Neuroses* (1898) a clearer picture begins to emerge, as described by Jean-Michel Quinodoz: "in this paper he elaborates on the idea of *deferred action*: the pathogenic effect of a traumatic event occurring in childhood maybe manifested not at the time it actually took place but retrospectively, when the child reaches a subsequent phase of sexual development (puberty, adolescence)."[2] Quinodoz goes on to describe the second phase of *nachträglichkeit* "which, for Freud, occurs after puberty, a new event revives the memory of the earlier incident, thereby giving rise to a traumatic impact which is much more important than the earlier event, by reason of the individual's newly acquired sexual maturity; this is the point at which the memory is repressed, 'retrospectively' or as a 'deferred action.'"[3] Freud's theorization of *nachträglichkeit* and indeed of trauma writ large comes from an analysis of specifically sexual and sexualized analyses. Freud's original analytical contextualization of trauma as a sexual experience is particularly applicable to Jessica's character as a victim, perpetuator, and survivor of sexual and mental trauma.

Since Freud's original theorization of the traumatic memory, the concept has been interpreted and reinterpreted throughout the last century and has most notably regained attention in literary and cultural studies discussions as a result of renewed theoretical interest in the artistic representations of trauma. Foremost among these critical engagements has been *Performance*

Research: On Trauma edited by Mick Wallis and Patrick Duggan, *The Performance of Violence and the Ethics of Spectatorship* by Lisa Fitzpatrick, *Visions and Revisions: Performance, Memory, Trauma*, edited by Bryoni Trezise and Caroline Wake, and, of course, *Unclaimed Experience: Trauma Narrative and History* by Cathy Caruth. Caruth's gloss of *nachträglichkeit* and indeed, her entire theorization of trauma is one of the foundational texts on the topic. Of particular interest to our conversation, Caurth theorizes the following regarding the importance of memory in the traumatized psyche:

> Traumatic experience, beyond the psychological dimension of suffering it involves, suggests a certain paradox: that the most direct seeing of a violent event may occur as an absolute inability to know it; that immediacy, paradoxically, may take the form of belatedness. The repetitions of the traumatic event—which remain unavailable to consciousness but intrude repeatedly on site—thus suggest a larger relation to the event that extends beyond what can simply be seen or what can be known, and is inextricably tied up with the belatedness and incomprehensibility that remain at the heart of this repetitive seeing.[4]

Caruthian trauma theory is not without its critics because of the emphasis it places on ideas such as *nachträglichkeit* and its interpretations of re-memory.[5] However, the series itself calls upon these theoretical processes as the basis for the main character's performance of trauma.

Performance theory scholars and scholarships have borrowed the terminology and theorization of trauma from these experts and applied the dialogue of trauma studies to dramatic representations and performances. Discourses of psychoanalysis and performance are often used to theorize the artistic expression of traumatic experiences.[6] Of significant import to our conversation is Ann Pellegrini's work with trauma and performance where she discusses the intersection between trauma theory and performance by describing the issue of intangibility and representation: "Of course, part of the problem with trauma is precisely its resistance to the literal, to the thing itself, and, yes, the theatrical such resonant sites through which to think about trauma anew."[7] The performance manifests the ineffable experience of trauma, and in doing so, invokes the trauma from the past, rewriting it as a new present: "There is a profound disconnect between what is experienced and what is apprehended or assimilated."[8] In other words, inherent in trauma is the temporal disconnect between the experience of trauma and the understanding of trauma. Performance and dramatic representation, however, have technical mechanisms to handle the problems of experience and chronological time. Moreover, because they already deal with the fantastic, these mediums allow for representations that are often difficult to explain or describe using other, more time-bound mediums. Specifically, we will focus on the technical use of flashback as the theatrical answer to the questions trauma creates about experience and re-memory.

"Do something": A Theory of Survivorship

Jessica's character theorizes the concept of trauma and traumatic revelation for the audience as an active-passive dialectic. In reference to her client's cheating partners, she describes that her clients' reactions follow one of two patterns: "Knowing it's real means they gotta make a decision. One, do something about it. Or two, keep denying it."[9] The audience knows Jessica's stance on traumatic revelation will be reactive as she ends her description with "Option two rarely pans out."[10] The intentional bracketing of the first episode and indeed the first season with this framework of activist resolve importantly establishes the character as one for whom the trauma is an ever-present reality, writing and rewriting the past with the present and vice versa. Another way to think about the importance of the character's theorization of traumatic revelation is to understand its opposite: the "keep denying it" faction. By denying the "realness" of the trauma, this faction must live in a nostalgic past, a time before the traumatic experience was made "real." They consciously reject the "realness" of the trauma, and isolate that trauma from bleeding into their fragile present. By "doing something about it," Jessica affirms her position as an actor in the traumatic performance.

With this theorization of survivor and victimhood framing the entire series, *Jessica Jones'* engagement with trauma becomes one of everyday performance and survival. The series' theatrical use of the flashback technique as a performance of traumatic memory comes with the very first moment of remembrance. For example, in the first episode, Luke Cage appears in the window and invokes the series' first moment of flashback. The audience is introduced to this moment by a narration from Jessica about the personal toll of private investigation: "In my line of work, you gotta know when to walk away. But some cases just won't let you go."[11] This moment is also her verbalization of the realities of living with trauma and the acknowledgment that the past is never fully past.

Next, the character trains her camera lens on the various vignettes offered by the city windows. The voyeurism, however, takes a marked turn when the camera falls on a man standing at the window staring out, possibly even staring at Jessica. With the gaze unexpectedly refocused, Jessica retreats to the corner of the fire escape and closes her eyes. In the background, the neon sign pulses purple, and the silhouette of a man—who the audience does not yet know as Kilgrave—drifts in from the left and is illuminated for only a moment before fading back to black. The man's voice whispers to Jessica from the past, "You want to do it. You know you do."[12] A sharp inhale yanks Jessica and the audience back to the present, signified by the signs turning back to pink and yellow. With her eyes wide open, she pants, illustrating the visceral sensation of the momentary time lapse. Her therapeutic mantra—

"Main Street. Birch Street. Higgins Drive. Cobalt Lane"—reaffirms the "real-ness" of the present.[13] For the audience, this moment comes out of order or at least out of context in a way that mimics the fragmentation of traumatic reenactment.[14] There is no specified significance of either the man at the window or the man in her mind. Other than the framing of the cause-and-effect, the audience must piece together the fragments of information linking these men to Jessica and to one another. The disordered and disruptive scene is offered without apology or clarification about these relationships or their significance. Instead, the audience experiences these moments just as the character does with no regard for the linear or logical. Alongside Jessica, the audience is likewise forced to survive these moments, reinforcing the irrationality of trauma.

The series itself unequivocally presents the dramatic flashbacks as a lingering symptom of the character's PTSD beginning in the first episode. Jessica's best friend, Trish Walker, links the trauma with the flashbacks: "This is just your PTSD […] Are you still having nightmares? Flashbacks?"[15] The naming of PTSD in this conversation is crucial to the audience's understanding of Jessica's character and her representation of this illness and its symptoms. It is equally as crucial that Jessica's flashbacks are linked directly to her PTSD, helping to irrevocably connect this dramatic technique and creative device to the character's experience of trauma.

In doing so, the series transcends the confines of its creative space and gestures towards socio-psychiatric conversations about PTSD and flashbacks. Flashbacks themselves are considered one of the primary diagnostic features of PTSD:

> The individual may experience dissociative states that last from a few seconds to several hours or even days, during which components of the event are relived and the individual behaves as if the event were occurring at the moment. Such events occur on a continuum from brief visual or other sensory loss of awareness of present surroundings. These episodes, often referred to as "flashbacks," are typically brief but can be associated with prolonged distress and heighted arousal.[16]

By alluding to these psychiatric roots, the series reinforces the "realness" of Jessica's representation of PTSD and situates their own use of flashbacks as a way to perform traumatic experience. PTSD, in other words, becomes the lens and the framework for the audience to view and understand the intrusion of Jessica's past on the present storyline in order to reinforce the recursive nature of the character's identity.

Interestingly, in the same conversation where Jessica's PTSD is dramatically and bluntly addressed, the audience also first learns of Jessica's time as a superhero. Jessica describes herself as the "tried and failed" hero, haunted by being "the person who tried to do something" but was "never the hero that [her sister] wanted [her] to be."[17] Later, Jessica's past as a superhero becomes slightly more fleshed out—even if it is never fully described in this first season—through a moment of flashback.[18] From this point in the chronology, however, the series makes clear that Jessica's attempt to be a superhero was not just unsuccessful but painfully so. Given the context of the conservation, the implication is that her failed heroism is the somehow linked to her PTSD and to Kilgrave—an implication that is realized later in the series. In the framing of this first conversation, however, we suspect that Jessica's heroism is one born from trauma and undone by trauma and that the Jessica in the first season is a hero *in medias res.*

Representing Trauma through Flashback

Jessica's traumatic heroism is developed and symbolized by the use of flashbacks. As a dramatic device, *Jessica Jones'* flashbacks serve two primary functions: first, to provide the audience with the character's backstory and second, to demonstrate the intrusion of her traumatic past on the present.[19] Often, these two functions coincide, since the first season focuses primarily on the traumatic story arc with Kilgrave as part of the character's backstory. In thinking about the role of flashbacks, it is important to remember—as the series asks the audience to—the connection between this technical device and the lived experiences of trauma. In this context, the flashback is a necessary intrusion of the past into the present, removing the subject from their firmed and fixed place in time.

It is important to understand that all but one of the flashbacks that the audience sees are through Jessica's eyes, through her experience, and through her memory. While this narrative decision gives the viewers a sense of immediacy and closeness with the character, they must also recognize that the information has been mediated, edited, written, and rewritten. The situation is further complicated by Jessica's characterization throughout the first season as a slightly unreliable narrator who turns to alcohol over therapy and physical comfort over mental well-being. This can lead to some gaps in the representation, which is itself part of the traumatic memory as Caruth describes: "The history that a flashback tells—as psychiatry, psychoanalysis, and neurobiology equally suggest—is, therefore, a history that literally *has no place*, neither in the past, in which it was not fully experienced, nor in the present, in which its precise images and enactments are not fully understood."[20] There are moments where Jessica cannot remember traumatic events such as the car accident and its immediate aftermath. There also moments where she chooses not to remember, such as such as the hotel room, which Jessica had clearly spent time in, but save for a few scraps of information, the audience has real sense of her experiences there. The audience is inclined to believe Jessica's flashbacks because of the pathos of her narrative and their proximity to her.

There are also moments where the flashbacks are corroborated by other characters, including Luke Cage, Trish Walker, Malcolm, and of course, Kilgrave himself. In one of the more haunting scenes in the first season, Kilgrave and Jessica face-off through flashbacks. In this scene, Kilgrave describes a time when they were together. Kilgrave's flashback begins with a subtle white light and soft music, as the image of Jessica standing on the rooftop terrace with Kilgrave appears. They kiss passionately, which Kilgrave claimed was from desire rather than command. Jessica, however, remembers that movement quite differently.[21] In her flashback, she is on the rooftop, but instead of kissing Kilgrave, she is fantasizing about jumping from the terrace and riding away on a white horse. Once the fantasy is over, the audience returns to the present for a moment before another flashback—whose the audience no longer knows—where Jessica stands on the terrace once again while Kilgrave commands her to come down from the ledge or to cut off her ears if she will not obey.[22] The audience is given "proof" in the present as Jessica reveals her scar behind her ear from the knife. Jessica's memory, while incomplete, is still accurate. Thus, while these moments of memory are mediated through the lens of time, trauma, and personality, the series does compel the audience to believe the flashbacks as real, or at least, real to Jessica.

The questions of time and memory are integral to the representations of traumatic flashbacks throughout the series. In order to represent these moments that occur outside of time, the series uses framing, editing, and effects to accompany the flashbacks and to symbolize of the ways traumatic memory can be invited and invoked. Jessica's memories of Kilgrave appear to claw at the character's present, a technique reinforced by the scraping and screeching sound effects that aurally symbolize the forceful, violent nature of these remembrances. By the end of the first episode, the audience knows such a flashback is about to occur since it is symbolized by sudden, jerky movements, infused with purple lighting. These flashbacks are violent in their suddenness and haunting in their darkness. They are framed to look like the film has been poorly edited, as if the frames from another part of the story—or another story entirely—have been superimposed on the current moment. They are often also moments triggered by places and people that Jessica interacted with during her time with Kilgrave. For instance, in the first episode, Jessica walks down the hallway at the hotel where, it is implied, she was once imprisoned by Kilgrave. The fire alarm blares and white lights flash around her in a scene that would seem more at home in a horror story than a superhero story. Between the flashes of white, the audience notices purple slowly seep into the white places as Jessica moves closer to the room where she believes him to be. The figure of a man appears in fits and spurts before her. In the room proper, the audience hears a man's voice whisper, "You miss me?" from the darkness as an arm begins to wrap itself around her shoulder seemingly out of the darkness.[23] For only a moment, a hand and face are visible in the shadows, but just as quickly disappear. The moment is startling, reminiscent of "jump scares" in horror movies. Technically speaking, it symbolizes how this past trauma tears itself and the present, reversing and revising any new story the character tries to write about herself. Even though Jessica's presence here is one of survivor and hero, the flashbacks concretize the memory of victimhood, reinforcing the fluidity of her performance of identity.

Kilgrave's intrusions on Jessica's everyday reality are not the only traumatic flashbacks represented in the series. Jessica herself experiences flashbacks to people and events in her past that remind the audience of the character's prolonged experiences with the traumatic and the character's mercurial sense of self-identity. Unlike the spontaneous and shocking qualities of the Kilgrave flashbacks, Jessica's flashbacks are bathed in white light, soft transitions, and quiet whirls, effortlessly transporting the character and the audience into the past. One of the more powerful examples is in the fifth episode where the audience learns of Jessica and Malcolm's first meeting. As Jessica attempts to intervene on Malcolm's behalf and remove him (or at least guard him) from Kilgrave's thrall, Malcolm unknowingly triggers a flashback when he protests, "You can't save me again."[24] Instantly, these words transport Jessica to a city sidewalk at night ushered in by a quiet, white light. The audience witnesses Jessica intervene in the mugging and potential murder of Malcolm. With the attacker fleeing, Jessica is interrupted by the sound of clapping. Jessica turns to face Kilgrave, not for the first time in the series, but for the first time in Jessica's chronology.[25] In this moment, the audience sees Jessica in between states of trauma: the trauma of her family's death but before the trauma of Kilgrave's thrall. It symbolizes Jessica's "do something" mindset where she steps from victim to survivor. Her agency in this moment is painfully fleeting. Kilgrave's presence and machinations undermine Jessica for the first time but not for the last time. In what should have been a powerful moment of self- affirmation, Jessica instead becomes a victim once again who the audience knows will go on to victimize others. The simultaneity of these roles and dramatization of their fluency symbolized through this flashback demonstrate the lived reality of traumatic experience.

Performing the Layers of Trauma

By linking the flashbacks to the character's PTSD, the flashbacks themselves become places where trauma is remembered and realized both for the character and the audience. As a result, many of the flashbacks are brought about abruptly through a "triggering" event, which is described in psychology terms: "Intense psychological distress or physiological reactivity often occurs when the individual is exposed to triggering events that resemble or symbolize an aspect of the traumatic event."[26] The exposure to traumatic events—real and represented—reinforces the series' use of flashbacks as moments were the unspeakable nature of trauma is represented and performed.

One of the most profound examples of a flashback caused by a traumatic triggering event is the reoccurring memory of Reva Connors' death. This moment is triggered several times throughout the series, including multiple times in the same episode.[27] The most dramatic and sustained return to this moment occurs in the third episode. The audience looks over Jessica's shoulder as she stares at newspaper clippings pronouncing, "Fatal Bus Crash Raises Concerns: Hell's Kitchen Resident Reva Connors Killed in Accident," "Commuters on Alert Following Fatal Bus Accident," and "Community Mourns Reva Connors in Wake of Tragic Accident."[28] A picture of Luke Cage standing near the graveside slides into view, taken presumably by Jessica in a previous moment of voyeurism. The scene cuts out momentarily, and the audience is returned to much later that night. Jessica appears more intoxicated than before the time jump. After a brief interlude, Jessica returns to the crumbled clipping. A sudden flash occurs and the audience is transported to the location in the clipping. Jessica stands on a city corner with blood on her hands. Kilgrave's familiar yet still mysterious voice screams in the background "Come back here!"[29] The entire scene is slowed and blurry as if it is taking place underwater.

Suddenly, a bus appears, rolls over, and hits the man still blurred in the background. Instantly, the audience is snapped back into the present but now instead of night at the office it is daytime on the city street.[30] This particular moment of flashback provides the most complete picture of the scene that the first season returns to most often. The audience experiences the flashback, not through Jessica's eyes, but through her perspective. The slowing down and skipping of time both inside and outside of the flashback mirrors the dissociative state common in sufferers of PTSD. Beyond this singular example, the repetition of this event underscores its overall importance to the development of Jessica's character as well as the progression of the plot. It also represents the nature of traumatic memory as an event "relived."[31] While this process often takes place in the untranslatable space of the mind, the repeated flashbacks to this traumatic event concretize this otherwise ineffable process and demonstrate how the past rewrites itself on the present.

The use of repetitive flashbacks to reinforce Jessica's traumatic reliving of the past is also present throughout the Hope Shlottman subplot. As Jessica follows leads on the missing Hope Shlottman, she eventually finds her way to an Asian restaurant that she had frequented with Kilgrave. Upon entering, the restaurant host intercepts her, and she begins asking questions about Hope and her companion, which Jessica eventually realizes is Kilgrave. While the host continues to describe the couple, Niku, the Asian fusion restaurant blurs and then fades away behind him until only the former Italian restaurant, Il Russo, is left. Jessica pushes past the host as the camera follows her through the now-crowded dining room. The scene slows, the images on the periphery blur, the scene blinks in and out sporadically, and voices of the spectral diners become indistinct. The character pushes her way to the back room where she sees herself dining with Kilgrave. The entire room is awash in purple, a color meant to symbolize him and his intrusions on her memory. Jessica stares at Kilgrave and the camera while the phantom Kilgrave sits with his back to the audience. She mimics all of his suggestions—loving the dinner he says she will love and smiling when he demands her to smile—in a haunting act of ventriloquism.

The scene jerks back to the present as the host continues the sentence he had started before the time disruption, reinforcing that Jessica alone experienced the slippage into the past. She quickly leaves the restaurant, bursting out of the doors and running out to the sidewalk so disoriented that she is unable to finish her anchoring mantra.[32] This moment is particularly interesting for its technical execution. The flashbacks splice into the scenery, recalling it from memory while simultaneously rewriting present. In doing so, the past and the present coalescence and become indistinguishable. The audience sees this superimposed reality through Jessica's eyes, and they are forced to experience the moment alongside her. The moment of trauma comes full circle as Jessica and the audience watch her and Kilgrave from the past in the present. Despite the time slippage, Jessica's identity remains unchanged: she is just as much Kilgrave's victim at this moment as she was when this scene initially took place. Jessica's isolation is further displayed by the fact that she and audience are the only witnesses to this shadow theatre. The host, completely unaffected, represents the ways trauma goes unrecognized and unrepresented outside of the world of the flashback.

Another example of the past superimposing itself on the present also occurs during the Hope Shlottman subplot when Jessica is searching for Kilgrave's other victims. In the fourth episode, Jessica convenes a group of witnesses who can testify to Kilgrave's existence. In order to ensure that the witnesses are telling the truth, Jessica personally interviews them. One man in particular describes giving Kilgrave his suit jacket, and Jessica asks him to stand up to see if he is the same size and body type as Kilgrave. As she looks over him, streaks of blue light flash around the man and Kilgrave's purple-tinged silhouette is superimposed upon him. Jessica looks away sickened and nods in confirmation of the story. This particular moment is important for the audience for three reasons. First, it demonstrates how traumatic memory intrudes on the present, changing the audience's understanding of the people, places, and events in the present moment. This linkage to the past taints the present. Jessica looks away from the remembrance of Kilgrave in disgust, but in doing so, also looks away from Kilgrave's victim in the same way. They are both connected by the intrusion of trauma and forever separated by it. Second, the moment is symbolic of how these traumatized characters possess the double consciousness of trauma where they are both of victim and survivor. Jessica and the male character behave as survivors in this scene, including bearing witness and testifying to the trauma. Yet, by rehearsing the circumstances of their victimhood, they are placed firmly back into the position of victim.

Finally, this brief moment demonstrates the everyday reality of trauma in the series. Both Jessica and the male character see and feel Kilgrave on their skin and in the clothes. Jessica is even physically disgusted by it. This moment reinforces a common reality in the series: while trauma might sometimes be ineffable, it is not unrepresentable. Rather, it is more often than not just beneath the surface of a character, haunting their everyday reality.

The superimposition of the past on the present is even more complicated with the introduction of other traumatic events in the character's timeline. In several episodes towards the end of the series, the past and present collide both mentally and physically when Kilgrave entices Jessica to meet him in her childhood home. Through flashbacks, the audience learns Jessica's background as she experiences it: fragmented and non-sequential. As the taxi pulls up to the house, Jessica watches her younger self have an argument with Dorothy, Jessica's new caretaker: "Jessica, I told you, we're not wasting anymore time looking for it" to which young Jessica replies, "it's under one of the floorboards."[33]

This scene ends with the entrance of Kilgrave from the side of the house and the three traumatic moments from her past—the death of her family, her separation from her childhood home, and her enthrallment with Kilgrave—collide in time and space. As these moments coalesce in the present, so do Jessica's identity as survivor and victim. The ghosts of her past and her past selves haunt her in the present and serve to confuse her role as hero and protector. Moreover, the episode after Jessica's homecoming begins in a flashback with Jessica's parents and younger brother preparing for the car trip that would end in their tragic deaths. Again, the past is superimposed on the present as Jessica watches her parents and younger brother walk past her as she stands in the doorway. She also sees her younger self walk past her down the staircase and out of the house. This moment obviously occurs chronologically before the argument with Dorothy, but again, the flashbacks are given according to experience rather than occurrence. In the same episode, the last flashback is actually the one that occurs first. Young Jessica in the backseat of the car with her brother arguing over a game. The argument distracts her father who turns to correct them, and in doing so, takes his eyes from the road. From context clues, the audience realizes that this causes him to disastrously rear-end a truck. All of these flashbacks are framed within the present where Kilgrave has forced Jessica into confronting them. In doing so, he hopes not to only conjure these ghosts, but to superimpose himself on them. Jessica alone stands at the confluence of these time streams, and the audience is able to witness the recursive and cyclic experience of trauma through these superimposed moments.

Haunted by Flashbacks

The decision to superimpose flashbacks onto the present necessarily forces the audience to recognize the impact of Jessica's past trauma on her everyday life. These superimposed flashbacks as well as others throughout the series seep into the seemingly innocuous moments, reinforcing the everyday reality of a character living with PTSD. Unlike physical trauma, Jessica's trauma, the result of mental, emotional, and sexual abuse, has left emotional and mental scars. The invisibility of this trauma makes it difficult for the audience to recognize and access it in the same way as physical abuse. Flashbacks, however, allow the series to perform certain ineffable characteristics of living with trauma, including the intrusion of trauma on the present, the double consciousness of survivor and victim, and the daily performance of traumatic identity.

There are many of these everyday moments of trauma littered throughout the series. In the first episode, for example, the audience sees Jessica sprawled out on the coffee table with her laptop glowing in the background and an overturned glass still cupped in her hand. The lighting unexpectedly shifts to purple and Kilgrave's silhouette appears. He aggressively licks the side of her face in a way that is meant to be dominating and humiliating. The moment abruptly ends when Jessica wakes, jumps to her feet, and recites her therapeutic mantra.[34] In this moment, the audience sees that even in sleep, Jessica's trauma is all pervasive, including in her unconscious life. Another example of the way trauma seeps into Jessica's everyday existence happens in the third episode when she opens the medicine cabinet at Luke Cage's apartment only to come face-to-face with a picture of Reva. Instantly, the picture springs to life, and the audience is transported back in time. The audience and Jessica watch Reva fall backwards as they have seen her do so many times before in the series.[35] In these moments, Jessica does not seek to confront her traumatic past as she does in other parts of the series. Rather, her traumatic past confronts her in these otherwise normal moments. The representation of them in the series is important for two reasons. First, they demonstrate the lived reality of trauma as something that can be triggered by seemingly insignificant experiences. Second, they perform the crucial function of representing how a person with PTSD lives with traumatic experiences every day even if there are no discernible signifiers of it. As a character, Jessica's past is always present even as she hopes that her present can rewrite the past.

The recognition and representation of living with trauma also reinforces how Jessica's identity is constantly in flux, not only for her but also for those around her. For instance, Jessica is attacked by a traumatic remembrance while riding the subway. The lights begin to flicker and suddenly the dark car turns purple. The silhouette of a man appears beside Jessica and screams in her ear, "come back here!"[36] Jessica punches at the shadow but ends up smashing the window of the car instead.[37] In the subway car, the voice of Kilgrave exists out of time and space, unconnected to her surroundings. The moment obviously surprises even Jessica herself who reacts with shock and anger. Unlike the triggered events, this flashback represents how Jessica's trauma is constantly reasserting itself in the present. The remembrance—only a few seconds long—moves her to react in the present, changing it and the perception of those around her. Even as the moment fades from purple to white, the haunted expressions of Jessica and the other riders demonstrate its lingering, haunting effects. The editing and framing effects such as the purple lighting and the suddenness of Kilgrave's presence underscore Jessica's helplessness in this moment. Ultimately, this flashback and others like it in the series underscore Jessica's day-to-day reality as a hero haunted by trauma.

This sentiment is reinforced in the concluding moments of the first season as Jessica reflects on heroism and her own unique relationship with it. Having been released from police custody without being charged in Kilgrave's death, Jessica reminisces on her feelings about heroism: "They say everyone is born a hero. But if you let it, life will push you over the line until you're the villain. The problem is, you don't always know that you've crossed that line. Maybe it's enough that the world thinks I'm a hero. Maybe if I work long and hard maybe I can fool myself."[38] In this final reflection, Jessica is still ambivalent towards her relationship with heroism, recalling the conversation of the "tried and failed" hero from the first episode.[39] While she has not convinced herself of her heroism, she is still willing to try—and possibly fail—again. In this sentiment, she provides a framework for ultimately understanding the traumatic hero who, like her own trauma, returns to the past to understand her present. The cyclical nature of traumatic memory, manifested throughout the series through flashbacks, is reinforced through this ultimate theorization of heroism as equally fluid. As a hero haunted by her trauma, the character of Jessica Jones performs the double consciousness of traumatic performance: at once victim and survivor, hero and villain. Through her flashbacks, the audience witnesses the traumatized psyche made manifest by bringing the ghosts of the past into the white, blurred lights of the present.

NOTES

1. Caroline Wake, "The Accident and the Account: Towards a Taxonomy of Spectatorial Witness in Theatre and Performance Studies," *Visions and Revisions: Performance, Memory, Trauma,* edited by Bryoni Trezise and Caroline Wake, 33–56 (Copenhagen: Museum Tusculanum Press, 2013). *Jessica Jones,* "AKA: It's Called Whiskey," television series, directed by David Petrarca, story by Liz Friedman, teleplay by Liz Friedman and Scott Reynolds (Netflix, 2015).

2. Jean-Michel Quinodoz, *Reading Freud: A Chronological Exploration of Freud's Writings* (London: Taylor & Francis, 2006), 34.

3. Jean-Michel Quinodoz, *Reading Freud,* 22.

4. Cathy Caruth, "Traumatic Awakenings," *Unclaimed Experience: Trauma, Narrative, and History* (Baltimore: The John Hopkins University Press, 1996), 91.

5. Recently, Alan Gibbs concluded his edited collection with the following summary: "the phenomenon of *Nachträglichkeit,* the belatedness of traumatic memory due to temporary amnesias, is far less ubiquitous than often suggested, despite its importance to Caruthian trauma studies." Alan Gibbs, "Conclusion," *Contemporary American Trauma Narratives,* ed. Alan Gibbs (Edinburgh: Edinburgh University Press, 2014), 241.

6. Trezise and Wake provide a concise outline of the history of the relationship between performance theory and trauma studies. Trezise and Wake, "Introduction: From Sight to Site," *Visions and Revisions: Performance, Memory, Trauma,* ed. Bryoni Trezise and Caroline Wake (Copenhagen: Museum Tusculanum Press, 2013), 11–28.

7. Ann Pellegrini, "Staging Sexual Injury: *How I Learned to Drive,*" *Critical Theory and Performance,* ed. Janelle G. Reinelt and Joseph R. Roach (Ann Arbor: University of Michigan Press, 2007), 415.

8. Ann Pellegrini, "Staging Sexual Injury: *How I Learned to Drive,*" 415.

9. *Jessica Jones,* "AKA Ladies Night," directed by S. J. Clarkson, written by Melissa Rosenberg.

10. *Ibid.*

11. *Ibid.*

12. *Ibid.*

13. *Ibid.*

14. *Ibid.*

15. *Ibid.*

16. American Psychiatric Association, *Diagnostic and Statistical Manual of Mental Disorders: DSM-V-TR* (Washington, D.C.: American Psychiatric Association, 2013), 275.

17. *Jessica Jones,* "AKA Ladies Night," directed by S. J. Clarkson, written by Melissa Rosenberg.

18. *Jessica Jones,* "AKA The Sandwich Saved Me," directed by Stephen Sujik, written by Dana Baratta.

19. While beyond the scope of this essay, the role of the audience as a silent witness to the character of Jessica Jones' trauma is tangentially germane to this discussion. My own conceptualization of audience is largely drawn from performance studies. See Caroline Wake, "The Accident and the Account: Towards a Taxonomy of Spectatorial Witness in Theatre

and Performance Studies," *Visions and Revisions: Performance, Memory, Trauma*, ed. Bryoni Trezise and Caroline Wake (Copenhagen: Museum Tusculanum Press, 2013), 33–56.

20. Cathy Caruth, "Recapturing the Past: Introduction," *Trauma: Explorations in Memory*, ed. Cathy Caruth (Baltimore: Johns Hopkins University Press, 1995), 153.

21. This is a classic example of *nachträglichkeit* as part of a cyclical relationship between past and present. Modell explains this aspect of Freud's original theorization of *nachträglichkeit* as, "the traumatic or unassimilated memories that are later revised—a view that is fully consistent with the 'working through' in the transference of the memory of an experience that had been traumatic, incomplete, or unassimilated." Modell, *Other Times, Other Realities: Toward a Theory of Psychoanalytic Treatment* (Cambridge: Harvard University Press, 1990), 62.

22. *Jessica Jones*, "AKA 1,000 Cuts," directed by Rosemary Rodriguez, written by Dana Baratta and Micah Schraft.

23. *Jessica Jones*, "AKA Ladies Night," directed by S. J. Clarkson, written by Melissa Rosenberg.

24. *Jessica Jones*, "AKA The Sandwich Saved Me," directed by Stephen Sujik, written by Dana Baratta.

25. *Jessica Jones*, "AKA The Sandwich Saved Me," directed by Stephen Sujik, written by Dana Baratta.

26. *Diagnostic and Statistical Manual*, 275.

27. Episodes that feature this moment include the second episode, "AKA Crush Syndrome," the third episode, "AKA It's Called Whiskey," the sixth episode, "AKA You're a Winner!," and the ninth episode, "AKA Sin Bin."

28. *Jessica Jones*, "AKA Crushed Syndrome," directed by S. J. Clarkson, written by Micah Schraft.

29. *Ibid.*

30. *Ibid.*

31. *Diagnostic and Statistical Manual*, 275.

32. *Jessica Jones*, "AKA Ladies Night," directed by S. J. Clarkson, written by Melissa Rosenberg.

33. *Jessica Jones*, "AKA Top Shelf Perverts," directed by Simon Cellan Jones, written by Jenna Reback and Micah Schraft.

34. *Jessica Jones*, "AKA Ladies Night," directed by S. J. Clarkson, written by Melissa Rosenberg.

35. *Jessica Jones*, "AKA: It's Called Whiskey," directed by David Petrarca, story by Liz Friedman, teleplay by Liz Friedman and Scott Reynolds.

36. *Jessica Jones*, "AKA Ladies Night," directed by S. J. Clarkson, written by Melissa Rosenberg.

37. *Ibid.*

38. *Jessica Jones*, "AKA Smile," directed by Michael Rymer, story by Jamine King and Scott Reynolds, teleplay by Scott Reynolds and Melissa Rosenberg.

39. *Jessica Jones*, "AKA Ladies Night," directed by S. J. Clarkson, written by Melissa Rosenberg.

Bibliography

American Psychiatric Association. "Post-Traumatic Stress Disorder (PTSD)." In *Diagnostic and Statistical Manual of Mental Disorders: DSM-V-TR*. Washington, D.C.: American Psychiatric Association, 2013.

Caruth, Cathy. "Recapturing the Past: Introduction." In *Trauma: Explorations in Memory*. Edited by Cathy Caruth, 151–157. Baltimore: Johns Hopkins University Press, 1995.

_____. "Traumatic Awakenings." In *Unclaimed Experience: Trauma, Narrative, and History*, 91–112. Baltimore: John Hopkins University Press, 1996.

Gibbs, Alan. "Conclusion." In *Contemporary American Trauma Narratives*. Edited by Alan Gibbs, 240–263. Edinburgh: Edinburgh University Press, 2014.

Modell, Arnold H. *Other Times, Other Realities: Toward a Theory of Psychoanalytic Treatment*. Cambridge: Harvard University Press, 1990.

Pellegrini, Ann. "Staging Sexual Injury: *How I Learned to Drive.*" In *Critical Theory and Performance.* Edited by Janelle G. Reinelt and Joseph R. Roach, 413–431. Ann Arbor: University of Michigan Press, 2007.
Quinodoz, Jean-Michel. *Reading Freud: A Chronological exploration of Freud's Writings.* London: Taylor & Francis, 2006.
Trezise, Bryoni, and Caroline Wake. "Introduction: From Sight to Site." In *Visions and Revisions: Performance, Memory, Trauma.* Edited by Bryoni Trezise and Caroline Wake, 11–28. Copenhagen: Museum Tusculanum Press, 2013.

Integrity, Family and Consent

The Ontological Angst of Jessica Jones

BRIAN FULLER *and* EMILY D. EDWARDS

Millennials Are Watching

Jessica Jones is a dick. A private dick. A sleuth. A shamus for hire. A gumshoe retained by the unlucky to chase down the unfaithful. The eponymous antiheroine of 2015's Netflix series is a detective so hard-boiled that Sam Spade (*The Maltese Falcon*, 1941), Phillip Marlowe (*The Big Sleep*, 1946), and Mike Hammer (*Kiss Me Deadly*, 1955) seem over easy by comparison. Hell's Kitchen, a turf she shares with Marvel peers Daredevil and Luke Cage, is a rotten bite of the Big Apple, a rude, sarcastic world in which human kindness and concern are acknowledged weaknesses. In that New York neighborhood, even intimacy is tainted with fury and affection with derisive insult.

Jones offers a dark narrative apparently popular with the cohort of Americans born between 1980 and the mid–2000s. The most diverse generation to date, these "millennials" represent one-third of the total U.S. population.[1] The exact number of 18–34-year-olds who watch *Jessica Jones* is, however, difficult to pin down. From its first original series, the Norwegian import *Lilyhammer,* Netflix has rather famously refused to release the ratings information that has been a standard of audience measurement for decades. The streaming service's chief content officer, Ted Sarandos, insists conventional ratings are irrelevant for programs that are both binge-watched and discovered over a course of years; accessed on multiple devices and platforms; and bankrolled by subscribers, not advertisers.[2]

Nielsen and other third parties nevertheless attempt to collect data, though studio executives complain the samples, "aren't wide enough and don't capture viewing from tablets and mobile devices."[3] Symphony Advanced Media "extrapolates audience figures from [15,000] panelists who download an app that runs in the background of their mobile devices or PCs, listening to identify the content they watch."[4] The tech firm gives *Jessica Jones* a 4.52 demo rating (based on the coveted 18–49 demographic) and 9.3 million total adult viewers during the first 35 days of availability.[5] If reliable, those figures sandwich *Jones* between Shonda Rhimes dramas (*Grey's Anatomy* [3.8], *How to Get Away with Murder* [3.5], and *Scandal* [3.5]) and ratings juggernaut *The Big Bang Theory* (5.8), the fourth highest rated broadcast show of the 2015–2016 season.[6]

Contested metrics elevate the importance of Netflix subscriber data as an indicator of viewer demographics. Here, the numbers are more clear-cut. "Netflix is most popular among the 16–24 demographic in the U.S., where an impressive 65% are now using it."[7] The service boasted 62 million paid-for accounts worldwide (that's 80 million U.S. users) in April 2015.[8] It went on to enjoy a significant subscriber bump of 3.28 million as it released high profile original shows—*Daredevil* and *Jessica Jones* among them—in the year's successive quarters.[9] Clearly, millennial audiences are hungry for Netflix and other streamed programming. And—if category searches across streaming services are any indication[10]—their appetites include film noir's traditions of style and content.

A Post-Traumatic Anti ("Super") Heroine

A thematic baton *Jessica Jones* certainly advances is noir's historic interest in complicated female characters. *Jones* pushed past even the genre's *femme fatale* stereotype to feature one of television's rarest species: the antiheroine.

Showrunner Melissa Rosenberg was keenly aware of the shortage: "We've had on cable these male characters who are very flawed and complex—Tony Soprano, Dexter Morgan, Vic Mackey. We've just begun to have that on cable for women in *Nurse Jackie* and *Weeds*."[11] *The Atlantic's* Akash Nikolas extended Rosenberg's list with *United States of Tara* and *The Big C*. Acknowledging Showtime's niche market, she also observed these are largely comedic roles. The women who carry drama series are unarguably strong, but they're still traditionally heroic. Patty Hewes (Glenn Close, *Damages*) and Claire Underwood (Robin Wright, *House of Cards*) might be outliers, but Nikolas convincingly argues the villainy of these characters is mitigated by good girls and bad men. Comparison demotes them to *femme fatale*.[12]

As writer and executive producer of *Dexter* from 2006 to 2009, Rosenberg spent four seasons co-creating Showtime's blackest antihero (a benevolent serial killer, of all things) and most-watched show. Yet her 2013 attempt to launch a female antihero, ABC's *Red Widow*, failed after only six episodes. Of the series' housewife-cum-mob-boss, Rosenberg admitted: "This is a very tricky character to sell to an audience because women are held to a higher standard.... I don't know where her character could go, she could be as bad as [*Breaking Bad*'s] Walter White."[13]

By the time Rosenberg was finally green-lighted for a 2015 Netflix run, she was fully committed to the cause of an on-screen antiheroine. "I love this character [Jessica]. That is an incredibly damaged, dark, complex female character that kicks ass. That's my favorite thing about it.... Jessica Jones is actually a former superhero with PTSD. So she is wrestling with having this damaged past and still trying to contribute something to the world."[14] Known variously through history as "irritable heart," "shell shock," and "combat fatigue," post-traumatic stress disorder (PTSD) is hardly confined to the experience of military combatants.[15] It may be expected in 17.6 percent of populations affected by torture and conflict.[16] Recalled Melissa Rosenberg: "My psychologist father-in-law said, 'I don't know why all superheroes aren't [suffering from] PTSD.'"[17]

"Intrusive recollection" constitutes PTSD's most distinctive symptom.[18] From a narrative perspective, the syndrome's signature nightmares and vivid, dissociative flashbacks seem tailor-made to complicate both characters and timelines. They force viewers to "co-experience the anguish and insecurity which are the true emotions of contemporary *film noir*," creating "a similar emotional effect: *that state of tension instilled in the spectator when the psychological reference points are removed.*"[19] "[PTSD is] not just a memory," says series star Krysten Ritter, "it's feeling like you're back in that situation."[20] The disorder's other symptoms of avoidance, estrangement, aggression, guilt, recklessness, and hyper-vigilance[21]—in significant addition to the frequent correlation between PTSD and substance abuse[22]—seem almost to co-opt classic descriptions of film noir.

Not surprisingly, PTSD is at the heart of an early noir classic, Arthur Ripley's 1946 thriller, *The Chase*. One of many genre screenplays adapted from a Cornell Woolwich novel, *The Chase* features Robert Cummings as a shell-shocked veteran whose vivid dreams disorient viewers and define the film's non-linear structure. Both pharmacological care and psychoanalytic therapy (then unfamiliar to post-war audiences) feature as central plot points. Cummings' character shares a therapist with the sadistic gangster he's fleeing.

Together, the manifestations of PTSD generate an emotional strain between "flight" and "fight" that fashions antiheroes from heroes, evident from the opening frame of Arisu Kashiwagi's title sequence:

> We based the concept off of Jessica's PTSD and alcoholism, her blurry, unreliable point of view, and translated that visually using paint strokes that smear and obfuscate the scenes. We wanted her visions and memories to be triggered by light, and floating in black negative space. So the scenes would appear only in small sections

of the frame, either blocked by a foreground element or contained inside of a silhou-etted framing device.[23]

Though Jones lost her parents in a horrific car crash for which she blames herself,[24] the wreck doesn't seem to be the source of her PTSD. As recently as 18 months before the first episode begins, Jessica is a dark but not atypical millennial who hates her 9-to-5 cubicle and enjoys barhopping with friends. She employs her intellect and her body with the breezy irresponsi-bility of most twenty-somethings.[25] Her PTSD, then, is likely the textbook response to rape endured by more than 50 percent of its survivors.[26]

Millennials, Rape and Mental Health

Millennials are history's best-educated generation. Fully one-third of adults aged 25 to 32 have at least a bachelor's degree[27]; about 61 percent have attended some college.[28] Because colleges and universities offer researchers manageable study populations high in situational risk factors (like peer pres-sure and underage drinking),[29] it is it not unreasonable to draw conclusions about millennials from campus trends of sexual assault, mental health, and activism.

Lingering stigmas, institutional disincentives, and a legacy of male priv-ilege no doubt contribute to inaccuracies of rape reportage. It is impossible to quantify the occurrence of rape, though it's become fashionable to simplify highlighted statistics from the 2007 Campus Sexual Assault Study (CSA).[30] Some interpreters of the study hold that one in five college women will be sexually assaulted by the time they graduate (a rate the study's lead author, Christopher Krebs, rejects as not "nationally representative"). Such an asser-tion "would mean that young American college women are raped at a rate similar to women in the Congo, where rape has been used as a weapon of war."[31]

Though rape's reported prevalence may be debated, milestones of social change are easier to pinpoint. Caroline Heldman and Baillee Brown identify four peaks of sexual violence activism[32]: the first follows the American Civil War; the second leads to the Civil Rights movement; the third is concurrent with the women's liberation movement of the 1960s and 70s. High-water marks of the fourth and current wave include greater networking through social media, a record fine for violation of the Cleary Act (2008),[33] two expan-sions of Title IX (2011[34] and 2014[35]), and Rolling Stone's 2014 publication and 2015 retraction of the discredited article "A Rape on Campus."[36]

Activists feared the magazine's high-profile misstep would compound existing problems of victim believability, a central theme of Jones's third episode. Hope Shlottman, a teenager Jessica is hired to find, claims Kilgrave forced her to kill her parents. United by common experience, Jessica naturally believes her. But Luke Cage and attorney Jeri Hogarth are skeptical. Both question Shlottman's sanity. Both demand empirical evidence.[37] The parallels are far from subtle. Those who level accusations of rape have, for years, endured similar skepticism.

It's hard to ignore as coincidental the national crusade against campus sexual assault and the near-simultaneous introduction of Marvel's first television female superhero. Yet, in a Television Critics Association panel, showrunner Melissa Rosenberg insisted, "We never walked into the writing room going, 'We are now going to take on rape and abuse and feminism.' We walked in telling a story for this character. And by being true to her character, it was true to the issues."[38] In a separate interview Rosenberg maintained, "The show's all about exploring the inner workings of Jessica Jones and her ensemble, their relationships, and Jessica's examination of her own trauma and healing."[39]

That the broader topic of emotional healing should concern millennial audiences also may be inferred by campus statistics. Across the Academy, student mental health has been described in "crisis" terms for nearly a decade.[40] Some practitioners claim 18-to-24-year-olds evince greater levels of stress and psychopathology than any previous generation.[41] Others are reluctant to join in disaster-mongering, pointing out that most data is subjectively self-reported by persons who may have been raised with unrealistic expectations of well-being.[42] In either case, Penn State's Center for Collegiate Mental Health (a consortium of 340 university and college counseling centers) reports that, from 2010 to 2015, "the average demand for counseling center services grew at least 5x faster than average institutional enrollment."[43] "Most university budgets do not support all the resources and staffing that's needed to provide instant service for anybody that walks in," says Dr. Dan Jones, director of Counseling and Psychological Services at Appalachian State University. "With students coming in greater numbers and more severity," Jones continued, "university mental health and counseling service centers are having a hard time keeping their head[s] above water."[44]

If statistics for college students offer one indicator of millennial demand for and access to mental health support, the armed services may offer another. 80.4 percent of active duty service members are below age 35, as are 85.3 percent of reservists.[45] As the country endures a sustained period of military activity, millennials are daily mustering out of service, thus lowering the average age of veterans. The resulting strain on psychiatric resources is significant. Of the 2.4 million deployed to wars in Afghanistan and Iraq since 2001, 30 percent experience mental health conditions requiring treatment. Sadly, fewer than half of them will receive care of any sort.[46] When care is available through the Veterans Health Administration or its approved contractors, it has not always proven timely. In the run-up to a scandal which deposed Secretary of

Veterans Affairs Eric Shinseki, the 2012 *Review of Veterans' Access to Mental Health Care* cited as endemic wait times at several representative facilities. Among them, "the Salisbury [Virginia] VA Medical Center had an average wait of 86 days for the psychiatrists' third next available appointment."[47] It should, therefore, surprise few to learn that 15.1 percent of all veteran suicides are committed by those aged 39 and younger,[48] or that suicide is the second leading cause of death among millennials in the general population.[49]

Of course, mental health isn't only the product of professional counseling resources. But, according to multiple studies by the Pew Research Center, millennials don't enjoy the broad support network of friends and religious affiliation[50] that their parents did. They are mistrustful of institutions[51] and further isolated by the delay of longtime romantic partnerships.[52] To put it succinctly, in or out of uniform, in our out of the classroom, millennials constitute the nation's most stressed generation.[53] And many of their stressors—environmental crises, political watersheds, and housing costs among them—seem beyond their power or permission. They are to be forgiven for seeing their own world mirrored in the noir of *Jessica Jones*, a show prominently questioning the limits of free will.

Out of Control: The Angst of Philosophical Conflict

"What are you having—a boy or a girl? Do you know yet?" The questions are typical of any baby shower. An expectant mother sensitive to the zeitgeist might well answer, "I won't know what gender it is until the kid tells me." Such an exchange is emblematic of a culturally pervasive metaphysical libertarianism, a celebration of free will, a belief that events are determined by human actions and decisions.[54] At its simplest, metaphysical libertarianism is expressed by the parental adage "When you grow up, you can be anything you want to be."

This philosophy offers a hopeful vision of personal agency. It must surely appeal to the progressive generation that elected an African American president and legalized gay marriage. Exceeding the 19th-century immigrant's dream of determining one's social class by willpower and effort, libertarianism suggests the boundaries of human experience can be redrawn by popular opinion, shaped by grassroots social activism.

On the other end of the philosophical spectrum is the worldview of determinism, held in common with our ancient Greek forebears. The puny humans of that era understood their place as pawns in the hands of the gods. They accepted many of their life's most important choices were matters of foregone conclusion, decided by the capricious denizens of Olympus.

Some hear echoes of determinism in the writings of 16th-century church reformers. Generally, the doctrine of Predestination holds that God invites humans to a pleasant afterlife. Since he is heaven's sovereign, the invitation to enter must originate with him. Thus, even when humans perceive they have "chosen" an eternity of delight, they are merely responding to an inexorable call. Calvin, Luther, and Zwingli (among other theologians) expanded this view from personal salvation to damnation and, indeed, all evil. Their notion of Double Predestination wonders, "If God invites some to heaven, does he not also sentence others to hell?" and "Does God ordain evil or merely permit it?"

At first blush, determinism seems dour. But it is not without appeal. The experience of "affluenza" defendant Ethan Couch suggests one can hardly be held responsible for circumstances imposed by deity, economy, biology, or politics. As another example, some might take comfort in a recent study indicating that—in obvious addition to environmental and lifestyle factors—even losing one's virginity may be a matter of genetic predisposition.[55]

Millennials' philosophical tensions might be illustrated in the strategies of LGBTQ activists. Gay men and lesbians have recently won a raft of legal victories by reasoning their affections are beyond their control, that some humans are biased from birth in favor of same-sex attraction (determinism). By contrast, members of the transgender community frequently assert a right to self-identify as a preferred gender—or no gender at all (metaphysical libertarianism). Torqued to the point of angst by philosophical conflict, millennials confront long-held assumptions. Marriage, college, children, home ownership, democracy—are desires for these intentional and authentic? Or have they been imprinted by suspect industry, religion, and tradition?

"How do I know *I* want the things I want?" This doubt is Kilgrave's[56] central epistemological threat. He not only forces victims to surrender or to act, but he subjects them to the deeper violation of making them *want*. In the finale's tense climax, Kilgrave doesn't just tell Trish to kiss him, he makes her desire the kiss.[57] In other episodes, he courts Jessica with subtle luxury—five-star hotels, gourmet food, haute couture—building a gilded enclosure he dares her to call a cage. Is such enticement rape or merely seduction? The sociopath is incapable of distinguishing one from the other. Often without knowing they've done so, his casualties embrace Kilgrave's hungers as their own. He erases their capacity for intentionality and self-definition—among the most treasured of millennial character traits.

Some are inclined to speak of Kilgrave's power as godlike. If so, he's a better fit for the ancient Greek model of divinity. Zeus moves. Athena countermoves. Each emotional god is apparently surprised by others, or even kicked off-balance by the occasional, unexpected human hero. Exceptional mortals (perhaps "demigods" better describes those with Jones's gifts) offer deities a rare temptation: the sporting adversary. Jessica's unpredictable willpower is catnip to Kilgrave. Though nearly omnipotent, he can't see the future. He is subject to the law of unintended consequences. Rendered largely proactive by his abilities, he is nevertheless obliged to respond strategically to clever or powerful opponents.

Probity and Family

By contrast, Allah, Yahweh, Jesus, and Brahman are generally credited with foreknowledge or omniscience. But Hell's Kitchen knows no such superpower. Its human analog is surveillance, the private detective's stock-in-trade. Gathered intelligence is a currency of such value that the view through a telephoto lens serves as gateway to the show. Jessica's tough-talking narration overlays a trumpet stolen from Jerry Goldsmith's *Chinatown* score. She follows adulterers to a car beneath a bridge. The cheaters' predictable appetites reward Jones with photographs. Later, from her bathroom, Jones surfs social media to borrow an identity which will help her serve a legal summons. Then it's off to a fire escape stakeout from which she surveils bar owner Luke Cage—all in the series' first ten minutes.[58] Whether by cyber-stalking or old-fashioned legwork, covertly collected data is the coin of this realm.

The tables turn in episode 3 when Jessica discovers that she is being watched by an unknown agent. She explores a purple room papered in photographs of herself. The music descends to a sinister register and the audience feels the sickening twist of obsession take hold.[59] Jessica answers Kilgrave's fixation with yet more surveillance, searching police video footage to discover her junkie neighbor, Malcolm, is spying for the purple Svengali.[60]

Apparently, Jessica's brand of surveillance is meant to be in some way noble. At least it seems noble by comparison to Kilgrave's. In this relativistic corner of Marvel's universe, absolutes of virtuous behavior are of dubious practicality. Jessica, and the audience for which she is proxy, understands it is wrong for a person to be held and traumatized against her will. Yet that is precisely Jones's strategy for dealing with Kilgrave. She drugs him, not with Rohypnol but with Sufentanil, locks him in an airtight chamber, and forces him to endure images of his childhood traumas in a scene reminiscent of *Clockwork Orange*. She beats him, hoping to force a confession. She assaults and restrains a police officer.[61] Extreme events loosen Jessica's moorings from norms of jurisprudence and morality, resulting "in the development of a profound sense of ontological lostness—the sense not just of being lost in the world, but of the loss of the world altogether … the fear that arises when the world ceases to make sense and the horror that accompanies the realization of lostness."[62]

A point of intersection with the noir aesthetic, a millennial's wandering compass of situational ambiguity rejects binary ethics. It further demands (or allows) redefinition of other personal particulars, as Rachel Dolezal demonstrated in 2015. Dolezal was former head of Spokane's chapter of the NAACP. Born to white parents, Dolezal for years "passed" as black, seldom correcting those who assumed her heritage to be African American. "I identify as black," she said.[63] Her parents, however, identify as Caucasian and were instrumental in "outing" their daughter as white.

Though roundly contested by scholars in the social and hard sciences, Dolezal's "transracial" claims illustrate a personal redefinition of ethnicity. Estrangement from her parents illustrates the personal redefinition of family. Such delineation is increasingly common and high profile. Consider the firestorm surrounding Olympic champion Simone Biles. Biles was adopted by her grandparents following a stint in foster care. Gymnastics announcer Al Trautwig refused to acknowledge their status, tweeting: "They may be mom and dad but they are NOT her parents." Both NBC and the announcer were deluged with negative feedback, forcing Trautwig's swift apology.[64]

Not surprisingly, fictional representations reflect contemporary family structures and ties. Since the 1990s, the narrative centrality of nuclear families on television (*I Love Lucy, Leave It to Beaver, The Adventures of Ozzie and Harriet, The Addams Family, Sanford and Son*) has given way to hand-picked companion groups (*Seinfeld, Friends, How I Met Your Mother*). No matter that Howard Wolowitz of *The Big Bang Theory* lives with his mother; her character is relegated to an off-screen voice. She, like the relatives of many millennial protagonists, is exiled on account of boorish or embarrassing behavior.

In the Stygian realm of *Jessica Jones*, however, family bonds are severed by trauma. Patricia Walker ostracizes her mother on grounds of past abuse. Jessica loses her parents to an automobile collision. Hope Shlottman murders her mom and dad, then aborts her child. Albert and Louise Thompson flee their son in fear. Suicide detaches fraternal twins Ruben and Robyn, Jessica's upstairs neighbors. Adultery and violence cost Jeri Hogarth her wife. Almost everyone in Jessica's world is deprived of the advisors and confidantes who know them best, the very people who are most motivated and best equipped to aid them in moral decision-making.

Friends and therapy groups are unlikely to offer guidance and comfort informed by the ideal family's reliability and shared experience. But this bygone archetype of close-knit kinsfolk may have only ever been an imagined average. Certainly by the end of the Second World War, family relationships were subject to profound renegotiation. Riveting Rosies had been summoned to the workforce by the bugle of patriotism. Controlling income streams of their own, this cohort of freshly-minted wage earners exerted unfamiliar, sometimes intimidating authority. A generation of their latchkey kids faced the fears of an atomic age and the modern temptations of rural electrification. Domestic upheavals inspired a grasp at vanishing national innocence. Competing political and religious philosophies were decried as threats to civic homogeneity. Even previously harmless amusements were subject to new ideological scrutiny, especially those which targeted America's impressionable youth.

Heralds of the Dark Age: The Dark Knight Returns and Watchmen

In 1954, publishers of sequential art authored a self-policing Comics Code Authority. Not unlike Hollywood's 1930 Production Code, the CCA forestalled a threat of government censorship in the wake of Senate hearings on juvenile delinquency. Thus, for decades, Rockwellian versions of Superman and his virtuous pals avoided extreme violence, ignoble sex, and gruesome horror.[65] Periodic erosions of the Code began in the 1970s. Popular comics occasionally and gingerly accommodated drug use and venal public officials[66] until 1986. That year, two titles appropriated the style and themes of film noir, plunging the medium into blackness, heralding a new and Dark Age of comics.[67]

Substantiating the impact of any genre often begins by specifying its unique set of visual and thematic codes.[68] But the battle to define (or to dismiss) noir has raged since the summer of 1946. When the German embargo was lifted on American films at the end of World War II, French theaters were flooded with a Hollywood backlog.

> From mid–July to the end of August, five movies flashed one after the other across Parisian screens, movies which shared a strange and violent tone, tinged with a unique kind of eroticism: John Huston's *The Maltese Falcon*; Otto Preminger's *Laura*; Edward Dmytryk's *Murder, My Sweet*; Billy Wilder's *Double Indemnity*; and Fritz Lang's *The Woman in the Window*.[69]

In a seminal review, critic Nino Frank referenced these movies collectively, coining the phrase "film noir."[70] Almost immediately (and to this day), many have cited exceptions and comparisons to challenge Frank's taxonomy. The canon is thus amorphous and debatable, less tidy than Science Fiction or Westerns.[71] Are its boundaries delimited by urban settings? By criminal plots? By morally ambiguous characters? By low-key lighting and unbalanced compositions? Perhaps few defenders of noir can do better than to appropriate Justice Potter Stewart's famous yardstick: "I know it when I see it."[72] Readers of *The Dark Knight Returns* and *Watchmen* undoubtedly "saw it."

Frank Miller wrote and penciled *The Dark Knight Returns,* casting the cynical Batman as a blood-spilling vigilante in a dystopia overrun by mass murderers and armored gangs. The comic's visual style, created in concert with inker Klaus Janson, was as black as its subject matter. Miller, Janson, and colorist Lynn Varley might well have cribbed ebony silhouettes from *The Big Combo* (1955) or doom-laden layouts from *The Lady from Shanghai* (1947). The creators so proudly acknowledged their debt to this cinematic tradition, they reissued a hardbound edition of the seminal comic without color, retitling it *Batman Noir: The Dark Knight Returns.*

The genre's signature aesthetic is perhaps less evident in the straightforward line work for Alan Moore's *Watchmen.* Artist Dave Gibbons's nine-panel grid generally steered clear of disorienting angles, intentionally rendering the "layout almost invisible or predictable."[73] But the story's leitmotifs of nihilism and corruption were stylistically affirmed by colorist John Higgins. Higgins "looked at movies and color photographs, to see how different base colors, human flesh or clothes, looked in shadow or in glaring neon light and tried to show how color changed … when passing into different light sources," or reflecting from various surfaces.[74] The result is a comic which is, by turns, both garish and muted,[75] depending on the narrative's emotional temperature. Moore described Higgins's strategy for *Watchmen*'s sixth issue: "It starts off really warm and cheerful … and on page five we make it a bit darker, and on page seven darker still, and it's like the lights are going down the entire issue, so when you get to the end it's really dark and really black."[76]

Batman Darkens the Screen

Batman (1989) was by no means the earliest comic film, but it was the first major studio superhero feature to succeed publication of *Watchmen* and *The Dark Knight Returns.* Taking cues from Moore and Miller,[77] director Tim Burton departed significantly from the sun-lit, aw-shucks heroes of Adam West, Lynda Carter, and Christopher Reeve. Critics traced *Batman*'s stylized grit to its antecedent film genre. "*Batman* … returns to the mood of the 1940s, the decade of *film noir* and fascism," said Roger Ebert.[78] "It was a shrewd choice for Burton to emulate the jarring angles and creepy lighting of *film noir*," declared *Variety.*[79] *The Hollywood Reporter* presaged the movie's Oscar win, observing its "disturbing portrait of a decaying society without structure or purpose. Production designer Anton Furst has created a Gotham City that is a dark, steaming cesspool, littered with waste."[80]

Batman was the year's biggest box office success. Worldwide, it grossed $411 million for comics giant DC and its parent corporation, Time Warner.[81] Meanwhile publishing rival Marvel slid toward bankruptcy. Its sale of film rights was motivated more by financial desperation than by creative strategy. When the company emerged from Chapter 11 protection in 1997, its character licenses were scattered across a panoply of studios: Men in Black and Spiderman were at Sony; The Fantastic Four, Daredevil, and X-Men were at Fox; Iron Man and Blade were at New Line; Captain America and Thor were at Artisan Entertainment; and Universal had The Incredible Hulk.

Adults Only: Jessica Jones in Print

Marvel's concurrent plan to boost magazine sales envisioned a wider base of adult readers. The CCA became a quaint relic of the Eisenhower era. Editors recruited writers and artists from "underground comix," whose content was frequently satirical and pornographic.[82] Their adult themes and explicit depictions were often sequestered from A-list superheroes under auxiliary corporate brands. One such subsidiary imprint was MAX, christened in 2001 with the inaugural volume of Alias (after Jessica Jones's detective firm, Alias Investigations). The new protagonist immediately specifies the periodical's mature parameters by dropping an "f-bomb" in the opening panel. "See, we can't have the kids picking up an issue of Alias looking for Wolverine and getting a mouth full of my potty, we just can't," acknowledged writer Brian Michael Bendis.[83] But Alias, co-created with Bendis by artist Michael Gaydos, wasn't merely shadowy and uncensored. It was heir apparent to the noir influences of Dark Age comics on both page and screen.

While a cinematographer captures brightness and hue simultaneously, a team of comic pencillers and inkers choose lighting values independent of the colorist's later work. Many images start with simple borders, relatively uniform in line width (figure 1). Shading and cross-hatching, inkers refine a continuum of gray. They let ebony pool in detail-obscuring shadows. Their "spot blacks" add depth, volume, and weight (figure 2). They designate mood and compositional emphasis.[84] Industry veteran Larry Hama takes seriously an artist's responsibility for lighting: "If the colorist has to ask if a scene takes place at night, you haven't done your job."[85]

Hama might have been writing the playbook for Gaydos's work on Alias. Smoky rooms striped by venetian blinds, depressing Manhattan rainstorms, even expositional conversations—they're all murky with ink, even before colorist Matt Hollingsworth blankets the panels with desaturated stains. Readers strain to distinguish facial features from shadows as Jessica recalls eight months of brainwashing:

> He fucking made me stand there and watch him fuck other girls. Telling me to wish it was me. Telling me to cry while I watched.... In my mind I can't tell the difference between what he made me do or say and what I do or say on my own. The only reason I know I wasn't in love with him is that I say to myself: How could I be? I hate him.[86]

Top: Figure 1: An example of basic rendering a comic artist might begin with in a panel. *Bottom*: Figure 2: An example of a further-refined panel (artwork by Tristan Fuller, used with permission).

Given the gravity of such dialogue, it could surprise no one if spot blacks were more important to *Alias* than to, say, *Archie*.

Any reader inclined to discount the comic's noir pedigree need only consult the flashbacks of issue 25, drawn in the slick style of the Silver Age by guest artist Mark Bagley. In them, Jessica recounts her time as Jewel, a carefree peacemaker in Spandex. Jewel drops into a downtown melee imagining she will make short work of a street fight. But the senseless mayhem

174 Jessica Jones, Scarred Superhero

can't be quieted. The brawlers are subject to the hypnotic influence of a man with purple skin, a smooth European who dines calmly amid a riot of his own making. When the bright flashbacks end, readers return to a gritty world rendered grittier by stylistic contrast. New York's Clinton neighborhood is a sick place. And its sickness has a name: Zebediah Killgrave.

Originally introduced as an antagonist for Daredevil in 1964, Killgrave was a Croatian physician who became a Soviet Bloc spy. Exposure to an experimental nerve gas turned his flesh a deep shade of amethyst and gave his pheromones the power to control others in his proximity.[87] His ambitions surely constrained by the CCA, Killgrave's goals seldom stretched beyond robbery over a half-dozen appearances culminating in the character's 1999 retirement.[88]

Bendis resurrected Killgrave in 2003, cruelly warping the Purple Man's 35-year backstory. Killgrave's psycho-sexual abuse of Jones coincides with his defeats at the hands of Daredevil. Says Jones, "he was doing this to me for every fucking time Daredevil beat the shit out of him."[89] Ultimately, Killgrave banishes the detective from his sight, hoping to simultaneously dispatch both Jones and Daredevil with one final fiat: "I want you to take a rusty pipe and I want you to shove it up Daredevil's stupid fucking ass!!"[90] The visual and thematic darkness uniting this trio of characters would prove significant a decade later when Hell's Kitchen became Marvel's nucleus of live-action noir.

MCU TV

Alias finished its print run in January 2004. Jessica Jones migrated to *Pulse*, a mainstream monthly in which she enjoyed greater interaction with established stars of Marvel's printed (generally brighter) universe. But a live-action macrocosm was only just beginning to take shape. Still disjointed by the earlier sale of character film rights, a Marvel Cinematic Universe (MCU) didn't coalesce until a deal with Merrill Lynch secured the wherewithal for the publisher to finance its own movies and regather its characters under a single roof. $525 million in revolving credit let Marvel Studios plant their flag with *Iron Man* and an initial phase of nine successive, interrelated films.[91]

For President of Production Kevin Feige, a suite of integrated narratives wasn't merely a financial strategy; it was a creative mirroring of the team and solo adventures that have characterized comics since the 1960s[92]:

> It's never been done before.... The other filmmakers aren't used to getting actors from other movies ... certain plot lines that are connected or certain locations that are connected but I think for the most part, in fact, entirely everyone was on board for it and thinks that it's fun.... My goal is that moviegoers have the same experience comic book readers had, that when you turn the page anybody can pop up and any other character can come into it.[93]

By almost any reckoning, Feige has parlayed the MCU into the world's highest-grossing box office franchise, with more than $10 billion in ticket sales as of summer 2016.[94]

Following Disney's purchase of Marvel Entertainment in 2009, a television expansion of the MCU to ABC (also Disney-owned) was predictable. Not long after the release of *Iron Man 3* (2013), the network began airing both *Agents of S.H.I.E.L.D.* (extending *The Avengers* big-screen narrative) and *Agent Carter* (a *Captain America* spinoff). But ABC passed on an initial *Jessica Jones* pilot.[95] "I think tonally it just wasn't quite the right fit," said *Jones* series creator Melissa Rosenberg.[96]

In a secretive 2013 negotiation,[97] Jeph Loeb, Head of Marvel Television, drafted an unprecedented streaming deal for a tetralogy, "set in the gritty world of heroes and villains of Hell's Kitchen, New York."[98] Netflix committed to four shows (*Daredevil*, *Jessica Jones*, *Luke Cage*, and *Iron Fist*) and a miniseries (*The Defenders*, which unites all four title characters), a total of no fewer than 60 episodes with almost no named talent then attached—testament to the strength of the Marvel brand.

First in the pipeline was *Daredevil*, the rights to which had reverted to Marvel when Fox missed a sequel production deadline. Showrunner Steven DeKnight and pilot director Phil Abraham envisioned a boundary-pushing, "modern-day *film noir*." But when filming started in July 2014, cinematographer Matthew Lloyd could identify only one camera, Red's Epic Dragon, capable of accommodating noir's low-light photography, slow-motion action sequences, and Netflix's anticipated rollout of Ultra HD streaming.[99] Some worried that television simply wasn't ready for true noir.

"Noir-Compatible" Televisions

The genre is amorphously defined but plainly named: *film* noir. Yet too little analysis considers the actual contribution of film technology and economy to visual style. In the 1940s and 50s, stocks like Kodak's Super-XX (used by Gregg Toland to shoot *Citizen Kane*) and Tri-X (used by Stanley Cortez to shoot *Night of the Hunter*) produced high speed negatives that withstood underexposure and push-processing. Cost-conscious studios embraced the stocks, particularly on "B" pictures, since doing so meant they could save money on lighting.[100]

Cheaper lighting and more sensitive emulsions freed John Alton, cinematographer of *T-Men* (Anthony Mann, 1947) and *The Big Combo* (Joseph H. Lewis, 1955), to pursue the storytelling possibilities of darkness. "When there is no light, one cannot see; and when one cannot see, his imagination starts to run wild. He begins to suspect that something is about to happen.

In the dark there is mystery."[101] Alton's pioneering book, *Painting with Light*, offers both technical instruction and philosophical reasoning for illuminating various scenes common to criminal dramas. He writes, "Interiors of a prison should never be bright, even in daylight scenes. For prisoners the sun never rises. There is a constant pressure overhead. Life in captivity is dark.... LIGHT IS LIBERTY AND LIBERTY IS LIFE."[102]

While film technology tailored noir to the silver screen, it simultaneously rendered the genre less suitable for television. Hired to film *I Love Lucy*, Karl Freund—ironically the cinematographer for expressionistic *noir* forbears *Metropolis* (Fritz Lang, 1927), *Dracula* (Tod Browning and Karl Freund, 1931), and *Mad Love* (Karl Freund, 1935)—established lighting standards to decrease film contrast, hoping to offset television's nascent image pickup system.[103] His high-key scheme, heavily dependent on unmotivated backlight to distinguish actors from background, defined the "look of most television for decades, in both comedy *and* drama, long after the transition to color."[104] Nuanced lighting, infrequently attempted between 1955 and 2005, seldom survived analog broadcast engineers instructed to normalize deep shadows before air.[105]

Not until the 21st century did digital television broadcast and manufacture accommodate the extreme contrast ratios associated with film noir. Even the best analog televisions were seldom capable of 30 shades of difference between solid black and solid white (a contrast ratio of only 30:1). Today, however, ratios of more than 5000:1 are not uncommon.[106] One might say only recently have televisions become "noir compatible." Even so, the Federal Communications Commission (FCC) obliges broadcasters and cable operators to function within certain technical parameters.

Imagine watching a string of NBC shows and commercials on a Thursday night. A sitcom might be made by Warner, a one-hour police procedural by Paramount, the ads by any number of agencies, the news by a local affiliate station. But all programming is produced to the network's uniform standards, then sent from a central engineering hub to American homes. Thus, from 8 to 11:30 p.m., viewers seldom adjust brightness, contrast, volume, gamma, or any of their television's myriad settings.

Compare that experience to watching a half-hour of YouTube. It wouldn't be unusual for three successive videos to share no common volume levels or even aspect ratios. The same shade of red might register as nearly orange in a compilation of cat antics, but purple in a confessional vlog. Because net-streamed and downloaded video aren't subject to the FCC's television conventions, the web is a Wild West of technical specifications.

Cinematographers of stream-native programming (Netflix and Hulu originals, for example) have been quick to pair these new freedoms with a digital work flow. In a roundtable that included the D.P.s of *Better Call Saul* and *Jessica Jones, Game of Thrones'* Director of Photography David Franco explains that low-light photography is cost effective as it never was before.

> "You see the end results right away, so you can push it as far as you can without having to do tests and figure out exactly how low [the lighting] can get." To shoot that dark a sequence on film, he explained, he would need to do a series of tests—half a day, he estimated, of filming and pre-lighting to test out how each shot looked. Financially, this would have been prohibitive, especially since they were shooting not in a studio but in an actual underground catacomb in Croatia.[107]

Thus, only as recently as 2013 (the year Netflix premiered *House of Cards*, its first in-house production) has distribution, regulation, and imaging technology, combined to make possible a television (laptop? internet? streaming?)[108] noir aesthetic as dark as cinema's—and *Daredevil* was primed to capitalize on the convergence.

Daredevil and a Definition of Noir

Echoing sentiments from across the blogosphere, Sulagna Misra readily identified the pilot's artistic pedigree: "The show is dark, certainly, but dark in a more *film noir* way, without needing to put on and point out its fedora. You've got dames with problems and constant cloudiness and calling in old favors, sure, but most of all, you have corrupt systems undergirding a city full of secrets."[109]

Though their strongly held opinions are easily accessible, it's hard to be certain freelance web contributors share the educated definition of film noir that arises from mindful, curated screenings of its texts. Credentialed journalists and academics alike lament the "Google-fueled, Wikipedia-based, blog-sodden collapse of any division between professionals and laymen, students and teachers, knowers and wonderers—in other words, between those of any achievement in an area and those with none at all."[110] The erosion of serious scholarship in pop-culture studies (to name but one branch of the humanities) constitutes a particular concern. It loosens the knot tethering criticism to historical and ideological context in favor of subjective, knee-jerk reviews. Given the average child's diet of six or more hours of daily screen time,[111] "art, especially art that seems to require the least amount of scholarly attention—reality TV, video games, comics—is precisely the art that *most* needs history, context, and deep study."[112]

To that end, a definition of noir probably lacks both context and nuance if it evokes images of a club bouncer who decides to admit or refuse entry based on some checklist of tropes. Alternatively, Imogen Sara Smith stipulates a spectrum of noir, "as alcoholic beverages are labeled by proof." She proposes four characteristics of the genre: (1) criminal or sinful plot elements, (2) a psychologically convoluted narrative method, (3) expressionistic visual style, and (4) "a tone of enveloping pessimism."[113]

In the Marvel/Netflix series *Daredevil* (2015), faith, justice, and mercy conflict against a background of all four characteristics. Like many a vigilante, Matt Murdock's mission is to close by force the loopholes through which the dark-hearted too often escape the law's noble intent. A blind lawyer by day, Murdock's heightened senses aid in Daredevil's nightly crusade against corruption in Hell's Kitchen.

Critics loved *Daredevil*'s first season.[114] They frequently praised show runners Drew Goddard and Steven DeKnight for daring to embrace a "PG-16" level of violence long suggested by the character in print. But even DeKnight understood that a spectrum like Smith's might accommodate even darker storytelling:

> I think once *Daredevil* was a hit and people were really responding positively, you can see the progression into more of an adult world in *Jessica Jones* where there are a lot of sexual situations, and for *Jessica Jones*, it's absolutely the right thing to do. Anyone who has read Brian Michael Bendis' amazing *Alias* storyline knows that…. If you look at *Jessica Jones*, it's a lot more graphically violent than *Daredevil* … but I think *Daredevil*'s success made them a little more comfortable about pushing it a little further.[115]

"Comic noir" antecedents of page and screen, franchise rights and corporate finances, digital technology and government regulation, even *Daredevil*'s "dry run"—all comprised the springboard from which *Jessica Jones* could, in the words of Louisa Ellen Stein, "rework the cinematic traditions of *film noir,* sometimes taking the form of self-conscious homage and sometimes surfacing in more incidental recreations of *noir* themes and aesthetics."[116] Stein's analysis of contemporary fandom identifies a millennial appetite for media texts that are melodramatic, taboo, and feminine, straddling the line between liminal and mainstream and "rife with issues of gender negotiation."[117] *Jessica Jones* clearly meets these qualifications. But that hardly makes the show's conflicted protagonist an example to be imitated.

Viewers might well sympathize with Jones as she navigates the issues of mental health with which her audience and gender are all too familiar. But none dare mimic her. She did, after all, snap a man's neck, having decided he was too evil to live. Thus she twists perilously between a victim's relived trauma and a hangman's burden of guilt. The struggle resonates as so authentic, other superheroes are one-dimensional by comparison.

But Jones doesn't compare herself to other superheroes. She has opted out of Spandex. She has retired her "Jewel" alter ego. Even so, she can't seem to shake an obligation to intervene in violent circumstances on behalf of weaker mortals. Liberated by fate's gift of super-strength, Jessica is simultaneously constrained by its resulting responsibilities. Viewers might well appreciate this paradox of free will as a metaphor for conflict in their own lives. Many of them are squeezed between the opportunities afforded the well-educated and the crippling onus of student debt—to choose but one millennial vise.

True to its literary and cinematic antecedents, *Jessica Jones*, resolves none of these conflicts. Its titular character defies emulation. Certainly, she knows right from wrong. Just as certainly, she is possessed of adamantine resolve. But—though her struggles are universal—her choices are her own. Her actions define principled decency on Jessica's own terms. Her behavior, her example, her success can't be copied or celebrated. She is not a role model. Indeed, the very notion of a role model challenges both genre conventions and the spirit of millennial angst. It might, therefore, be more apt to name Jessica Jones a reassuring dark angel who survives noir's darker universe.

NOTES

1. *15 Economic Facts About Millennials* (Washington, D.C.: The Council of Economic Advisors, October 2016), 5, Accessed August 3, 2016, https://www.whitehouse.gov/sites/default/files/docs/millennials_report.pdf.

2. Nellie Andreeva, "Netflix Won't Release *Lilyhammer* Ratings, Company's Ted Sarandos Explains Why," *Deadline Hollywood*, February 7, 2012, http://deadline.com/2012/02/netflix-wont-release-lilyhammer-ratings-companys-ted-sarandos-explains-why-227285/#more-227285.

3. Joe Flint and Ben Fritz, "Netflix Viewership Finally Gets a Yardstick," *The Wall Street Journal*, August 26, 2015, http://www.wsj.com/articles/netflix–viewership-finally-gets-a-yardstick-1440630513.

4. Jeanine Poggi, "Inside the Company Behind Netflix's Measurement War," *Advertising Age*, January 19, 2016, http://adage.com/article/digital/inside-company-claims-measure-netflix/302187.

5. Daniel Holloway, "TV Ratings: Amazon's *Transparent* Lags Behind Netflix, Hulu Shows," *Variety*, June 21, 2016, http://variety.com/2016/digital/news/amazon-transparent-hulu-netflix-making-a-murderer-112263-catastrophe-1201798269.

6. Tony Maglio, "25 Highest Rated Broadcast TV Shows of 2015–2016 Season," *The Wrap*, June 9, 2016, http://www.thewrap.com/25-highest-rated-tv-shows-nfl-empire-big-bang-cbs-nbc-fox-abc/?mode=3.

7. Jason Mander, "Netflix Has Twice as Many American Users as Subscribers," *Global Web Index*, April 20, 2015, http://www.globalwebindex.net/blog/netflix-has-twice-as-many-american-users-as-subscribers.

8. *Ibid.*

9. Shalini Rakmachandran and Maria Armental, "At Netflix, Big Jump in Users—and Costs," *The Wall Street Journal*, July 15, 2015, http://www.wsj.com/articles/netflix-reports-jump-in-streaming-users-1436991166.

10. See https://www.netflix.com/browse/genre/7687 and https://www.culturedvultures.com/film-noir-streaming, among many other online category search resources.

11. Goeff Berkshire, "*Red Widow:* Melissa Rosenberg plans a 'cable-esque' show for network television," *zap2it*, January 10, 2013, http://zap2it.com/2013/01/red-widow-melissa-rosenberg-plans-a-cable-esque-show-for-network-television.

12. Nikolas Akash, "Where Is the Female Tony Soprano?" *The Atlantic*, June 27, 2013, http://www.theatlantic.com/entertainment/archive/2013/06/where-is-the-female-tony-soprano/277270.

13. Berkshire, "*Red Widow.*"

14. Jami Philbrick, "Exclusive: Screenwriter Melissa Rosenberg talks *AKA Jessica Jones*," *I Am Rogue*, November 9, 2011, http://www.iamrogue.com/news/movie-news/item/5226-exclusive-screenwriter-melissa-rosenberg-talks-aka-jessica-jones.html.

15. Nancy C. Andreasen, "Posttraumatic Stress Disorder: A History and a Critique," *Annals of the New York Academy of Sciences*, October 2010, http://www.brainline.org/content/2011/01/posttraumatic-stress-disorder-a-history-and-a-critique_pageall.html.

16. Zachary Steel, Tien Chey, Derrick Silove, Claire Marnane, Richard A. Bryant, and Mark van Ommeren, "Association of torture and other potentially traumatic events with mental health outcomes among populations exposed to mass conflict and displacement: a systematic review and meta-anaylsis," *Journal of the American Medical Association* 302:5 (August 5, 2009): 538. doi: 10.1001/jama.2009.1132.

17. Jami Philbrick, "Exclusive: Screenwriter Melissa Rosenberg talks *AKA Jessica Jones*," *I Am Rogue*, November 9, 2011, http://www.iamrogue.com/news/movie-news/item/5226-exclusive-screenwriter-melissa-rosenberg-talks-aka-jessica-jones.html.

18. Terence M. Keane, Jessica Wolfe, and Kathryn L. Taylor, "Post-traumatic stress disorder; Evidence for diagnostic validity and methods of psychological assessment," *Journal of Clinical Psychology* 43, no.1 (January 1987): 36. doi: 10.1002/1097–4679(198701)43:1<32::AID-JCLP2270430106>3.0.CO;2-X.

19. Raymond Borde and Etienne Chaumeton, "Towards a Definition of *Film Noir*," trans. Alain Silver in *Film Noir Reader*, ed. Alain Silver and James Ursini (Compton Plains, NJ: Limelight, 1996), 25.

20. Libby Hill, "Krysten Ritter on playing anti-superhero, Jessica Jones," *Los Angeles Times*, November 18, 2015, http://www.latimes.com/entertainment/tv/la-et-st-krysten-ritter-jessica-jones-20151118-story.html.

21. *Posttraumatic Stress Disorder Fact Sheet* (Arlington, VA: American Psychiatric Association, 2013), 1, accessed May 30, 2016, http://www.dsm5.org/Documents/PTSD %20Fact %20Sheet.pdf.

22. Joseph Volpicelli, et al., "The Role of Uncontrollable Trauma in the development of PTSD and Alcohol Addiction," *Alcohol Research and Health* 23:4 (1999): 258.

23. Will Perkins, "Marvel's Jessica Jones," *Art of the Title*, March 1, 2016, http://www.artofthetitle.com/title/jessica-jones.

24. *Marvel's Jessica Jones*, "AKA WWJD?" Season 1, Episode 8, Netflix, November 20, 2015.

25. *Marvel's Jessica Jones*, "AKA The Sandwich Saved Me," Season 1, Episode 5, Netflix, November 20, 2015.

26. Ronald C. Kessler, et al., "Posttraumatic stress disorder in the National Comorbidity Survey," *Archives of General Psychiatry* 52:12 (December 1995): 1052. doi:10.1001/archpsyc.1995.03950240066012.

27. "The Rising Cost of Not Going to College," *Pew Research Center*, February 11, 2014, http://www.pewsocialtrends.org/2014/02/11/the-rising-cost-of-not-going-to-college.

28. *15 Economic Facts About Millennials* (Washington, D.C.: The Council of Economic Advisors, 2014), October 2014, https://www.whitehouse.gov/sites/default/files/docs/millennials_report.pdf.

29. Anya Kamenetz, "The History of Campus Sexual Assault," *NPR Ed*, November 30, 2014, http://www.npr.org/sections/ed/2014/11/30/366348383/the-history-of-campus-sexual-assault.

30. Christopher P. Krebs, et al., *The Campus Sexual Assault (CSA) Study*, December 2007, https://www.ncjrs.gov/pdffiles1/nij/grants/221153.pdf.

31. Emily Yoffe, "The College Rape Overcorrection," *Slate*, December 7, 2014, http://www.slate.com/articles/double_x/doublex/2014/12/college_rape_campus_sexual_assault_is_a_serious_problem_but_the_efforts.html.

32. Caroline Heldman and Baillee Brown, "Campus Rape: A Brief History of Sexual Violence Activism in the U.S.," *Feminist Fight Club*, August 8, 2014, https://carolineheldman.me/2014/08/08/campus-rape-a-brief-history-of-sexual-violence-activism-in-the-u-s.

33. Geoff S. Larcom, "Eastern Michigan University to pay $350,000 in federal fines over Laura Dickinson case," *Ann Arbor News*, June 6, 2008, http://blog.mlive.com/annarbornews/2008/06/eastern_michigan_university_to.html.

34. Russlyn Ali, "Dear Colleague Letter," *U.S. Department of Education Office for Civil Rights*, April 4, 2011, http://www2.ed.gov/print/about/offices/list/ocr/letters/colleague-201104.html.

35. Theodore R. Delwiche, Noah J. Delwiche, and Andrew M. Duehren, "Law School Found in Violation of Title IX after Years-Long Probe," *The Harvard Crimson*, December 30, 2014, http://www.thecrimson.com/article/2014/12/30/law-school-violation-title-ix.

36. Sheila Coronel, Steve Coll, and Derek Kravitz, "'A Rape on Campus' What Went Wrong?" *Rolling Stone*, April 5, 2015, http://www.rollingstone.com/culture/features/a-rape-on-campus-what-went-wrong-20150405.

37. *Marvel's Jessica Jones*, "AKA It's Called Whiskey," Season 1, Episode 3, Netflix, November 20, 2015.

38. Maureen Ryan, "How *Jessica Jones'* Creative Team Tackled Assault, Consent and Sexuality," *Variety*, January 18, 2016, http://variety.com/2016/tv/news/jessica-jones-sex-assault-consent-1201682069.

39. Dominic Patten, "*Marvel's Jessica Jones* EP Melissa Rosenberg on Luke Cage, Season 2, *Supergirl* & Gender Parity in Hollywood," *Deadline Hollywood*, November 18, 2015, http://deadline.com/2015/11/jessica-jones-spoilers-marvel-melissa-rosenberg-krysten-ritter-luke-cage-1201628832.

40. "The State of Mental Health on College Campuses: A Growing Crisis," *American Psychological Association*, 2011, http://www.apa.org/about/gr/education/news/2011/college-campuses.aspx.

41. Gregg Henriques, "The College Student Mental Health Crisis," *Psychology Today*, February 15, 2014, https://www.psychologytoday.com/blog/theory-knowledge/201402/the-college-student-mental-health-crisis.

42. Loretta G. Breuning, "Why I Don't Believe Reports of a Mental Health Crisis," *Psychology Today*, February 23, 2014, https://www.psychologytoday.com/blog/your-neuro-chemical-self/201402/why-i-don-t-believe-reports-mental-health-crisis.

43. *2015 Annual Report* (State College, PA: Center for Collegiate Mental Health, 2016), 2, January 2016, http://ccmh.psu.edu/wp-content/uploads/sites/3058/2016/01/2015_CCMH_Report_1–18–2015.pdf.

44. Tyler Kingkade, "Using College Mental Health Services Can Lead to Students Getting Removed From Campus," *The Huffington Post*, October 7, 2014, http://www.huffingtonpost.com/2014/10/07/college-mental-health-services_n_5900632.html.

45. *2012 Demographics: Profile of the Military Community* (Washington, D.C.: Office of the Deputy Assistant Secretary of Defense, 2012), 36, 86–87, 2012, http://download.military onesource.mil/12038/MOS/Reports/2012_Demographics_Report.pdf.

46. *Meeting the Behavioral Health Needs of Veterans: Operation Enduring Freedom and Operation Iraqi Freedom* (Washington, D.C.: National Council for Behavioral Health, 2012), 2, November 2012, http://www.thenationalcouncil.org/wp-content/uploads/2013/02/Veterans-BH-Needs-Report.pdf.

47. *Review of Veterans' Access to Mental Health Care* (Washington, D.C.: VA Office of Inspector General, 2012), 7, April 23, 2012, http://www.va.gov/oig/pubs/VAOIG-12–00900–168.pdf.

48. Janet Kemp and Robert Bossarte, *Suicide Data Report, 2012* (Washington, D.C.: Department of Veterans Affairs, February 2013), 22, http://www.va.gov/opa/docs/suicide-data-report-2012-final.pdf.

49. *Suicide: Facts at a Glance* (Atlanta: Centers for Disease Control and Prevention 2015), 2, http://www.cdc.gov/violenceprevention/pdf/suicide-datasheet-a.PDF.

50. *America's Changing Religious Landscape* (Washington, D.C.: Pew Research Center, May 12, 2015), 5, http://www.pewforum.org/files/2015/05/RLS-08–26-full-report.pdf.

51. *Millennials in Adulthood: Detached from Institutions, Networked with Friends* (Washington, D.C.: Pew Research Center, 2014), March 7, 2014, http://www.pewsocialtrends.org/files/2014/03/2014–03–07_generations-report-version-for-web.pdf.

52. *Millennials: Confident. Connected. Open to Change* (Washington, D.C.: Pew Research Center, 2010), 11, February 2010, http://www.pewsocialtrends.org/files/2010/10/millennials-confident-connected-open-to-change.pdf.

53. Michelle Castillo, "Millennials are the most stressed generation, survey finds," *CBS News*, February 11, 2013, http://www.cbsnews.com/news/millennials-are-the-most-stressed-generation-survey-finds.

54. Galen Strawson, "Free Will," *Rutledge Encyclopedia of Philosophy* (London: Routledge, 2011), doi: 10.4324/9780415249126-V014-2.

55. Day, Felix, et al., "Physical and neurobehavioral determinants of reproductive onset and success," *Nature Genetics* 48, no.6 (June 2016): 622, doi: 10.1038/ng.3551.

56. Unlike the comic villain, the television character's *nom de guerre* is spelled with one "L."

57. *Marvel's Jessica Jones*, "AKA Smile," Season 1: Episode 13, Netflix, November 20, 2015.

58. *Marvel's Jessica Jones*, "AKA Ladies Night," Season 1: Episode 1, Netflix, November 20, 2015.

59. *Marvel's Jessica Jones*, "AKA It's Called Whiskey," Season 1: Episode 3, Netflix, November 20, 2015.

60. *Marvel's Jessica Jones*, "AKA 99 Friends," Season 1: Episode 4, Netflix, November 20, 2015.

61. *Marvels Jessica Jones*, "AKA Sin Bin," Season 1: Episode 9, Netflix, November 20, 2016.

62. Jeffrey Andrew Weinstock, "Lostness (Blair Witch)," in *Nothing That Is: Millennial Cinema and the Blair Witch Controversies*, ed. Sarah L. Higley and Jeffrey Andrew Weinstock (Detroit: Wayne State University Press, 2002), 237, 242.

63. Greg Botelho, "Ex-NAACP leader Rachel Dolezal: 'I identify as black,'" CNNwww, June 17, 2015, http://www.cnn.com/2015/06/16/us/washington-rachel-dolezal-naacp.

64. Erik Brady and Rachel Axon, "NBC's Al Trautwig apologizes for comments on Simone Biles' parents," *USA Today*, August 8, 2016. http://www.usatoday.com/story/sports/olympics/rio-2016/2016/08/08/al-trautwig-apology-simon-biles-parents/88402048.

65. David Hajdu, *The Ten-Cent Plague: The Great Comic-Book Scare and How It Changed America* (New York: Farrar, Straus and Giroux, 2008), 128–130.

66. Don and Maggie Thompson, *Crack in the Code*, Newfangles, February 1971, accessed July 10, 2016, http://www.ebay.com/itm/NEWFANGLES-44-FANZINE-1970-DON-AND-MAGGIE-THOMPSON-/390654950738.

67. Mark Vogler, *The Dark Age: Grim, Great & Gimmicky Post-Modern Comics* (Raleigh, NC: TwoMorrows Publishing, 2006), 21.

68. Alain Silver, Introduction to *Film Noir Reader*, ed. Alain Silver and James Ursini (Compton Plains, NJ: Limelight, 1996), 7–10.

69. Raymond Borde and Etienne Chaumeton, *A Panorama of American Film Noir (1941–1953)*, trans. Paul Hammond (San Francisco: City Lights, 2002), 1.

70. Nino Frank, "Un nouveau genre 'policier': L'aventure criminelle," *L'Ecran français*, August 28, 1946, 14.

71. Richard Brody, "'Film Noir': The Elusive Genre," *The New Yorker*, July 23, 2014, http://www.newyorker.com/culture/richard-brody/film-noir-elusive-genre-2.

72. *Jacobellis v. Ohio*, 378 U.S. 184 (1964).

73. "Illustrating *Watchmen*: Q&A with Dave Gibbons," WatchmenComicMoviewww, October 23, 2008, http://www.watchmencomicmovie.com/102308-dave-gibbons-watchmen-comic-illustrator.php.

74. Andrea Fiamma, "From *Watchmen* to *Orfani*: A Colorists' Roundtable," *The Comics Journal*, March 30, 2016, http://www.tcj.com/from-watchmen-to-orfani-a-colorists-roundtable.

75. "Bristol: Gibbons & Higgins Talk *Watchmen*," *Comic Book Resources*, May 20, 2009, http://www.comicbookresources.com/?page=article&id=21282.

76. "A Portal to Another Dimension: Alan Moore, Dave Gibbons, and Neil Gaiman," *The Comics Journal*, June 6, 2012, http://www.tcj.com/a-portal-to-another-dimension-alan-moore-dave-gibbons-and-neil-gaiman.

77. Tim Burton, "Batman," in *Burton on Burton*, ed. Mark Salisbury (London: Faber and Faber, 2006), 71.

78. Roger Ebert, "Batman," *Chicago Sun-Times*, June 23, 1989.

79. "Review: *Batman*" (excerpt), *Variety*, 1989, accessed July 23, 2016, http://variety.com/1988/film/reviews/batman-2-1200428063.

80. "*Batman*: THR 's 1989 Review," *The Hollywood* Reporter, accessed July 23, 2016, http://www.hollywoodreporter.com/news/batman-thrs-1989-review-801339.

81. "Batman," *Box Office Mojo,* accessed August 2, 2016, http://www.boxofficemojo. com/movies/?id=batman.htm.

82. Roger Sabin, *Comics, Comix & Graphic Novels: A History of Comic Art* (London: Phaidon Press, 1996), 94–95.

83. Brian Michael Bendis, "Farewell to *Alias," Jessica Jones: Alias,* January 2004, 23.

84. Michael Cho, "The Importance of Light and Shadow," class lecture handout, February 3, 2009, http://chodrawings.blogspot.com/2009/02/few-notes-about-inking.html.

85. Larry Hama, "Larry Hama's Ten Rules for Drawing a Comic Book Page," *The Beat* (blog), August 27, 2013, http://www.comicsbeat.com/larry-hamas-10-rules-for-drawing-a-comic-book-page.

86. Brian Michael Bendis, Michael Gaydos, and Mark Bagley, "Purple Part Two," *Alias,* October 2003, 13, 16.

87. Stan Lee and Joe Orlando, "Killgrave, the Unbelievable Purple Man!" *Daredevil,* October 1964, 19.

88. Terry Kavanagh and Mike Miller, "Behind the Curtain," *X-Man,* November, 1999, 10.

89. Brian Michael Bendis, Michael Gaydos and Mark Bagley, "Purple Part Two," *Alias,* October 2003, 14.

90. *Ibid.,* 18.

91. Devin Leonard, "Marvel Goes Hollywood," *Fortune,* May 23, 2007.

92. Tom Russo, "Super Group," *The Boston* Globe, April 29, 2012.

93. Jami Philbrick, "Kevin Fiege Talks *Iron Man 2, The Avengers* and More," *MovieWeb,* accessed July 10, 2016, http://movieweb.com/exclusive-kevin-fiege-talks-iron-man-2-the-avengers-and-more.

94. Nash Information Services, "Box Office History for Marvel Cinematic Universe Movies," *The Numbers,* accessed August 2, 2016, http://www.the-numbers.com/movies/franchise/Marvel-Cinematic-Universe#tab=summary.

95. David Hinckley, "ABC announces *The Hulk* TV series in development for 2013–14 season," *New York Daily News,* July 3, 2012, http://www.nydailynews.com/entertainment/tv-movies/abc-announces-hulk-series-development-2013–14-season-article-1.1078588.

96. Melissa Rosenberg, *Writer Talks Fitting Jessica Jones Into the MCU,* Video, 07:32, November 17, 2015, http://www.ign.com/videos/2015/11/19/writer-talks-fitting-jessica-jones-into-the-mcu.

97. Nellie Andreeva, "Marvel Preps 60-Episode Package of Four Series & A Mini for VOD & Cable Networks," *Deadline Hollywood*, October 14, 2013, http://deadline.com/2013/10/marvel-preps-60-episode-package-of-four-series-a-mini-for-vod-cable-networks-611826.

98. David Lieberman and Nellie Andreeva, "Netflix Picks Up Four Marvel Live-Action Series & A Mini Featuring Daredevil, Jessica Jones, Iron Fist, Luke Cage For 2015 Launch," *Deadline Hollywood*, November 7, 2013, http://deadline.com/2013/11/disney-netflix-marvel-series-629696.

99. Noah Kadner, "Without Fear," *American Cinematographer,* May 2015, 58–59.

100. David Mullen, "Film Noir B&W film stocks," *Cinematography.com: Forums.* September 29, 2014. http://www.cinematography.com/index.php?showtopic=65047.

101. John Alton, *Painting with Light* (Berkeley: University of California Press, 1995), 44.

102. *Ibid.,* 55–56.

103. Leigh Allen, "Filming the *I Love Lucy* Show," *American Cinematographer* January 1952, 27.

104. Matthew Dessem, "Why TV Shows Are Darker Than They've Ever Been," *Slate,* June 29, 2016, http://www.slate.com/articles/arts/television/2016/06/cinematographers_from_game_of_thrones_jessica_jones_and_better_call_saul.html.

105. *Ibid.*

106. Geoffrey Morrison, "What Is TV Contrast Ratio?" *CNET,* March 19, 2015, http://www.cnet.com/news/what-is-contrast-ratio.

107. Matthew Dessem, "Why TV Shows Are Darker Than They've Ever Been," *Slate,* June 29, 2016, http://www.slate.com/articles/arts/television/2016/06/cinematographers_from_game_of_thrones_jessica_jones_and_better_call_saul.html.

108. Chris Bennion, "Netflix's *Daredevil*—spoiler-free series review: Essential viewing even if you're not a Marvel fan," *The Independent*, May 1, 2015, http://www.independent.co.uk/arts-entertainment/tv/reviews/daredevil-netflix-spoiler-free-series-review-essential-viewing-even-if-youre-not-a-marvel-fan-10217790.html.

109. Sulagna Misra, "*Daredevil* Series Premiere Recap: Let the Devil Out," *Vulture*, April 10, 2015, http://www.vulture.com/2015/04/daredevil-recap-season-1-episode-1.html#.

110. Tom Nichols, "The Death of Expertise," *The Federalist*, January 17, 2014, http://thefederalist.com/2014/01/17/the-death-of-expertise.

111. Jane Wakefield, "Children spend six hours or more a day on screens," *BBC News*, March 27, 2015, http://www.bbc.com/news/technology-32067158.

112. Amanda Ann Klein and Kristen Warner, "Erasing the Pop-Culture Scholar, One Click at a Time," *The Chronicle of Higher Education*, July 6, 2016, http://chronicle.com/article/Erasing-the-Pop-Culture/237039.

113. Imogen Sara Smith, *In Lonely Places: Film Noir Beyond the City* (Jefferson, NC: McFarland, 2011), 4–5.

114. "Marvel's Daredevil Season 1 (2015)," accessed April 12, 2016, *Rotten Tomatoes*, https://www.rottentomatoes.com/tv/daredevil/s01.

115. James Bean, "*Daredevil* Show Runner Steven DeKnight details grisly deleted scenes," *Hypable*, December 9, 2015, http://www.hypable.com/daredevil-deleted-scenes-steven-deknight-interview.

116. Louisa Ellen Stein, *Millennial Fandom: Television Audiences in the Transmedia Age* (Iowa City: University of Iowa Press, 2015), 77.

117. *Ibid.*, 78.

Bibliography

Akash, Nikolas. "Where is the Female Tony Soprano?" *The Atlantic*, June 27, 2013. http://www.theatlantic.com/entertainment/archive/2013/06/where-is-the-female-tony-soprano/277270.

Ali, Russlyn. "Dear Colleague Letter." *U.S. Department of Education, Office for Civil Rights*, April 4, 2011. http://www2.ed.gov/print/about/offices/list/ocr/letters/colleague-201104.html.

Allen, Leigh. "Filming the *I Love Lucy* Show." *American Cinematographer*, January 1952.

Alton, John. *Painting with Light*. Berkeley: University of California Press, 1995.

America's Changing Religious Landscape. Report. Washington, D.C.: Pew Research Center, May 12, 2015. 1–200. http://www.pewforum.org/files/2015/05/RLS-08-26-full-report.pdf.

Andreasen, Nancy C. "Posttraumatic Stress Disorder: A History and a Critique." *Annals of the New York Academy of Sciences*, October 2010. http://www.brainline.org/content/2011/01/posttraumatic-stress-disorder-a-history-and-a-critique_pageall.html.

Andreeva, Nellie. "Marvel Preps 60-Episode Package of Four Series & A Mini for VOD & Cable Networks." *Deadline Hollywood*, October 14, 2013. http://deadline.com/2013/10/marvel-preps-60-episode-package-of-four-series-a-mini-for-vod-cable-networks-611826.

Andreeva, Nellie. "Netflix Won't Release *Lilyhammer* Ratings, Company's Ted Sarandos Explains Why." *Deadline Hollywood*, February 7, 2012. http://deadline.com/2012/02/netflix-wont-release-lilyhammer-ratings-companys-ted-sarandos-explains-why-227285/#more-227285.

"Batman." *Box Office Mojo*. http://www.boxofficemojo.com/movies/?id=batman.htm.

"Batman: THR's 1989 Review." *The Hollywood Reporter*. http://www.hollywoodreporter.com/news/batman-thrs-1989-review-801339.

Bean, James. "*Daredevil* Show Runner Steven DeKnight details grisly deleted scenes." *Hypable*. December 9, 2015. http://www.hypable.com/daredevil-deleted-scenes-steven-deknight-interview.

Bendis, Brian Michael, Michael Gaydos, and Mark Bagley. "Purple Part 2." *Alias*, October 2003.

Bendis, Brian Michael. "Farewell to *Alias*." *Alias*, January 2004.

Bennion, Chris. "Netflix's Daredevil—spoiler-free series review: Essential viewing even if you're not a Marvel fan." *The Independent*, May 1, 2015. http://www.independent.co.uk/arts-entertainment/tv/reviews/daredevil-netflix-spoiler-free-series-review-essential-viewing-even-if-youre-not-a-marvel-fan-10217790.html.

Berkshire, Geoff. "*Red Widow:* Melissa Rosenberg plans a cable-esque' show for network television." *zap2it.* January 10, 2013. http://zap2it.com/2013/01/red-widow-melissa-rosenberg-plans-a-cable-esque-show-for-network-television.

Borde, Raymond, and Etienne Chaumeton. *A Panorama of American Film Noir (1941–1953).* Translated by Paul Hammond. San Francisco: City Lights, 2002.

Borde, Raymond, and Etienne Chaumeton. "Towards a Definition of *Film Noir.*" Translated by Alain Silver. In *Film Noir Reader*, edited by Alain Silver and James Ursini. Compton Plains, NJ: Limelight, 1996.

Botelho, Greg. "Ex-NAACP leader Rachel Dolezal: 'I identify as black.'" *CNN.com.* June 17, 2015. http://www.cnn.com/2015/06/16/us/washington-rachel-dolezal-naacp.

Brady, Erik, and Rachel Axon. "NBC's Al Trautwig apologizes for comments on Simone Biles' parents." *USA Today*, August 8, 2016. http://www.usatoday.com/story/sports/olympics/rio-2016/2016/08/08/al-trautwig-apology-simon-biles-parents/88402048.

Breuning, Loretta G. "Why I Don't Believe Reports of a Mental Health Crisis." *Psychology Today*, February 23, 2014. https://www.psychologytoday.com/blog/your-neurochemical-self/201402/why-i-don-t-believe-reports-mental-health-crisis.

"Bristol: Gibbons & Higgins Talk *Watchmen.*" *Comic Book Resources*, May 20, 2009. http://www.comicbookresources.com/?page=article&id=21282.

Brody, Richard. "'Film Noir': The Elusive Genre." *The New Yorker*, July 23, 2014. http://www.newyorker.com/culture/richard-brody/film-noir-elusive-genre-2.

Burton, Tim "Batman." In *Burton on Burton*, edited by Mark Salisbury, 70–83. London: Faber & Faber, 2006.

Castillo, Michelle. "Millennials are the most stressed generation, survey finds." *CBS News*, February 11, 2013. http://www.cbsnews.com/news/millennials-are-the-most-stressed-generation-survey-finds.

Cho, Michael. "The Importance of Light and Shadow." Class lecture handout, February 3, 2009. http://chodrawings.blogspot.com/2009/02/few-notes-about-inking.html.

Coronel, Steve Coll, and Derek Kravitz. "'A Rape on Campus' What Went Wrong?" *Rolling Stone*, April 5, 2015. http://www.rollingstone.com/culture/features/a-rape-on-campus-what-went-wrong-20150405.

Day, Felix, Hannes Helgason, Daniel I. Chasman, Lynda M. Rose, Po-Ru Loh, Robert A. Scott, Agnar Helgason, Austine Kong, Gisli Masson, Olafur Th Magnusson, Daniel Gudbjartsson, Unnur Thorsteinsdottir, Julie E. Buring, Paul M. Ridker, Patrick Sulem, Kari Stefansson, Ken K. Ong, and John R. B. Perry. "Physical and neurobehavioral determinants of reproductive onset and success." *Nature Genetics* 48, no. 6 (June 2016): 617–623. doi: 10.1038/ng.3551.

Delwiche, Theodore, Noah J. Delwich, and Andrew M. Duehren. "Law School Found in Violation of Title IX after Years-Long Probe." *The Harvard Crimson*, December 30, 2014. http://www.thecrimson.com/article/2014/12/30/law-school-violation-title-ix.

Dessem, Matthew. "Why TV Shows Are (Literally) Darker Than They've Ever Been." *Slate*, June 29, 2016. http://www.slate.com/articles/arts/television/2016/06/cinematographers_from_game_of_thrones_jessica_jones_and_better_call_saul.html.

Ebert, Roger. "Batman," *Chicago Sun-Times,* June 23, 1989.

Fiamma, Andrea. "From *Watchmen* to *Orfani:* A Colorists' Roundtable." *The Comics Journal*, March 30, 2016. http://www.tcj.com/from-watchmen-to-orfani-a-colorists-roundtable.

15 Economic Facts About Millennials. Report. Washington, D.C.: The Council of Economic Advisors, October 2014. 1–49. https://www.whitehouse.gov/sites/default/files/docs/millennials_report.pdf.

Flint, Joe, and Ben Fritz. "Netflix Viewership Finally Gets a Yardstick." *The Wall Street Journal*, August 26, 2015. http://www.wsj.com/articles/netflix-viewership-finally-gets-a-yardstick-1440630513.

Frank, Nino. "Un nouveau genre 'policier': L'aventure criminelle.'" *L'Ecran français*, August 28, 1946.

Hajdu, David. *The Ten-Cent Plague: The Great Comic-Book Scare and How It Changed America*. New York: Farrar, Straus and Giroux, 2008.

Henriques, Gregg. "The College Student Mental Health Crisis." *Psychology Today*, February 15, 2014. https://www.psychologytoday.com/blog/theory-knowledge/201402/the-college-student-mental-health-crisis.

Heldman, Caroline, and Baillee Brown. "Campus Rape: a Brief History of Sexual Violence Activism in the U.S." *Feminist Fight Club*, August 8, 2014. https://carolineheldman.me/2014/08/08/campus-rape-a-brief-history-of-sexual-violence-activism-in-the-u-s.

Hill, Libby. "Krysten Ritter on playing anti-superhero, Jessica Jones." *Los Angeles Times*, November 18, 2015. http://www.latimes.com/entertainment/tv/la-et-st-krysten-ritter-jessica-jones-20151118-story.html.

Hinckley, David. "ABC announces *The Hulk* TV series in development for 2013–14 season." *New York Daily News*, July 3, 2012.

Holloway, Daniel. "TV Ratings: Amazon's *Transparent* Lags Behind Netflix, Hulu Shows." *Variety*, June 21, 2016. http://variety.com/2016/digital/news/amazon-transparent-hulu-netflix-making-a-murderer-112263-catastrophe-1201798269.

"Illustrating Watchmen: Q&A with Dave Gibbons." Watchmencomicmovie.com. October 23, 2008. http://www.watchmencomicmovie.com/102308-dave-gibbons-watchmen-comic-illustrator.php.

Jacobellis v. Ohio. 378 U.S. 184 (1964).

Kadner, Noah. "Without Fear," *American Cinematographer*, May 2015.

Kamenetz, Anya. "The History of Campus Sexual Assault." *NPR Ed*, November 30, 2014. http://www.npr.org/sections/ed/2014/11/30/366348383/the-history-of-campus-sexual-assault.

Kavanagh, Terry, and Mike Miller. "Behind the Curtain." *X-Man*, November 1999.

Keane, Terence M., Jessica Wolfe, and Kathryn L. Taylor. "Post-traumatic stress disorder: Evidence for diagnostic validity and methods of psychological assessment." *Journal of Clinical Psychology* 43, no.1 (January 1987): 32–43. doi: 10.1002/1097–4679(198701)43:1<32::AID-JCLP2270430106>3.0.CO;2-X.

Kessler, Ronald C., Amanda Sonnega, Evelyn Bromet, Michael Hughes, and Christopher B. Nelson. "Posttraumatic stress disorder in the National Comorbidity Survey." *Archives of General Psychiatry* 52, no.12 (December 1995): 1048–1060. doi:10.1001/archpsyc.1995.03950240066012.

Kingkade, Tyler. "Using College Mental Health Services Can Lead to Students Getting Removed From Campus." *The Huffington Post*, October 7, 2014. http://www.huffingtonpost.com/2014/10/07/college-mental-health-services_n_5900632.html.

Klein, Amanda Ann, and Kristen Warner. "Erasing the Pop-Culture Scholar, One Click at a Time." *The Chronicle of Higher Education*, July 6, 2016. http://chronicle.com/article/Erasing-the-Pop-Culture/237039.

Krebs, Christopher P., Christine H. Lindquist, Tara D. Warner, Bonnie S. Fisher, and Sandra L. Martin. *The Campus Sexual Assault (CSA) Study*, December 2007. https://www.ncjrs.gov/pdffiles1/nij/grants/221153.pdf.

Larcom, Geoff S. "Eastern Michigan University to pay $350,000 in federal fines over Laura Dicknson case." *Ann Arbor News*, June 6, 2008. http://blog.mlive.com/annarbornews/2008/06/eastern_michigan_university_to.html.

Lee, Stan, and Joe Orlando. "Killgrave, the Unbelievable Purple Man!" *Daredevil*, October 1964.

Leonard, Devin. "Marvel Goes Hollywood." *Fortune*, May 23, 2007.

Lieberman, David, and Nellie Andreeva. "Netflix Picks Up Four Marvel Live-Action Series & A Mini Featuring Daredevil, Jessica Jones, Iron Fist, Luke Cage For 2015 Launch." *Deadline Hollywood*, November 7, 2013. http://deadline.com/2013/11/disney-netflix-marvel-series-629696.

Maglio, Tony. "25 Highest Rated Broadcast TV Shows of 2015–2016 Season." *The Wrap*, June 9, 2016. http://www.thewrap.com/25-highest-rated-tv-shows-nfl-empire-big-bang-cbs-nbc-fox-abc/?mode=3.

Mander, Jason. "Netflix has twice as many American users as subscribers." *Global Web Index*, April 20, 2015. http://www.globalwebindex.net/blog/netflix-has-twice-as-many-american-users-as-subscribers.

"Marvel Reaches Agreement to Emerge from Bankruptcy." *The New York Times*, July 11, 1997.
"Marvel's Daredevil Season 1 (2015)." *Rotten Tomatoes*. https://www.rottentomatoes.com/tv/
    daredevil/s01.
Marvel's Jessica Jones. Season 1. Netflix. November 20, 2015.
*Meeting the Behavioral Health Needs of Veterans: Operation Enduring Freedom and Operation
    Iraqi Freedom*. Report. Washington, D.C.: National Council for Behavioral Health, 2012.
    1–13. November 2012. http://www.thenationalcouncil.org/wp-content/uploads/2013/02/
    Veterans-BH-Needs-Report.pdf.
Millennials: Confident. Connected. Open to Change. Report. Washington, D.C.: Pew Research
    Center, 2010. 1–140. February 2010. http://www.pewsocialtrends.org/files/2010/10/
    millennials-confident-connected-open-to-change.pdf.
Millennials in Adulthood: Detached from Institutions, Networked with Friends. Report. Wash-
    ington, D.C.: Pew Research Center, 2014. 1–68. March 7, 2014. http://www.pewsocialtrends.
    org/files/2014/03/2014-03-07_generations-report-version-for-web.pdf.
Misra, Sulagna. "*Daredevil* Series Premiere Recap: Let the Devil Out." *Vulture*, April 10, 2015.
    http://www.vulture.com/2015/04/daredevil-recap-season-1-episode-1.html#.
Morrison, Geoffrey. "What is TV Contrast Ratio?" *CNET*, March 19, 2015. http://www.cnet.
    com/news/what-is-contrast-ratio.
Mullen, David. "Film Noir B&W film stocks." *Cinematography.com: Forums*, September 29,
    2014. http://www.cinematography.com/index.php?showtopic=65047.
Nash Information Services. "Box Office History for Marvel Cinematic Universe Movies." *The
    Numbers*. http://www.the-numbers.com/movies/franchise/Marvel-Cinematic-Universe
    #tab=summary.
Nichols, Tom. "The Death of Expertise." *The Federalist*, January 17, 2014. http://thefederalist.
    com/2014/01/17/the-death-of-expertise.
Patten, Dominic. "*Marvel's Jessica Jones* EP Melissa Rosenberg on Luke Cage, Season 2, *Super-
    girl* & Gender Parity in Hollywood." *Deadline Hollywood*, November 18, 2015. http://
    deadline.com/2015/11/jessica-jones-spoilers-marvel-melissa-rosenberg-krysten-ritter-
    luke-cage-1201628832.
Perkins, Will. "Marvel's Jessica Jones." *Art of the Title*, March 1, 2016. http://www.artofthetitle.
    com/title/jessica-jones.
Philbrick, Jami. "Exclusive: Screenwriter Melissa Rosenberg talks *AKA Jessica Jones*." *I Am
    Rogue*, November 9, 2011. http://www.iamrogue.com/news/movie-news/item/5226-
    exclusive-screenwriter-melissa-rosenberg-talks-aka-jessica-jones.html.
_____. "Kevin Feige Talks *Iron Man 2, The Avengers* and More." *MovieWeb*. http://movieweb.
    com/exclusive-kevin-feige-talks-iron-man-2-the-avengers-and-more.
Poggi, Jeanine. "Inside the Company Behind Netflix's Measurement War." *Advertising Age*,
    January 19, 2016. http://adage.com/article/digital/inside-company-claims-measure-
    netflix/302187.
"A Portal to Another Dimension: Alan Moore, Dave Gibbons, and Neil Gaiman." *The Comics
    Journal*, June 6, 2012. http://www.tcj.com/a-portal-to-another-dimension-alan-moore-
    dave-gibbons-and-neil-gaiman.
Posttraumatic Stress Disorder Fact Sheet. Report. Arlington, VA: American Psychiatric
    Association, 2013, 1–2. http://www.dsm5.org/Documents/PTSD%20Fact%20Sheet.pdf.
Rakmachandran, Shalini, and Maria Armental. "At Netflix, Big Jump in Users—and Costs."
    The Wall Street Journal. July 15, 2015. http://www.wsj.com/articles/netflix-reports-jump-
    in-streaming-users-1436991166.
"Review: *Batman*" (excerpt). *Variety*, 1989. http://variety.com/1988/film/reviews/batman-2-
    1200428063.
Review of Veterans' Access to Mental Health Care. Report. Washington, D.C.: VA Office of Inspec-
    tor General, April 23, 2012. 1–63. Accessed August 2, 2016. http://www.va.gov/oig/pubs/
    VAOIG-12–00900–168.pdf.
"The Rising Cost of Not Going to College." *Pew Research Center*. February 11, 2014. http://
    www.pewsocialtrends.org/2014/02/11/the-rising-cost-of-not-going-to-college.
Rosenberg, Melissa. *Writer Talks Fitting Jessica Jones Into the MCU*. Video. November 17, 2015.
    http://www.ign.com/videos/2015/11/19/writer-talks-fitting-jessica-jones-into-the-mcu.

Russo, Tom. "Super Group." *The Boston Globe*, April 29, 2012.

Ryan, Maureen. "How *Jessica Jones'* Creative Team Tackled Assault, Consent and Sexuality." *Variety*, January 18, 2016. http://variety.com/2016/tv/news/jessica-jones-sex-assault-consent-1201682069.

Sabin, Roger. *Comics, Comix & Graphic Novels: A History of Comic Art*. London: Phaidon Press, 1996.

Silver, Alain. *Film Noir Reader*. Edited by Alain Silver and James Ursini. Compton Plains, NJ: Limelight, 1996.

Smith, Imogen Sara. *In Lonely Places: Film Noir Beyond the City*. Jefferson, NC: McFarland, 2011.

"The State of Mental Health on College Campuses: A Growing Crisis." *American Psychological Association*. 2011. http://www.apa.org/about/gr/education/news/2011/college-campuses. aspx.

Steel, Zachary; Tien Chey; Derrick Silove; Claire Marnane; Richard A. Bryant; and Mark van Ommeren. "Association of torture and other potentially traumatic events with mental health outcomes among populations exposed to mass conflict and displacement: a systematic review and meta-anaylsis." *Journal of the American Medical Association* 302, no .5 (August 5, 2009): 537–549.

Stein, Louisa Ellen. *Millennial Fandom: Television Audiences in the Transmedia Age*. Iowa City: University of Iowa Press, 2015.

Strawson, Galen. "Free Will." *Rutledge Encyclopedia of Philosophy*. London: Routledge, 2012. doi: 10.4324/9780415249126-V014–2.

Suicide Data Report, 2012. Report by Janet Kemp and Robert Bossarte. Washington, D.C.: Department of Veterans Affairs, February 2013. 1–59. http://www.va.gov/opa/docs/ suicide-data-report-2012-final.pdf.

Suicide: Facts at a Glance. Report. Atlanta, GA: Centers for Disease Control and Prevention, 2015. 1–2. http://www.cdc.gov/violenceprevention/pdf/suicide-datasheet-a.PDF.

Thompson, Don, and Maggie. "Crack in the Code." *Newfangles*, February 1971. http://www. ebay.com/itm/NEWFANGLES-44-FANZINE-1970-DON-AND-MAGGIE-THOMPSON-/390654950738.

2015 Annual Report. Report. State College, PA: Center for Collegiate Mental Health, 2016. 1–40. http://ccmh.psu.edu/wp-content/uploads/sites/3058/2016/01/2015_CCMH_Report_ 1-18-2015.pdf.

2012 Demographics: Profile of the Military Community. Report. Washington, D.C.: Office of the Deputy Assistant Secretary of Defense, 2012. 1–191. http://download.militaryone source.mil/12038/MOS/Reports/2012_Demographics_Report.pdf.

Vogler, Mark. *The Dark Age: Grim, Great & Gimmicky Post-Modern Comics*. Raleigh, NC: TwoMorrows Publishing, 2006.

Volpicelli, Joseph; Geetha Balaraman; Julie Hahn; Heather Wallace; and Donald Bux. "The Role of Uncontrollable Trauma in the development of PTSD and Alcohol Addiction." *Alcohol Research and Health* 23, no. 4 (1999): 256–262.

Wakefield, Jane. "Children spend six hours or more a day on screens." *BBC News*. March 27, 2015. http://www.bbc.com/news/technology-32067158.

Weinstock, Jeffrey Andrew. "Lostness (Blair Witch)." In *Nothing That Is: Millennial Cinema and the Blair Witch Controversies*. Edited by Sarah L. Higley and Jeffrey Andrew Weinstock, 229–244. Detroit: Wayne State University Press, 2002.

Yoffe, Emily. "The College Rape Overcorrection." *Slate*, December 7, 2014. http://www.slate. com/articles/double_x/doublex/2014/12/college_rape_campus_sexual_assault_is_a_ serious_problem_but_the_efforts.html.

From the Hellmouth to Hell's Kitchen

Analyzing Aesthetics of Women Survivors and Spaces in Buffy the Vampire Slayer *and* Jessica Jones

COURTNEY LEE WEIDA

Superhuman Strength, Superhero Healing and Human Survival

Superhero and private detective Jessica Jones, "is not above humor, or beauty, or faith; she is neither weak nor helpless."[1] In all its multiplicity, Marvel's *Jessica Jones* is revolutionary in its diverse depiction of women's life experiences and relationships. Finding its home on Netflix's streaming service after being passed over by network television,[2] the show stands to extend a small continuum of cult media representations of powerful women superheroes and their complex female friendships. Jessica Jones herself (as represented through showrunner Melissa Rosenberg's creative vision) is somewhat ambivalent about the implications of her powers: superhero strength, speed, and healing, as well as the responsibilities and burdens those powers may incur. With common threads of a compelling, if somewhat unwilling, complex female heroine, this essay will draw comparisons between *Jessica Jones* and Joss Whedon's *Buffy the Vampire Slayer* (*BTVS*), a 1997–2003 show in which the female lead, Buffy Summers, possesses strikingly comparable superhuman power (enhanced strength, speed, and healing) and also responds to a calling to protect others.

In parallel fashion, Jessica Jones and Buffy Summers' wars against evil forces in Hell's Kitchen and the Hellmouth are frequently supported and even

189

facilitated by their nuanced female friendships and collaborative communities. This analysis explores relationships between the *Jessica Jones* and *Buffy the Vampire Slayer* television series, not purely between the two deadpan title heroines, but also addressing comparisons of their relationships with supporting female characters. I will outline several possibilities and problems that both shows present in the creation of feminist communities and gendered space around psychological issues of extraordinary strength and of human frailty.

This essay focuses on the complex, sometimes overlooked feminist aesthetics of the superhero(ine) as a symbol of survival within these visually rich and richly symbolic series, with additional characters representing strength of character as much as physical strength when tested by extreme trauma and its aftermath. The dark color palettes, symbolic fashion aesthetics, and surreal spaces of each show reflect a great deal about the stories and characters, particularly in terms of their growth and development as survivors.

Support Groups for Superheroes and Survivors of the Supernatural

Jones and Summers are skillful warriors, yet each is intellectually and psychologically uncertain about the nature of heroism. Drawn into a plot early in season one involving her nemesis Kilgrave's latest victim: Hope Shlottman, Jessica initially seeks to flee Kilgrave and abandon her detective and superhero roles. It is Jessica's friend and adoptive sister, Trish Walker, who recalls her to her duties of stopping Kilgrave, by emphasizing that she is the only person who can. Similarly, Buffy Summers vacillates between her all-encompassing identity as a superhero (vampire slayer) and a few attempts at escape by running away or turning away. Buffy is recalled to slaying by pleas from her own close-knit community of family and friends, as well as supernatural events that take place in new settings and demand her attention as slayer. As well, Buffy struggles in balancing slaying duties with her similarly all-encompassing roles as a daughter, romantic partner, friend, student, employee, and caregiver. The hardships of ordinary life balanced with superhero callings weigh heavily on both women. I couldn't help but relate these struggles for work-life balance as hyperbolic versions of those that many young women encounter as they juggle extraordinary caregiving and work expectations. In navigating these challenges, Jessica's experience of trauma plays a marked role. So too, Buffy has several encounters with therapists and counselors in attempts to cope with the aftermath of violence and loss.

While Jessica's formalized therapy occurs before season one, she also inadvertently helps form a trauma support group. Attorney Jeri Hogarth (the first openly lesbian character in Marvel cinema and television) gathers a vast group of people who all claim to have suffered from mind-control. This is a public (albeit, somewhat empty) gesture in order to lend credence to her defense of Hope Shlottman's murder of her parents as a result of Kilgrave's control. Those New Yorkers who respond to the call include individuals who appear to be mentally ill, those who perhaps are lying in hopes of personal gain, as well as genuine victims who are able to identify characteristics and stories that reflect Kilgrave's actual appearance and tendencies, thus proving their credibility to Jessica. All the respondents may be victims, but not all are victimized by Kilgrave.

As viewers, we too bear witness to fragments of these stories spoken in Hogarth's practice and a subsequent support group in a coffee shop. The conversations are often heartbreaking because they are so unbelievable as supernatural events. Yet these stories can also seem, at times, more like tragic human failings of the victims. A father who abandoned his child and ends up losing his marriage because of it, might easily be seen as a deadbeat dad and perhaps a druggie, rather than the victim of Kilgrave's power. Could any deadbeat dad and drug abuser perhaps then also be a victim, not of Kilgrave, but of other circumstances? These questions reverberate with ambiguity throughout the first season.

Besides Jessica's immediate goal of lending credibility to Hope, the act of bearing witness to these survivors also gives Jessica additional leads to fight Kilgrave and, importantly, reveals stories more tragic than her own. Notably, although the support group of survivors forms from the gathering of witnesses, Jessica does not attend the group regularly. She stresses that part of the reason she doesn't attend the group or talk through her issues elsewhere is because although her story is "shitty," someone else's suffering is always greater. She does refer New York City Police officer Will Simpson to the group in order to process his brutal attack on Trish and her home while under Kilgrave's control. This referral is ambiguous because Jessica expresses doubts about Simpson's motives as well as the efficacy of the support group.

Some critics have characterized Jessica's disdain for the support group she and Hogarth unintentionally inspire as a criticism of support groups themselves. *The Feminist Frequency*, a feminist popular culture blog, suggests:

> The show shuns the opportunity to depict something akin to a genuine attempt at recovery in favor of portraying Jones as being above such things. A support group is formed for people who have been violated by the villain, Kilgrave, but Jessica never participates. In reality, many people who have been traumatized carry around a tremendous amount of shame and do avoid opportunities for help and support.

However, having the show's hero be the one character who doesn't ask for help suggests that it's stronger and braver not to seek help, when it's actually just the opposite.[3]

While the myth of the magically strong superhero impervious to trauma is indeed misleading, I would also suggest that Jessica's relationship to the support group (and perhaps to most relationships) is representative of her flaws and sense of hopelessness than her strength and judgment. Jessica provides various reasons as to why she will not attend the group or allow herself to dwell on her emotional scars elsewhere. She notes that her approach to her trauma chiefly includes repression and self-medication. By referring to these destructive tendencies in a clinically and self-aware admission of poor judgment, she asserts her conscious (albeit questionable) choices to drink excessively and to operate in survival mode.

Further, we might characterize Jessica's response to trauma as evidence of the difficulty of processing trauma while actively experiencing it. Kilgrave is still victimizing Jones and others, and all of her energy is directed into the seemingly hopeless task of resisting him. Importantly, Jessica only revisits her traumas in attempts to solve crimes against others and defeat Kilgrave. She revisits her own memories, appearing as both witness and victim, with her witness self a sort of private detective of her own life, seeking details that connect to Hope's plight.

Strange Patients: Pitfalls of Superheroine Therapies

Jessica's past is generally repressed, with memories surfacing to connect dots in her detective work. Jessica inverts the truism, "what doesn't kill us makes us stronger" by substituting the word "stranger" as her own personal maxim. Buffy also experiences strangeness and estrangement from her world after experiencing trauma. After her death and supernatural resurrection, Buffy wonders if she is not fully human, if she is has become a "thing." Both Buffy and Jessica have been diagnosed with post-traumatic stress disorder (PTSD), with Jones' PTSD's reoccurrence as the reason for Trish's initial disbelief that Kilgrave has actually returned. Meanwhile, Buffy's PTSD is diagnosed by Janina Scarlet, a popular culture blogger and psychologist who chronicles Buffy's suffering and symptoms throughout the series.[4]

Jones' therapy occurs before the series, with traces evident in the mantra she has adopted to stave off her panic attacks. Over its seven seasons, BTVS presents several of Buffy's complicated encounters with counseling, but each ends poorly if not disastrously. In high school, Buffy has a mandatory meeting with guidance counselor Stephen Platt. She opens up to Platt cautiously at their first meeting, generalizing and sanitizing her struggles within her breakup with Angel to remove any references to the supernatural. Drawn in by his compassion, Buffy warms to Platt and begins to disclose deeper feelings of fear about Angel's violence. Buffy also blurts out her fears that if she spoke openly to her friends or to Rupert Giles (her watcher/mentor), they would have her committed. During a subsequent session, Buffy is horrified (and further traumatized) to realize Platt has been killed and cannot hear her confession. Giles also attempts some rudimentary therapeutic discussions with Buffy about Angel's subsequent death. He fabricates a story about a spell that requires her to share details about Angel's death, which he admits was a ploy to help her open up and discuss this traumatic event. Buffy recaps the events of Angel's death quickly and tonelessly, not really taking the bait.

In college, Buffy speaks perhaps most freely with recently-sired vampire and psychology student, Holden Webster, who she must ultimately annihilate at the close of their "session," staking him in the heart as is her slayer duty. Their conversation about her difficulties relating with men could be seen as having the potential to be an ultimate therapy, a clearly defined relationship where confidentiality, distance, and closure is literally guaranteed. At the same time, the therapeutic relationship is obviously limited and compromised by the same demonic forces that traumatized (and continue to traumatize) the patient. Buffy spars with Holden verbally and physically, giving the impression that her "session" with Holden is also a bit of a ruse, which of course, it is.

Buffy subsequently admires and socializes more earnestly with her college professor and mentor, psychologist Maggie Walsh. This relationship has an element of therapy and of parenting to it. Similarly to Holden, Dr. Walsh succumbs to darker forces (not just demons, but her own immorality, greed, and power). In a complex plot, Walsh turns on Buffy and is killed by her own demon-Frankensteinesque creation. As each of these therapeutic experiences becomes more and more dangerous for Buffy and for her counselors, her final psychiatric encounter is a demon-induced dream in which she is institutionalized and her psychiatrists inform her that the vampire slaying is all a delusion; she can return to a peaceful home were her mother is still living and even married to her father. Eerily still, Buffy admits to her close friend Willow Rosenberg that her parents had actually briefly institutionalized her when she first began slaying demons and vampires. We may recall this possibility remained as Buffy's fear throughout the series, looking back to her sessions with Platt.

Both Jessica and Buffy struggle to maintain their specialized roles and hyper-focused visions of reality and morality as superheroes, often finding the perspective of mental health to be incompatible with that vision. The particular examination of self and reality associated with therapy is largely inappropriate, if not perilous, for these women. Though both Jessica and

Buffy encourage friends and acquaintances to seek professional help, they themselves are largely unable to do so. As women, perhaps many aspects of their heroine roles are particularly fragmented by the conflicting expectations of caregiving and crime-fighting, leaving little room for self and self-analysis.

Superhero as Traumatized Witness/Seer

The opening credits for the show serve as a reminder of Jessica's dark and scrutinizing view of her strange world in Hell's Kitchen, panning black and purple shadows and ending on what appears to be Jessica's eye. This closing detail is important because Jessica Jones is the narrator of the show and the viewer tends to see what she sees (through close-ups, flashbacks, and other visuals). She is the ultimate observer, a private *eye*, as well as the jaded storyteller of her own unfolding tale.

A select few characters appear and act in the show in the absence of Jessica's watchful eye. The camera grants these major characters the temporary solitary space to speak and see as Jessica does. One such exception is her neighbor Malcolm Ducasse. At first, Jessica views him somewhat benevolently, as he appears to be a kind and rather harmless heroin addict. We only see what Jessica sees, and Jessica doesn't look too closely at Malcolm initially. Jessica later discovers Malcolm has been under the constant control of Kilgrave as his spy for surveillance of Jessica, and that he has been coerced to take drugs. Jessica's own direct submission to this surveillance by sending Kilgrave a "selfie" each day frees Malcolm from Kilgrave's grasp.

She also desperately implores Malcolm to resist his addiction (thus making her self-sacrifice significant), to save her "for once" by saving himself. In recovering from addiction and processing his traumas, Malcolm appears in his own scenes to wonder who he is now, after surviving. In contrast with Jessica and apart from her, Malcolm models the use of survivor support communities in his world view, personal healing, and growth: observing that talking itself helps him and questioning if his own past drug use is solely the fault of Kilgrave, or if these actions were always a deeper part of him. It is this process that leads him to become a collaborative leader like Trish: a hero on the sidelines whose caring and fortitude about helping others exceeds Jessica's at times. Malcolm is, arguably, a somewhat more developed version of BTVS' Xander Harris or Rupert Giles: a male observer/"watcher"/helper on the periphery of a girl gang of sorts. Given the countless male superheroes from comic books, films, and television shows, this inversion is striking. These male characters sometimes highlight the possibility of intelligent, caring men who are not threatened by powerful women, but rather are proud to be feminist male allies.

Feminist Allies, Coalitions in Conflict

Counterparts to Jessica Jones' superheroine allies exists in the Buffy-verse: Buffy benefits greatly from her smaller support system prior to the arrival of other potential slayers. Core collaborators and supporters include her mother, Willow, Buffy's sister Dawn Summers, Xander, and Giles. Buffy models many different kinds of development and learning within this group, including academic, experiential, and spiritual.[5] Specifically, there are various forms of support and specialized learning through her relationships that challenge and guide Buffy in her heroism against vampires and other demons, from Giles' research, to Willow's witchcraft, her mother's mentoring, learning to care for Dawn, Riley's military training, new friend and former demon Anya's firsthand knowledge of other demons, Angel's past as a vampire, fellow vampire Spike's particular history with past vampire slayers, and others.

However, the potential slayers of the show's final season join this inner circle as trainees/refugees and residents of Buffy's home. The potentials serve as a specific role reversal for Buffy to not only save, but to also train and mentor others in the specifics of slaying and importantly to share her power among them. This power shift goes so far that Buffy is effectively exiled from her home and leadership role, while other slayers literally take her place. This reversal is echoed in the efforts of the aforementioned Kilgrave support group, who mobilize not against Kilgrave, but against Jessica. As survivors, they come to blame and attempt to act out violently against a fellow victim. This plot too has a sense of things going ridiculously too far, and also represents power shifting in terms of problems.

Admittedly, I did not like watching many of the characters from Jessica Jones' Kilgrave support group, nor did I enjoy most of the plot lines of Buffy's potential slayers. The writing and character development felt, from my perspective, weaker and less nuanced than in other areas of both shows. That being said, these groups function as important elements of the female super-hero story, advocating for a shared space and shifting and sharing of power that defines the heroes, imperfect though they all may be. Perhaps the frustration many feel as viewers when a powerful and often female group with such potential flounders under the strain of such petty issues mirrors real life problems of feminist coalitions. The fantasy that a strong female leader and those women that understand and support her cause will always or easily win out is too simplistic. The small victories of hard earned collaborations of sisterhood (Buffy, Dawn, and Willow; or Jones, Trish, and nurse Claire Temple) become more meaningful. Feminist power sharing also becomes more nuanced. This is not a solitary approach to heroism; indeed, it shows that women can work together.

Sexual Politics and the Possibility of Sex-Positive Conversations

These groups and friendships also can contribute to personal growth and learning in romantic relationships and surviving domestic violence situations. In her survivor space at home, Buffy also opens up to her friends about the violence and verbal abuse perpetrated by Angel when he is literally wrestling with his demons. She later grapples with her anguish over her complex sexual relationship with another vampire: Spike, whose treatment of her is troubled, troubling, and for Buffy, confusing and sometimes guilt-inducing. Buffy particularly opens up to Tara Maclay, who has also encountered abuse in her past. For many viewers, Buffy's serial experiences with these supernatural lovers/villains echoes the ambiguity and confusion of love, hate, mental illness, sexism, consent, and sex. What constitutes rape, stalking, and/or BDSM? It is not entirely clear to Buffy, and she deliberates on boundaries as she draws support from her friends and decides on her own definitions.

Meanwhile, Jones' complex but often sex-positive and consensual encounters with Luke Cage have been mis-read as abusive or harmful by a *New York Times* reviewer.[6] In its first season, Jessica Jones is not at the point of processing her trauma from Kilgrave and her childhood; she often rejects Trish's home as a healing space and seeks her closest friend only out of desperation. The time and space for Jones to come to terms with Kilgrave's crimes against her, the traumatic deaths of her family, and her own fear and guilt associated with these events is still to be determined.

Superhero Feminist Fashion: A Dress with High Top Sneakers

The complex psychological armor of these women is often echoed in their fashion choices. From an aesthetic perspective, *Jessica Jones* employs rich visual references from fashion to scenery: from the grey scale of the noir genre that is to be expected among private detective stories, to more surprising and fantastically surreal touches of vivid color which pop up in Jessica's flashback and dream sequences. Jessica Jones emerges iconically from a pile of urban trash during the darker parts of the season, clad in her well-worn black clothing and ready to plod on in her grim and often thankless tasks. Jones' signature look is also described as "a hot punk Daria in shredded Citizens of Humanity jeans and red lipstick."[7] But Jessica also imagines herself escaping from the grasp of Kilgrave by leaping off a New York building, while wearing a long and yellow floral gown against a cerulean sky.

With respect to this particular fantasy, it may be recalled that Jessica possesses the power to fly, but she has not yet developed her skill. This flight is symbolic of her hidden power to escape, literally and metaphorically, and also to be fearless of falling/failing. The color blue itself is also significant. Jessica's former therapist had apparently trained her to cope with her post-traumatic stress disorder from Kilgrave's abuses with a calming and grounding mantra that includes repetition of the words "Cobalt Lane" which is a beautiful phrase, and evokes the deepest, sought-after blue pigment.

Jessica lands from her imagined leap gracefully and mounts a gorgeous white horse that carries her off into the city. Jessica symbolically becomes her own white knight: savior and rescuer to herself. The horse itself is widely significant in feminist aesthetics. Many female artists, such as Leonora Carrington (1917–2011), have employed the horse symbol widely as a sign of freedom and independence, linking female figures with wild nature. Meanwhile, developmental theorists noted that the horse (which appears prominently in so many female children's drawings) can express escape and movement within the creative growth of young girls as "a symbol of running, dashing freedom that is part of the joy of growing up."[8] A white horse might also evoke biblical imagery of death, or the apocalypse. Perhaps Jessica, like Buffy, must be seen as bringing the gift of death along with the power of saving lives.

Like her horse, Jessica's one appearance in a long yellow dress is not as simplistic as it may seem, when considered alongside the remembrance of her neighbor that young Jessica wore dresses with her high top sneakers. The child's juxtaposition of dress and athletic shoe shows a powerful juxtaposition and balancing of formal/functional, aesthetic/active. Adult Jessica's yellow dress is paired not with sneakers, but with equally practical black combat boots. Jessica is consistently feminine, yet also athletic and moving. She is not an object; she can choose to be defiant, and even defiantly feminine. The yellow of her dress is echoed in the warmer colors of Hope's beige coat, and even her hospital and prison clothing. The contrast is often apparent: When Jessica is dark, Hope is bright.

So too, BTVS episodes compellingly employed long (though often white) dresses alongside dark leather jackets and powerful weaponry, incredible and literal leaps of faith, and fairy-tale inspired heroines pitted again mythic monsters. One visually-stunning BTVS episode evokes the genre of silent film. In "Hush," Buffy assumes the role of princess warrior/savior by screaming (literally using the magical power of her voice) to destroy fairy-tale inspired monsters who have stolen the voices and (more gruesomely) the hearts of victims. In parallel fashion, Willow and her soon-to-be love interest, Tara, employ magic to move heavy objects into the path of the monsters and keep themselves safe. The women characters collectively employ the feminist powers of female voice and collaborative witchcraft as weapons.

While this noir episode of BTVS was generally popular among fans (and was the sole Emmy-nominated BTVS episode), *Jessica Jones'* online viewers and critics were less receptive to the dress/horse sequence (e.g., *New York Times* reviews, Reddit users' comments, a C+ review of the episode by The AV Club, and others). I would argue that the horse plot was symbolically more complex than it appeared, if viewed alongside BTVS. Jessica's escape fantasy plays into a rich history of horse symbolism, free movement, and strength for girls and women where other spatial imagery casts them as weak. So too, both Jessica and Buffy fantasize about and even attempt to run away from their homes in Hell's Kitchen and the Hellmouth, and the burdens of their callings.

Trouble in the Dream House: Superheroines Defying Symbols of Dolls and Homes

Buffy's hometown is shared with demons, making it a threshold space to Hell (a Hellmouth), whereas Jessica's dark city home (haunted by urban crime, the interdimensional wars of the Avengers, and most recently, Kilgrave) is Hell's Kitchen. The shattering of everyday objects by supernatural forces is a thematic element in each show, as worlds literally collide. Importantly, the childhood symbols and spaces of dolls, particularly Mattel's Barbie and her dream house, figure subtly but eerily in *Jessica Jones* to foreshadow its villains' victimization of female characters.

Police officer Simpson backs up his claim to Trish that he has spent his life protecting people with a childhood memory of burning his sister's Barbie dream house and all his own G.I. Joe toy soldiers in an effort to save Barbie from a catastrophe he himself invented. Simpson's story of protective intentions nearly compromised by extremely violent execution foreshadows his near-fatal attack of Trish and the demise of her home while he is under Kilgrave's control. Additionally, the sacrifice of all his G.I. Joe soldiers predicts the unnecessary loss of his fellow officers in his unwanted later attempts to aid Jessica against Kilgrave. Simpson's gradual descent into drug-induced violence renders many of his actions indivisible from those committed under Kilgrave's control. Viewers are led to question the complexities of the violence Kilgrave actually creates, versus the suffering he merely encourages somewhat passively, and in contrast with the trauma he actually suffers alongside his victims.

There is a symmetry to Kilgrave and Simpson, echoed in their Barbie references and various attacks on women's homes. Jessica notes to Trish that Kilgrave has purchased and eerily restored the house she once lived in with her family prior to the car accident that killed all of her family. Kilgrave's recreation of Jessica's childhood home is an effort to lure and then undo her, and Jessica describes the space as a nightmare version of Barbie's dream house. After deliberation, Jessica places her desire to protect Hope over any need for personal revenge against Kilgrave. She will not kill him, nor will she sacrifice herself to try to reform him. Jessica is focused on her original quest to free Hope. In a parallel fashion, she tries to recall Simpson to the moral imperative of his original role as a police officer, reminding him to "serve and protect" when he doggedly tortures Kilgrave's defenseless employee.

Simpson continuously persists in sacrificing human lives and laws in relentless pursuit of his increasingly drugged and distorted view of his mission. Kilgrave and Simpson are effectively "cut from the same societal cloth"[9] (though Simpson may often look more the part of the White Knight). Disastrously, Kilgrave and Simpson believe women are dolls, playthings; that they can decide and dictate what females in their lives should do. Buffy's characterization echoes this concept complexly, as Whedon initially conceived her as a sort of Barbie, but one that would possess "kung fu grip" and evoke icons like Wonder Woman.[10] Perhaps Buffy is then a complex action figure, defying her dollness through her actions.

So too, Jones and Trish defy male attempts to make them compliant, to make them things. Neither woman is ultimately defeated by the delusions of Simpson and the manipulations of Kilgrave. Jessica rejects Kilgrave, even in his potential for good, rather than sacrifice herself to him. Trish is not won over by Simpson's offers of reconciliation (nor his rather tone deaf and patronizing additional offers of steak cooked rare with cheesecake, or perhaps health food: tofu and wheat berries). His gifts seem almost like the tainted offerings of Trish's manipulative mother, mere bargaining chips to gain power over her and access to information about Jessica. Integral to *Jessica Jones* and *Buffy the Vampire Slayer* is the message that we honor one another greatly through the hard-earned gifts of our friendship and trust. Although Jessica cannot ultimately keep Hope alive despite great efforts and gyrations, she does pledge her love to and rescue Trish. This moment echoes Buffy's absolute love and sacrifices for Dawn and for Willow. For these heroines, friendship is a source of supreme strength, and sisterhood an underlying superpower.

Tentative Conclusions for Superwomen and Other Survivors

This essay has examined various roles of heroic women in supernatural and traumatic contexts. Perhaps most significantly, the two series represent symbolic, adoptive, or even magical sisterhoods as defining roles and responsibilities of the female protagonists. Namely, Jessica and Trish's adoptive sister relationship and collaborative partnership might be productively compared with that of Buffy and Willow. Where Willow brings intelligence, computing prowess, and the supernatural power of witchcraft, Trish offers thoughtful organizational strategy, martial arts training, and unwavering moral support. In another parallel, Jessica's fierce protection of Hope Shlottman could be seen as symbolically akin to the sibling-cum-guardian relationship that develops between Buffy with Dawn. Dawn and Trish are in many ways aspects of Buffy and Jessica, representing heroism without supernatural strength, sisterhood, and the human (rather than superhuman) soul. Dawn is a sort of key to another world and a threat to the human one, while Trish is the key to Jessica's tragic past.

Rather than gloss over the extraordinary qualities of these incredible events and heroines, the supernatural contexts of settings and plots echo the murkiness and difficulties of naming, responding to, and recovering from trauma. My mother, a forensic psychologist, once noted the unreality and difficulty of disclosing/discussing extreme trauma by very brutalized patients and prisoners of war, reflecting perhaps their sense of a certain unbelievable quality somewhat parallel to these fictional survivor stories. Extreme suffering exists outside the bounds of typical human experience, and thus can defy (or be thought to defy) typical therapies. Accordingly, Jones' avoidance of therapeutic response to trauma and Buffy's challenges within therapeutic situations reflect their similar foundational challenges to relate through words and through relationships.

In my view, both the suffering and hard-won survivor status of heroines like Jessica Jones is often related to their strength and struggles as women. So far in its first season, the *Jessica Jones* series addresses a wide range of compelling (and often challenging) major life events women may encounter outside of mainstream media representations, including rape, substance addiction, lesbian sexuality and domestic violence, abortion, and post-traumatic stress disorder. Further, ensemble New Yorkers and main characters alike are also victimized by villain Kilgrave's manipulation and mind control, including men and involving intersecting categories of identity such as class, culture, and race. With a somewhat more diverse cast than other popular television series, the show does not shy away from issues of gender and racial discrimination (e.g., Jessica Jones' African American neighbor, Malcolm, remarks, "Everyone's a little racist"). Further, the show offers additional perspectives aside from Jessica's. Though BTVS had a rather white-washed cast, it also tackled sexual assault, addiction, plotlines pertaining to LGBTQ+++ experiences, and PTSD suffering, opening the door for richer representations.

The ensemble cast of Kilgrave's survivors form and attend a diverse and sometimes healing support group throughout much of the first season of *Jessica Jones*, sharing traumas that fractured their lives. The achievements and ultimate disbanding of this group raise questions about the nature of communities of abuse survivors, and human capabilities to process and respond to crises individually and through collective dialogue. So too, Buffy's experiences with therapy dramatize the difficulties of communication and relationships for survivors. Accordingly, therapies for trauma are evoked in the most traditional and primal form for female superheroines, through healing partnerships and communities of women. The value of feminist communality with its complexities, conflicts, and power echoes into our contemporary world.

NOTES

1. Sonia Sairya, "Jessica Jones: Marvel's Newest Show Makes Trauma a Superpower," *Slate*, accessed November 22, 2015, http://www.salon.com/2015/11/22/jessica_jones_marvels_newest_show_makes_surviving_trauma_a_superpower.
2. Molly Freeman, "How Netflix Saved Jessica Jones From Becoming a Crime Procedural," *Screenrant*, accessed June 17, 2016, http://screenrant.com/jessica-jones-melissa-rosenberg-netflix-abc.
3. Anita Sarkeesian, "Some Thoughts on Jessica Jones," *The Feminist Frequency*, accessed December 1, 2015, http://femfreq.tumblr.com/post/134336278616/some-thoughts-on-jessica-jones.
4. Janina Scarlet, "The Psychology of Inspirational Women: Buffy the Vampire Slayer," *The Mary Sue*, accessed March 5, 2015, http://www.themarysue.com/the-psychology-of-inspirational-women-buffy-the-vampire-slayer.
5. Christine Jarvis, "Real stakeholder education? Lifelong learning in the Buffyverse," *Studies in the Education of Adults* 37:1 (2005): 31–46.
6. Simon Abrams, "Jessica Jones Episode 1: The Worst in People." *The New York Times,* accessed November 20, 2015, http://www.nytimes.com/2015/12/13/arts/television/jessica-jones-netflix-episode-1-review.html.
7. Emily Nussbaum, "Graphic, Novel: Marvel's Jessica Jones and the Superhero Survivor," *The New Yorker* December 21, 2015.
8. Viktor Lowenfeld and W. Lambert Brittain, *Creative & Mental Growth* (New York: Prentice Hall, 1987), 310.
9. Edeline Wrigh, "Toxic Masculinity in *Jessica Jones*: Kilgrave as a 'Nice Guy' and Will Simpson as Misogynistic Hero," *The Mary Sue*, accessed December 11, 2015, http://www.themarysue.com/toxic-masculinity-in-jessica-jones-kilgrave-as-a-nice-guy-and-will-simpson-as-misogynistic-hero.
10. Tasha Robinson, "Interview: Joss Whedon." *A. V. Club.*, accessed September 5, 2001, http://www.avclub.com/article/joss-whedon-13730.

BIBLIOGRAPHY

Abrams, Simon. "Jessica Jones Episode 1: The Worst in People." *The New York Times*, November 20, 2015, http://www.nytimes.com/2015/12/13/arts/television/jessica-jones-netflix-episode-1-review.html.
Freeman, Molly. "How Netflix Saved Jessica Jones From Becoming a Crime Procedural." *Screenrant*, June 17, 2016, http://screenrant.com/jessica-jones-melissa-rosenberg-netflix-abc.
Jarvis, Christine. "Real stakeholder education? Lifelong learning in the Buffyverse." *Studies in the Education of Adults* 37:1 (2005): 31–46.

Lowenfeld, Viktor, and W. Lambert Brittain. *Creative & Mental Growth*. New York: Prentice Hall, 1987.

Nussbaum, Emily. "Graphic, Novel: Marvel's Jessica Jones and the Superhero Survivor." *The New Yorker*, December 21, 2015.

Sairya, Sonia. "Jessica Jones: Marvel's Newest Show Makes Trauma a Superpower." *Slate*, November 22, 2015.

Sarkeesian, Anita. "Some Thoughts on Jessica Jones." *The Feminist Frequency*, December 1, 2015, http://femfreq.tumblr.com/post/134336278616/some-thoughts-on-jessica-jones.

Scarlet, Janina. "The Psychology of Inspirational Women: Buffy the Vampire Slayer." *The Mary Sue*, March 5, 2015, http://www.themarysue.com/the-psychology-of-inspirational-women-buffy-the-vampire-slayer.

Wrigh, Edeline. "Toxic Masculinity in *Jessica Jones*: Kilgrave as a 'Nice Guy' and Will Simpson as Misogynistic Hero." *The Mary Sue*, December 11, 2015.

Battling Bluebeard, Fighting for Hope

The Heroine's Journey

VALERIE ESTELLE FRANKEL

Seen in the most popular stories, from ancient myths to modern film, the heroine's journey is a metaphor for facing the dark side of the self and emerging stronger than before. Most often the protagonist is innocent, such as Dorothy Gale of Oz or Lucy Pevensie of Narnia, confronting sterility, power, and evil in the figure of the wicked queen. Other times, however, the questing heroine may be a wounded, traumatized figure, more like *The Hunger Games'* Katniss Everdeen, who struggles to deal with her PTSD and fear of intimacy as well as an evil tyrant. Such a figure is television's Jessica Jones.

Her *Alias* comics' alter-ego spends three-quarters of her story as a private investigator aiding superheroes. Only after, does she face her greatest challenge—her suppressed trauma from her nemesis the Purple Man.[1] By defeating him in comic and show, Jessica finally achieves healing and ends the villain's threat. She also must deal with her own dark, often self-destructive impulses. Beyond all this, Jessica's is a story of self-definition. "*Alias* as a title for the series as a whole indicates that it is a book about all the people Jessica has been—daughter, orphan, mother, lover, sister, hero, drunk, slut, detective, and moral agent; it is a title linked to our discovery of who Jessica actually is," explains Roz Kaveney, author of *Superheroes! Capes and Crusaders in Comics and Films.*[2] Certainly, she frees herself from the conventional definition of superhero and thus creates a new image of the woman with powers, though one who resists a hero nickname and costume as she struggles to fix the world. Scholar and mythologist Joseph Campbell writes:

> All these different mythologies give us the same essential quest. You leave the world that you're in and go into a depth or into a distance or up to a height. There you come

to what was missing in your consciousness in the world you formerly inhabited. Then comes the problem either of staying with that, and letting the world drop off, or returning with that boon and trying to hold onto it as you move back into your social world again. That's not an easy thing to do.[3]

Indeed, this is the damaged heroine's path through her thirteen-episode saga.

Accepting the Quest

Television's Jessica, a cynical private investigator, spends her days tracking cheating spouses and serving violent lowlifes with subpoenas. As she comments, "People do bad shit. I just avoid getting involved with them in the first place. That works for me. Most of the time."[4] As an outsider observing their lives from a distance and barely living her own, she's clearly struggling with trauma. Flashbacks burst into her ordinary life, like a man's voice saying, "You want to do it. You know you do," and a hand stroking her hair. Creative filming angles up drains and in mirrors similarly stress her dissociation. The camera confusedly blurs and spins. In the comic, she's better off, if only a little. *SlashFilm* critic Jacob Hall notes:

> In *Alias*, Jessica is mess, but she's a controlled mess. She drinks too much. She sleeps around with strange men. She gets into trouble of the personal and professional varieties. She's flawed, but she has her act together. You get the impression that she pays her rent on time, even though crushing pain and trauma are always lurking at the fringes of her everyday existence.
>
> Netflix Jessica is a disaster zone. Her apartment and office are continuously trashed, she gets thrown out of bars into literal piles of garbage, and she might as well have vomit stains all over that badass leather jacket.[5]

Both are suffering, though the one in the comics has a handle on her life. Show-Jessica often stands frozen, unable to do more than recite her street names and wait for the shaking to stop. Hall adds, "Her pain is all too real, her psychic wounds deep and painful. It helps that the series devotes an episode to her life prior to Kilgrave. Seeing the admittedly sarcastic and slightly maladjusted Jessica before she was fundamentally damaged makes her story all the more heartbreaking."[6]

Suddenly, a case intrudes that shatters Jessica's careful life and provides the classic Call to Adventure. The Shlottmans have journeyed from Omaha seeking their missing daughter Hope. As Jessica investigates and recognizes the girl's purchases of lingerie and dinner, she realizes the horrors of her own past have resurfaced. Attempting to flee, as per the hero's traditional refusal of the call, she begs her employer for money, then, desperate, goes to Trish Walker, her successful foster sister whom she's avoided for six months. Trish doesn't encourage Jessica to run but to step up and be a hero, adding, "I know one thing, you are far better equipped to deal with that animal than some innocent girl from Omaha. You're still the person who tried to do something."

Jessica backs away. "Tried and failed. That's what started this. I was never the hero that you wanted me to be."[7] She is the damaged ex-superhero, shattered by what she's faced at Kilgrave's hand and determined to never wear a costume again. Critic Sadie Gennis examines how Jessica's trauma affects her decision to pursue and vanquish Kilgrave once and for all:

> The trauma Jessica endured from Kilgrave goes far beyond rape. As she explains, he "violated every cell in my body and every thought in my goddamn head," even making her kill for him. Though most survivors aren't struggling with the weight of murder, how Jessica flagellates herself over what happened is powerfully resonant. She isolates herself from everyone, convinced that she is hopelessly broken and only burdens those around her. And that—the shame, the self-loathing, the self-doubt—is often the trauma hardest for survivors to overcome.[8]

Succumbing to her morals, Jessica invades Kilgrave's hotel and valiantly carries the mind-controlled girl out by force, saving this younger copy the way she would have wanted to be saved herself. After, she offers Hope her own lessons in coping, insisting she recite her street names and say it wasn't her fault. As Jessica adds, "His control, whatever it is, it wears off. But it takes time and distance, so we're both getting out of here."[9]

To her horror, Hope suddenly shoots both her parents and passes on a message from Kilgrave, telling Jessica to smile. Horrified, Jessica gets a taxi, but before she can leave, she abruptly takes Trish's advice. No longer will she run from her past. She is crossing over and accepting the quest at last.

Thus television Jessica sets out not only to stop Kilgrave but also to save his newest victim. As Jessica's successor, Hope is the closest mirror for the superheroine. Jessica's *Alias* character has a similar struggle, as she helps several damaged teen superheroes like a high schooler claiming she's a mutant and Mattie Franklin, the third Spider-Woman. As the latter tells a story of drug addiction, of being controlled externally, and watching her life as if it's on a television, Jessica tells her, "I know *exactly* what you mean." Reassembling these shattered heroines represents fixing herself. Critic John R. Parker observes, "At any moment Jones seems in danger of losing herself completely, of letting the weight of her past and the grisly realities of life dragging her down. It's a war of attrition with Jones, a constant battle to get just one more thing right than she gets wrong."[10]

Comic-book Jessica also faces fragments of herself as she helps male heroes. First, Jessica discovers Captain America's identity just as his girlfriend is murdered. She also protects Matt Murdock after he's exposed as Daredevil. Both jobs emphasize the dangers of being a superhero, especially one with a secret identity. All the heroes have flaws and aren't nearly as perfect as they

believe themselves to be. From there, she runs across a Rick Jones impersonator and, spending time with this perpetual sidekick, is reminded of her own
former idolization of the Avengers, before everything changed. She cheats J.
Jonah Jameson, emphasizing how she still wants to do good even in small
ways like helping the homeless on his dime. All these cases pull the ambivalent
ex-superheroine back into the traditional Marvel world step by step, breaking
down her denial as Hope's case does on the show.

Still, for both series, all Jessica's cases involve loss and misery of some
kind, with more realistic endings than happy ones. Life is no longer a comic
book, the book and show both imply. Further, the books emphasize the danger
of being a peripheral superhero not in the inner circle: the Avengers' supe-
riority and self-assuredness nearly got Jessica killed. Thus, dealing with them
means dealing with her past trauma. Parker adds, "that's what *Alias* is really
about: recovery. Taking the pain others have given you and turning it into
something better, making the world a better place in whatever small way possible."[11] He then explains Jessica's conflict in more detail:

> From a missing teenage superhero to a group of family members seeking an admis-
> sion of guilt from the villain who killed them, every case forms some link to Jessica's
> personality or past. Some of those connections are obvious, but it's mostly implied:
> it's up to the reader to understand what piece of herself Jessica sees in a teenage run-
> away from a mutant-hating town; it's incumbent upon you to puzzle out the trauma
> that withered away at this once-gleaming protector of the innocent and reduced her
> to an outwardly cynical and hopeless alcoholic.[12]

It is simpler in the show's world of non-costumed heroes to introduce an
innocent girl victim rather than an actual Spider-Woman or mutant wannabe.
At the same time, this changed metaphor fails to address the intense vulnerability of superheroines. True, they have strength and powers, but they are
also often the victims in comics, killed and injured to drive the male characters. Thus *Alias* makes it even clearer that Jessica is rescuing the superhero
side of herself, while the show focuses more on her human side as Hope
struggles for public understanding.

Gathering Allies

Collecting friends and allies is an important stage of the journey. They
often reflect parts of the heroine's will (or unsubtle mind, heart, and courage
in a story like in *The Wizard of Oz*), emphasizing skills she needs to develop.
They can also reflect the vulnerable, innocent part of the heroine—healing
or protecting them means healing or protecting herself. While Hope is an
obvious foil, the other survivor of the story is Jessica's closest companion,
Trish.

Though on the show, Trish is the non-superpowered sister, Marvel Comics tells a far different story. The show describes her childhood stardom as redheaded icon Patsy, a reference to the character's history. Patsy Walker actually dates back to *Miss America Magazine* #2 (Nov. 1944), written by Ruth Atkinson and published by Marvel's precursor Timely Comics. With red hair and a wholesome all-American family, she wasn't a superhero but a friendly girl-next-door type who clashed with her straight-laced parents, partied with her boyfriend Buzz, and exchanged barbs with her black-haired nemesis Hedy Wolfe. She appeared in in issues of *Miss America, Teen Comics,* and *Girls' Life,* then finally her own teen-humor *Patsy Walker* series, followed by *Patsy and Hedy* and *Patsy and Her Pals.* As a contemporary, realistic series, it survived the death and resurgence of superhero comics, stretching from the 1940s through 1967. The series remains a reminder of an earlier time for Marvel, one of wholesome values and everyday life.

In 1976, Marvel comics rebranded Patsy Walker as the superheroine Hellcat (as she appropriated the costume abandoned by the sixties heroine, The Cat). In a yellow unitard and black mask and gloves, she battled alongside the Avengers, then the Defenders. The superheroine Moondragon trained her in psychic ability and advanced barefoot martial arts, granting her superpowers of a sort. After training, she could move small objects telekinetically, resist mental control, and later, sense the presence of demons.

Even with all these powers, she's still vulnerable to child abuse. As comic-book Patsy notes of her mother, "She wasn't a good person … when she got sick … she … she tried to make a deal with a demon to save herself. For me to die instead."[13] In *The Defenders* #89, her mother dies. At the graveside, Patsy says, "You always told me not to cry—to act like a grownup—whether you were dragging me to modeling school or an agency. I guess that's part of the reason we never got along. You wanted me to *be* perfect. The ideal daughter. Something I could never live up to." Patsy describes a childhood as tomboy daughter to the ultimate stage mother, with her mother's friend Millie the Model trying to get her jobs. When Patsy wouldn't cooperate, her mother wrote fiction about her as a teen romance star. Poor Patsy describes feeling like "a freak." As she adds, her mother had had such big dreams for her, "sometimes I felt she couldn't tell the difference between me and the fictional Patsy in the magazines."[14]

The comics version thus has a double life, as fictional magazine heroine and real-life superhero, both sides struggling with identity. The television series spoofs the two eras with Patsy Walker comics and a children's television show. However, it subverts these with the child abuse and stage mom behavior often linked to child stardom. Young Patsy is miserable and needs the fiery Jessica to defend her, stopping the overbearing mother from bruising her and making her throw up. Jessica thus spends her teenage years defending her more vulnerable adoptive sister. As grown women, however, Trish has become a powerhouse on her own.

In episode three, Jessica discovers that Trish now lives with a steel-reinforced door, bulletproof windows, video surveillance, and a safe room. At this evidence of Trish's fright, Jessica asks if her mother is back, but Trish replies that she no longer needs Jessica's protection—she's even learning Krav Maga like her comic alter ego. Trish replies, "No one touches me anymore unless I want them to. I let you fight my battles for too long."[15] Many fans believe television-Trish will evolve into Hellcat, as she has already tried the supersoldier drugs and trained in unarmed combat. Now all she needs is a nickname. Jacob Hall, comparing the show and the *Alias* comic, asks:

> After all, why would the series establish this enthusiastic do-gooder of a sidekick as being a capable martial artist if they weren't planning to stick her in a costume at some point? In any case, Trish is one of the best characters on the show, even though Marvel diehards will grumble that her proper comic name, Patsy, is disregarded on the show as a childhood nickname.[16]

In 2016, Marvel introduced a new comic called *Patsy Walker, AKA Hellcat* written by Kate Leth with art by Brittney L. Williams. Jessica Jones even visits in issues #5–7, presumably as a nod to the show. Meanwhile, Patsy, like Trish, deals with her ex-stardom as she builds a new image and forms an agency for superheroes seeking work. With the emphasis on life's practicalities, her superhero stunts are small, dealing with her reputation rather than galactic threats. It's compared by many to *Squirrel Girl*, a fun, girly Marvel comic that emphasizes friendship and compromise over fighting. As such, Patsy is once more contrasted with the far harder Jessica with her own gritty comics.

Television Trish, like the 2016 comic character, provides help through legal and star-power means more than superheroics. Encouraged by Trish and the lawyer Jeri Hogarth, Hope does a radio interview and shares her story. Of course, Jessica, who's never done the same for herself, is horrified at this turn of events:

> **Trish:** We're doing a live remote with Hope from the prison.
> **Jessica:** No.
> **Trish:** Jess, you asked me to defend her.
> **Jessica:** Yeah, not to drag her out in public with her guts hanging out.
> **Trish:** Hey, it's me. I'm on her side. I'll go easy.
> **Jessica:** Trish, he'll be listening. He wouldn't miss it. Probably not. He'll be listening to her and thinking about me.
> **Trish:** He's already thinking about you. Hope wants to fight back and I want to help her.[17]

Courageous Trish is right; Kilgrave is already stalking Jessica, and all his victims need to go on the attack. Taking the position of Jessica's defender, the best friend who lends strength when needed, Trish actually challenges Kilgrave on the air: "So yes, I think he's out there, this sick, perverted man.... He is preying on the hopeless so he can feel powerful, probably terrified of his own weakness, which suggests impotence.... Probably suggests some serious Oedipal issues...."[18] Jessica panics at this defiance and pulls the plug. In this scene, Jeri embodies her sense of caution, Hope her vulnerability, and Trish her courage and determination, all showing Jessica what she must do.

Another important step is the support group. Though Jessica starts it for selfish reasons, she subconsciously is trying to fix the other victims, and thus fix the victimized part of herself. Nonetheless, she adamantly refuses to join them.

> **Jessica:** I told them to keep in touch. Talk.
> **Hogarth:** You starting a support group? Will you be participating?
> **Jessica:** Like I'd waste my time circle jerking with a bunch of whiners.
> **Hogarth:** Yes, you are a paragon of mental health.
> **Jessica:** I'm using them, Hogarth. I wanna know everything they did with him, everywhere they went, every word that was said, particularly about me, and what the hell he's gonna do next.[19]

Still, the therapy seems to help some of them. In group, Malcolm (who had been training to be a social worker before Kilgrave turned him into a junkie to make him spy on Jessica) says, "It's not just the things that he made me do that keep me up. It's the question of who I am. I mean, he turned me into an addict, a liar, a thief. He did that. But I don't know if it was in me to begin with or ... or if it's part of who I am now."[20] Jessica heals him with more than the support group as she handcuffs him in the bathroom (admittedly with a blanket, pillow, water bottle, and peanut-butter sandwich) to get clean. She gives him the freedom she always wanted for himself, forgiving all he's done but telling him he can determine his own life. She says:

> You have a choice now.... The whole time he had me, there was some part of me that fought. There was some tiny corner of my brain that tried to get out. And I'm still fighting. I won't stop fighting. But if you give up.... I lose. Do you get that? He did this to you to get at me. To isolate me. To make me feel like an infection, one more person dead or dying because of me. So why don't you remember how to be a goddamn human being again instead of this self-pitying piece of shit that he turned you into, and save me for once? You choose.[21]

She tosses Malcolm the drugs she has confiscated from him, but he flushes them, making a decision to do better.

On the heroine's quest, these friends are known as the Animus, the masculine voices in the heroine's head guiding her. This Animus, "evokes masculine traits within her: logic, rationality, intellect. Her conscious side, aware of the world around her, grows, and she can rule and comprehend the exterior world," as explained in my own *From Girl to Goddess: The Heroine's Journey through Myth and Legend.*[22] Malcolm is the most obvious of these, balancing her passion and rage with caution.

As the heroine grows, her Animus is replaced by increasingly wiser versions: initiative and planning, then rule of law, and wisdom, while her enemies follow the same process of growth to challenge her.[23] First influencing Jessica is Kilgrave, the voice of brutality and cruelty. Through the series, he grows smarter, not only increasing his power but relying on hostages, backup security, and trickery. With Jessica's lovesick, helpless neighbor Ruben (whose twin sister acts more like his babysitter) and Malcolm the junkie, Jessica has little support. After this, however, she transforms Malcolm the junkie into Malcolm the clever friend and sympathetic counselor. Kilgrave kills Ruben, a tragedy that symbolically removes the weakened support around Jessica and pushes her to strike back. Further, she makes new allies. With supersoldier Simpson, Jessica begins planning and works out a plan focused on justice for Hope rather than revenge. Later come the seasoned police chief and Kilgrave's father, whose respective city authority and scientific knowledge might be able to stop Kilgrave.

A final male friend is, of course, Luke Cage, played by Mike Colter. Colter adds:

> The way that I was able to see how Luke dealt with Jessica, he's a supporter. He could have intervened with Kilgrave, but that was something she had to deal with for herself. He couldn't come to her rescue because that wouldn't change the horror of what she'd been through. In that regard, it defined who he was and how he looked at her, as a person who's a complete individual that can do things for herself, but if she needed him, he was there for her.[24]

He is another reflection of Jessica, the only other superpowered person. Both are determined not to be Avengers but ordinary people getting through their days. "Luke has never bought into most of the stock but unneeded aspects of superheroing—the costume, the mask, the secret identity—and he has always been 'hero for hire'—a mercenary. He is not Captain America, nor does he pretend to be; he is not the embodiment of an ideal, just a working stiff with powers," Kaveney explains.[25] He aids in Jessica's planning, though his experience also brings touches of righteousness and wisdom. With his example, Jessica finally faces her old nemesis.

The Enemy

Luke Cage is positioned against the villain of the story, Kilgrave himself. As Luke is the altruist, Kilgrave is the narcissist—not just a villain but a threat to Jessica's sense of self. He would take her over completely and turn her into a compliant doll if he could; and indeed, he's done so before.

The Purple Man did not employ physical sexual abuse as a weapon against Jessica, although he raped other women under his power, ordering Jessica to watch. However, he instructed her to love him, then to beg him for sex, and, as she grimly recounts, "I would beg him to fuck me—I would beg him 'til I cried" (14, no. 25). Jessica's slavery is total: "I lay at his feet. I slept on his floor. I bathed him" (ibid). Despite the horror of this, it is Jessica's description of how this false consciousness feels which may be the most disturbing aspect of this story: "In your head—it doesn't feel any different than when you think it yourself, you see? It's almost soothing. In my mind, I can't tell the difference between what he made me do or say and what I do or say on my own" (16, no. 25).[26]

She knows it wasn't her doing, but as she says, "it doesn't change the fact that I did it or said it." In fact, his influence is especially terrible since it feels like part of Jessica; as she explains on the show, he "violated every cell in my body and every thought in my goddamn head."[27] In the course of their acquaintance, Kilgrave has imprisoned and raped her, but also ordered her to enjoy it. He turned her into a murderer (the one moment so horrific it helped her break free). He even desecrates the childhood street names she uses to ground herself when he moves into her childhood home. After her enslavement, Jessica is devastated on every level. Sadie Gennis explains in her essay, "How Jessica Jones Got Rape Stories Right": "She isolates herself from everyone, convinced that she is hopelessly broken and only burdens those around her. And that—the shame, the self-loathing, the self-doubt— is often the trauma hardest for survivors to overcome."[28]

He has stolen her agency, but worse, he leaves her fearing that some part of her consented, however much it isn't true. Though he's attempted to make Jessica fall in love with him and always asks her to enjoy herself in his company, when she resists he tells her to slice off her own ear. "His only evidence that she chose to have this happen to her? That she didn't walk off a ledge to her death to get away from him. Choosing to live is consent enough for Kilgrave," protests Brian Formo in his essay, tellingly titled "Why *Jessica Jones* and *Spotlight* Are a Step Forward for Victims of Abuse."[29] Because she didn't kill herself fast enough, Kilgrave believes she willingly stayed with him.

Of course, this battle echoes that of many women trapped in abusive relationships. Karen Healy, discussing the series' feminism, adds, "This particular false consciousness is chemically induced, but this could easily be a description of the patriarchally-imposed ideological false consciousness, with Killgrave as its smirking representative."[30] He, a white male with mind control powers, believes other people don't matter. Thus, her battling his smothering authority becomes a feminist stand. Jessica, fighting for an identity as a superheroine, then simply as an individual, is struggling to reclaim the agency her enslaver stole from her in a feminist quest rarely seen in male-centric Marvel storylines. However, it's common in myth and fairytales.

Among these, the Bluebeard figure is a classic antagonist for the heroine. In the fairytale of this name, he marries the innocent heroine and forbids her to go into a room of his house. When she does, she discovers the bodies of his previous wives. Thus, she's married to a killer and must fight for her very existence within the domestic space. Bluebeard is the vicious Animus who has devoured the entire psyche. The heroine must strike back, defending those emotional parts of herself, such as intuition and autonomy, that the creature most wants to control. In short, the heroine must battle for her very sense of identity. Jessica manages a compromise: she smiles for Kilgrave and even moves in with him, but maintains a set of rules. Inside Jessica's childhood home, they play a cat and mouse game of hidden tricks and hostages as each tries to stay safe and control the other. She's determined to remain her essential self and even stay heroic. In her celebrated book *Women Who Run with the Wolves*, Clarissa Pinkola Estés explains, "To restrain the natural predator of the psyche it is necessary for women to remain in possession of all their instinctual powers," listing among them intuitive healing, tenacious loving, and creativity.[31]

All Jessica's compromises, all the times she gives in to Kilgrave, she does it to save the innocents he holds hostage. When she gives him a taste of saving lives and he tells her, "I can't do it without you," she actually considers staying with him to make him into a good person. This combination of guilt and obligation is the heroine's biggest trap. "Many women have literally lived the Bluebeard tale. They marry while they are yet naive about predators, and they choose someone who is destructive to their lives. They are desperate to 'cure' that person with love," comments Estés.[32] Jessica is not naïve, but she recognizes that Kilgrave does care for her and can delight in doing good. Like many heroines, she finds herself in a destructive relationship, with the savage male pleading with her to devote her altrusim to him and redeem him. Though the compassionate heroine is always tempted, she must learn to deny pity and turn her back on him. Estés adds, "Today, it is generally understood that the romantic and spiritual man-god—the male ideal worthy of a woman's self-sacrifice and worship, for whom she is expected to set aside herself and her life—simply does not exist."[33]

Kilgrave is most certainly not such a man. "Which part of staying in five-star hotels, eating in all the best places, doing whatever the hell you wanted, is rape?" he protests. He believes he has improved Jessica's life through the luxuries he has offered, showing his complete obliviousness to the demands of a mutual relationship. Further, he insists, as many abusers do, that he has no way of knowing she did not consent. The one thing he does not do is ask. As Gennis protests, "The fact that Kilgrave is seemingly unclear about whether Jessica did or didn't consent doesn't make him any more sympathetic. It makes him more terrifying, because the notion of a man abusing women without full comprehension of his actions is not fantastical. It's bleakly real."[34]

"Given the low percent of rape that is actually reported, and the extremely-high percent of PTSD from victims, this a perfect parallel for what a rapist actually does: exert power over someone's body and mind; and although creator Melissa Rosenberg is very subtle about this, Kilgrave clearly has no clue what consent is," explains Formo.[35] While Kilgrave seems unable to grasp this concept, he is responsible for his own actions and for the trauma they cause. Other excuses follow, as Kilgrave mentions that his parents abused him and disavows responsibility for Jessica's drinking problem.[36] Jessica, like many women in abusive relationships, struggles through the arguments that sound so logical on the surface.

His constant insistence on her smiling is a metaphor for controlling Jessica, but also making her cover the abuse and pretend all is fine, as Gennis points out:

> Without showing a single rape onscreen, showrunner Melissa Rosenberg captures the atrocity of Kilgrave's actions with a single word: smile. Each time Kilgrave orders Jessica to smile, the threat feels chillingly familiar. It's something every woman has experienced in her life walking down the street. And though cat-calling rarely escalates to a physical or sexual assault, there is always the acute awareness that it could and that you might not be strong to stop it. These are the very real fears Kilgrave taps into. He is the embodiment of misogyny, both casual and determined, and he doesn't even know it.[37]

In the midst of her trauma, Jessica finds a path to wholeness in her female friends. Once again, Trish parallels Jessica, offering her own support, as she too has experienced abuse. Episode three has Kilgrave sending Will Simpson, the cop and ex-supersoldier, to kill Trish, beating and half-strangling her. After, Trish manages to move past this attack and have a sexual relationship with him. As such, Trish remains a model for Jessica of healing from the trauma and finding a way to welcome men into her life. Jessica, keeping Luke Cage at arm's distance, struggles with the concept of love, but tries to connect with Luke through the first season arc.

Trish and Jessica's overwhelming trauma is especially symbolized by doors. Jessica begins by destroying her own door, shattered just as her PI life is about to be torn apart. Trish tries to have the door fixed, but Jessica insists she'll repair it herself. Though neighbors and clients also comment that she is not safe with her door open, Jessica feels it has been blasted open; she has no blocks, no defense, no cover. Perhaps this is why she never goes into hiding, not as a superhero or under threat. Later, doorways suggest a major step forward in trust: Jessica and Luke lurk outside each other's doors, hoping for permission to approach. Trish and Simpson sit against the two sides of her door for hours and chat before she invites him to step through the door …

and goes to bed with him. Later, Simpson destroys their trust along with Jessica's glass door, after he takes a few red pills that make him uncontrollably violent. Jessica brings Luke to her place in episode twelve and specifically unlocks the door, reaching through the sharp-edged window and letting him in (suggesting her defenses have been blasted once again, but this time only partially). Meanwhile, goons clean up Simpson and the corpses he left, invading Trish's and Jessica's homes; Jessica tells Trish to invest in better security. The heroine's classic symbol is the home—in this case, one Jessica and Trish are each steadily rebuilding, like building the borders of the self towards a strong, defended exterior.

The comics also add an even darker edge of abuse than strangling when Patsy Walker joins the story, as long-time readers quickly recognized. Patsy, married to Defenders teammate Daimon Hellstrom—the Son of Satan—goes down to Hell to rescue him. However, when she sees her husband's dark side, she's driven mad.[38] A later comic has an insane Patsy narrate as her husband comes home. Upstairs, she chants to herself, "Kisses and horror shows…. I brought you back, Daimon. Brought you back for kisses and got nothing but horror shows. I brought you back…." When her sanity returns, Patsy cries for hours because she still loves him. "Imagine that. Dragging the only man you've ever really loved back from death … and discovering he wasn't worth the bother."[39] This devotion to someone so unworthy is every superheroine's greatest fear. She finally commits suicide in *Hellstorm Prince of Lies* #14, though her eventual rescue from Hell follows.[40] Thus, this Bluebeard relationship parallels Jessica's total abuse, physical and mental. Nonetheless, both women find a way through darkness and into light.

Jessica Jones's best friend in *Alias*, Carol Danvers, the former Ms. Marvel, has just as disturbing an abuse story. *Avengers* #200 (1980) begins with Carol's having a baby, with a mysterious full term pregnancy that has only lasted three days. When the Wasp calls her lucky, Carol bursts out, "I've been used! That isn't my baby. I don't even know who the father is."[41] She finally meets her "son," only to be overwhelmed with the artificial feelings he has created for her and blissfully goes off with him. As Carol A. Strickland protests in her "The Rape of Ms. Marvel," writers Jim Shooter and his male staff "slaughtered Marvel's symbol of modern women, Ms. Marvel. They presented her as a victim of rape who enjoyed the process, and even wound up swooning over her rapist and joining him of her 'free' will."[42] Like Ms. Marvel, Jessica has to live knowing most of her friends cannot understand the severity of her trauma. Kaveney adds, connecting the pair:

> Not only was she grotesquely abused by her lover/child (who then aged into senility as fast as he had matured), but her colleagues in the Avengers failed to notice that she was hardly in her right mind when she agreed to all of this, and let her go off without thinking things through. The superhero community has let both Carol and Jessica

down, largely by being unthinking men with a tendency to think women capable of any irrational behavior, and not to examine the possible causes.[43]

In Chris Claremont's *Avengers Annual* #10 (1981), Carol finally gets a chance to speak up for herself as she tells the Avengers how furious she is: "I didn't love Marcus! I *never* loved Marcus! Don't any of you realize what happened months ago, what Marcus *did* to me?" She explains that she never left of her own free will, adding:

> You took everything Marcus said at face value. You didn't question, you didn't doubt. You simply let me go with a wave and a bouncy Bon Voyage. That was your mistake for which I paid the price. My mistake was trusting you. After a trauma like mine, it's easy to wallow in bitterness and self-pity. But both grief and ... guilt ... have to be faced, dealt with, exorcised. There's more ... there *has* to be more ... to being heroes than simply defeating villains. You have a role, a purpose far greater than yourselves. You have to set examples, lead the way. You represent what we *should* be, what we dream of becoming, not what we are. You screwed up, Avengers. That's human. What is also human is the ability to learn from those mistakes. To grow. To mature. If you do that ... even a little ... then perhaps what I went through will have a positive meaning. It's your choice.[44]

Thus, as Jessica spends time with Carol or Trish, each guides her to express her hurt and loss of control, then move beyond it and find healing. Both have suffered from abusive, controlling men who took over their bodies and sanity. Still, both stand as examples that healing is finally possible.

Death and Empowerment

As a hero, Jessica takes massive responsibility for everything, especially Kilgrave's actions. When Kilgrave threatens more hostages, he adds, "There would've been a rash of suicides across the neighborhood, and who would've been to blame?" When she denies bearing any guilt here, he retorts, "You keep telling yourself that. Maybe you'll actually believe it someday."[45]

Still, she insists on keeping Kilgrave alive for one reason: so he can take public responsibility for his crimes, exonerating Hope but also in many ways, Jessica. "For Jones—and any survivor—her physical torment won't go away simply by killing her abuser. But making sure that he can never commit it again and that he is properly punished—judicially—makes his horrors known, and could likely benefit more survivors, because such a public display could get more survivors to come forward," Formo explains.[46]

> The show also highlights the need for the police, the legal system and other members of society to believe and support victims, rather than blame them. Because sadly, the fact that Hope (Erin Moriarty) is the one who winds up in jail after being raped and abused by Kilgrave rings true. Every year, victims are arrested after reporting their

own rape. Women are repeatedly written off as "crazy" and unreliable narrators of their own story, particularly when their rapists are wealthy, attractive white men, such as Kilgrave.

That's why the small, but crucial decision to have Jessica fight not for vengeance against Kilgrave, but to force the world to believe his victims is so important. The tendency to blame victims for their own assaults is why so [many] rapes go unreported (68 percent) and unprosecuted. And even if they do make it to court, they rarely result in any jail time (2 percent), creating a cycle that revictimizes rape survivors and shelters the attackers. This sad truth is what eventually drives Jessica to realize there is no possibility for justice within the established legal system, and why she is ultimately forced to resort to more guerrilla tactics.[47]

While Jessica attempts to legally prove Kilgrave's crimes, pushing him to use his powers on camera and before witnesses, she fails and Kilgrave recaptures Hope. In his cruelty, Kilgrave realizes how much Jessica wants to save her and thus prove that she can save the damaged part of herself. He smirks, "She'll never kill me. Despite her calloused, hard-bitten, and, frankly, poorly-styled facade, despite her several problems, she still hopes that, at her core, she might just be a hero. But only if she can save you. The ultimate innocent victim."[48] Hope, despairing, kills herself so Jessica will finally destroy Kilgrave. At this loss, Jessica crumples in anguish.

On her mythic journey, the heroine experiences death and through this, battles the darkness and grows stronger. This need not be her own death, as the loss of another can affect her just as strongly. Indeed, Hope's sacrifice gives her the strength to take down Kilgrave and end his wickedness. Estés writes, "This is our meditation practice as women, calling back the dead and dismembered aspects of ourselves, calling back the dead and dismembered aspects of life itself. The one who re-creates from that which has died is always a double-sided archetype. The Creation Mother is always the Death Mother and vice versa."[49] Jessica emerges from Hope's death stronger and angrier, determined to protect the world as cruel vigilante, not law-abiding superhero.

Kilgrave next turns on Luke, Jessica's new love interest, and when Luke escapes his burning bar, he shows he has been "Kilgraved" and attacks Jessica until she's forced to shoot him. In the hospital, talking to Nurse Temple, she rejects blaming herself for Luke's dramatic injuries. "I did have a choice and I chose to survive," she decides. Still, Luke's brush with death hurts her, as she has just opened herself up to feeling again. She thinks: "Pain is always a surprise. I try to avoid landmines. Avoid caring. I can even see it coming. But until it hits, you have no idea what pain is."[50]

On cue, Kilgrave takes over the hospital intercom and pushes Jessica to blame herself once more: "Should have known you'd save your own skin, boyfriend be damned. Selfish as ever. Clearly, it's not better to have loved and lost."[51] He voices her inner self-hate spiral, encouraging Jessica to despair and isolate herself.

Determined to end his reign over her life, Jessica finally walks into Kilgrave's trap. This is her own descent into the underworld, as she's prepared to face her worst demon and surrender to his control again to end the violence. *From Girl to Goddess* concludes, "These journeys into darkness represent death—only by completely surrendering to the unknown can the heroine transcend her existence, and learn the wisdom and magic of mortality."[52] There on the docks, she follows his orders, admits her own flaws, and finally lets him take her beloved Trish. Now she knows her worst fears can no longer destroy her. Meanwhile, allowing herself to surrender to Kilgrave convinces him she is under his control. When she turns passive, he joyfully rushes to her and says: "My God. It's finally over. You're mine now. No more fighting. No more of these ugly displays. You'll be with me now. Look, after a while … however long it takes…. I know…. I know you will feel what I feel. Let's start with a smile."

Obeying his favorite command, she smiles for him, then, throwing the word back at him, she snaps his neck. Actress Krysten Ritter concludes:

> For Jessica, that final victorious, triumphant moment when she kills Kilgrave, I found that very conflicting, in terms of her head space. He's the reason why she got up, every day. He's the reason why she went out in the world. It really gave her a purpose. And I don't think that the past trauma just goes away with his death.[53]

Indeed, the psychological damage Kilgrave has caused does not disappear. "The world still does not believe his victims, despite the mounting number of those who've come forward. Kilgrave's death has not erased Jessica's PTSD, nor has it helped her recognize her own self-worth, a feat that is now probably made harder by the rising body count for which she blames herself."[54] Still, her facing Kilgrave and removing his threat has given her a little peace.

Further, as the first Marvel superhero starring in her own television narrative, she is striking a blow for women's power, destroying her rapist utterly. Critic Karen Healy likewise sees the comics' insertion of the character into Silver Age history—a time in which many sweet and unassertive heroines like Sue Storm and the schoolgirl Jean Grey were invented—as "neatly performing the feminist process of recovering marginalized, hitherto unspoken, female narratives."[55] Adding her to the few female superheroes of the Silver Age retroactively creates a touch more feminism. In both versions, hers is a tale of brutalization by a patriarchal figure, then her battle to escape him—and in fact all the Avengers—and make a life for herself beyond their tradition of costumed team-ups and public fame. The show likewise emphasizes that Marvel's women can have their own epics without pretending to be incompetent like Agent Carter or teaming up under male leadership like Skye and Melinda May from *Agents of S.H.I.E.L.D.*, or Scarlet Witch and Black Widow. Jessica answers to no one but herself.

Television's Jessica Jones ends the story in her own office, trashed and shattered by male rage, the glass in the door in shards so anyone can walk in. Nonetheless, it is only halfway broken—better than at the series beginning—and all the violent men are out of the picture. Only her kindly neighbor Malcolm enters, eager to support Jessica on her hero path. She does not yet commit to Luke the way she does in the comic. Still, she has assembled her team of Trish and Malcolm, and with them, she has gained a little wisdom. More importantly, she is still protecting the world as a healing woman returning to heroism at last.

NOTES

1. Brian Michael Bendis and Michael Gaydos, *Alias Ultimate Collection Book 2* (New York: Max Comics, 2010).
2. Roz Kaveney, *Superheroes!: Capes and Crusaders in Comics and Films* (London: I.B. Tauris, 2008), 68.
3. Joseph Campbell with Bill Moyers, *The Power of Myth*, ed. Betty Sue Flowers (New York: Doubleday, 1988), 190.
4. *Marvel's Jessica Jones*, "AKA Ladies Night," directed by S. J. Clarkson, written by Melissa Rosenberg. Netflix, November 20, 2015.
5. Jacob Hall, "Jessica Jones vs. Alias: How Marvel's New Netflix Series Compares to the Comic That Inspired It," *SlashFilm*, November 23 2015, http://www.slashfilm.com/jessica-jones-vs-alias.
6. *Ibid.*
7. *Marvel's Jessica Jones*, "AKA Ladies Night."
8. Sadie Gennis, "How Jessica Jones Got Rape Stories Right," *TV Guide*, December 3 2015, http://www.tvguide.com/news/jessica-jones-rape-sexual-assault-stories/.
9. *Marvel's Jessica Jones*, "AKA Ladies Night."
10. John R. Parker, "*Alias* Jessica Jones: A Critical Look Back at Marvel's Mature Readers Hero and New Netflix Star," *Comics Alliance*, November 5 2014, http://comicsalliance.com/alias-omnibus-review.
11. *Ibid.*
12. *Ibid.*
13. Kate Leth and Brittney L Williams, *Patsy Walker, AKA Hellcat #7* (New York: Marvel, 2016).
14. Ed Hannigan, et al., *The Defenders #89* (New York: Marvel, 1980).
15. *Marvel's Jessica Jones*, "AKA It's Called Whiskey," directed by David Petrarca, written by Liz Friedman and Scott Reynolds. Netflix, November 20, 2015.
16. Hall.
17. *Marvel's Jessica Jones*, "AKA It's Called Whiskey."
18. *Ibid.*
19. *Marvel's Jessica Jones*, "AKA 99 Friends," directed by David Petrarca, written by Hilly Hicks, Jr. Netflix, November 20, 2015.
20. *Marvel's Jessica Jones*, "AKA You[apost]re a Winner!" directed by Stephen Surjik, written by Edward Ricourt. Netflix, November 20, 2015.
21. *Marvel's Jessica Jones*, "AKA The Sandwich Saved Me," directed by Stephen Surjik, written by Dana Baratta. Netflix, November 20, 2015.
22. Valerie Estelle Frankel, *From Girl to Goddess: The Heroine's Journey through Myth and Legend* (Jefferson, NC: McFarland, 2010), 22.
23. Marie Louise Von Franz, "The Process of Individuation," ed. Carl Jung, *Man and His Symbols* (New York: Doubleday, 1964), 206.
24. Christina Radish, "*Jessica Jones* Cast on Season 2 Possibilities, Sex Scenes, and *Luke Cage*," *Collider*, 28 January 2016, http://collider.com/jessica-jones-season-2-sex-scenes-luke-cage.

25. Kaveney, *Superheroes!* 84.
26. *Ibid.*, 68.
27. *Marvel's Jessica Jones*, "AKA WWJD?" directed by Simon Cellan Jones, written by Scott Reynolds. Netflix, November 20, 2015.
28. Gennis.
29. Brian Formo, "Why *Jessica Jones* and *Spotlight* Are a Step Forward for Victims of Abuse," *Collider*, 9 December 2015, http://collider.com/jessica-jones-spotlight-sexual-abuse.
30. Karen Healy, "The Secret Origins of Jessica Jones: Multiplicity, Irony and a Feminist Perspective on Brian Michael Bendis's *Alias.*" 2006. http://girl-wonder.org/papers/healey.html.
31. Clarissa Pinkola Estés, *Women Who Run With the Wolves* (New York: Ballantine Books, 1992), 44.
32. *Ibid.*, 50.
33. Carol Pearson and Katherine Pope, *The Female Hero in American and British Literature* (New York: R.R. Bowker, 1981), 35.
34. Gennis.
35. Formo.
36. *Marvel's Jessica Jones*, "AKA WWJD?"
37. Gennis.
38. Rafael Nieves and Michael Bair, *Hellstorm Prince of Lies* #3 (New York: Marvel, 1993).
39. Warren Ellis and Peter Gross, *Hellstorm Prince of Lies* #14 (New York: Marvel, 1994).
40. Kurt Busiek and Norm Breyfogle, *Avengers Annual* 2000 (New York: Marvel, 2000).
41. Jim Shooter and George Pérez, *Avengers* #200 (New York: Marvel, 1980), Marvel Unlimited. Marvel.com.
42. Carol A. Strickland, "The Rape of Ms. Marvel," http://carolastrickland.com/comics/msmarvel.
43. Kaveney, *Superheroes!*, 80.
44. Chris Claremont and Michael Golden, *Avengers Annual* #10, *Essential Ms. Marvel. Vol. 1* (New York: Marvel, 2007).
45. *Marvel's Jessica Jones*, "AKA 1,000 Cuts," directed by Rosemary Rodriguez, written by Dana Baratta and Micah Schraft. Netflix, November 20, 2015.
46. Formo.
47. Gennis.
48. *Marvel's Jessica Jones*, "AKA 1,000 Cuts."
49. Estés 33.
50. *Marvel's Jessica Jones*, "AKA Smile," directed by Michael Rymer, story by Jamie King and Scott Reynolds, teleplay by Scott Reynolds and Melissa Rosenberg Netflix, November 20, 2015.
51. *Ibid.*
52. Frankel, 124.
53. Radish.
54. Gennis.
55. Healy.

Bibliography

Bendis, Brian Michael, and Michael Gaydos. *Alias Ultimate Collection Book 2.* New York: Max Comics, 2010.
Busiek, Kurt, and Norm Breyfogle. *Avengers Annual* 2000. New York: Marvel, 2000.
Campbell, Joseph, with Bill Moyers. *The Power of Myth.* Edited by Betty Sue Flowers. New York: Doubleday, 1988.
Claremont, Chris, and Michael Golden. *Avengers Annual* #10, *Essential Ms. Marvel. Vol. 1.* New York: Marvel, 2007.
Ellis, Warren, and Peter Gross. *Hellstorm Prince of Lies* #14. New York: Marvel, 1994.
Estés, Clarissa Pinkola. *Women Who Run With the Wolves.* New York: Ballantine Books, 1992.

Formo, Brian. "Why *Jessica Jones* and *Spotlight* Are a Step Forward for Victims of Abuse." *Collider*, 9 December 2015. http://collider.com/jessica-jones-spotlight-sexual-abuse.

Frankel, Valerie Estelle. *From Girl to Goddess: The Heroine's Journey through Myth and Legend.* Jefferson, NC: McFarland, 2010.

Hall, Jacob. "Jessica Jones vs. Alias: How Marvel's New Netflix Series Compares to the Comic That Inspired It," *SlashFilm*, November 23 2015. http://www.slashfilm.com/jessica-jones-vs-alias.

Hannigan, Ed, et al. *The Defenders* #89. New York: Marvel, 1980.

Healy, Karen. "The Secret Origins of Jessica Jones: Multiplicity, Irony and a Feminist Perspective on Brian Michael Bendis's *Alias*." 2006. http://girl-wonder.org/papers/healey.html.

Kaveney, Roz. *Superheroes! Capes and Crusaders in Comics and Films.* London: I.B. Tauris, 2008.

Leth, Kate, and Brittney L Williams. *Patsy Walker, AKA Hellcat* #7. New York: Marvel, 2016.

Marvel's Jessica Jones. "AKA It's Called Whiskey." Episode no. 103. Directed by David Petrarca. Written by Liz Friedman and Scott Reynolds. Netflix, November 20, 2015.

Marvel's Jessica Jones. "AKA Ladies Night." Episode no. 101. Directed by S. J. Clarkson. Written by Melissa Rosenberg. Netflix, November 20, 2015.

Marvel's Jessica Jones. "AKA 99 Friends." Episode no. 104. Directed by David Petrarca. Written by Hilly Hicks, Jr. Netflix, November 20, 2015.

Marvel's Jessica Jones. "AKA 1,000 Cuts." Episode no. 110. Directed by Rosemary Rodriguez. Written by Dana Baratta and Micah Schraft. Netflix, November 20, 2015.

Marvel's Jessica Jones. "AKA Smile." Episode no. 113. Directed by Michael Rymer. Story by Jamie King and Scott Reynolds. Teleplay by Scott Reynolds and Melissa Rosenberg Netflix, November 20, 2015.

Marvel's Jessica Jones. "AKA The Sandwich Saved Me." Episode no. 105. Directed by Stephen Surjik. Written by Dana Baratta. Netflix, November 20, 2015.

Marvel's Jessica Jones. "AKA WWJD?" Episode no. 108. Directed by Simon Cellan Jones. Written by Scott Reynolds. Netflix, November 20, 2015.

Marvel's Jessica Jones. "AKA You're a Winner!" Episode no. 106. Directed by Stephen Surjik. Written by Edward Ricourt. Netflix, November 20, 2015.

Nieves, Rafael and Michael Bair. *Hellstorm Prince of Lies* #3 (New York: Marvel, 1993).

Parker, John R. "*Alias* Jessica Jones: A Critical Look Back at Marvel's Mature Readers Hero and New Netflix Star," *Comics Alliance*, November 5 2014. http://comicsalliance.com/alias-omnibus-review.

Pearson, Carol, and Katherine Pope. *The Female Hero in American and British Literature.* New York: R.R. Bowker, 1981.

Radish, Christina. "*Jessica Jones* Cast on Season 2 Possibilities, Sex Scenes, and *Luke Cage*." *Collider*, 28 January 2016. http://collider.com/jessica-jones-season-2-sex-scenes-luke-cage.

Sadie, Gennis. "How Jessica Jones Got Rape Stories Right," *TV Guide*, December 3, 2015. http://www.tvguide.com/news/jessica-jones-rape-sexual-assault-stories/.

Shooter, Jim and George Pérez. *Avengers* #200. New York: Marvel, 1980.

Strickland, Carol A. "The Rape of Ms. Marvel." http://carolastrickland.com/comics/msmarvel.

Von Franz, Marie Louise. "The Process of Individuation." *Man and His Symbols.* Edited by Carl Jung. New York: Doubleday, 1964.

"Is that real or is it just in my head?" "Both"

Chronotopal Representations of Patriarchal Villainy and the Feminist Antihero in Marvel's Jessica Jones

JUSTIN WIGARD

As a superhero, Jessica Jones occupies a somewhat unusual position due to the conflicts she faces. This becomes most apparent when compared with similar Marvel properties such as *Daredevil*, which places a heavy emphasis on physical fighting and on Matt Murdock being physically powerful enough to defeat standard, publicly visible supervillains (such as the Kingpin). Jessica Jones, on the other hand, faces enemies that are more ideologically pervasive in nature; Kilgrave exerts dominance over everyone around him, but is seen more frequently controlling women and undermining Jessica's identity. She has the power of super strength, yet the villainy she faces is insidious and nearly invisible, which can be viewed as representations of patriarchy.

This essay, then, will argue that Jessica Jones represents something rather unique in the Marvel Cinematic Universe (MCU): a feminist superhero whose conflicts expose problematic aspects of gender relations in American society. First, the villainy in *Daredevil* will be examined in order to show how Daredevil establishes a standard superhero narrative of good versus evil, while Jessica Jones builds off this foundation to offer a more gender-driven narrative. M. Bakhtin's notion of the chronotope operates as a theoretical lens through which to view *Jessica Jones*, as it allows a reading of the show through its historical, cultural, and generic context. By viewing Jessica as a product of her historical position and cultural influences, it becomes apparent that, as a superhero, she acts as a champion of feminism. In response, the villains at work within the show operate as and represent agents of patriarchal oppression, often overtly and covertly suppressing Jessica's agency and identity. Each of Jessica's conflicts with these villains (Kilgrave, and to a lesser degree, Will Simpson) will ultimately be shown to problematize and subvert American gender norms.

"It's not how you hit the mat, it's how you get up"

From a cinematic standpoint, Marvel's films and television shows are generally considered to be lighter in chromatic, tonal, and thematic elements than other comic book film properties. Recently, in DC Comics' *Man of Steel* and *Batman V. Superman: Dawn of Justice* films, the superheroes are clearly defined by their colorful costumes, which Peter Coogan allots as being a critical component as, "the costume announces the superhero and places him or her within the superhero community."[1] Iron Man, Captain America, and even the Incredible Hulk are prominent fixtures of the box office, dominating the superheroic landscape since Marvel's *The Incredible Hulk* was released in 2008. This string of superhero films from Marvel Studios runs somewhat formulaically, with superheroes developing superpowers, battling villains, and saving the world from would-be disaster. That is to say, the MCU was narratively safe: films, and their various network television shows, routinely deal with the end of the world or the universe, but pointedly shy away from mature or grim themes like sexual assault or realistic depictions of violence. The public popularity and subsequent scrutiny of Marvel's film franchise meant that, if Marvel wanted to explore uncharted and dark territory, they needed to expand their market for release, eventually collaborating with streaming giant Netflix to present shorter, grittier superhero stories that could not be shown on networks like CBS or ABC.

In Netflix's first Marvel-owned show, *Daredevil*, Matt Murdock works as a defense lawyer by day, serving the broken and penniless citizens of Hell's Kitchen in New York City, and defends these same citizens by night as a violent vigilante superhero named Daredevil. His intrinsic superpower stems from his blindness: when his sight was lost in a car accident as a child, Murdock's other senses heightened in compensation, allowing him to utilize complex martial arts to a deadly degree, regardless of his ability to see properly.[2] Eschewing the traditionally light-hearted tone of the MCU, the first action sequence of *Daredevil*'s first episode finds the titular hero mercilessly bludgeoning would-be human traffickers on a wharf at night, going so far as to snap one criminal's femur.[3] This tone-setting scene establishes that Matt Murdock, as Daredevil, uses extreme physical force in taking down criminals, as well as establishes the kinds of criminals he faces: rapists, gangsters, and mobsters. Rather than facing extradimensional beings or power-hungry billionaires, Murdock faces real-world criminal activity on the streets of Hell's Kitchen in New York City. Elements of gratuitous violence, bleak criminal acts, as well as scenes of sex and nudity, quickly delineate that *Daredevil* represents something new for the MCU: dark, grim, violent, and mature.

Initially wearing a black hood over his eyes, a form-fitting black shirt, darkly-colored cargo pants, and combat boots, Murdock quickly becomes known as "The Man in Black" around Hell's Kitchen before donning his iconic "Devil" costume and the Daredevil persona. He adopts the color red to better project this "Devil of Hell's Kitchen" identity, but also in honor of his late father, "Battlin'" Jack Murdock, who also wore red so his opponents "can't tell how much [he's] bleeding."[4] Moreover, Daredevil actively chooses to be visible to his enemies, or barring that, leaves visible evidence of his handiwork as a warning to others. At the end of the first episode, "Into the Ring," Murdock leaves the battered, but still-breathing, body of a would-be assailant on the steps of the *New York Bulletin* for reporters to find. This sends two messages to both the denizens of Hell's Kitchen and its criminal underworld: Daredevil is physically stronger and more violent than most criminals, and wants those criminals to be afraid.

As Frank Verano notes, "the archenemy represents an inversion of the hero's values and is a figure with whom the hero is constantly at odds—physically, mentally, and ideologically,"[5] and the Kingpin (crime lord Wilson Fisk) acts as a perfect inversion of Daredevil. To say that the Kingpin is physically large is an understatement, as he naturally towers over all who stand next to him, including Daredevil, most clearly shown when Matt Murdock meets the Kingpin in an art gallery.[6] Moreover, the Kingpin's fighting style is one of brute strength, exercising giant fists and body slams instead of finesse or martial arts. Unlike Daredevil, the Kingpin is deliberately invisible: his criminal empire is founded upon acts of gratuitous violence spread through word of mouth down his ranks, acts like ruthlessly smashing an underling's skull in an SUV door until it becomes pulp just because he "embarrassed" the Kingpin.[7] In the very first episode, Fisk's right-hand man, Wesley, issues a chilling reminder to Fisk's peers: "We don't say his name." Yet, when Fisk does finally make a public appearance, he gives a televised speech about a plan to "make this city a better place"[8]; that plan, unbeknownst to the public, is to tear down as much of the city as possible, control the organized crime in the area, and rebuild it in his own image.

Given these comparisons, *Daredevil* features a nuanced, but straightforward, superhero narrative. Murdock plays the part of superhero savior, defending Hell's Kitchen from corporate evil by day as a lawyer and doling out vigilantism by night as the Daredevil. Both tracks of this superhero narrative find Murdock on the side of good, or what Stanford W. Carpenter defines as "positive values" in society that embodies "culturally defined value systems" of responsibilities and irresponsibilities.[9] As a lawyer, Murdock works to ensure Wilson Fisk is held accountable for his criminal activity through legal means, while as Daredevil, Murdock has a duty to enforce justice by whatever means necessary, legal or otherwise. In doing so, Murdock is upholding a responsibility to justice and actively combatting criminally-sanctioned violations of justice. By contrast, the Kingpin believes that he has a responsibility to make Hell's Kitchen better; the problem lies in his homicidal and criminal methodology, marking him as a supervillain. Instead of spending his time, energy, and resources into creating positive change in the city, Kingpin expends these resources into dismantling Hell's Kitchen to rebuild it.

In effect, then, Daredevil may be defined, in part, by his adherence to generic superhero conventions like the traditional costume and heroic mission, but he is truly defined by the villainy he faces, and how he responds. After months of building a legal case against the Kingpin, Murdock's pursuit of a legal capture and imprisonment of the Kingpin ultimately proves to be fruitless. He is released shortly after being called into court, leaving Murdock only one option: don the Daredevil suit, and bring Fisk in by whatever means necessary. The climactic end battle between Daredevil and the Kingpin revolves around physical strength: Daredevil is much smaller, more agile, and trained in martial arts, while the Kingpin is almost comically (in the comedic sense) larger and stronger than the Devil of Hell's Kitchen. After exchanging blows, the Kingpin is standing over the hero, exerting physical dominance by savagely beating Daredevil with his own billy club, revealing that physical strength, and that alone, is the key to this conflict. The Kingpin asks, broken and bloodied, "You really think one man in a silly looking costume will make a difference?" Daredevil literally rises to the occasion, takes back his billy clubs (symbolically taking the power back in the fight), and knocks the Kingpin out. This ultimately reveals that, as a superhero, Daredevil must be physically stronger than his opponents to fulfill his primary goal of defending Hell's Kitchen.

"New York may be the city that never sleeps, but it sure does sleep around"

Given this context of modern and grim superheroism, M. M. Bakhtin's theoretical notion of the chronotope offers a unique avenue for analyzing the villainy and heroism in *Jessica Jones*. Bakhtin contents that the chronotope (defined as "time/space,")[10] is an accounting of the historical period and cultural ideology surrounding a work of literature; when looked at in conjunction with the genre of a text, the chronotope of a work further reveals the signifiers at work within a text. Though Bakhtin is primarily concerned with literature, the historical settings and cultural signifiers of television and film properties can be examined just the same, as Jason Bainbridge argues. He finds that because Marvel uses real-world locations like San Francisco and New York City, "New York City is therefore not only the spine of the Marvel Universe, it is a suture—suturing the Marvel Universe to the real world, providing a material context for these iconic forms."[11] Expanding on this concept, Joseph Michael Sommers notes that not only are superheroes especially culturally relevant due to the rise in popularity of superhero films, but that through a chronotopal reading, it becomes apparent that the medium of film acquires "the contemporality of the moment of the films' construction … becom[ing] artifacts of their own time period."[12] Therefore, superhero films, and by proxy television series, operate as textual and cultural artifacts, when their historical, cultural, and generic context is exposed.

Returning to the foundation of *Daredevil* as *Jessica Jones'* most significant Marvel contemporary, a short comparison reveals the two Netflix shows have much in common. Both feature superheroes that utilize physical violence when necessary (though Jones is much more loathe to use her superpower for violence and is traumatized by it, in some cases). Each show deals with mature themes, ranging from sexual violence to child kidnapping, but the particular treatment of the superhero genre is what serves as the greatest separation here. *Daredevil* is defined partially by its adherence to the procedural-crime genre as much as to the traditional superhero narrative, following different cases brought to Murdock's law firm, Nelson & Murdock, while a parallel storyline tracks the evolution and rise of Daredevil the superhero. Seemingly in direct contrast to *Daredevil*, *Jessica Jones* distances itself through a wholly different genre: neo-noir.

Because the genre of a text is central to understanding its historical and cultural signifiers, according to Bakhtin, understanding how and why *Jessica Jones* fits into the neo-noir genre is critical to understanding its subversive nature. Though film studies critics readily debate some of the definitive elements of the neo-noir genre, beyond that it stems directly from the noir film genre, a working definition of neo-noir is needed nonetheless. Drawing on one of the forerunners of the neo-noir movement, Foster Hirsch in *Detours and Lost Highways*, Jerold J. Abrams finds that "social issues, like race, class, and gender, already latent in noir, [are] at the forefront of dark cinema," due in part to their prominence within society itself.[13] According to Hirsch, then, neo-noir is defined primarily by its direct engagement with social issues. Expanding on Hirsch's notion, Mark T. Conard explains that neo-noir filmmakers are cognizant of their position within the existing noir framework, and as such, cause neo-noir and noir films to share much in common, such as "the same alienation, pessimism, moral ambivalence, and disorientation."[14] Robert Schwartz extends this genre to feature five qualities: color and integration of cinematographically advanced technology; violence, sexual activity, and mature themes; modernized "hard-boiled" detective fiction; good/bad cops; and "the emergence of the serial killer."[15] What materializes is a complicated image of the neo-noir genre: a deliberate engagement with social issues, morally ambivalent characters and narratives, and cinematic qualities that subvert the film noir genre before it.

From the outset, the claustrophobic introduction sequence and jazz-inspired musical theme serve to establish *Jessica Jones* as belonging to the neo-noir genre. Silhouettes and shadows of Jones and other citizens of Hell's Kitchen are depicted under a purple and yellow color filter, offering a modern take on the classic black-and-white aesthetic of bygone noir films. Suddenly, the lilting and playful jazz piano is overlaid with a jarring electric guitar riff, again delineating *Jessica Jones* into the "neo" camp of noir television according to Schwartz's cinematic qualities. Much of this sequence feels claustrophobic as a result of the perspective: the viewer is treated to views of silhouettes and shadows from around corners, through window curtains, and behind chain-link fences. As the guitar riff crescendos, the collaged and watercolor images coalesce into a blinking eye, panning backward to reveal that the eye is both female and presumably Jones' eye, still observing, watching, recording. Jeffrey A. Brown notes that, with regards to conflicts pertaining to power, gender, and identity, "the ability to see clearly in cinema is equated with power,"[16] bringing into focus a generic element of *Jessica Jones*, namely Jones' profession as a private detective. Through this introductory sequence, *Jessica Jones* subtly informs the viewers of its capacity to undermine and subvert traditionally male cinematic norms through a visual refrain, reminding the viewer that Jessica has investigative clarity, and therefore, power.

Following the tone set forth in the opening sequence, Jones offers an internal monologue and narration of events unfolding in front of the viewer's eyes, filling the role of hard-boiled detective in a classic noir film before following tropes closer to the neo-noir genre. During the opening narration for episode 1, "AKA Ladies' Night," Jessica drolly claims that New York City "may be the city that never sleeps, but it sure does sleep around," snaps photos of a couple having sex underneath of a seedy bridge in Hell's Kitchen, and derisively explains her work as a private detective looking, "for the worst in people … clients hire [her] to find dirt … and [she] finds it,"[17] all while a sullen jazz saxophone undercuts her monologue. In quick succession, Jessica gets into a disagreement with a client over the photos, gets screamed at, and puts the client's head through a glass window on her door, still falling in line with the hard-boiled private eye of the noir genre. However, the next scene's synth-infused score and narration of Jones claiming that "people do bad shit"[18] signals a sharp evolution into neo-noir narrative territory. Jones is established as being an incredibly effective private investigator due to her "questionable methods" to get the job done, as Jones' on-again/off-again employer and high-power lawyer Jeri Hogarth laments. Jones readily lies to get information about cases, actively breaks the law by impersonating medical personnel,[19] and in one case, holds a spouse before an oncoming train to obtain a signature on divorce papers.[20] This paints Jones as a morally ambivalent private investigator, one that the audience laughs with as she cheerfully mocks a sleazy bar owner, yet one whom the audience leers at over her continued mistreatment of everyone in close proximity.

The special effects on *Jessica Jones* are used very selectively within the narrative, primarily to depict when superpowered individuals are using their abilities. Some of these effects are obvious, such as when Luke Cage's bullet-proof skin is shown to be on fire in "AKA I've Got the Blues," but for Kilgrave, the effects are much more subtle. Shade VFX CEO Bryan Godwin explains that "[actor] David Tennant's skin is tinted purple in a few key scenes as a nod to 'The Purple Man,'" revealing that these instances are when Kilgrave applies his mind control.[21] This follows suit with Abrams' assertion that in the neo-noir genre, the focus is to be on the self; in this case, Godwin's visual effects, "are just there to support the story," augmenting the case and subtly shifting the viewer's perception of the show. This can further be seen as Jessica begins to fall asleep in various episodes,[22] where the viewer sees a traumatic vision of Kilgrave creeping into her consciousness. As this unfolds, the neon pink lights gradually shift down in hue to purple, as does the general ambient light of the environment. These neo-noir effects, subtle but not imperceptible, also identify these characters as superpowered in addition to their outward and extrinsic uses of their superpowers (lifting cars, stopping bullets, commanding others to jump to their death).

Within the first ten minutes of *Jessica Jones*, most of Schwartz's qualities are fulfilled: the introduction sequence features technical film animation; nudity and violence are both shown, literally through Jessica's eyes; and Jessica establishes a private-eye narrative by breaking down her clientele's wants, needs, and policies. Since *Jessica Jones* exemplifies the neo-noir genre, the show's position within the genre becomes integral for a chronotopal reading due to Hirsch's defining element of social issues and Schwartz's remaining qualities found in Jones' conflicts with the serial killer (Kilgrave) and good/bad cops (Will Simpson in both cases). According to comics scholars like Geoff Klock, Peter Coogan, and Johnson, superheroes are more than just costumed crusaders battling the forces of evil, instead they represent societal issues, fears, and trends. Since *Jessica Jones* inarguably features superheroes (Jones with super strength, Luke Cage with indestructible skin), supervillains

(Kilgrave and Will Simpson), and conflicts between the two forces, *Jessica Jones* is rooted firmly within the superhero genre. That being said, much as the superhero herself embodies certain real-world ideologies, it can be extended that the supervillain is representative of societal issues as well, returning to Verano's assertion that the archenemy represents not just the inverse of the superhero, but the inverse of their ideals. Given this intersection of both the superhero and neo-noir genres, Jones and Kilgrave will be analyzed for the social issues they embody in order to reveal what their superheroic conflict throughout the series signifies.

"God didn't do this. The Devil did. And I'm going to find him"

American superhero narratives have a long and sordid correlation with societal trends, as Johnson claims that "changes within popular superheroes' stories reflect the period's important social trends."[23] While Johnson takes a decadal view of the intersecting points between societal movements and comic book trends in a broad sense, this essay focuses on a specific period in history and American culture during that time period which coincides with the release of *Jessica Jones*. Because *Jessica Jones* operates within a specific historical setting, from 2014 to 2015,[24] the show acts as a mirror of New York during this same time. An increasingly public clash between feminists advocating for equal rights for women and the ideologically conservative defenders of systematic patriarchy within the United States rose to the American consciousness, and it is this ideological conflict that makes up the historical time and cultural space in which *Jessica Jones* occupies. Women began speaking out in droves about being sexually assaulted, laying bare their experiences and their ensuing trauma, topics which were not only taboo but actively hidden from the public. During this time, feminism gained a massive amount of traction due to movements like Emma Watson's #HeforShe campaign, President Barack Obama's "It's on Us" initiative, and general public support of feminism as more celebrities, politicians, and citizens embraced the label "feminist."[25] Returning to Bainbridge's notion that the fictional NYC in superhero narratives bridges the consciousness of the real-world New York, this increased public awareness and subsequent feminist activism is the element of American consciousness that Jones represents within her narrative as a superhero.

These facets of feminism bleed into both Jones' personality and her narrative. As a superhero, Jones is independent, relying on her own superpowers and professional skills in order to put an end to Kilgrave's nefarious narrative. Throughout the first season, men often try to take over her investigation and suggest that they're more capable of taking down Kilgrave than Jones is. Will

Simpson, a police officer who had been controlled by Kilgrave in the third episode "AKA It's Called Whiskey" offers to utilize police resources in his off-hours to take Kilgrave down. Over the course of the season, Simpson descends from shining paragon of police ethics to become an abusive, homicidal, and disgraced police officer, falling in line with Schwartz's notion of the neo-noir genre as featuring both good and bad cops. Each time that Simpson interferes with Jones' investigation, consequences both arise and worsen. When Jones, Simpson, and Walker work together to capture Kilgrave, Simpson tries to end Kilgrave's life, even though Jones needs him alive.[26] After Simpson interferes, they are all beaten by thugs while Kilgrave gets away.

Similar instances of interference and repercussion can be seen in further episodes of Simpson's narrative, as he ingests an experimental steroid pill that gives him super strength, but erodes his moral judgment in the process. When Simpson helps out with Kilgrave's interrogation, he questions Jessica's methods, and later kills Detective Oscar Clemons because of a personal vendetta against Kilgrave; Simpson even goes so far as to recruit a bunch of his "boys" to put a hit out on Kilgrave, which is almost lazily thwarted by Kilgrave sending a kamikaze woman with a bomb to kill him and his boys. Even though Simpson has special forces military training, has access to governmental super strength steroid pills, and has the resources of the entire New York Police Department at his disposal, Jones is the only person to be outside of Kilgrave's control, and therefore, the single person who is solely qualified to be stopping Kilgrave. Her heroic capacity is constantly undermined and threated by male intruders like Simpson, but within the neo-noir and superhero generic intersection, this misogynistic underpinning has further ideological ramifications.

If the Kingpin acts as an inverse of the core of Daredevil, so too does Kilgrave represent an inversion of Jessica's identity and values. Jones' personal narrative throughout the show is primarily based around her ongoing conflict with Kilgrave and his psychological, sexual, and physical abuse of Jessica, past and present. Early in the show, Jones experiences a recurring flashback of Kilgrave saying (in slow motion and with blurred effects, again marking the use of new technology), "Get back here Jessica," shortly before a truck is shown crashing in front of the pair.[27] This flashback occurs and reoccurs when Jones's trauma is reopened, a process that Dominick Labara defines as "acting out,"[28] referring to the victim's inability to discern present from traumatized past. While the typical hard-boiled detective in a film noir typically drinks regularly, Jones self-medicates with excessive drinking to both get to sleep and to block off her trauma, as shown in "AKA Ladies' Night." Jones reveals that Kilgrave used his mind-controlling superpowers to place Jones under his influence, then continuously raped her,[29] though he claims and thoroughly believes it was a loving relationship.[30]

This qualitative difference in their superpowers, and how they use them, offers a clear distinction between the two: whereas Jessica's superpower manifests in the form of super-strength, Kilgrave's chemically altered brain allows him to control the minds of other people. The manner in which he does this, controlling others through vocalizing commands, depicts Kilgrave as a manipulative and authoritative man preferring to have his victims act out his whims and machinations. Regarding her own powers, Jones explains to Luke Cage, "I'm not hiding, but I'm not advertising," revealing that Jones actively chooses not to oppress or traumatize people around her, instead primarily using her powers in a (mostly) positive manner as a private investigator. One key clue that escapes Jessica's notice, until it is too late to act, is that Hope Shlottman is still under Kilgrave's control when she shoots and kills her parents.[31] As has been established, a vital element of Kilgrave's persona is the color purple, due to his suits, the color that emanates when he uses his powers, and when Jessica relives her traumatic past with Kilgrave. Hope seemed free of Kilgrave's grasp: she showed agency, free will, and perhaps most importantly, remorse over her actions. Yet, in the elevator, Hope is carrying a flannel bag that conceals a pistol, a bag that just so happens to be purple in color. While more than enough material exists to offer a visual rhetoric breakdown of both *Jessica Jones* and *Daredevil*, the key here is the insidious nature of Kilgrave's control: Hope's actions were invisibly controlled by the machinations of Kilgrave as he mentally influenced her entire worldview, shaping it to his liking.

Once Jones finds Kilgrave through a long bout of sleuthing and makes a visible stand to end his scheming, Kilgrave reveals that he has been spying on her for months, leaving behind a room covered in photographs of Jones, taken without her express permission or consent. Reversing the roles here, Kilgrave shows that he has been observing Jones, disorienting the superhero as she struggles to determine how these pictures were taken, and by which agent of Kilgrave's. Undermining the private investigator's power in this fashion is reminiscent of the real-world "Gamergate" events that played an important role in the latest rise of feminism. In response to feminist video game and cultural scholarship, anonymous men's rights activists and online harassers coalesced into launching vitriolic and anti-feminist attacks specifically on female game developers like Zoë Quinn, as well as feminist critics like Jessica Valenti and Anita Sarkeesian.[32] Because these attacks originate online, the perpetrators are virtually anonymous, only guided by a larger movement. Likewise, Jessica can never be certain which random passerby might be an agent of Kilgrave's, mirroring the anonymity of the insidious online misogyny within the United States.

The conflicts between Jones and Kilgrave reveal a very pointed ideological discussion when viewed through the lens of the chronotope. Because

Jones ascribes to the neo-noir genre, the show, by its construction, is overtly conscious in its engagement with social issues, which is, more specifically, the increasingly tense clash between feminists and societal patriarchy. In "Aka Ladies' Night," Jones has a chance to run; she has an opportunity to flee the city, the state, even the country. She chooses to instead face Kilgrave, a serial rapist who controls everyone around him, a man who kept her imprisoned and literally restricted her agency as a human being. Returning to Verano's notion that the supervillain operates as an inverse of the superhero, it stands to reason that since Kilgrave is a superpowered inverse of Jones, so too is he an ideological inverse. If Jones is representative of a feminist politic in America, Kilgrave can be seen as standing in for a dangerous, overtly patriarchal, politic in the same vein. Jones ultimately confronts Kilgrave, snaps his neck, and ends his reign of systematic and misogynistic abuse, control, and torture. While Kilgrave's death is certainly a drastic end, what *Jessica Jones* the television show is advocating for is a drastic end to the systemic patriarchy in place today.

Through Bakhtin's notion of the chronotope, we see that the intersection of this particular historical period and cultural context, in combination with the neo-noir and superhero genres, reveals Jessica Jones (the character) as a feminist antihero. Likewise, we also see the main antagonist, Kilgrave, as a misogynist and patriarchal villain. By putting these two in direct conflict with one another, a very specific trajectory appears of a feminist champion overcoming a patriarchal villain, paralleling a similar trajectory of more recent instances of feminism coming into direct conflict with patriarchal norms in American society. Given all of this, Jessica Jones seems to be a direct call to action for women to start taking charge of their lives, and to start challenging systematic oppression at the hands of male privilege.

NOTES

1. Peter Coogan, "The Hero Defines the Genre, the Genre Defines the Hero," *What Is a Superhero?*, ed. Robin S. Rosenberg and Peter Coogan (New York: Oxford University Press, 2013), 6.
2. *Daredevil*, "Into the Ring," directed by Phil Abraham, written by Drew Goddard, Netflix, April 10, 2015.
3. *Daredevil*, "Into the Ring."
4. *Daredevil*, "Cut Man," directed by Phil Abraham, written by Drew Goddard, Netflix, April 10, 2015.
5. Frank Verano, "Superheroes Need Supervillains," *What Is a Superhero?*, 83.
6. *Daredevil*, "Speak of the Devil," directed by Nelson McCormick, written by Christos Gage and Ruth Fletcher Gage, Netflix, April 10, 2015.
7. *Daredevil*, "Into the Ring."
8. *Daredevil*, "Shadows in the Glass," directed by Steven Surjik, written by Steven S. DeKnight, Netflix, April 10, 2015.
9. Stanford W. Carpenter, "Superheroes need Superior Villains," *What Is a Superhero?*, 89.
10. Mikhail Mikhailovich Bakhtin, "Forms of Time and of the Chronotope in the Novel,"

The Dialogic Imagination, ed. Michael Holquist, trans. Caryl Emerson and Michael Holquist (Austin: University of Texas Press, 1981), 84.

11. Jason Bainbridge, "'I am the City': Spider-Man, New York City and the Marvel Universe," *Comics and the City: Urban Space in Print, Picture and Sequence*, ed. Jorn Aherns and Arno Meteling (New York: Continuum, 2010), 175.

12. Joseph Michael Sommers, "The Traumatic Revision of Marvel's Spider-Man: From 1960s Dime-Store Comic Book to Post-9/11 Moody Motion Picture Franchise," *Children's Literature Association Quarterly* 37, no. 2 (2012): 192.

13. Jerold J. Abrams, "Space, Time, and Subjectivity in Neo-Noir Cinema," *The Philosophy of Neo-Noir*, ed. Mark T. Conard (Lexington: University Press of Kentucky, 2007), 8.

14. Mark T. Conard, "Introduction," *The Philosophy of Neo-Noir*, ed. Mark T. Conard (Lexington: University Press of Kentucky, 2007), 2.

15. Ronald Schwartz, *Neo-Noir: The New Film Noir Style from Psycho to Collateral* (Lanham, MD: Scarecrow Press, 2005), xi.

16. Jeffrey A. Brown, *Dangerous Curves: Action Heroines, Gender, Fetishism, and Popular Culture* (Jackson: University Press of Mississippi, 2011), 209.

17. *Jessica Jones*, "AKA Ladies Night," directed by S.J. Clarkson, written by Melissa Rosenberg, Netflix, November 20, 2015.

18. *Ibid.*

19. *Ibid.*

20. *Jessica Jones*, "AKA Top Shelf Perverts," directed by Simon Cellan Jones, written by Jenna Reback and Micah Schraft, Netflix, November 20, 2015.

21. Sidney Fussell, "This is the small team behind the special effects in 'Daredevil' and 'Jessica Jones,'" *TechInsider*, January 25, 2016, Accessed Aug. 11, 2016, http://www.techinsider.io/daredevil-jessica-jones-special-effects-shade-vfx-2016-1.

22. *Jessica Jones*, "AKA Ladies Night."

23. Johnson, 2.

24. *Jessica Jones*, "AKA Ladies Night."

25. Rebecca Solnit, "Listen Up, Women Are Telling Their Story Now," *The Guardian*, December 30, 2014, accessed August 15, 2016, https://www.theguardian.com/news/2014/dec/30/-sp-rebecca-solnit-listen-up-women-are-telling-their-story-now.

26. *Jessica Jones*, "AKA The Sandwich Saved Me," directed by Stephen Surjik, written by Dana Baratta, Netflix, November 20, 2015.

27. *Jessica Jones*, "AKA Crush Syndrome," directed by S.J. Clarkson, written by Micah Schraft, Netflix, November 20, 2015.

28. Dominick LaCapra, *Writing History, Writing Trauma* (Baltimore: John Hopkins University Press, 2014), 21–22.

29. *Jessica Jones*, "AKA Ladies Night."

30. *Ibid.*

31. *Ibid.*

32. Shira Chess and Adrienne Shaw, "A Conspiracy of Fishes, or, How We Learned to Stop Worrying about #GamerGate and Embrace Hegemonic Masculinity," *Journal of Broadcasting & Electronic Media* 59, no. 1 (2015): 210, 212.

BIBLIOGRAPHY

Abrams, Jerold A. "Space, Time, and Subjectivity in Neo-Noir Cinema." In *The Philosophy of Neo*-Noir. Edited by Mark T. Conard, 7–20. Lexington: University Press of Kentucky, 2007.
Bainbridge, Jason. "'I Am the City': Spider-Man, New York City and the Marvel Universe." In *Comics and the City: Urban Space in Print, Picture and Sequence*. Edited by Jorn Aherns and Arno Meteling. 163–82. New York: Continuum, 2010.
Bakhtin, Mikhail Mikhailovich. "Forms of Time and of the Chronotope in the Novel." In *The Dialogic Imagination*. Edited by Michael Holquist. Translated by Caryl Emerson and Michael Holquist, 84–258. Austin: University of Texas Press, 1981.
Brown, Jeffrey A. *Dangerous Curves: Action Heroines, Gender, Fetishism, and Popular Culture.* Jackson: University Press of Mississippi, 2011.

Carpenter, Stanford W. "Superheroes need Superior Villains." In *What Is a Superhero?* Edited by Robin S. Rosenberg and Peter Coogan, 89–93. New York: Oxford University Press, 2013.

Chess, Shira, and Adrienne Shaw. "A Conspiracy of Fishes, or, How We Learned to Stop Worrying about #GamerGate and Embrace Hegemonic Masculinity." *Journal of Broadcasting & Electronic Media* 59, no. 1 (2015): 208–220.

Conard, Mark T. "Introduction." In *The Philosophy of Neo-Noir*. Edited by Mark T. Conard, 1–4. Lexington: University Press of Kentucky, 2007.

Coogan, Peter. "The Hero Defines the Genre, the Genre Defines the Hero." In *What Is a Superhero?* Edited by Robin S. Rosenberg and Peter Coogan, 3–10. New York: Oxford University Press, 2013.

Daredevil. "Cut Man." Directed by Phil Abraham. Written by Drew Goddard. Netflix, April 10, 2015.

Daredevil. "Into the Ring." Directed by Phil Abraham. Written by Drew Goddard. Netflix, April 10, 2015.

Daredevil. "Speak of the Devil." Directed by Nelson McCormick. Written by Christos N. Gage and Ruth Fletcher. Netflix, April 10, 2015.

Fussell, Sidney. "This is the small team behind the special effects in *Daredevil* and *Jessica Jones*." *TechInsider*. January 25, 2016. Accessed August 11, 2016. http://www.techinsider.io/daredevil-jessica-jones-special-effects-shade-vfx-2016–1.

Jessica Jones. "AKA Crush Syndrome." Directed by S.J. Clarkson. Written by Micah Schraft. Netflix, November 20, 2015.

Jessica Jones. "AKA Ladies Night." Directed by S.J. Clarkson. Written by Melissa Rosenberg. Netflix, November 20, 2015.

Jessica Jones. "AKA Top Shelf Perverts." Directed by Simon Cellan Jones. Written by Jenna Reback and Micah Schraft. Netflix, November 20, 2015.

Johnson, Jeffrey K. *Super-History: Comic Book Superheroes and American Society, 1938 to the Present*. Jefferson, NC: McFarland, 2012.

LaCapra, Dominick. *Writing History, Writing Trauma*. Baltimore: John Hopkins University Press, 2014.

Schwartz, Ronald. *Neo-Noir: The New Film Noir Style from Psycho to Collateral*. Lanham, MD: Scarecrow Press, 2005.

Solnit, Rebecca. "Listen Up, Women Are Telling Their Story Now." *The Guardian*, December 30, 2014. Accessed August 15, 2016, https://www.theguardian.com/news/2014/dec/30/-sp-rebecca-solnit-listen-up-women-are-telling-their-story-now.

Sommers, Joseph Michael. "The Traumatic Revision of Marvel's Spider-Man: From 1960s Dime-Store Comic Book to Post-9/11 Moody Motion Picture Franchise." *Children's Literature Association Quarterly* 37, no. 2 (2012): 188–209.

Verano, Frank. "Superheroes need Supervillains." In *What Is a Superhero?* Edited by Robin S. Rosenberg and Peter Coogan, 83–87. New York: Oxford University Press, 2013.

About the Contributors

Daniel **Binns** is a screenwriter, producer and researcher, and he runs intensive studios on media archaeology, transmedia storytelling and film theory at RMIT University, Melbourne, Australia. He has written and produced documentary and lifestyle programming for Fox Sports, National Geographic and the Seven Network.

Janis **Breckenridge** is an associate professor of Spanish at Whitman College, specializing in socially committed narrative and visual cultures of Latin America and Spain. Her scholarship on Hispanic comics has appeared in the *International Journal of Comic Art, Chasqui, Confluencia* and *Ergocomics*.

Lillian **Céspedes González** is Ph.D. candidate at the University of Winchester, UK. Her research interests include the Viking Age, gender, comic books, audience studies and depictions of Old Norse women in TV series and comics.

Emily D. **Edwards** was a journalist and media producer before she joined the faculty at the University of North Carolina at Greensboro, where she is a professor. The writer/ producer/director of many films, she has also published books and articles on popular media.

Valerie Estelle **Frankel** is an award-winning author or editor of some 60 books on pop culture. Many of her books focus on women's roles in fiction, from her heroine's journey guide *From Girl to Goddess* and *Superheroines and the Epic Journey* to *Empowered: The Symbolism, Feminism, and Superheroism of Wonder Woman*.

Brian **Fuller** is a media educator and an Emmy Award–winning filmmaker. His films regularly appear in festivals, competitions, broadcast outlets and high-profile venues. He also researches and lectures on the intersection of media production skills and character virtues.

Melissa C. **Johnson** is the chair of and associate professor in the Department of Focused Inquiry at Virginia Commonwealth University. She has published and presented on women writers, depictions of women in popular culture and the scholarship of teaching and learning in addition to her poetry.

Abigail **Keyes** is a writer and researcher with a background in performance studies and wellness. She is the author of *The Salimpour School of Dance Compendium, Vol. 1*, a survey of Middle Eastern dance history.

Aleah **Kiley** is a film and media studies graduate student at the University of California, Santa Barbara. Her work focuses on tracing difference, identity, and power through media industries and histories.

Nicholas William **Moll** is a lecturer and researcher at Federation University, Australia. His research interests focus on popular culture, franchising and notions of genre, specifically the translation and adaptation of tropes across narrative, media, form and marketplace boundaries.

Christopher J. **Olson** is a Ph.D. candidate in the English Department at the University of Wisconsin, Milwaukee, with a media, cinema and digital studies concentration. He has taught classes on masculinity, interracial communication, ethics and superheroes, film as art and game studies.

Sharon **Packer**, MD, was an assistant professor of psychiatry and behavioral sciences for the Albert Einstein College of Medicine and the Icahn School of Medicine at Mt. Sinai. She maintains a private practice and is the author of several books and essays.

Tim **Rayborn** is the author of three books, *The Violent Pilgrimage* (2013), *Against the Friars* (2014), and *A New English Music* (2016), all from McFarland, as well as two popular arts histories, *Beethoven's Skull* (2016) and *Shakespeare's Ear* (2017), both from Skyhorse. He has also written dozens of articles for various journals and magazines, in both the U.S. and the UK.

CarrieLynn D. **Reinhard** is an associate professor of communication arts and sciences at Dominican University. She has published numerous articles and book chapters on reception studies, primarily concerning digital communication technologies.

Zak **Roman** is a Ph.D. candidate in the School of Journalism and Communication at the University of Oregon. His research interests include cinema studies, popular culture and the political economy of the mass media.

Melissa **Wehler** is the dean of Humanities and Sciences at Central Penn College. Her publications include essays in edited collections, and her research interests include the gothic, feminism, performance and culture.

Courtney Lee **Weida** directs the Art Education graduate program at Adelphi University. As an associate professor, she has designed courses in arts education, studio art and art history. Her research addresses art and education through contemporary crafts, book arts and 'zines and gender and popular culture.

Justin **Wigard** is a Ph.D. Fellow at Michigan State University, where he studies the heroic tradition in popular culture. His work appears in the *Critical Insights* volume on Neil Gaiman, where he offered a biographical sketch of the writer.

Index